Oracle Data Guard 11gR2 Administration Beginner's Guide

Learn how to build and maintain Data Guard configurations with real-life, practical examples

Emre Baransel

Nassyam Basha

[PACKT] PUBLISHING

enterprise
professional expertise distilled

BIRMINGHAM - MUMBAI

Oracle Data Guard 11gR2 Administration Beginner's Guide

First published: June 2013

Production Reference: 1170613

Published by Packt Publishing Ltd.
Livery Place
35 Livery Street
Birmingham B3 2PB, UK.

ISBN 978-1-84968-790-4

www.packtpub.com

Cover Image by Sandeep Babu (sandyjb@gmail.com)

Credits

About the Authors

Emre Baransel is a graduate of Electrical and Electronic engineering and has two Master's, one in Business Administration and the other one in Information Systems. He has been working in the IT industry for the past 10 years. He has worked for one of the largest fixed-line and GSM technology-based companies in Turkey. He was nominated as an Oracle ACE in 2012. He's an Oracle Certified Professional (OCP), a founding member of TROUG (Turkish Oracle User Group), and a blogger at emrebaransel.blogspot.com. He has spoken at the Oracle Open World in the US and at user group conferences in different countries of Europe. He has also contributed to the *Oracle RMAN 11g Backup and Recovery* book in 2010. He has focused specially on high database availability and disaster recovery solutions, cloud technologies, and database security.

First of all, I would like to thank the love of my life, my wife Tulay, for her patience and support during the time I was writing this book, and my super sweet son Demir for his presence in my life. I would also like to thank my co-author Nassyam for his great effort on this book under intense work pressure, the technical reviewers Jaffar, Joel, and Michael for their valuable time, and the Packt Publishing team for all their help and labor on this book. Thousands of hours were spent on this book by many different people. Thank you all who made this book possible.

Nassyam Basha is a Database Administrator. He has around seven years of IT experience of which the last five years have been as a Production Oracle DBA. He is a post graduate who holds a master's degree in Computer Applications from the University of Madras. He started working with dBase and FoxPro, and has participated in several projects with FoxPro and Oracle database starting from Oracle 7. He is an Oracle 10*g* Certified Professional having good knowledge in Oracle technologies such as Data Guard, RMAN, RAC, and performance tuning. He has completed more than 90 Data Guard setups on all platforms, from RAC to non-RAC and successful cluster migrations with switchovers and failovers for many business-critical production databases with major Data Guard-related issues. He actively participates in Oracle-related forums such as OTN, having 9000+ posts, using the profile Freelists (`https://forums.oracle.com/forums/profile.jspa?editMode=true&user ID=651869`). He maintains an Oracle technology-related blog, (`www.oracle-ckpt.com`) and he is reachable at `nassyambasha@gmail.com`.

Above and beyond all others, I have to thank my Almighty Allah and my parents N. Abdul Aleem and Rahimunnisa. Without them I wouldn't have been able to be what I am today. A special thanks to my brother Nawaz Basha who has been with me all the time, in joy and even in sadness, and to my family members Zaheer Ahamed, Farhana, Riyana, niece Fathima Zehra, and my nephew Azzoo. I would also like to express my gratitude to Oracle professionals such as Shahbaz, Mohammad Farhan, Syed Jaffar Hussain, Chinar Aliyev, Michael Seberg, Uwe Hesse, Mohamed Houri, Adi Narayana, and all my friends along with my favorite authors Larry Carpenter and Joseph Meeks. I shall not forget to thank my clients and colleagues who have provided me with invaluable opportunities to expand my knowledge and shape my career. My heartfelt appreciation goes to the technical reviewers of this book, Syed Jaffar Hussain, Michael Seberg, and Joel Perez for the time they have spent reviewing this book, and to Packt Publishing's team members, Stephanie Moss, Leena Purkait, and Martin Bell for their support. Thanks to all of them and to their team members for giving me the opportunity to write this book. Last but not the least, I would like to say a big thanks to Emre Baransel who gave me the opportunity to co-author this book with him. His help, along with his direction were strong assets to write. Thank you Emre.

About the Reviewers

Syed Jaffer Hussain has been an Oracle Database Expert for over 14 years in his 20 years of Information Technology (IT) career. Over the past 14 years of his Oracle journey, he has been associated with several local and large-scale international banks where he implemented and managed very complex cluster and non-cluster environments with hundreds of business critical databases. Recognizing his efforts and contribution towards the community, Oracle awarded him the prestigious Best DBA of the year award in 2011, and bestowed him with the Oracle ACE Director status. He has also acquired a number of industry best-Oracle credentials, such as Oracle Certified Master (OCM), Oracle RAC Expert, and OCP DBA 8*i*, 9*i*, 10*g*, and 11*g* in addition to ITIL expertise.

Syed is an active Oracle speaker. He regularly presents technical sessions and webinars on various Oracle technologies at many Oracle events. You can visit his technical blog at `http://jaffardba.blogspot.com`, where he discusses and writes about workarounds/ solutions for the issues confronted by him in his day-to-day activities.

Apart from being a part of the core Technical Review committee for a few Oracle technology-oriented books, he has also co-authored the books *Oracle 11g R1/R2 Real Application Cluster Essentials* and *Oracle Expert RAC*.

I would like to thank the Almighty and my parents for giving me everything I needed to become what I am today in life. Also, I owe a very big thanks to my wife Ayesha and my three champs (Ashfaq, Arfan, and Aahil) for allowing me to concentrate on my work by sacrificing their family time. Last but not the least, from the bottom of my heart, I would like to thank every individual who stood behind me and supported me morally during my ups and downs and encouraged me all through my life.

Michael Seberg has worked with Oracle since Version 7.3 in programming and administration. In the spring of 2010, Michael took on data protection for his employer, designing a complete failover site for Oracle using Data Guard. He has done extensive testing of switchover, failover, and monitoring of Data Guard. An Oracle generalist, Michael also works with Fusion Middleware, Forms and Reports, PHP, JSP, and Linux. He also does development in PL SQL, Object Pascal, and Java. Michael maintains a large personal website dedicated to Oracle technologies. He is a frequent contributor to the Oracle Technology Network (OTN) forum.

I would like to thank my wife Andrea for her commitment and patience with me.

Joel Perez is an expert DBA with over 12 years of specialized experience in several database areas with special focus on high availability and disaster recovery solutions (RAC, RMAN, Data Guard, and so on), upgrades, backup and recovery, database hardening, performance tuning, and others. During these years, Joel has worked as a Senior Consultant with a large number of companies and clients in various countries namely Venezuela, Panama, Costa Rica, Dominican Rep., Haiti, Nicaragua, Guatemala, Colombia, Honduras, Ecuador, Mexico, India, and others. Joel is a frequent speaker at many events such as OTN LAD TOUR. Among other complementary activities, Joel teaches high availability courses in Oracle University of several countries in Latin America and publishes articles for OTN LAD. Joel was the first Latin American to be named OTN Expert in the year 2003. Joel has been an Oracle ACE since 2004 and an Oracle ACE Director since 2012.

www.PacktPub.com

Support files, eBooks, discount offers and more

You might want to visit www.PacktPub.com for support files and downloads related to your book.

Did you know that Packt offers eBook versions of every book published, with PDF and ePub files available? You can upgrade to the eBook version at www.PacktPub.com and as a print book customer, you are entitled to a discount on the eBook copy. Get in touch with us at service@ packtpub.com for more details.

At www.PacktPub.com, you can also read a collection of free technical articles, sign up for a range of free newsletters and receive exclusive discounts and offers on Packt books and eBooks.

http://PacktLib.PacktPub.com

Do you need instant solutions to your IT questions? PacktLib is Packt's online digital book library. Here, you can access, read and search across Packt's entire library of books.

Why Subscribe?

- Fully searchable across every book published by Packt
- Copy and paste, print and bookmark content
- On demand and accessible via web browser

Free Access for Packt account holders

If you have an account with Packt at www.PacktPub.com, you can use this to access PacktLib today and view nine entirely free books. Simply use your login credentials for immediate access.

Instant Updates on New Packt Books

Get notified! Find out when new books are published by following @PacktEnterprise on Twitter, or the *Packt Enterprise* Facebook page.

Table of Contents

Preface

Data Guard is the Oracle technology that meets high availability, disaster recovery, and data protection requirements for the Oracle Database, and is the market leader product for this scope. In enterprise systems, Data Guard is very widely used, so managing Data Guard configurations is a common task of Oracle DBAs. This administration task is not just about installing and keeping standby databases synchronized with the primary database. DBAs also provide standby databases for reporting and testing purposes, recovering partial data by using them, performing role transitions for disaster recovery testing or for planned maintenance operations, integrating Data Guard with the existing Oracle environment, and so on. As an Oracle DBA, you need to learn how to install and maintain Data Guard and benefit from it as much as possible.

In this practical book, you'll not only be introduced to Oracle Data Guard, you'll also see all aspects of Data Guard administration with examples, recipes, and best practices. We'll start by learning about the fundamental components of Data Guard, and then continue with configuring physical and logical standby databases of Data Guard. The important details and best practices of Data Guard administration will be covered later on.

What this book covers

Chapter 1, *Getting Started*, includes an introduction to Oracle Data Guard. Configuration elements, the architecture of the physical and logical standby databases, Data Guard services, the history of Data Guard, and a comparison with other replication solutions are covered in this chapter.

Chapter 2, *Configuring the Oracle Data Guard Physical Standby Database*, explains how to prepare the configuration from scratch, create a physical standby database including post tasks with a step-by-step approach, and verify the physical standby database recovery including real-time apply.

Chapter 3, Configuring Oracle Data Guard Logical Standby Database, shows you how to prepare a logical standby database configuration with pre and post steps. Customization and management in a logical standby database are also covered.

Chapter 4, Oracle Data Guard Broker, explains the detailed implementation of the Data Guard broker, monitoring and managing Data Guard using the broker, troubleshooting the Data Guard broker, and configuring fast-start failover (FSFO).

Chapter 5, Data Guard Protection Modes, focuses on the three data protection modes of Oracle Data Guard. You'll learn how to choose the correct mode for your requirements and how to change modes using SQL*Plus, the Data Guard broker, and Enterprise Manager Cloud Control.

Chapter 6, Data Guard Role Transitions, will include the necessary steps to accomplish successful switchover and failover operations in the physical and logical standby database environments. It also covers different tools to perform role transitions.

Chapter 7, Active Data Guard, Snapshot Standby, and Advanced Techniques, explains what Active Data Guard is, how to integrate applications with Active Data Guard, and several advantages of using it, such as performing Data Pump exports, gathering ASH reports, and advanced compression. This chapter also describes how to use snapshot standby, implement cascade standby databases, configure the cross-platform Data Guard setup, and also provides a brief on Data Guard tuning.

Chapter 8, Integrating Data Guard with the Complete Oracle Environment, explains the configuration steps required to integrate Data Guard with Enterprise Manager Grid Control, RMAN, and RAC. Integrating Data Guard with these products is crucial to make an efficient configuration and take advantage of all of these products together.

Chapter 9, Data Guard Configuration Patching, explains how to apply one-off patches and patch set updates to databases in a Data Guard environment, and some best practices of patching.

Chapter 10, Common Data Guard Issues, gives practical information for dealing with some very common issues in Data Guard that every administrator needs to know and experience.

Chapter 11, Data Guard Best Practices, includes very important information regarding how to make a Data Guard configuration perfect and take maximum advantage of Data Guard properties. Connection failover, deletion of archived log files, using flashback, database rolling upgrade using transient logical standby and corruption detection, and prevention and automatic repair with Oracle Data Guard are covered.

What you need for this book

In order to follow the exercises in this book, you must install the Oracle Database 11*g* Release 2 software on two separate database servers (primary and standby). You can use a virtual machine to create virtual database servers on your PC. Also, a database has to be created on the primary database server. The Oracle management software, Enterprise Manager 12*c* Cloud Control, needs to be installed to follow specific exercises using this tool.

Who this book is for

If you are an Oracle DBA who wants to configure and administer Data Guard and improve your knowledge on Data Guard with a step-by-step approach and hands-on scenarios, this book is for you. With a basic understanding of Oracle database administration you'll easily be able to follow the book.

Conventions

In this book, you will find several headings appearing frequently.

To give clear instructions of how to complete a procedure or task, we use:

Time for action – heading

1. Action 1
2. Action 2
3. Action 3

Instructions often need some extra explanation so that they make sense, so they are followed with:

What just happened?

This heading explains the working of tasks or instructions that you have just completed.

You will also find some other learning aids in the book, including:

Pop quiz – heading

These are short multiple-choice questions intended to help you test your own understanding.

Have a go hero – heading

These are practical challenges that give you ideas for experimenting with what you have learned.

You will also find a number of styles of text that distinguish between different kinds of information. Here are some examples of these styles, and an explanation of their meaning.

Code words in text, database table names, folder names, filenames, file extensions, pathnames, dummy URLs, user input, and Twitter handles are shown as follows: The LOG_ARCHIVE_DEST_n parameters must be configured properly on every instance of primary and standby databases to show remote archiving destinations.

A block of code is set as follows:

```
LOG_ARCHIVE_CONFIG =
{
  [ SEND | NOSEND ]
  [ RECEIVE | NORECEIVE ]
  [ DG_CONFIG=(remote_db_unique_name1, ... remote_db_unique_name9) |
NODG_CONFIG ]
```

When we wish to draw your attention to a particular part of a code block, the relevant lines or items are set in bold:

```
2   DBMS_SCHEDULER.CREATE_JOB (
3   JOB_NAME => 'REFRESH_EMPDEPT_MV_PRIMARY' ,
4   JOB_TYPE => 'PLSQL_BLOCK',
```

Any command-line input or output is written as follows:

```
RFS LogMiner: Registered logfile [/u01/app/oracle/archive_
std/1_106_791552282.arc] to LogMiner session id [1]

...

LOGMINER: Begin mining logfile for session 1 thread 1 sequence 106, /u01/
app/oracle/archive_std/1_106_791552282.arc

LOGMINER: End  mining logfile for session 1 thread 1 sequence 106, /u01/
app/oracle/archive_std/1_106_791552282.arc
```

New terms and **important words** are shown in bold. Words that you see on the screen, in menus or dialog boxes for example, appear in the text like this: Expand the **Data Guard Performance** category and click on the **Estimated Failover Time** section.

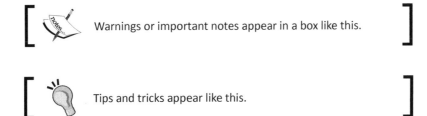

Warnings or important notes appear in a box like this.

Tips and tricks appear like this.

Reader feedback

Feedback from our readers is always welcome. Let us know what you think about this book—what you liked or may have disliked. Reader feedback is important for us to develop titles that you really get the most out of.

To send us general feedback, simply send an e-mail to feedback@packtpub.com, and mention the book title through the subject of your message.

If there is a topic that you have expertise in and you are interested in either writing or contributing to a book, see our author guide on www.packtpub.com/authors.

Customer support

Now that you are the proud owner of a Packt book, we have a number of things to help you to get the most from your purchase.

Downloading the example code

You can download the example code files for all Packt books you have purchased from your account at http://www.packtpub.com. If you purchased this book elsewhere, you can visit http://www.packtpub.com/support and register to have the files e-mailed directly to you.

Errata

Although we have taken every care to ensure the accuracy of our content, mistakes do happen. If you find a mistake in one of our books—maybe a mistake in the text or the code—we would be grateful if you would report this to us. By doing so, you can save other readers from frustration and help us improve subsequent versions of this book. If you find any errata, please report them by visiting http://www.packtpub.com/submit-errata, selecting your book, clicking on the **errata submission form** link, and entering the details of your errata. Once your errata are verified, your submission will be accepted and the errata will be uploaded to our website, or added to any list of existing errata, under the Errata section of that title.

Piracy

Piracy of copyright material on the Internet is an ongoing problem across all media. At Packt, we take the protection of our copyright and licenses very seriously. If you come across any illegal copies of our works, in any form, on the Internet, please provide us with the location address or website name immediately so that we can pursue a remedy.

Please contact us at copyright@packtpub.com with a link to the suspected pirated material.

We appreciate your help in protecting our authors, and our ability to bring you valuable content.

Questions

You can contact us at questions@packtpub.com if you are having a problem with any aspect of the book, and we will do our best to address it.

1
Getting Started

The objective of this chapter is to make you familiar with the Oracle Data Guard 11gR2 environment. We will discuss the definition, properties, and history of Data Guard. You will become accustomed with the concepts of standby databases and how Data Guard provides the robust solution of high availability and disaster recovery.

In this chapter, we will discuss the following topics:

◆ The definition and features of Data Guard

◆ The evolution of Data Guard

◆ The architecture and topology of Data Guard

◆ Comparison of Data Guard with other replication solutions

Let's get on with learning what Oracle Data Guard is and its primary features are.

What is Data Guard?

Data Guard, which was introduced as the standby database in Oracle database Version 7.3 under the name of Data Guard with Version 9i, is a data protection and availability solution for Oracle databases. The basic function of Oracle Data Guard is to keep a synchronized copy of a database as standby, in order to make provision, incase the primary database is inaccessible to end users. These cases are hardware errors, natural disasters, and so on. Each new Oracle release added new functionalities to Data Guard and the product became more and more popular with offerings such as data protection, high availability, and disaster recovery for Oracle databases.

Using Oracle Data Guard, it's possible to direct user connections to a Data Guard standby database automatically with no data loss, in case of an outage in the primary database. Data Guard also offers taking advantage of the standby database for reporting, test, and backup offloading. Corruptions on the primary database may be fixed automatically by using the non-corrupted data blocks on the standby database. There will be minimal outages (seconds to minutes) on the primary database in planned maintenances such as patching and hardware changes by using the switchover feature of Data Guard, which changes the roles of the primary and standby databases. All of these features are available with Data Guard, which doesn't require an installation but a cloning and configuration of the Oracle database.

A Data Guard configuration consists of two main components: primary database and standby database. The primary database is the database for which we want to take precaution for its inaccessibility. Fundamentally, changes on the data of the primary database are passed through the standby database and these changes are applied to the standby database in order to keep it synchronized.

The following figure shows the general structure of Data Guard:

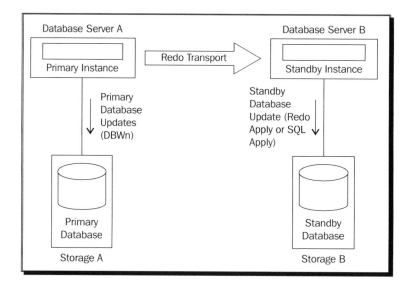

Let's look at the standby database and its properties more closely.

Standby database

It is possible to configure a standby database simply by copying, cloning, or restoring a primary database to a different server. Then the Data Guard configurations are made on the databases in order to start the transfer of redo information from primary to standby and also to start the apply process on the standby database.

Primary and standby databases may exist on the same server; however, this kind of configuration should only be used for testing. In a production environment, the primary and standby database servers are generally preferred to be on separate data centers.

Data Guard keeps the primary and standby databases synchronized by using redo information. As you may know, transactions on an Oracle database produce redo records. This redo information keeps all of the changes made to the database. The Oracle database first creates redo information in memory (redo log buffers). Then they're written into online redo logfiles, and when an online redo logfile is full, its content is written into an archived redo log.

 An Oracle database can run in the `ARCHIVELOG` mode or the `NOARCHIVELOG` mode. In the `ARCHIVELOG` mode, online redo logfiles are written into archived redo logs and in the `NOARCHIVELOG` mode, redo logfiles are overwritten without being archived as they become full. In a Data Guard environment, the primary database must be in the `ARCHIVELOG` mode.

In Data Guard, transfer of the changed data from the primary to standby database is achieved by redo with no alternative. However, the apply process of the redo content to the standby database may vary. The different methods on the apply process reveal different type of standby databases.

There were two kinds of standby databases before Oracle database Version 11*g*, which were: physical standby database and logical standby database. Within Version 11*g* we should mention a third type of standby database which is snapshot standby. Let's look at the properties of these standby database types.

Physical standby database

The Physical standby database is a block-based copy of the primary database. In a physical standby environment, in addition to containing the same database objects and same data, the primary and standby databases are identical on a block-for-block basis. Physical standby databases use Redo Apply method to apply changes. Redo Apply uses **Managed recovery process (MRP)** in order to manage application of the change in information on redo.

In Version 11*g*, a physical standby database can be accessible in read-only mode while Redo Apply is working, which is called Active Data Guard. Using the Active Data Guard feature, we can offload report jobs from the primary to physical standby database.

Physical standby database is the only option that has no limitation on storage vendor or data types to keep a synchronized copy of the primary database.

Logical standby database

Logical standby database is a feature introduced in Version 9*i*R2. In this configuration, redo data is first converted into SQL statements and then applied to the standby database. This process is called SQL Apply. This method makes it possible to access the standby database permanently and allows read/write while the replication of data is active. Thus, you're also able to create database objects on the standby database that don't exist on the primary database. So a logical standby database can be used for many other purposes along with high availability and disaster recovery.

Due to the basics of SQL Apply, a logical standby database will contain the same data as the primary database but in a different structure on the disks.

One discouraging aspect of the logical standby database is the unsupported data types, objects, and DDLs. The following data types are not supported to be replicated in a logical standby environment:

- BFILE
- Collections (including VARRAYS and nested tables)
- Multimedia data types (including Spatial, Image, and Oracle Text)
- ROWID and UROWID
- User-defined types

The logical standby database doesn't guarantee to contain all primary data because of the unsupported data types, objects, and DDLs. Also, SQL Apply consumes more hardware resources. Therefore, it certainly brings more performance issues and administrative complexities than Redo Apply.

Snapshot standby database

Principally, a snapshot standby database is a special condition of a physical standby database. Snapshot standby is a feature that is available with Oracle Database Version 11*g*. When you convert a Physical standby database into a snapshot standby database, it becomes accessible for read/write. You can run tests on this database and change the data. When you're finished with the snapshot standby database, it's possible to reverse all the changes made to the database and turn it back to a physical standby again.

An important point here is that a snapshot standby database can't run Redo Apply. Redo transfer continues but standby is not able to apply redo.

Oracle Data Guard evolution

It has been a long time that the Oracle Data Guard technology has been in the database administrator's life and it apparently evolved from the beginning until 11*g*R2. Let's look at this evolution closely through the different database versions.

Version 7.3 – stone age

The functionality of keeping a duplicate database in a separate server, which can be synchronized with the primary database, came with Oracle database Version 7.3 under the name of standby database. This standby database was constantly in recovery mode waiting for the archived redo logs to be synchronized. However, this feature was not able to automate the transfer of archived redo logs. Database administrators had to find a way to transfer archived redo logs and apply them to the standby server continuously. This was generally accomplished by a script running in the background.

The only aim of Version 7.3 of the standby database was disaster recovery. It was not possible to query the standby database or to open it for any purpose other than activating it in the event of failure of the primary database. Once the standby database was activated, it couldn't be returned to the standby recovery mode again.

Version 8*i* – first age

Oracle database Version 8*i* brought the much-awaited features to the standby database and made the archived log shipping and apply process automatic, which is now called managed standby environment and managed recovery, respectively. However, some users were choosing to apply the archived logs manually because it was not possible to set a delay in the managed recovery mode. This mode was bringing the risk of the accidental operations to reflect standby database quickly.

Along with the "managed" modes, 8*i* made it possible to open a standby database with the read-only option and allowed it to be used as a reporting database.

Even though there were new features that made the tool more manageable and practical, there were still serious deficiencies. For example, when we added a datafile or created a tablespace on the primary database, these changes were not being replicated to the standby database. Database administrators had to take care of this maintenance on the standby database. Also when we opened the primary database with resetlogs or restored a backup control file, we had to re-create the standby database.

Version 9*i* – middle age

First of all, with this version Oracle8*i* standby database was renamed to Oracle9*i* Data Guard. 9*i* Data Guard includes very important new features, which makes the product much more reliable and functional. The following features were included:

◆ *Oracle Data Guard Broker* management framework, which is used to centralize and automate the configuration, monitoring, and management of Oracle Data Guard installations, was introduced with this version.

◆ Zero data loss on failover was guaranteed as a configuration option.

◆ *Switchover* was introduced, which made it possible to change the roles of primary and standby. This made it possible to accomplish a planned maintenance on the primary database with very less service outage.

◆ Standby database administration became simpler because new datafiles on the primary database are created automatically on standby and if there are missing archived logs on standby, which is called gap; Data Guard detects and transmits the missing logs to standby automatically.

◆ Delay option was added, which made it possible to configure a standby database that is always behind the primary in a specified time delay.

◆ Parallel recovery increased recovery performance on the standby database.

In Version 9*i* Release 2, which was introduced in May 2002, one year after Release 1, there were again very important features announced. They are as follows:

◆ Logical standby database was introduced, which we've mentioned earlier in this chapter

◆ Three data protection modes were ready to use: Maximum Protection, Maximum Availability, and Maximum Performance, which offered more flexibility on configuration

◆ The Cascade standby database feature made it possible to configure a second standby database, which receives its redo data from the first standby database

Version 10*g* – new age

The 10*g* version again introduced important features of Data Guard but we can say that it perhaps fell behind expectations because of the revolutionary changes in release 9*i*. The following new features were introduces in Version 10*g*:

◆ One of the most important features of 10*g* was the Real-Time Apply. When running in Real-Time Apply mode, the standby database applies changes on the redo immediately after receiving it. Standby does not wait for the standby redo logfile to be archived. This provides faster switchover and failover.

◆ Flashback database support was introduced, which made it unnecessary to configure a delay in the Data Guard configuration. Using flashback technology, it was possible to flash back a standby database to a point in time.

◆ With 10*g* Data Guard, if we open a primary database with resetlogs it was not required to re-create the standby database. Standby was able to recover through resetlogs.

◆ Version 10*g* made it possible to use logical standby databases in the database software rolling upgrades of the primary database. This method made it possible to lessen the service outage time by performing switchover to the logical standby database.

10*g* Release 2 also introduced new features to Data Guard, but these features again were not satisfactory enough to make a jump to the Data Guard technology. The two most important features were Fast-Start Failover and the use of Guaranteed restore point:

◆ **Fast-start failover** automated and accelerated the failover operation when the primary database was lost. This option strengthened the disaster recovery role of Oracle Data Guard.

◆ **Guaranteed restore point** was not actually a Data Guard feature. It was a database feature, which made it possible to revert a database to the moment that Guaranteed restore point was created, as long as there is sufficient disk space for the flashback logs. Using this feature following scenario became possible: Activate a physical standby database after stopping Redo Apply, use it for testing with read/write operations, then revert the changes, make it standby again and synchronize it with the primary. Using a standby database read/write was offering a great flexibility to users but the archived log shipping was not able to continue while the standby is read/write and this was causing data loss on the possible primary database failure.

Version 11*g* – modern age

Oracle database version 11*g* offered the expected jump in the Data Guard technology, especially with two new features, which are called Active Data Guard and snapshot standby. The following features were introduced:

◆ Active Data Guard has been a milestone in Data Guard history, which enables a query from a physical standby database while the media recovery is active.

◆ Snapshot standby is a feature to use a physical standby database read/write for test purposes. As we mentioned, this was possible with 10*g*R2 Guaranteed restore point feature but 11*g* provided the continuous archived log shipping in the time period that standby is read/write with snapshot standby.

- It has been possible to compress redo traffic in a Data Guard configuration, which is useful in excessive redo generation rates and resolving gaps. Compression of redo when resolving gaps was introduced in 11gR1 and compression of all redo data was introduced in 11gR2.

- Use of the physical standby databases for the rolling upgrades of database software was enabled, aka Transient Logical Standby.

- It became possible to include different operating systems in a Data Guard configuration such as Windows and Linux.

- Lost-write, which is a serious data corruption type arising from the misinformation of storage subsystem on completing the write of a block, can be detected in an 11g Data Guard configuration. Recovery is automatically stopped in such a case.

- RMAN fast incremental backup feature "Block Change Tracking" can be run on an Active Data Guard enabled standby database.

- Another very important enhancement in 11g was Automatic Block Corruption Repair feature that was introduced with 11gR2. With this feature, a corrupted data block in the primary database can be automatically replaced with an uncorrupted copy from a physical standby database in Active Data Guard mode and vice versa.

We've gone through the evolution of Oracle Data Guard from its beginning until today. As you may notice, Data Guard started its life as a very simple database property revealed to keep a synchronized database copy with a lot of manual work and now it's a complicated tool with advanced automation, precaution, and monitoring features. Now let's move on with the architecture and components of Oracle Data Guard 11gR2.

Oracle Data Guard architecture

The main architecture of Oracle Data Guard 11gR2 includes a primary database, up to 30 standby databases, the redo transport services, (which automatically ship the redo log data from the primary to standby server), and Apply Services (which applies the changes in redo on the standby database). There are of course some background processes special to a Data Guard configuration, which run the services in question.

In a Data Guard configuration, the switchover and failover concepts are also very important. By performing a switchover, it's possible to change the roles of the primary and standby databases and change the direction of the redo shipping. Failover is the option that we must use to open a standby database to user connection in read/write mode, when the primary database is inaccessible.

The last Data Guard components that we'll mention in this chapter are user interfaces to monitor and administrate a Data Guard configuration. These are SQL*Plus, Oracle Enterprise Manager Cloud Control, and Data Guard broker command-line interface (DGMGRL).

Data Guard services

These services are the vital points of a Data Guard configuration. Database administrators should decide and use the proper configuration to supply the business needs and tune these services to comply with SLAs.

Redo transport services

In a primary database, when a user commits a transaction, the relevant redo data is written into online redo logfiles from memory (Redo Log Buffer). After the online redo log group becomes full it is archived into an archived redo logfile with a log switch. It's possible to configure Data Guard sending the redo data to standby databases from the log buffer as the transactions are committed (by LGWR process) or from the online redo logfiles when they're being archived (by ARCn processes). Shipping redo data with ARCH will result in more data loss in the case of primary database failure because the data change information in the current online log of primary will be lost.

The following diagram shows the Data Guard configuration with ARCH transportation mode:

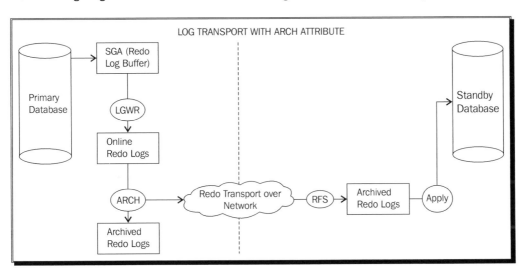

Here are the important properties of the log transport with the ARCH attribute:

- Logs are sent by the ARCH process; the LNS process is not in use
- Standby redo logs are not mandatory on the standby database
- Data in the unarchived online redo log will be lost in a failover

If LGWR is used for the redo transportation, it's possible to guarantee zero data loss failovers by creating a Data Guard configuration in which the primary database waits for confirmation from the standby database that redo has been received, before it informs that the commit is completed. This configuration is called **Synchronous redo transport (SYNC)**. However, this may affect the performance of the primary database.

The following diagram shows the Data Guard configuration with LGWR and SYNC transportation mode:

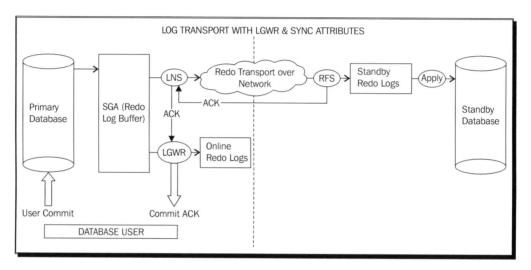

The following points explain the diagram in a better way:

♦ Redo is read and sent to the standby database directly from the log buffer by the LNS process

♦ Acknowledgment needed from the standby database (RFS to LNS and LNS to LGWR) to send COMMIT ACK to the database user

♦ It's mandatory to use standby redo logs

♦ Zero data loss in failover can be guaranteed with this configuration

♦ There maybe slower response times on the primary database

♦ The primary database stops giving service in a network disruption incident between primary and standby

If SYNC redo transport is chosen in an 11*g* Data Guard configuration, the performance decrease on the primary database will be less than the earlier releases. Previously, the primary database used to finish writes to the online redo log first and then send redo to the standby database. There were two consecutive I/O operations that the primary database needs to wait for in order to complete the commit. In 11*g* these two I/O operations run in parallel. The primary database does not wait for finishing writes to online redo log and it sends the redo data to standby at the same time.

The other option is to use the **Asynchronous redo transport (ASYNC)** method, which avoids the impact to primary database performance. In this method, the primary database never waits for any acknowledgment from the standby database in order to complete the commit. In the ASYNC redo transport method we have the performance gain; however, this method does not guarantee zero data loss failovers because it does not guarantee all the committed transactions being received by the standby database at any moment.

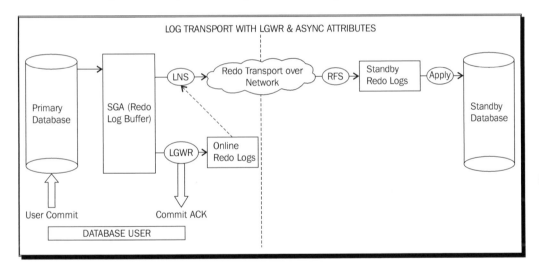

The following points explain the diagram in a better way:

♦ No acknowledgment needed from standby to send the COMMIT ACK to the database user

♦ Redo is read and sent to standby from the Redo Log Buffer or online redo logs by the LNS process. If LNS cannot catch the send data in the Redo Log Buffer before it is recycled, it automatically reads and sends redo data from the online redo log.

♦ The committed transactions that weren't shipped to standby yet, may be lost in a failover

♦ Potential slower response time on primary database with SYNC mode is not valid here

Protection modes

Data Guard offers three data protection modes, which serve different business needs in terms of data protection and performance. You can find the properties of these modes in the following comparison table:

Mode	Redo transport	Action with no standby database connection	Risk of data loss
Maximum Protection	SYNC and LGWR	The primary database needs to write redo to at least one standby database. Otherwise it will shut down.	Zero data loss is guaranteed.
Maximum Availability	SYNC and LGWR	Normally works with SYNC redo transport. If the primary database cannot write redo to any of its standby databases, it continues processing transactions as in ASYNC mode.	Zero data loss in normal operation, but not guaranteed.
Maximum Performance	ASYNC and LGWR/ARCH	Never expects acknowledgment from the standby database.	Potential for minimal data loss in a normal operation.

Apply services

Data Guard automatically transfers redo data from the primary to standby database and applies it on the standby database. Redo transport services work independent of apply services and never wait for Redo Apply but if there's a problem on redo transportation, apply services normally stop and wait for the new redo to arrive. The most important categorization in apply services is the Redo Apply and SQL Apply. These apply methods create the infrastructure of physical and logical standby databases.

As a property of Data Guard, both in Redo Apply and SQL Apply, the standby database validates the redo data in order to prevent physical corruptions that may occur at the primary database from reflecting to the standby database. By default, the standby database writes received redo data into the standby redo logfiles and apply services do not apply redo until the standby redo log is archived as an archived redo log. If we use the **real-time apply** feature, which became available with 10*g*, the apply services don't wait for the archival operation and apply the redo data as it's received and written into the standby redo logs.

It's also possible to specify a delay value to keep the standby database behind the primary database with the specified minutes. This may be chosen to prevent human error operations on the primary database to be applied to standby immediately. However, as we discussed previously, after the support of flashback database, there's no need to define a delay in Data Guard configuration.

Redo Apply (physical standby databases)

Redo Apply keeps a block-by-block copy of the primary database. By default, Redo Apply automatically runs a parallel apply processes, which is equal to the number of CPUs of the standby database server minus one. These parallel recovery processes are controlled by the MRP process, which is the background process responsible for the application of redo data.

Redo Apply has the following benefits for its users:

◆ There are no unsupported data types, objects, and DDLs

◆ Redo Apply has higher performance when compared with SQL Apply or any other replication solutions

◆ It offers simple management by keeping the database structure exactly the same as the primary database with its fully automated architecture

◆ It's possible to take advantages of Active Data Guard and snapshot standby for reporting and testing

◆ Backups taken from physical standby databases are ready to be restored to primary. So we can offload the backup from primary

◆ Redo Apply offers a strong corruption detection and prevention mechanism.

◆ It's possible to use physical standby databases for the rolling upgrades of the database software, which is known as transient logical standby

◆ The real-time apply feature applies the redo as it's received. This feature makes it possible to query real-time or near real-time data from the standby database

By offering these features, Redo Apply (physical standby database) has become a very popular and widely used-technology for the high availability and disaster recovery of Oracle databases.

Monitoring Redo Apply

While Redo Apply runs on the standby database, administrators need to monitor the status of the apply process and check if it's working in accordance with the selected configuration. As mentioned, the MRP process is responsible from the Redo Apply process and monitoring the status of this process will give us valuable information on what's going on with Redo Aapply.

Time for action – monitoring Redo Apply

We'll install Data Guard configuration beginning with *Chapter 2, Configuring Oracle Data Guard Physical Standby Database*. So, you will not be able to perform the actions in this chapter on the test environment. Please just read the actions to consolidate the given theoretical information mentioned earlier.

We'll query the `v$managed_standby` view on the standby database for monitoring. The Data Guard configuration is in the Maximum Performance mode with `ASYNC` and `LGWR` attributes. We'll change the redo transport and apply characteristic and monitor the behavior of Data Guard.

1. For our first test, a one hour delay is defined. Let's check this by running the following query on the primary database:

```
SQL> select name, value from v$parameter where name like
'log_archive_dest_2';
NAME                       VALUE
------------------         ----------------------------------------
log_archive_dest_2         SERVICE=TEST_STANDBY LGWR ASYNC
                           VALID_FOR=(ONLINE_LOGFILES,PRIMARY_ROLE)
                           DB_UNIQUE_NAME=TEST DELAY=60
```

We can see that a 60-minute delay is defined on the primary database. This doesn't mean that the redo data will be sent with a 60-minute delay. This setting means the redo data will be sent immediately but the standby database will not apply the redo that was received in the last 60 minutes.

> **Downloading the example code**
>
> You can download the example code files for all Packt books you have purchased from your account at `http://www.packtpub.com`. If you purchased this book elsewhere, you can visit `http://www.packtpub.com/support` and register to have the files e-mailed directly to you.

2. So let's see what's happening on the standby side by running the following query on the standby database. (Note: We can connect to a standby database from the standby database server with the `sqlplus / as sysdba` command. This allows us to connect to the database as a sys user and with password file authentication.)

```
SQL> select process, status, thread#, sequence#, block#, blocks
from v$managed_standby;

PROCESS    STATUS         THREAD#   SEQUENCE#      BLOCK#      BLOCKS
--------   ------------   -------   ---------      ------      ----------
ARCH       CONNECTED      0         0              0           0
ARCH       CONNECTED      0         0              0           0
MRP0       WAIT_FOR_LOG   1         461            0           0
RFS        IDLE           0         0              0           0
RFS        IDLE           1         469            1727085     40
```

3. The output shows that the log with the sequence `469` is being received from primary, but the `MRP` process is still waiting for the log with the sequence number `461`. Let's check if this log has been received:

```
SQL> select name, archived from v$archived_log where
sequence#=461;
```

```
NAME                                                          ARC
------------------------------------------------------------  --
+FRA/test/archivelog/2012_08_08/thread_1_seq_461.2606.7908  YES
```

4. So the log sequence `461` was received but `MRP` is not applying it because of the configured 60-minute delay on the primary database. We can see this situation more clearly on the alert log:

```
RFS[1]: Archived Log:
'+FRA/test/archivelog/2012_08_08/thread_1_seq_461.2606.79081019
9'
Wed Aug  8 22:31:28 2012
RFS[1]: Archive log thread 1 sequence 461 available in 60
minute(s)
Wed Aug  8 23:14:48 2012
Media Recovery Log +FRA/test/archivelog/2012_08_08/thread_1_
seq_460.2841.790809291
Media Recovery Delayed for 60 minute(s)
```

The highlighted line in the previous code shows that the log sequence `461` was received at `22:31` but will be available to use only after 60 minutes.

5. Now let's cancel the delay on the media recovery and monitor again. On the primary database perform the following:

```
SQL> alter system set log_archive_dest_2='SERVICE=TEST_STANDBY
LGWR ASYNC VALID_FOR=(ONLINE_LOGFILES,PRIMARY_ROLE)
DB_UNIQUE_NAME=TEST';
System altered.
```

6. After a few minutes on the standby database perform the following:

```
SQL> select process, status, thread#, sequence#, block#, blocks
from v$managed_standby;
```

PROCESS	STATUS	THREAD#	SEQUENCE#	BLOCK#	BLOCKS
ARCH	CONNECTED	0	0	0	0
ARCH	CLOSING	1	470	3432448	403
MRP0	**WAIT_FOR_LOG**	**1**	**471**	**0**	**0**
RFS	IDLE	0	0	0	0
RFS	**IDLE**	**1**	**471**	**878728**	**2**

We can see that, the `MRP` is not waiting for any old sequence; it's waiting for the log sequence that is on the way from primary to standby. (Because the LGWR attribute is used on log transport, this log is the current log sequence on the primary.)

7. Let's look at the alert log again:

```
Thu Aug 09 00:27:16 2012
Media Recovery Log +FRA/test/archivelog/2012_08_09/thread_1_
seq_470.515.790820745
Thu Aug 09 00:27:57 2012
Media Recovery Waiting for thread 1 sequence 471 (in transit)
```

As you can see there's no text in alert log about the delay, because it was cancelled. The MRP process applied the log sequence 470 and started to wait for the next log (471) to completely arrive and get archived. It also indicates that the next log is in transit, which means it is currently being received by RFS.

8. Let's convert the Redo Apply mode to real-time apply and see how Data Guard will apply the redo as it received from the primary database. First we'll stop Redo Apply on the standby database and start again in the real-time apply mode:

```
SQL> ALTER DATABASE RECOVER MANAGED STANDBY DATABASE CANCEL;
Database altered.
SQL> ALTER DATABASE RECOVER MANAGED STANDBY DATABASE USING
CURRENT LOGFILE DISCONNECT FROM SESSION;
Database altered.
```

9. After a few minutes we will check the status of the processes:

```
SQL> select process, status, thread#, sequence#, block#, blocks
from v$managed_standby;
```

PROCESS	STATUS	THREAD#	SEQUENCE#	BLOCK#	BLOCKS
ARCH	CONNECTED	0	0	0	0
ARCH	CLOSING	1	472	3432448	403
MRP0	**APPLYING_LOG**	1	473	1985328	4096000
RFS	IDLE	0	0	0	0
RFS	**IDLE**	1	473	1985957	11

Now it's obvious that MRP is applying the log as it arrives to standby. The RFS process is transferring the log sequence 473, which is the current log on the primary side, and at the same time the MRP process is applying the same log sequence. Look at the block number column; we can see that MRP is applying the redo blocks that have just arrived.

You should also know that, even there is a DELAY value specified on the primary database; if the apply mode is real-time apply on the standby database, the DELAY will be ignored. You'll see the following lines in the standby alert log in such a case:

```
Managed standby recovery started with USING CURRENT
LOGFILE
Ignoring previously specified DELAY 60 minutes
```

What just happened?

You have just seen the Redo Apply behavior on different Data Guard configurations such as delayed, non-delayed, and real-time apply. You learned how to query the status of the important Data Guard processes MRP and RFS on the standby database.

Pop quiz – real-time apply consideration

Q1. What's the risk of using real time apply and how can we overcome this risk?

SQL Apply (logical standby databases)

The SQL Apply technology resides on mining the standby redo logs, building SQL transactions that apply the changes in question, and finally, executing the SQL on the standby database, which is read/write accessible. This process is more expensive in terms of hardware resource usage as a matter of course. The LSP process manages the application of changes to a logical standby database.

The general purpose of building a logical standby database is reporting the needs with read/write access requirement. SQL Apply is not suitable for disaster recovery and high availability as much as Redo Apply because of the unsupported data types and logically different database infrastructure.

SQL Apply offers the following benefits to its users:

◆ The logical standby database is always read/write accessible while SQL Apply is running; so that users may run reports, create temporary tables and indexes for performance issues. Also it's possible to create objects and keep data on the standby database, which do not exist on primary.

◆ The logical standby database is open for read/write activity. But normally there are no writes possible on the standby objects, which exist on primary. This feature maintains the consistency of the replicated primary data.

◆ It's possible to upgrade the Oracle database software version with almost no downtime using a logical standby database.

Role transitions

Role transitions basically enable users to change the roles of the databases in a Data Guard configuration. There are two role transition options in Data Guard, which are **switchover** and **failover**.

Switchover

In a basic Data Guard configuration with one primary and one standby database, a switchover operation changes the roles of these databases, and so the direction of the redo shipping. In a correctly designed configuration, archived log shipping in the opposite direction starts immediately after switchover and clients do not need to change their connection descriptions in order to connect the new primary database.

If there is more than one standby database in a Data Guard configuration, it's possible to perform switchover between the primary and any of the standby databases. After the switchover, the new primary database can continue to send redo to all of the standby databases in the configuration.

Regardless of the configuration of Data Guard, a switchover operation always guarantees zero data loss. This brings high reliability to switchover and thus it's widely used for planned maintenance operations, such as hardware or operating system upgrades, database software rolling upgrade, and other infrastructure maintenances. Switchover reduces the downtime for these maintenance operations by a significant amount of time.

Failover

Failover is the operation of converting a standby database to a primary database, because of a failure in the original primary database. If the flashback database is disabled on the primary database, failover is an operation with no return. In other words, we have to flashback the failed primary database to a state before failover in order to re-establish the configuration. Without flashback, Data Guard configuration needs to be built from scratch.

A manual database failover may be performed in the case of failure with the initiative of the database owner. However, this will require extra outage for the decision making. If fast-start failover is used, which is a 10*g* release 2 feature, the failover operation will perform automatically.

Fast-start failover

This property of automating the failover operation can only be used in Data Guard broker enabled configuration. The observer process which runs on a different server from the primary and standby databases, continuously monitors the accessibility of the primary database. If both the observer and the standby database cannot reach the primary database for a predefined length of time, a fully-automated failover process is started. With 11*g* Release 2, we call it fully automated, because this process includes changing the role of the standby as primary, starting the database services on the new primary database, disconnecting the client from the failed primary database, and redirecting them to the new primary database.

If the observer establishes the connection with the original primary database again after the failover, it informs the database that the failover was performed and it will automatically reinstate the database using flashback. In order to configure fast-start failover, we need to specify the fast recovery area and enable flashback on the primary and standby databases.

Keep in mind that in Version 11*g*, Data Guard must be on Maximum Availability or Maximum Performance mode in order to use fast-start failover. In 10*g* Release 2, only Maximum Availability mode is supported for fast-start failover.

User interfaces for administering Data Guard

There are three options for a database administrator to manage a Data Guard environment, which are SQL*Plus command-line interface, Oracle Enterprise Manager, and Data Guard broker command-line interface (DGMGRL). In almost every IT infrastructure management interface, command-line tools offer great flexibility and detailed options and the graphical interfaces are user friendly, simple, and automated.

SQL*Plus

SQL*Plus provides all kinds of administration and monitoring operations for the administrators, but you'll need to access each server in the Data Guard configuration and do the operations separately. It's also sometimes painful to have easy readable outputs from SQL*Plus.

DGMGRL

Data Guard broker command-line interface (DGMGRL) is the Data Guard broker tool that automates and centralizes Data Guard management. Using DGMGRL we can run some consecutive operations such as switchover and failover with just one command. Also, the status of the Data Guard configuration can be queried with special Data Guard broker commands via DGMGRL. Outputs are designed to be easily readable.

Enterprise Manager

Enterprise Manager offers an integrated graphical user interface for Data Guard broker enabled Data Guard configurations. It's possible to graphically monitor the general configuration information, performance, synchronization status of Data Guard, and also perform administration tasks such as switchover, failover, adding, and removing standby database from configuration.

Time for action – using interfaces to monitor Data Guard

1. At the first step we will use SQL*Plus to gather information from Data Guard and monitor its status. The connection to the standby database must be from the standby database server with password file authentication if the standby database is on mount mode and so not accessible from outside. If Active Data Guard is enabled, it's also possible to connect a standby database remotely. Let's connect to the standby database and gather the main Data Guard configuration information:

```
$sqlplus / as sysdba
SQL> select database_role,open_mode,protection_mode from
v$database;


DATABASE_ROLE        OPEN_MODE             PROTECTION_MODE
----------------     --------------------  --------------------
PHYSICAL STANDBY     READ ONLY WITH APPLY  MAXIMUM PERFORMANCE


SQL> select recovery_mode from v$archive_dest_status where
recovery_mode !='IDLE';


RECOVERY_MODE
----------------------
MANAGED REAL TIME APPLY
```

We have a physical standby database with the Maximum Performance mode. The value of the OPEN_MODE column is READ ONLY WITH APPLY, which indicates that Active Data Guard is enabled. The output of the second query shows that real-time apply is being used as the recovery mode.

2. Now let's check the status of the Data Guard synchronization:

```
SQL> select name, value from v$dataguard_stats;
NAME                     VALUE
------------------------ ----------------
transport lag            +00 00:00:00
apply lag                +00 00:00:00
apply finish time
estimated startup time   231
```

The output shows that we have a fully synchronized standby database, where there is no redo transport and apply lag. The **estimated startup time** value is **231** seconds, which is an estimate of the time needed to start and open the standby database.

3. Now we'll see an example about how to use Data Guard broker command-line interface (DGMGRL) to gather information about the Data Guard status. We can run DGMGRL on the primary database server and connect locally or we can also connect from a remote server. Let's connect from the primary database server locally:

```
$dgmgrl
DGMGRL> connect sys/password;
Connected.
We have connected to the primary database with the sys user.
Now we can check the configuration.
DGMGRL> show configuration;
Configuration - TEST
  Protection Mode: MaxPerformance
  Databases:
    Turkey    - Primary database
    India     - Physical standby database

Fast-Start Failover: DISABLED

Configuration Status:
SUCCESS
```

4. We had the general configuration information with the `show configuration` command. At the end of the output we see the configuration status as SUCCESS, which means, everything in the broker configuration is working properly. However, we can also see a status of warning or error. We can also run the `show database` command for some general information:

```
DGMGRL> show database 'India';
Database
  Name:            India
  Role:            PHYSICAL STANDBY
  Enabled:         YES
  Intended State:  ONLINE
  Instance(s):
    india
Current status for "India":
SUCCESS
```

 In order to gather detailed information from the databases in the Data Guard configuration, we use the keyword `verbose` in the `show database` command such as `show database verbose 'India'`.

5. The last interface to monitor and manage a Data Guard configuration is the Enterprise Manager Cloud Control, with the former name Enterprise Manager Grid Control. The following screenshot shows the interface for the monitoring and administration of Data Guard. Detailed information will be given in *Chapter 8, Integrating Data Guard with the Complete Oracle Environment*, about using Enterprise Manager Cloud Control for Data Guard management:

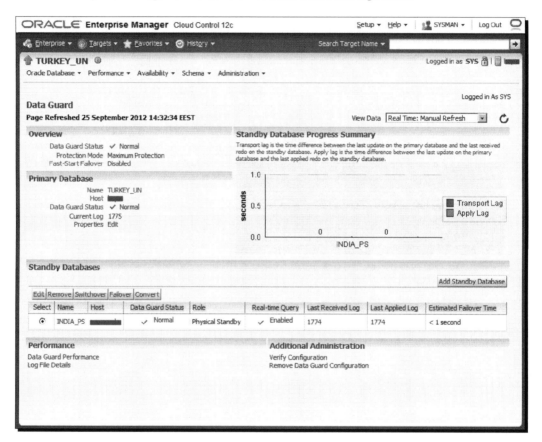

What just happened?

You have just seen examples of monitoring the Data Guard environment with three different interfaces. These examples are just intended to give you a first impression of what these interfaces look like. Properties and details of the tools in question will be covered in the next chapters.

All of these interfaces can be used to monitor and manage the Data Guard; however, they all have their own pros and cons. If you already use Enterprise Manager Cloud Control in your current IT infrastructure, Data Guard installations must be added as targets in order to take advantage of its visual and easy monitoring and management potential. If you don't have Cloud Control but have multiple Data Guard installations, you should think about using it to overcome the challenges of central monitoring.

Data Guard background processes

In a Data Guard configuration we can see some Oracle Data Guard specific background processes in both, primary and standby databases. These processes perform the operations of redo transport and apply services. Data Guard broker also has some specific background processes. We can see the description and duties of the most important Data Guard processes as follows:

- **MRP0 (Managed Standby Recovery Process)** coordinates the read and apply process of redo in a physical standby database.

- **RFS (Remote File Server)** is responsible for receiving the redo data, which is sent by the primary database to the standby database.

- **LSP0 (Logical Standby Coordinator Process)** coordinates the SQL Apply processes, which are the mining processes and apply processes.

- **LSP1 (Logical Standby Dictionary Build Process)** is used on the logical standby databases when a switchover or failover is in action.

- **LSP2 (Logical Standby Set Guard Process)** is used to operate Database Guard settings. Database Guard specifies which objects will be protected for modification in a logical standby database.

- **NSAn (Redo Transport NSA1 Process)** is used on the primary database to ship redo data to the standby database when ASYNC mode is being used. There may be multiple NSA processes such as NSA1 and NSA2.

- **NSSn (Redo Transport NSA1 Process)** is also used on the primary database to ship redo data to the standby database. However, only when the SYNC mode is being used.

- **DMON (Data Guard Broker Monitor Process)** runs on every instance in a Data Guard broker configuration. It communicates with local database and DMON processes of the remote databases. The broker-related requests and the monitoring information are transferred on this communication channel.

- **FSFP (Data Guard broker fast-start failover pinger process)** is used for the management of fast-start failover status.

Other replication solutions and Data Guard

There are many options to replicate an Oracle database data to a remote system. In the scope of disaster recovery, Oracle Data Guard and storage-based replication solutions such as EMC Symmetrix Remote Data Facility (SRDF), HP Continuous Access, Hitachi Universal Replicator and TrueCopy, IBM Global Mirror, and Metro Mirror are the main players in the market. When talking about Oracle database replication we also have to mention Oracle's well-known replication technologies GoldenGate and Streams. However, these products were not developed for disaster recovery fundamentally. Their primary aim is replication for ETL and data warehouse.

There are also some third-party tools capable of replicating Oracle database data, but here we'll mention about the most commonly-used technologies: Data Guard, storage-based replication solutions, GoldenGate, and Streams.

Storage-based replication solutions

Storage-base replication solutions technologies are based upon the storage-array based replication of data. Thus, the source of data does not matter. All kinds of application and database data can be replicated to a remote location, where Data Guard is only able to replicate Oracle databases.

In general there are two kinds of storage-based replication: synchronous and asynchronous replication. Synchronous replication means that each update to the source storage unit must also be updated in the target storage unit before another update can process. This guarantees zero data loss in the case of primary site failure. However, synchronous replication affects the I/O respond performance of the primary system depending on the distance between sites and network capacity. Therefore, this technology is distance limited. Synchronous replication technologies support up to 300 km distance between sites in the current technology level.

Asynchronous replication provides a long-distance replication solution with minimal impact on performance. In some products, the main problem with the asynchronous mode is the data consistency on the secondary site. The primary site sends a periodic, incremental copy of updates to the secondary site instead of a constant stream of updates. So there is no guarantee that dependent write operations on the primary site are transferred and applied to the remote destination in the same sequence.

Using storage-based replication solutions, it's not possible to start an Oracle instance and query database on the secondary site using the disks with the replicated data because of the data inconsistency issue. However Data Guard offers Active Data Guard, which enables users to query the standby database while replication is on the go. Some other advantages of Data Guard over storage-based replication solutions are enhanced corruption detection and prevention, automated database failover (fast-start failover), and RMAN backup offloading features that may not benefit from the use of storage-based replication solutions.

GoldenGate and Streams

GoldenGate is a data replication and integration tool for heterogeneous environments. It provides real-time capture, transformation, routing, and delivery of database transactions across heterogeneous systems (Oracle, DB2, MySQL, SQL Server, Sybase, Teradata, Netezza, and so on). Oracle agreed to acquire GoldenGate software in 2009 and then released 10.4, 11.1, and 11.2 versions with new enhancements. On the other hand, Streams is a built-in feature of the Oracle database that was first announced with database Version 9.2 and allows information sharing within an Oracle database or between Oracle databases.

Their common property is their capability of capturing, propagating, and applying data changes between Oracle databases.

On the other hand their main differences are:

+ The heterogeneous platforms and data integration support of GoldenGate is different from that of Streams
+ License conditions for Streams is included in the Oracle Enterprise Edition license and GoldenGate is a self-licensed product

Because of the GoldenGate's wider technology infrastructure and flexibility over Streams, Oracle announced that Oracle Streams will continue to be supported, but will not be actively enhanced and the best elements of Oracle Streams will be evaluated for inclusion with Oracle GoldenGate. It was also indicated that GoldenGate is the strategic product of Oracle on data distribution and data integration.

 Oracle recommends Data Guard for full Oracle database protection with the high availability and disaster recovery purpose and recommends GoldenGate for information distribution and consolidation, application upgrades, changes, and also applications desiring flexible high availability needs.

An important feature of GoldenGate that makes the product different from its counterparts is the bidirectional replication capability, which is also called active-active replication. With this feature the primary and standby concepts are replaced by two active primary sites. Updates on site A are replicated to site B, and updates on site B are replicated to site A. The main challenges here are conflict handling and loop detection. A conflict is likely to occur in a bi-directional environment, where the same row or field is being updated at both sides and the changes are replicated. In this situation, a decision needs to be made if both transactions fail, or one transaction overwrites the other. The other key point is loop detection. If an update is replicated from site A to site B and then the same update from site B to site A, and so on, this loop needs to be detected and solved. The following diagram shows the general structure of an active-active GoldenGate configuration:

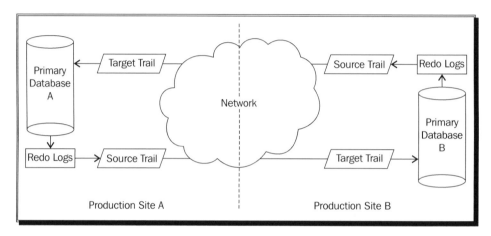

GoldenGate is a preferred solution to extract data from production databases in order to feed the data warehouse. It offers much flexibility to select specific data on the database and if needed transform the data before it hits the target.

The replication market's leaders, namely, Data Guard, storage-based replication products, and GoldenGate are compared in the following table with their most important features. Streams is out of this comparison because of the strategy mentioned by Oracle on its replication products:

	Data Guard	Storage-based replication	GoldenGate
Hardware independency	Supported. Possible to choose different server/ storage vendors for primary and standby.	Not Supported. Must use the same storage vendor on both sides.	Supported. Possible to choose different server/ storage vendors for primary and standby.
Software independency	Not supported. Only Oracle database replication.	Supported. All kinds of database and application data can be replicated.	Limited support. Different database products can be replicated.
Zero data loss capability	Supported with Maximum Protection mode.	Limited support with synchronous replication (distance limitation about 300 km).	Not supported.
Corruption detection and prevention	Supported.	Not supported.	Not supported.
Bidirectional replication within one database	Not supported.	Not supported.	Supported. Two active sites may send updates to each other.
Query standby data	Supported with Active Data Guard and Snapshot standby features.	Not supported.	Supported with continuously read/ write accessible target databases.
Inside database selective replication	Limited support with logical standby databases.	Not supported.	Supported. Data may be selected and transformed before it hits the target.
Automatic database failover	Supported with fast-start failover feature.	Not supported.	Not supported.
GUI based management	Supported.	Supported.	Supported.
RMAN backup offload	Supported. The primary database RMAN backups can be offloaded to a physical standby and backups will physically be the same.	Not supported.	Supported. In a full replication of primary, RMAN backups may be offloaded but backups will only logically be the same, not physically.

	Data Guard	Storage-based replication	GoldenGate
Cascaded destinations for replication	Supported.	Supported.	Supported.
License	License required only for Active Data Guard. Otherwise no extra license required.	License required for storage replication software.	License required for GoldenGate software.

 The information on this table reflects the general characteristics of the storage-based replication products. All vendor products don't offer the exact same features; also the features for the same objective may have different capabilities and restrictions.

After reviewing the comparison table, it's obvious that Data Guard has better properties for high availability and disaster recovery purposed Oracle database replication. Storage-based replication products offer disaster recovery solution for the complete IT infrastructure data; however, when the case is Oracle databases, they cannot offer the Oracle integrated, flexible, and automatized features as in Data Guard. On the other side, we can see that GoldenGate was positioned especially for ETL and data integration requirements and it has great flexibility in this field. However, it also cannot reach Data Guard standards on data protection and disaster recovery.

Summary

You've reached the end of this chapter. This chapter provided the foundation for the rest of this book. We covered the definition, general properties, and history of Oracle Data Guard.

It's very important to know the capabilities and general properties of similar products when implementing an IT solution. We have now gained an understanding of what Data Guard and the other main Oracle database replication products offer to its users. We're able to make decisions for the implementation of our replication requirements.

The next chapter will explain the configuration process of a physical standby database in detail.

2

Configuring the Oracle Data Guard Physical Standby Database

In this chapter, the installation of the physical standby database will be covered in three steps. The first step will be to prepare the environment for the installation, especially the preinstallation tasks on the database. Then the second step for creating a physical standby database will be covered. In the last step, the Data Guard installation will be verified to see if it is installed correctly.

In this chapter, we'll discuss the following topics:

- ◆ Planning and understanding requirements
- ◆ Preparation for the configuration
- ◆ Step-by-step instructions to create the physical standby database
- ◆ Verifying the physical standby database configuration (post-installation steps)

Before preparing the configuration, you should know the business criticality of your database, how to avoid failures, and how much data you are ready to lose.

Preconfiguration for Data Guard

The Data Guard configuration contains a primary database that transmits redo data to a standby database. The standby database is remotely located from the primary database for disaster recovery and backup operations. You can also configure the standby database at the same location as the primary database. However, for disaster-recovery purposes and to make it highly available, it's strongly recommended to configure standby in a geographically remote location.

Before implementing a Data Guard configuration, take into account concepts such as high data availability, efficient systems utilization, and data protection.

- **Availability**: Outages should be tolerated transparently and should be recovered quickly in case of server failures or any network failures
- **Protection**: Ensure minimum data loss; standby data should be isolated from production faults such as storage failures, site failures, data corruptions, or operator errors
- **Utilization**: Standby resources should be utilized for productive use in case of any planned maintenance or for application access

Data loss consideration

Before implementing any high-availability solution, you need to determine the acceptable amount of data loss. Data loss should not be calculated in terms of time (for example, seconds or minutes); it should be calculated in terms of transactions. The following example is drafted from a production database. Notice how much data can be lost in 60 seconds. During the peak hours of your business, run the `Stats` pack or AWR snapshot at periodic intervals 2-3 times. In the report, take a look at the **Load profile** section. The **Per second** column of the **Redo size** row is the redo generation rate of your database:

Load profile		
	Per second	**Per transaction**
Redo size	16615645.13	9172093.26

Instance activity stats			
Statistic	**Total**	**Per second**	**Per transaction**
Redo size	16615645.13	16615645.13	9172093.26

In the **Instance activity stats** table, the redo size generated is 16615645.13 bytes per second—that is nearly 15.9 MB per second and nearly 950 MB per minute. Are you ready to lose 950 MB of data? You may want to rethink your recover plan. It must be calculated in terms of transactions.

Based on your transactions rate, calculate how much redo is generated and how much data loss is acceptable. You can configure Data Guard to have **zero data loss**.

These load profiles and statistics can be gathered using the following utilities:

- **After 9i**: To execute the AWR report, use `SQL>@?/rdbms/admin/awrrpt.sql`
- **Oracle 9i**: To execute the `Stats` pack report, use `SQL>@?/rdbms/admin/spreport.sql`

Network bandwidth consideration

We need to determine the network bandwidth required for a Data Guard physical standby implementation. Network latency is a huge factor in the amount of redo you will be able to transport from your primary site to the standby site. This value is unique to your network, and if you have a high latency network you might not be able to sustain the required rate of redo shipping. The wide area network between the primary site and standby site may be used by more than just Data Guard. So, the bandwidth requirements have to be sorted out. The formula used by Oracle, assuming a conservative TCP/IP network overhead of 30 percent, is as follows:

Required bandwidth (Mbps) = ((Redo rate bytes per sec. / 0.7) * 8) / 1,000,000

Based on this formula, according to the redo size from the preceding example, the required bandwidth is equal to 189.8930872 mbps (((16615645.13/ 0.7) * 8) / 1,000,000). Of course, according to the preceding example, bandwidth should be very high, because it's an example taken during a huge job with lot of DML activity. This means that the peak redo generation rate is a good indicator of your Data-Guard-related network requirements. Make sure that, while specifying your network requirements with your network service provider, you also consider other applications and their **Service Level Agreements (SLAs)** using the same network. The preceding formula indicates the network bandwidth that should be available to Data Guard; it does not indicate what the entire network bandwidth should be between your primary and DR data centers.

Preparing the primary database

This topic describes Data Guard parameters and how to prepare the standby database creation and configuration. What prerequisites are mandatory to be completed before configuring the standby database? We will discuss each and every task that needs to be accomplished.

Archive log mode

For any primary database, there are some basics you should configure. One of these is to run the primary database in the **archive log mode**, which is a mandatory step. You can create a database in the archive log mode or the **noarchive log mode** and you can change this later.

If the primary database is already in the archive log mode, you can skip this step and proceed with the next one. If this has not been done, perform the following procedure to put the primary database in the archive log mode.

Time for action – enabling the archive log mode

Perform the following steps on the primary database:

1. Check whether archiving has been enabled or disabled, as follows:

```
SQL> archive log list
Database log mode               No Archive Mode
Automatic archival              Disabled
Archive destination             USE_DB_RECOVERY_FILE_DEST
Oldest online log sequence      6
Current log sequence            8
```

2. Perform a clean shutdown, as follows:

```
SQL> shutdown immediate
Database closed.
Database dismounted.
ORACLE instance shut down.
```

 Ensure that you have performed a clean shutdown; if not, you may see this error: **ORA-00265: instance recovery required, cannot set ARCHIVELOG mode**.

3. Start the database in the mount state.

```
SQL>startup mount
ORACLE instance started.
Total System Global Area    818401280 bytes
Fixed Size                  2217792 bytes
Variable Size               515901632 bytes
Database Buffers            297795584 bytes
Redo Buffers                2486272 bytes
Database mounted.
```

4. Enable the archive log mode.

```
SQL> alter database archivelog;
Database altered.
```

5. Open the database as follows:

```
SQL> alter database open;
Database altered.
```

6. Check if archiving has been enabled or not.

```
SQL> archive log list
Database log mode              Archive Mode
Automatic archival             Enabled
Archive destination            USE_DB_RECOVERY_FILE_DEST
Oldest online log sequence     6
Next log sequence to archive   8
Current log sequence           8
```

 After enabling the archive log mode, perform a log switch and check whether the archive log is created or not from the `v$archived_log` view, as follows:

```
SQL> select * from v$archived_log;
```

What just happened?

After mentioning some considerations about Data Guard, we've completed the mandatory task of enabling the archive log mode on the primary database.

Force logging

For a physical standby to be a mirror copy, it must receive redo for the changes made to the primary database. In the primary database, when a segment is defined with the NOLOGGING attribute and if a NOLOGGING operation updates the segment, the online redo logfile will be updated with minimal information. This is preferred to complete operations faster but it's not supported in a primary database with the Data Guard configuration. When the redo/ archived logfile containing the NOLOGGING operation is used to recover the datafiles on the standby database, Oracle invalidates such blocks and the error ORA-26040 along with error ORA-1578 are reported by SQL statements in the next block reads. You can see the following errors if operations are performed by NOLOGGING:

```
ORA-01578: ORACLE data block corrupted (file # 4, block # 84)
ORA-01110: data file 4: ' /u01/app/oracle/oradata/orcl/users01.dbf'
ORA-26040: Data block was loaded using the NOLOGGING option
```

Time for action – enabling force logging

Perform the following steps on the primary database:

1. Check the force logging status as follows:

```
SQL> select name, force_logging from v$database;

NAME       FOR

--------- ---

ORCL      NO
```

2. Enable the force logging mode as follows:

```
Enabling Force Logging on Primary Database is mandatory.

SQL> alter database force logging;

Database altered.
```

3. Check the force logging status again as follows:

```
SQL> select name,force_logging from v$database;

NAME       FOR

--------- ---

ORCL      YES
```

In the alert log, you'll see following lines:

```
alter database force logging

ALTER DATABASE FORCE LOGGING command is waiting for existing
direct writes to finish. This may take a long time.

Completed: alter database force logging
```

What just happened?

We've put the primary database in the force logging mode, which is required for the Data Guard physical standby database to work properly.

Standby redo logs

Standby redo logfiles are used by a standby database to store the redo received from the primary database. The redo received by a standby database via redo transport is written to the current SRL group by the **Remote File Server (RFS)** background process. When a log switch occurs on the primary database, RFS writes the redo to the next standby redo log group and the previously used standby redo log group is archived on the standby database by an ARCn process.

Configuring the standby redo logfiles on the primary database is optional. After a switchover, the primary database role will be changed to standby; if SRLs were configured, the new standby will be ready to receive redo data and write them into the standby redo logfiles.

The SRL files must be the same size as your **online redo log (ORL)** files. You also need to have enough SRL groups; that is, one more than the number of ORL groups. Let's suppose you have three ORL groups in the primary database; then, n+1 (that is, four) SRL groups should be configured. On RAC databases you should create n+1 SRL groups for each thread. For example, in an RAC primary database with two instances and three ORL groups per instance, we should create $2*(3+1)$ SRL groups (that is, 8 groups).

 We'll use the RMAN duplicate method to create the physical standby database; if SRLs exist on primary, they'll be automatically created on standby.

Some other considerations on creating SRL groups are as follows:

- ◆ In RAC, do not forget to create SRLs for each thread by specifying the thread number on the shared disks.

- ◆ If you add any ORLs in the primary database later, you'll have to add SRLs on primary and each standby database. If you resize ORLs, you have to resize SRLs too.

- ◆ It's not recommended to multiplex SRLs, because multiplexing may adversely affect redo transport performance and SRL availability is not crucial as ORL availability is.

Time for action – configuring standby redo logs on primary

Run the following procedures on the primary database to create standby redo logfiles:

1. Check the ORL's members and the sizes of each member as follows:

```
SQL> select a.group#, a.status, a.bytes/1024/1024 SizeMB, b.member
from v$log a, v$logfile b where a.group#=b.group# order by group#;


GROUP# STATUS      SizeMB MEMBER
------ --------- ---------- -------------------------------------
     1 INACTIVE      100 /u01/app/oracle/oradata/orcl/redo01.log
     2 CURRENT       100 /u01/app/oracle/oradata/orcl/redo02.log
     3 INACTIVE      100 /u01/app/oracle/oradata/orcl/redo03.log
     4 INACTIVE      100 /u01/app/oracle/oradata/orcl/redo04.log
```

In this single instance of the primary database, we have four redo log groups, each with one member and a size of 100 MB. We should create at least five standby redo log groups.

2. Add the standby redo logfiles as shown in the following example:

```
SQL> alter database add standby logfile group 11 ('/u01/app/
oracle/oradata/orcl/standby_redo01.log') size 100m;

SQL> alter database add standby logfile group 12 ('/u01/app/
oracle/oradata/orcl/standby_redo02.log') size 100m;

SQL> alter database add standby logfile group 13 ('/u01/app/
oracle/oradata/orcl/standby_redo03.log') size 100m;

SQL> alter database add standby logfile group 14 ('/u01/app/
oracle/oradata/orcl/standby_redo04.log') size 100m;

SQL> alter database add standby logfile group 15 ('/u01/app/
oracle/oradata/orcl/standby_redo05.log') size 100m;
```

3. Check the status of new the standby redo logfiles:

```
SQL> select group#,bytes,status from v$standby_log;

GROUP#    BYTES        STATUS
------    ---------    ----------

11    104857600    UNASSIGNED
12    104857600    UNASSIGNED
13    104857600    UNASSIGNED
14    104857600    UNASSIGNED
15    104857600    UNASSIGNED
```

What just happened?

We've completed the optional task of creating standby redo logs on the primary database. Again, if the standby redo logs were created on primary, the RMAN duplicate will create them on standby automatically.

Fast recovery area (FRA)

Prior to 11*g* R2, FRA stood for **Flash Recover Area**, but since Oracle Database 11*g* R2, FRA stands for **Fast Recovery Area**. It's a place on the disk where the database automatically manages naming, retention, and deletion of recovery-related files. FRA can contain control files, online redo logfiles, archived redo logs, flashback logs, and RMAN backups. It's not mandatory but strongly recommended to configure FRA.

In order to enable FRA, you need to set two initialization parameters and you don't need to shut down and restart the database. Note that, in Oracle RAC, these parameters should have the same values across instances and the location must be on shared storage.

Time for action – enabling FRA

Perform the following steps on the primary database now. We'll be enabling FRA on the standby database later.

1. Check the default FRA location as follows:

   ```
   SQL> show parameter db_recovery_file_dest

   NAME                                  TYPE          VALUE
   ------------------------------------- ----------- -----------

   db_recovery_file_dest                 string
   ```

2. Configure the FRA size.

   ```
   SQL> alter system set db_recovery_file_dest_size=4g;

   System altered.
   ```

3. Configure the FRA destination.

   ```
   SQL> alter system set db_recovery_file_dest='/u01/app/oracle/
   flash_recovery_area';

   System altered.
   ```

4. Control the FRA configuration.

   ```
   SQL> show parameter db_recovery_file_dest

   NAME                           VALUE
   ---------------------------    -----------------------

   db_recovery_file_dest          /u01/app/oracle/flash_recovery_area
   db_recovery_file_dest_size     4G
   ```

 In RAC databases, use the keyword `sid='*'`; this ensures that the change will apply to all instances in the cluster.

What just happened?

We've enabled the Fast Recovery Area on the primary database, which is not mandatory but a recommended step. When preparing `init.ora` for a standby instance and starting this instance in the following steps, we'll also set FRA-related initialization parameters for standby, so FRA will also be enabled on the standby database.

Understanding initialization parameters

In the primary database, there are some parameters that are related to the Data Guard configuration and need to be verified or modified. Now we're going to look into the details of these parameters.

> When changing an initialization parameter, if you are using a PFILE, you need to edit the file and execute an ALTER SYSTEM SET command, parameter= 'value' scope=memory, to load the change into the system. If you use an SPFILE, you can just execute the ALTER SYSTEM SET command, parameter= 'value' scope=both, which will set the change in memory and write it to the SPFILE to make the change valid at the next database restart.

DB_NAME

The DB_NAME parameter specifies the database identifier up to eight characters. This parameter must be the same in all the instances of the RAC database and also in the physical standby database. This parameter is validated at MOUNT status when the instance reads the control file; if the DB_NAME parameter does not match the name of the database mentioned in the control file, you will get the following error:

```
"ORA-01504: database name 'Dummy' does not match parameter db_name
'orcl'"
```

You don't need to configure or change this parameter in the Data Guard physical standby configuration.

DB_UNIQUE_NAME

This parameter specifies a unique name for each database having the same DB_NAME parameter. This parameter must be different on the primary, standby, or logical standby database. The DB_UNIQUE_NAME parameter is limited to 30 characters. It can contain alphanumeric, underscore (_), dollar ($), and pound (#) characters but must begin with an alphabetic character. This parameter is static, so it requires bouncing the database in order to change this parameter. If this parameter is not set explicitly, its value will be the same as that of the DB_NAME parameter. You can use the following statement to change the value of the DB_UNIQUE_NAME parameter:

```
SQL> alter system set db_unique_name='turkey_un' scope=spfile;
```

- The DB_UNIQUE_NAME parameter allows a location-specific alias to be created for a database. It is better to avoid using names related to the role, such as primary and standby. These names work well until a switchover is performed, at which point the switchback operation can be very confusing. Therefore, always try to use a geographical value for the DB_UNIQUE_NAME parameter, such as Turkey or India.

◆ The `DB_UNIQUE_NAME` parameter will be the same in all RAC databases across all instances. In RAC databases, only the instances are hosted in different nodes but they are using only one database. Database-unique names can be different in primary and standby because they are sharing neither configuration files nor datafiles.

The following table shows the naming format that we're going to use for the physical standby Data Guard configuration example:

Parameter	Primary	Physical standby
Instance name	TURKEY	INDIA
DB_NAME	ORCL	ORCL
DB_UNIQUE_NAME	TURKEY_UN	INDIA_UN
Net service name	TURKEY	INDIA

LOG_ARCHIVE_CONFIG

Using this parameter, you can enable or disable sending/receiving redo logs to/from databases. You also specify the list of the `DB_UNIQUE_NAME` parameter of each database in the Data Guard configuration with this parameter.

Use the following syntax to change this parameter:

```
LOG_ARCHIVE_CONFIG =
{
 [ SEND | NOSEND ]
 [ RECEIVE | NORECEIVE ]
 [ DG_CONFIG=(remote_db_unique_name1, ... remote_db_unique_name9) |
NODG_CONFIG ]
 }
```

Its default value is `SEND, RECEIVE, NODG_CONFIG` and we only need to update the `DG_CONFIG` part as follows:

```
SQL> alter system set log_archive_config= 'DG_CONFIG=(turkey_un,india_
un)' scope=both;
```

This is a dynamic parameter in which you can add or remove the `DB_UNIQUE_NAME` parameters from the configuration. It's mandatory to set this parameter for RAC databases in Data Guard. However, it's also recommended to set this for single-instance databases. The order of unique names doesn't matter and all unique names in the Data Guard configuration should be included.

LOG_ARCHIVE_MAX_PROCESSES

This parameter specifies the number of archiver processes in a database. In Data Guard, it's important to have enough archiver processes on the primary database. Think of the value of this parameter as the number of channels where redo can be transferred to the standby database. In peak database times and in gap resolution, if the number of the LOG_ARCHIVE_MAX_PROCESSES value is not sufficient on the primary database, redo shipping may suffer.

Its default value is 2 in 10g (which is generally not sufficient in Data Guard) and 4 in 11g. Depending on the number of remote destinations and redo activity on the primary database, you may need to increase the value. Keep in mind that increasing the value means more resource usage and database start/stop times will also be affected.

> It's also important to set a sufficient value for LOG_ARCHIVE_MAX_PROCESSES on the standby database for switchover purposes, and especially if the cascade Data Guard configuration is in use and the standby database is sending redo to another destination.

LOG_ARCHIVE_DEST_n

These parameters, where n is from 1 to 31 in 11g R2, are used to define destinations to the archive redo data. The LOCATION or SERVICE attribute must be defined with this parameter and indicates a local disk destination and remote database destination respectively. It's an important part of the Data Guard configuration and shows the redo transport flow and its properties.

> When you have already configured LOG_ARCHIVE_CONFIG=DG_CONFIG(...) and you try to set/change the attributes of log_archive_dest_n without specifying DB_UNIQUE_NAME, the following errors will occur:
>
> ◆ **ORA-02097**: The parameter cannot be modified because the specified value is invalid
> ◆ **ORA-16052**: The DB_UNIQUE_NAME attribute is required
>
> You must use one of the DB_UNIQUE_NAME parameters of DG_CONFIG in every modification of this parameter.

There are many attributes of the LOG_ARCHIVE_DEST_n parameter and we'll learn most of the important ones in the following sections. Keep in mind that the destination must contain either a LOCATION or SERVICE attribute; the other attributes are optional.

LOCATION and SERVICE

As mentioned earlier, each destination must specify a valid attribute, either of LOCATION or SERVICE, to identify either a local location or a remote destination where redo transport services will send redo data.

The destinations from LOG_ARCHIVE_DEST_1 through LOG_ARCHIVE_DEST_10 can contain either the LOCATION or SERVICE attribute, while destinations from LOG_ARCHIVE_ DEST_11 through LOG_ARCHIVE_DEST_31 can contain only the SERVICE attribute, which does not support the LOCAL destination. For the LOCAL destination, you can specify a disk location or FRA. When specifying the SERVICE attribute, a valid Oracle Net Service name that identifies the remote Oracle database instance is used, where the redo data will be sent.

The following is the example for the LOCATION attribute:

```
SQL> alter system set log_archive_dest_1='LOCATION=/u01/app/oracle/
oraarch';
```

If you are using FRA, it will be as follows:

```
SQL> alter system set log_archive_dest_1='LOCATION=USE_DB_RECOVERY_FILE_
DEST';
```

The following is an example for the SERVICE attribute:

```
SQL> alter system set log_archive_dest_2='SERVICE=india db_unique_
name=india_un';
```

VALID_FOR

This attribute specifies in which states the destination will be valid. It's optional when setting the LOG_ARCHIVE_DEST_n parameter but has to be specified for each redo transport destination of the Data Guard databases so that the redo transport continues after a role transition. This attribute works with two pair of keywords, which are REDO_LOG_TYPE and DATABASE_ROLE.

REDO_LOG_TYPE can be set to the following values:

♦ ONLINE_LOGFILE is valid only when archiving online redo logfiles

♦ STANDBY_LOGFILE is valid only when archiving standby redo logfiles

♦ ALL_LOGFILES is valid when archiving either ORLs or SRLs

`DATABASE_ROLE` can be set to the following values:

- ♦ `PRIMARY_ROLE` is valid only when the database role is primary
- ♦ `STANDBY_ROLE` is valid only when the database role is standby
- ♦ `ALL_ROLES` is valid when the database is either primary or standby

When the `VALID_FOR` attribute is not specified, online redo logfiles and standby redo logfiles will be archived depending on the role of the database. The destination will be enabled even if the role is primary or standby. This is equivalent to the `ALL_LOGFILES`, `ALL_ROLES` setting on the `VALID_FOR` attribute.

> It makes sense to use the `ALL_LOGFILES`, `ALL_ROLES` mode in the `LOCAL` archiving destinations.

SYNC and ASYNC

Remember that synchronous and asynchronous redo transport modes were covered in *Chapter 1, Getting Started*. The `SYNC` and `ASYNC` keywords are used to specify whether the redo transport mode will be synchronous or asynchronous.

`SYNC` will be specified when you want to send redo using the synchronous method. In order to commit a transaction on the primary database, related redo data needs to be received by all the destinations that are set with the `SYNC` attribute. This protection mode is used in either Maximum Protection or Maximum Availability mode. The `SYNC` attribute does not support destinations from `LOG_ARCHIVE_DEST_11` through `LOG_ARCHIVE_DEST_31`. The `SYNC` attribute example is shown as follows:

```
SQL> alter system set log_archive_dest_2='SERVICE=india LGWR SYNC db_
unique_name=india_un';
```

The redo data generated by a transaction doesn't need to be received by a destination that has the `ASYNC` attribute before that transaction can commit. This attribute will be selected by default if you do not specify either the `SYNC` or `ASYNC` keyword. This method is used in the Maximum Performance mode:

```
SQL> alter system set log_archive_dest_2='SERVICE=india LGWR ASYNC db_
unique_name=india_un';
```

AFFIRM and NOAFFIRM

These attributes control when the destination database acknowledges received redo data. Two options are before and after writing to the standby redo log. The AFFIRM attribute ensures that a redo transport destination will send an acknowledgment after writing it to the standby redo logfiles; NOAFFIRM ensures that the redo transport destination will send an acknowledgment before writing it to the standby redo log. This attribute is used with the SERVICE attribute when specifying remote destinations. To view the attribute configuration, you can use the v$archive_dest view with the AFFIRM column.

If both AFFIRM and NOAFFIRM are not specified, it defaults to AFFIRM when the SYNC attribute is specified and NOAFFIRM when the ASYNC attribute is specified.

```
SQL> alter system set log_archive_dest_2='SERVICE=india SYNC AFFIRM DB_
UNIQUE_NAME=india_un';

System altered.


SQL> select affirm from v$archive_dest where dest_id=2;

AFF

---

YES
```

COMPRESSION

This attribute is used to specify whether redo data is compressed before transmission. Compression of redo is useful when there is a bandwidth issue in the network between primary and standby databases. The amount of redo data passing over the network decreases, which improves redo transport performance.

You should remember that compression is a CPU-intensive operation and this compression is an option of Oracle Advanced Compression; so, in order to enhance this feature you must purchase a license. The COMPRESSION attribute example is as shown follows:

```
SQL> alter system set log_archive_dest_2='SERVICE=india
COMPRESSION=ENABLE DB_UNIQUE_NAME=INDIA_UN';
```

MAX_CONNECTIONS

This specifies the number of connections to the redo destination when sending archived redo logfiles. MAX_CONNECTIONS will be used only if the redo transport services use ARCH. You can set the MAX_CONNECTIONS value from 1 through 5. However, it's limited with the number of ARCn processes that is specified with LOG_ARCHIVE_MAX_PROCESSES.

Any standby database using ARCn processes will not use standby redo logs if the MAX_CONNECIONS attribute is specified. So we cannot use real-time Redo Apply with MAX_CONNECTIONS.

```
SQL> alter system set log_archive_dest_2='SERVICE=india MAX_CONNECTIONS=3
db_unique_name=india_un';
```

```
SQL> select MAX_CONNECTIONS from v$archive_dest where dest_id=2;
MAX_CONNECTIONS
---------------
              3
```

MAX_FAILURE

This attribute defines how many times the database will attempt to reconnect to a failed standby database before giving up. When you set the MAX_FAILURE attribute, you also have to set the REOPEN attribute. Once the failure count is greater than or equal to the value you specified, the REOPEN attribute value will set to zero internally. This will cause the database to transport redo data to an alternate destination corresponding to the ALTERNATE attribute.

```
SQL> alter system set log_archive_dest_1='LOCATION=USE_DB_RECOVERY_FILE_
DEST REOPEN=8 MAX_FAILURE=4';
System altered.
```

```
SQL> select MAX_FAILURE,FAILURE_COUNT,REOPEN_SECS from v$archive_dest
where dest_id=1;
MAX_FAILURE FAILURE_COUNT REOPEN_SECS
----------- ------------- -----------
          4             0           8
```

REOPEN

The redo transport services will try to reopen the failed remote destination after a specified number of seconds. By default, the database attempts to reopen failed destinations at the set log-switch time. You can use this attribute to shorten the interval of redo transport reconnect attempts.

```
SQL> alter system set log_archive_dest_2='SERVICE=INDIA reopen=90 db_
unique_name=INDIA_UN';
System altered.
```

```
SQL> select reopen_secs,max_failure from v$archive_dest where dest_id=2;
REOPEN_SECS MAX_FAILURE
----------- -----------
         90           0
```

NET_TIMEOUT

This attribute is used only with the `SYNC` redo transport mode. Depending on the value of the `NET_TIMEOUT` attribute, the LGWR process will block and wait for acknowledgment from a redo transport destination. If the acknowledgment is not received within the time specified, an error will be logged and the transport session to that destination is terminated. If not set, its default value is 30 seconds.

Before setting this attribute, consider your network bandwidth. If you specify lower values such as 1 to 5 seconds, the primary database may often disconnect from the standby database due to transient network errors. A minimum value of 10 should be considered.

```
SQL> alter system set log_archive_dest_2='SERVICE=INDIA SYNC NET_
TIMEOUT=20 db_unique_name=india_un';

System altered.


SQL> select net_timeout from v$archive_dest where dest_id=2;
NET_TIMEOUT
-----------
         20
```

DELAY

This attribute is used to set a delay between the primary and standby databases. When `DELAY` is used, redo is sent to the standby database with no delay but Redo Apply waits for the delay time before applying the archived log.

```
SQL> alter system set log_archive_dest_2='SERVICE=india delay=10 db_
unique_name=india_un';

System altered.


SQL>  selectdelay_mins,destination from v$archive_dest where dest_id=2;
DELAY_MINS DESTINAT
---------- --------
        10 india
```

If real-time apply is used on the standby database, this attribute will be ignored even if you specify it. You can also override this parameter by using the NODELAY option in the managed recovery command.

```
SQL> ALTER DATABASE RECOVER MANAGED STANDBY DATABASE NODELAY;
```

 Now we've finished learning the most important attributes of the LOG_ARCHIVE_DEST_n parameter. Remember that these optional attributes should be used depending on the need. You should use the defaults in the initial configuration and consider changing the defaults later depending on the necessity.

LOG_ARCHIVE_DEST_STATE_n

These parameters, where n is from 1 to 31, indicate the state of the related redo log destination configured by the LOG_ARCHIVE_DEST_n parameter. The default value is ENABLE, which means the redo destination is active. If you want to make the destination inactive, you can set the LOG_ARCHIVE_DEST_STATE_n parameter to DEFER. This destination will be excluded until it is reenabled. If any log archive destination has been configured as a failover archive location, the LOG_ARCHIVE_DEST_STATE_n status will be ALTERNATE.

```
SQL> alter system set log_archive_dest_state_2='defer';

System altered.

SQL> show parameter log_archive_dest_state_2
NAME                          TYPE          VALUE
----------------------------- ------------- -------
log_archive_dest_state_2      string        defer
```

 This parameter is useful in planned maintenance on databases. For example, when patching the primary database, you can stop sending redo to standby locations.

What just happened?

We've gone through the preconfiguration steps of the Data Guard physical standby database installation. We also learned the properties and options of primary database initialization parameters related with Data Guard. Now we're going to start installing the physical standby database.

Creating the physical standby database

In order to create a physical standby database, we first need to install Oracle database binaries to the standby database server and then start a standby database instance. Installing Oracle binaries is out of this book's scope, so it's assumed a standby server is ready with the Oracle database software installed. We will start by covering a standby database instance and copying database files from primary to standby, but first let's look at the initialization parameters that we need to set on standby before starting the instance.

Standby database related initialization parameters

The following are the important Data-Guard-related initialization parameters we set on physical standby databases.

FAL_SERVER

This parameter specifies from where the standby database should request missing archived logs if there is a gap in the logs. It is used only when the database is in the standby role and has a gap in the received archived logs.

A redo gap occurs when the redo transport doesn't run for a while. A maintenance operation on the standby server or a network interruption may cause this. Setting this parameter allows the standby to find the missing redo and have it transported.

On the standby database, you need to set the Oracle Net Service name of the primary database as the value of this parameter. Also, taking account of a possible switchover, don't forget to set FAL_SERVER on the primary database with the value of the standby database service name.

> The FAL_CLIENT parameter is no longer required in 11*g*. In earlier releases, you set the FAL_CLIENT parameter on the standby database, and the value is the Oracle Net Service name that the primary database uses to connect the standby database. In 11*g*, when it's not set, the primary database will obtain the client service name from the related LOG_ARCHIVE_DEST_n parameter.

STANDBY_FILE_MANAGEMENT

The STANDBY_FILE_MANAGEMENT parameter is used only for the environment of the physical standby databases. By default, its value is MANUAL. By setting this parameter to AUTO, we'll make sure that, when we add or drop datafiles on our primary database, those files are also added or dropped on the standby database. Setting this parameter to AUTO can cause files to be created automatically on the standby database and it can even overwrite existing files; we should be careful when we set both DB_FILE_NAME_CONVERT and STANDBY_FILE_MANAGEMENT and ensure that the existing datafiles on standby won't be overwritten.

```
SQL> alter system set standby_file_management='AUTO';
System altered.
```

When the parameter is set to MANUAL, if any datafile is added in primary, you'll see the following errors:

```
File #5 added to control file as 'UNNAMED0007' because
the parameter STANDBY_FILE_MANAGEMENT is set to MANUAL
The file should be manually created to continue.
MRP0: Background Media Recovery terminated with error 1274
Some recovered datafiles maybe left media fuzzy
Media recovery may continue but open resetlogs may fail
```

DB_FILE_NAME_CONVERT

In some cases, the directory structure may not be the same in source/primary and destination/standby database locations. The DB_FILE_NAME_CONVERT parameter is used to convert the file locations of datafiles. When you add a datafile in the primary database, assuming you have a STANDBY_FILE_MANAGEMENT parameter setting of AUTO, it will create a datafile on the standby database according to the settings of the DB_FILE_NAME_CONVERT parameter. Before setting DB_FILE_NAME_CONVERT, make sure that filesystem exists and is writable.

When setting this parameter, we must specify one or more paired strings. The first string is the pattern of the primary database file location whereas the second string is the pattern of the standby database file location.

The following is an example of DB_FILE_NAME_CONVERT:

```
alter system set db_file_name_convert= "'/u01/app/oracle/oradata/turkey_
un', '/u01/app/oracle/oradata/india_un'" scope=spfile;
```

When using ASM, the settings are very simple. We need to mention only the disk groups of primary and standby as follows:

```
alter system set db_file_name_convert="'+DATA_AREA','+DATA_STBY'"
scope=spfile;
```

Note that this is a static parameter and it requires the instance to restart for the change to become active.

LOG_FILE_NAME_CONVERT

This parameter plays a similar role to `DB_FILE_NAME_CONVERT` and is valid for online and standby redo logfiles. The `LOG_FILE_NAME_CONVERT` parameter converts the file location of a new logfile on the primary database to the desired location on the standby database.

```
SQL> alter system set log_file_name_convert= "'/u01/app/oracle/oradata/
turkey_un', '/u01/app/oracle/oradata/india_un'" scope=spfile;
```

 The `DB_FILE_NAME_CONVERT` and `LOG_FILE_NAME_CONVERT` parameters can be used for physical standby databases and RMAN Duplicate/**TSPITR (Tablespace Point-in-Time Recovery)** operations. It cannot be used on logical standby databases and for RMAN restore operations.

The physical standby database instance

Now it's time to start a database instance on the standby server. In our example, we're going to start a single database instance, not RAC. If an RAC standby database is going to be configured, you need to start instances on RAC nodes and then register the instances to cluster. Considerations about RAC standby databases will be covered in *Chapter 8, Integrating Data Guard with the Complete Oracle Environment*.

Time for action – starting the physical standby instance and making it ready for the RMAN duplicate

Execute the following steps to start a database instance on the standby server and make it ready for the RMAN duplicate operation.

1. Create a service in Windows.

   If you are creating a Data Guard configuration in Windows, you must create a service using the `oradim` utility as follows:

   ```
   oradim -NEW -SID <sid> -STARTMODE manual -PFILE C:\app\oracle\
   product\11.2.0\admin\<sid>\pfile\init.ora
   ```

   You can skip this step if the environment is not Windows.

2. Set the standby database initialization parameters:

Copy the `PFILE` from the primary system to the standby system under the `$ORACLE_HOME/dbs` directory with the proper name (`initINDIA.ora` in our example). Make changes as needed if the control file locations will be different on the standby database and then change locations. The diagnostic destination and memory must be checked. You also need to set the standby-related parameters we've just covered. Use the following example to compare parameters of the primary and standby databases.

We haven't set Data-Guard-related parameters on the primary database yet. We'll set them after the RMAN duplicate operation finishes successfully. The following primary initialization parameters will be the final status.

 In this example, the database files on the primary database are under the `/u01` directory and the database files on the standby database are under the `/u02` directory. This has been configured intentionally to show you the settings of the related initialization parameters.

The following are the primary database parameters:

```
control_files='/u01/app/oracle/oradata/orcl/control01.ctl','/u01/
app/oracle/flash_recovery_area/orcl/control02.ctl'

db_name='orcl'

db_file_name_convert='/u02/app/oracle/oradata/orcl','/u01/app/
oracle/oradata/orcl'  # for switchover purpose

db_recovery_file_dest='/u01/app/oracle/flash_recovery_area'

db_recovery_file_dest_size=4070572032

db_unique_name='turkey_un'

diagnostic_dest='/u01/app/oracle'

fal_server='INDIA'  # for switchover purpose

instance_name='TURKEY'

local_listener='LISTENER'

log_archive_dest_1='LOCATION=USE_DB_RECOVERY_FILE_DEST VALID_
FOR=(ALL_LOGFILES,ALL_ROLES)'

log_archive_dest_2='SERVICE=INDIA LGWR ASYNC VALID_FOR=(ONLINE_
LOGFILES,PRIMARY_ROLE) DB_UNIQUE_NAME=INDIA_UN'

log_archive_config='DG_CONFIG=(turkey_un,india_un)'

log_archive_max_processes=8

log_file_name_convert='/u02/app/oracle/oradata/orcl','/u01/app/
oracle/oradata/orcl'  # for switchover purpose
```

```
memory_target=822083584

remote_login_passwordfile='EXCLUSIVE'

standby_file_management='AUTO' # for switchover purpose
```

The following are the standby database parameters:

```
control_files='/u02/app/oracle/oradata/orcl/control01.ctl','/u02/
app/oracle/flash_recovery_area/orcl/control02.ctl'

db_name='orcl'

db_file_name_convert='/u01/app/oracle/oradata/orcl','/u02/app/
oracle/oradata/orcl'

db_recovery_file_dest='/u02/app/oracle/flash_recovery_area'

db_recovery_file_dest_size=4070572032

db_unique_name='india_un'

diagnostic_dest='/u02/app/oracle'

fal_server='TURKEY'

instance_name='INDIA'

local_listener='LISTENER'

log_archive_dest_1='LOCATION=USE_DB_RECOVERY_FILE_DEST VALID_
FOR=(ALL_LOGFILES,ALL_ROLES)'

log_archive_dest_2='SERVICE=TURKEY LGWR ASYNC VALID_FOR= (ONLINE_
LOGFILES,PRIMARY_ROLE) DB_UNIQUE_NAME=turkey_un' # for switchover
purpose

log_archive_config='DG_CONFIG=(turkey_un,india_un)'

log_archive_max_processes=8

log_file_name_convert='/u01/app/oracle/oradata/orcl','/u02/app/
oracle/oradata/orcl'

memory_target=822083584

remote_login_passwordfile='EXCLUSIVE'

standby_file_management='AUTO'
```

3. After preparing the standby instance parameter file, set the Oracle user environment variables and start the standby instance in the No Mount status.

```
[oracle@oracle-stby ~]$ export ORACLE_HOME= /u01/app/oracle/
product/11.2.0/db_1

[oracle@oracle-stby ~]$ export ORACLE_SID=INDIA

[oracle@oracle-stby ~]$ sqlplus / as sysdba

SQL*Plus: Release 11.2.0.1.0 Production on Sun Aug 12 12:17:01
2012
```

```
Copyright (c) 1982, 2009, Oracle.  All rights reserved.

Connected to an idle instance.


SQL>startup nomount

ORACLE instance started.

Total System Global Area   818401280 bytes

Fixed Size                   2217792 bytes

Variable Size              507513024 bytes

Database Buffers           306184192 bytes

Redo Buffers                 2486272 bytes


SQL> select host_name,status from v$instance;

HOST_NAME             STATUS

-------------------- ------------

oracle-stby           STARTED
```

4. The following are the SQL*Net configurations.

   With 11*g*, we can use RMAN duplicate without the need of primary database backup. The RMAN duplicate using the active database feature reads from the original database files. In order to use this feature, we have to perform static registration of the service to the listener. To do this, we configure both the listener and TNS names. The standby database instance must be in the NOMOUNT state before the duplicate command. In the NOMOUNT state, the database instance will not self-register with the listener. Another item to note is that you must use a dedicated server to connect when the database is in the NOMOUNT state.

   Before we jump into configuration, let's describe static service information. Static service information is normally not required in the listener.ora configuration file. In order to perform duplicate using active database to connect instance in NOMOUNT status, we are using static listener entry. The parameters required for static service information are SID_NAME, GLOBAL_DBNAME, and ORACLE_HOME.

   ❑ SID_NAME: The Oracle SID is the instance identifier, as in the INSTANCE_NAME parameter of the parameter file

   ❑ GLOBAL_DBNAME: The GLOBAL_DBNAME parameter is typically a concatenation of the DB_DOMAIN and DB_NAME parameters in the parameter file or the same as the SERVICE_NAMES parameter in the parameter file

   ❑ ORACLE_HOME: It's the installation directory of the Oracle database software

Configure the listener and TNS configuration on both the primary and standby databases. The following is the example of the standby database's `listener.ora` configuration:

```
LISTENER=
  (DESCRIPTION=
      (ADDRESS_LIST=
          (ADDRESS=(PROTOCOL=tcp)  (HOST= oracle-stby)(PORT=1521))
          (ADDRESS=(PROTOCOL=ipc)(KEY=extproc))))
SID_LIST_LISTENER =
  (SID_LIST =
      (SID_DESC =
          (SID_NAME = PLSExtProc)
          (ORACLE_HOME = /u01/app/oracle/product/11.2.0/db_1)
          (PROGRAM = extproc))
      (SID_DESC =
          (GLOBAL_DBNAME = india_un)
          (SID_NAME = INDIA)
          (ORACLE_HOME = /u01/app/oracle/product/11.2.0/db_1)))
```

The following will be the TNS entry primary database used to connect the standby database:

```
INDIA =
  (DESCRIPTION =
    (ADDRESS = (PROTOCOL = TCP)(HOST = oracle-stby)(PORT = 1521))
    (CONNECT_DATA =
      (SERVER = DEDICATED)
      (SERVICE_NAME = india_un)))
```

> PMON automatically registers with the listener listening on the default port, 1521. If the listener is listening from a non-default port, or if this is an RAC database, the `LOCAL_LISTENER` parameter must be set to register PMON with the listener. Set the `LOCAL_LISTENER` parameter to the local listener alias, the name of the listener in the `listener.ora` file. Also, the `LOCAL_LISTENER` value has to be resolved using the `tnsnames.ora` file or in an Oracle Names Server.

5. Now start the listeners on both the primary and standby servers.

```
$lsnrctl start
```

When the listener is running, check the database accessibility and response time, using `tnsping` from both primary to standby and standby to primary databases.

The registered services with the listener of primary should be similar to the following screenshot:

```
[oracle@oracle-primary admin]$ lsnrctl status

LSNRCTL for Linux: Version 11.2.0.1.0 - Production on 04-AUG-2012 12:00:46

Copyright (c) 1991, 2009, Oracle.  All rights reserved.

Connecting to (DESCRIPTION=(ADDRESS=(PROTOCOL=IPC)(KEY=EXTPROC1521)))
STATUS of the LISTENER
------------------------
Alias                     LISTENER
Version                   TNSLSNR for Linux: Version 11.2.0.1.0 - Production
Start Date                04-AUG-2012 11:49:50
Uptime                    0 days 0 hr. 10 min. 56 sec
Trace Level               off
Security                  ON: Local OS Authentication
SNMP                      OFF
Listener Parameter File   /u01/home/oracle/product/11.2.0/db_1/network/admin/listener.ora
Listener Log File         /u01/app/oracle/diag/tnslsnr/oracle-primary/listener/alert/log.xml
Listening Endpoints Summary...
  (DESCRIPTION=(ADDRESS=(PROTOCOL=ipc)(KEY=EXTPROC1521)))
  (DESCRIPTION=(ADDRESS=(PROTOCOL=tcp)(HOST=192.168.180.10)(PORT=1521)))
Services Summary...
Service "PLSExtProc" has 1 instance(s).
  Instance "PLSExtProc", status UNKNOWN, has 1 handler(s) for this service...
Service "orclXDB" has 1 instance(s).
  Instance "TURKEY", status READY, has 1 handler(s) for this service...
Service "turkey_un" has 2 instance(s).
  Instance "TURKEY", status UNKNOWN, has 1 handler(s) for this service...
  Instance "TURKEY", status READY, has 1 handler(s) for this service...
The command completed successfully
[oracle@oracle-primary admin]$
```

The registered services with the listener of standby are as follows:

```
[oracle@oracle-stby admin]$ lsnrctl status

LSNRCTL for Linux: Version 11.2.0.1.0 - Production on 04-AUG-2012 12:03:06

Copyright (c) 1991, 2009, Oracle.  All rights reserved.

Connecting to (DESCRIPTION=(ADDRESS=(PROTOCOL=IPC)(KEY=EXTPROC1521)))
STATUS of the LISTENER
------------------------
Alias                     LISTENER
Version                   TNSLSNR for Linux: Version 11.2.0.1.0 - Production
Start Date                04-AUG-2012 11:50:20
Uptime                    0 days 0 hr. 12 min. 46 sec
Trace Level               off
Security                  ON: Local OS Authentication
SNMP                      OFF
Listener Parameter File   /u01/home/oracle/product/11.2.0/db_1/network/admin/listener.ora
Listener Log File         /u01/app/oracle/diag/tnslsnr/oracle-stby/listener/alert/log.xml
Listening Endpoints Summary...
  (DESCRIPTION=(ADDRESS=(PROTOCOL=ipc)(KEY=EXTPROC1521)))
  (DESCRIPTION=(ADDRESS=(PROTOCOL=tcp)(HOST=192.168.180.20)(PORT=1521)))
Services Summary...
Service "PLSExtProc" has 1 instance(s).
  Instance "PLSExtProc", status UNKNOWN, has 1 handler(s) for this service...
Service "india_un" has 2 instance(s).
  Instance "INDIA", status UNKNOWN, has 1 handler(s) for this service...
  Instance "INDIA", status BLOCKED, has 1 handler(s) for this service...
The command completed successfully
[oracle@oracle-stby admin]$
```

6. Copy the password file from the primary system to standby. You can find this file under the `$ORACLE_HOME/dbs` directory with the name `orapwSID`. Copy it to the same directory on the standby server and rename correspondingly.

7. If you have configured the encryption wallet on the primary database, copy the wallet to the standby system. If you have more than one standby database, you must copy these files to every standby location. You can access the encrypted data from standby when the wallet module contains the master encryption key from the primary database.

What just happened?

We're ready to start the RMAN duplicate. Let's revisit the actions that have been performed on the primary and standby systems:

Task	Primary	Standby
Instance status	Open	No mount
Archive log mode	Enabled	N/A
FRA	Enabled	Enabled
Force logging	Enabled	N/A
SQL* net configuration	Configured	Configured
PFILE/SPFILE	Exists	Copied, renamed, and modified
Password file	Exists	Copied and renamed
Control file	Exists	Will be created automatically (standby CF)
Standby redo logs	Created	Will be duplicated
Data files	Exists	Will be duplicated

Using RMAN duplicate to create physical standby databases

In order to create a physical standby database, we have several methods depending on the release features. We've already mentioned that we'll use the RMAN duplicate from the active database method. In this method, there's no need to take a backup in primary and copy it on the standby system.

Here is an overview of the other methods used to create a standby database:

♦ **Hot backups**: Backups taken from the primary database by executing the `ALTER DATABASE BEGIN BACKUP` command can be used to create a standby database.

♦ **RMAN backups**: Full (level 0) RMAN database backups can also be used for the standby configuration.

◆ **Cloud Control**: This is the only graphical interface we can use to create a standby database configuration. It offers online duplicates, existing or new RMAN backups, and handles the steps of copying the `init.ora` file and the password file.

[For the first two methods, all the preconfigurations we've set until now are still needed.]

When creating the active database duplicate, RMAN copies the datafiles directly from the primary database to the standby database over the network; in such cases, the primary database must be opened or mounted. Before we start creating the RMAN duplicate, we start the standby instance in the NOMOUNT status; after successful duplication, RMAN leaves the instance in the MOUNT status.

Time for action – running an RMAN duplicate

Perform the following steps to create a standby database with the RMAN duplicate method:

1. Check the primary database status; it must be either open or mount.

   ```
   SQL> select db_unique_name,database_role,open_mode from
   v$database;

   DB_UNIQUE_  DATABASE_ROLE     OPEN_MODE

   ----------  ----------------  --------------------

   turkey_un   PRIMARY           READ WRITE
   ```

2. Run the RMAN command from the standby system. Connect the primary and standby instances using Oracle Net Service names.

   ```
   [oracle@oracle-stbydbs]$ rman target sys/free2go@turkey auxiliary
   sys/free2go@india

   Recovery Manager: Release 11.2.0.1.0 - Production on Thu Jul 26
   18:41:06 2012

   Copyright (c) 1982, 2009, Oracle and/or its affiliates.  All
   rights reserved.

   connected to target database: ORCL (DBID=1316772835)

   connected to auxiliary database: ORCL (not mounted)
   ```

   RMAN will show the connected sessions as shown previously, which provided the primary status—either open or mounted. Also, standby is in the NOMOUNT status.

3. Now execute the DUPLICATE command.

RMAN> duplicate target database for standby from active database;

The output will be similar to the one as shown in the following screenshot:

```
[oracle@oracle-stby ~]$ rman target sys/free2go@turkey auxiliary sys/free2go@india

Recovery Manager: Release 11.2.0.1.0 - Production on Fri Aug 3 21:27:10 2012

Copyright (c) 1982, 2009, Oracle and/or its affiliates.  All rights reserved.

connected to target database: ORCL (DBID=1316772835)
connected to auxiliary database: ORCL (not mounted)

RMAN> duplicate target database for standby from active database;

Starting Duplicate Db at 03-AUG-12
using target database control file instead of recovery catalog
allocated channel: ORA_AUX_DISK_1
channel ORA_AUX_DISK_1: SID=19 device type=DISK
```

The tail of the output logfile will be as follows:

```
Starting Duplicate Db at 26-JUL-12
using target database control file instead of recovery catalog
allocated channel: ORA_AUX_DISK_1
channel ORA_AUX_DISK_1: SID=19 device type=DISK
...
contents of Memory Script:
{
   backup as copy current controlfile for standby auxiliary format
'/u02/app/oracle/oradata/orcl/control01.ctl';
   restore clone controlfile to  '/u02/app/oracle/flash_recovery_
area/orcl/control02.ctl' from
 '/u02/app/oracle/oradata/orcl/control01.ctl';
}
executing Memory Script
....
sql statement: alter database mount standby database
...
Starting backup at 26-JUL-12
using channel ORA_DISK_1
channel ORA_DISK_1: starting datafile copy
input datafile file number=00001 name=/u01/app/oracle/oradata/
orcl/system01.dbf
output file name=/u02/app/oracle/oradata/orcl/system01.dbf
tag=TAG20120726T160751
channel ORA_DISK_1: datafile copy complete, elapsed time: 00:01:04
channel ORA_DISK_1: starting datafile copy
...
```

```
sql statement: alter system archive log current
contents of Memory Script:
{
   switch clone datafile all;
}
executing Memory Script
datafile 1 switched to datafile copy
input datafile copy RECID=2 STAMP=789667774 file name=/u02/app/
oracle/oradata/orcl/system01.dbf
...
Finished Duplicate Db at 26-JUL-12
```

> When a restore is in progress, you can monitor how much is complete and how much is still pending using the v$session_longops view from the primary database.

4. Configure the primary database initialization parameters required for Data Guard.

```
SQL> alter system set log_archive_dest_2='SERVICE=INDIA LGWR ASYNC
VALID_FOR=(ONLINE_LOGFILES,PRIMARY_ROLE) DB_UNIQUE_NAME=INDIA_UN'
scope=both sid='*';

SQL> alter system set log_archive_config= 'DG_CONFIG=(turkey_
un,india_un)' scope=both sid='*';

SQL> alter system set log_archive_max_processes=8 scope=both
sid='*';
```

Configure the following parameters in order to make the Data Guard configuration ready for a role-change operation:

```
SQL> alter system set fal_server='INDIA' scope=both sid='*';
SQL> alter system set standby_file_management='AUTO' scope=both
sid='*';
SQL> alter system set db_file_name_convert= '/u02/app/oracle/
oradata/orcl','/u01/app/oracle/oradata/orcl' scope=spfile sid='*';
SQL> alter system set log_file_name_convert= '/u02/app/oracle/
oradata/orcl','/u01/app/oracle/oradata/orcl' scope=spfile sid='*';
```

Note that the last two settings are made on SPFILE; therefore, a database restart is required to make the changes valid.

What just happened?

We've successfully restored the standby database with the standby role using Oracle 11*g* RMAN duplicate of the active database method. We've also discussed different methods used to create a standby database from primary.

Post-installation steps

In this section, we'll verify the standby database status, start Redo Apply to synchronize the standby database with the primary database, and see how we check the status of Redo Apply at the end.

Verifying the standby database configuration

After creating the physical standby database and enabling redo transport services, you may want to verify the standby database configuration and also check if the database changes are being successfully transmitted from the primary database to standby.

Time for action – verifying the standby database configuration

Run the following actions to verify the standby database configuration and redo transport services:

1. Connect the standby database using SQL*Plus and check for the database role and status to ensure the database role is the physical standby.

   ```
   SQL> select db_unique_name,database_role,open_mode from
   v$database;

   DB_UNIQUE_NAME   DATABASE_ROLE     OPEN_MODE
   --------------   ---------------   --------------------

   india_un         PHYSICAL STANDBY MOUNTED
   ```

2. Check the standby database, SPFILE.

   ```
   SQL> show parameter spfile

   NAME    TYPE    VALUE
   ------  ------  ------------------------------------------------

   spfile  string  /u01/app/oracle/product/11.2.0/db_1/dbs/
   spfileINDIA.ora
   ```

 If you have started the standby instance with PFILE, you should create an SPFILE and start an instance again using the new SPFILE.

3. Use the `v$datafile` view to check the location of the datafiles in the standby database. The standby database datafile must be under the `/u02` directory because of the `DB_FILE_NAME_CONVERT` parameter setting.

```
SQL>  select name from v$datafile;

NAME
-----------------------------------------------
/u02/app/oracle/oradata/orcl/system01.dbf
/u02/app/oracle/oradata/orcl/sysaux01.dbf
/u02/app/oracle/oradata/orcl/undotbs01.dbf
/u02/app/oracle/oradata/orcl/users01.dbf
/u02/app/oracle/oradata/orcl/example01.dbf
```

4. Use the `v$logfile` view to check the location of online and standby redo logfiles in the standby database.

```
SQL> select group#,type,member from v$logfile;

    GROUP# TYPE    MEMBER
---------- ------- -----------------------------------------------
         3 ONLINE  /u02/app/oracle/oradata/orcl/redo03.log
         2 ONLINE  /u02/app/oracle/oradata/orcl/redo02.log
         1 ONLINE  /u02/app/oracle/oradata/orcl/redo01.log
         4 ONLINE  /u02/app/oracle/oradata/orcl/redo04.log
        10 STANDBY /u02/app/oracle/oradata/orcl/standby_redo01.log
        11 STANDBY /u02/app/oracle/oradata/orcl/standby_redo02.log
        12 STANDBY /u02/app/oracle/oradata/orcl/standby_redo03.log
        13 STANDBY /u02/app/oracle/oradata/orcl/standby_redo04.log
        14 STANDBY /u02/app/oracle/oradata/orcl/standby_redo05.log
```

Note that the online redo logfiles and standby redo logfiles in the primary database are created under the `/u01` directory, whereas logfiles in the standby database are under `/u02`. This change occurred because of the settings of the `LOG_FILE_NAME_CONVERT` parameter.

```
SQL> show parameter log_file_name_convert
NAME                    TYPE         VALUE
----------------------- ------------ ----------------------------
log_file_name_convert   string       /u01/app/oracle/oradata/orcl,
                                      /u02/app/oracle/oradata/orcl
```

5. Verify if the redo transport service is active using the `v$managed_standby` view on the standby database:

```
SQL> SELECT THREAD#,SEQUENCE#,PROCESS,CLIENT_PROCESS,STATUS,BLOCKS
FROM V$MANAGED_STANDBY;

  THREAD#  SEQUENCE# PROCESS   CLIENT_P STATUS        BLOCKS
---------- ---------- --------- -------- ------------ ----------
        1        148 ARCH      ARCH     CLOSING           6
        1        147 ARCH      ARCH     CLOSING           8
        1        149 RFS       LGWR     IDLE              1
        0          0 RFS       UNKNOWN  IDLE              0
```

You must see RFS processes running on the standby database, which are responsible for writing redo information that the primary database sends to standby.

What just happened?

We've verified the standby database mode, status, and database files. We've also seen that the redo transport service is actively working between primary and standby.

Managing Redo Apply

As discussed in *Chapter 1*, *Getting Started*, Redo Apply is the synchronization method of the physical standby databases. Now let's see how can we start, stop, and monitor Redo Apply.

Time for action – starting, stopping, and monitoring MRP

Before starting Redo Apply services, the physical standby database must be in the MOUNT status. From 11*g* onwards, the standby database can also be in the OPEN mode. If the redo transport service is in the ARCH mode, the redo will be applied from the archived redo logfiles after being transferred to the standby database. If the redo transport service is in LGWR, the **Log network server (LNS)** will be reading the redo buffer in SGA and will send redo to Oracle Net Services for transmission to the standby redo logfiles of the standby database using the RFS process. On the standby database, redo will be applied from the standby redo logs.

Redo apply can be specified either as a foreground session or as a background process; it can also be started with real-time apply.

 To execute the following commands, the control file must be a standby control file. If you execute these commands in a database in the primary mode, Oracle will return an error and ignore the command.

1. Start Redo Apply in the foreground.

Connect to the SQLPlus command prompt and issue the following command. If the media recovery is already running, you will run into the error **ORA-01153: an incompatible media recovery is active**.

```
SQL> ALTER DATABASE RECOVER MANAGED STANDBY DATABASE;
Database altered.
```

Whenever you issue the preceding command, you can monitor the Redo Apply status from the alert logfile. Managed standby recovery is now active and is not using real-time apply. The SQL session will be active unless you terminate the session by pressing *Ctrl + C* or kill the session from another active session. Press *Ctrl + C* to stop Redo Apply.

```
SQL> ALTER DATABASE RECOVER MANAGED STANDBY DATABASE;
 ALTER DATABASE RECOVER MANAGED STANDBY DATABASE
*
ERROR at line 1:
ORA-16043: Redo apply has been canceled.
ORA-01013: user requested cancel of current operation
```

> After starting media recovery, you may see errors such as the following, which are expected. This is in fact an enhancement to the Data Guard technology introduced in 10gR2 to improve speed of switchover/failover. In previous versions, role transition would require us to clear the online redo logfiles before it can become a primary database. Now, the database attempts to clear the ORLs when starting Redo Apply. If the files exist, they will be cleared; if they do not exist, it reports one of the following errors. It attempts to create the online redo logfiles before starting recovery. Even if this is not possible because of different structure or `log_file_name_convert` is not set, Redo Apply does not fail.

2. Start Redo Apply in the background.

In order to start the Redo Apply service in the background, use the `disconnect from session` option. This command will return you to the SQL command line once the Redo Apply service is started. Run the following statement on the standby database:

```
SQL> alter database recover managed standby database disconnect
from session;
Database altered.
```

3. Check the Redo Apply service status.

From SQL*Plus, you can check whether the **Media Recover Process** (**MRP**) is running using the V$MANAGED_STANDBY view:

```
SQL> SELECT THREAD#,SEQUENCE#,PROCESS,CLIENT_PROCESS,STATUS,BLOCKS
FROM V$MANAGED_STANDBY;
```

THREAD#	SEQUENCE#	PROCESS	CLIENT_P	STATUS	BLOCKS
1	146	ARCH	ARCH	CLOSING	1868
1	148	ARCH	ARCH	CLOSING	6
0	0	ARCH	ARCH	CONNECTED	0
1	147	ARCH	ARCH	CLOSING	8
1	149	RFS	LGWR	IDLE	1
0	0	RFS	UNKNOWN	IDLE	0
0	0	RFS	UNKNOWN	IDLE	0
0	0	RFS	N/A	IDLE	0
1	149	MRP0	N/A	APPLYING_LOG	204800

```
9 rows selected.
```

From the PROCESS column, you can see that the background process name is MRP0; Media Recovery Process is ACTIVE and the status is APPLYING_LOG, which means that the process is actively applying the archived redo log to the standby database. From the OS, you can monitor the specific background process as follows:

```
[oracle@oracle-stby ~]$ ps -ef|grep mrp
oracle    5507    1  0 19:26 ?        00:00:02 ora_mrp0_INDIA
```

From the output, you can simply estimate how many standby instances are running with background recovery. Only one Media Recovery Process can be running per instance.

Also, you can query from v$session.

```
SQL> select program from v$session where program like '%MRP%';
PROGRAM
------------------------
oracle@oracle-stby (MRP0)
```

4. Stop Redo Apply.

To stop the MRP, issue the following command:

```
SQL> ALTER DATABASE RECOVER MANAGED STANDBY DATABASE CANCEL;
Database altered.
```

From the alert logfile, you will see the following lines:

```
Sun Aug 05 21:24:16 2012
ALTER DATABASE RECOVER MANAGED STANDBY DATABASE CANCEL
Sun Aug 05 21:24:16 2012
MRP0: Background Media Recovery cancelled with status 16037
Errors in file /u02/app/oracle/diag/rdbms/india_un/INDIA/trace/
INDIA_mrp0_5507.trc:
ORA-16037: user requested cancel of managed recovery operation
Managed Standby Recovery not using Real Time Apply
Recovery interrupted!
```

After stopping the MRP, no background process is active and this can be confirmed by using the V$MANAGED_STANDBY or V$SESSION view shown as follows:

```
SQL> SELECT THREAD#,SEQUENCE#,PROCESS,CLIENT_PROCESS,STATUS,BLOCKS
FROM V$MANAGED_STANDBY;
```

THREAD#	SEQUENCE#	PROCESS	CLIENT_P	STATUS	BLOCKS
1	146	ARCH	ARCH	CLOSING	1868
1	148	ARCH	ARCH	CLOSING	6
0	0	ARCH	ARCH	CONNECTED	0
1	147	ARCH	ARCH	CLOSING	8
1	149	RFS	LGWR	WRITING	1
0	0	RFS	UNKNOWN	IDLE	0
0	0	RFS	UNKNOWN	IDLE	0
0	0	RFS	N/A	IDLE	0

```
8 rows selected.


SQL>  select program from v$session where program like '%MRP%';
no rows selected
```

5. Start real-time apply.

To start Redo Apply in real-time apply mode, you must use the USING CURRENT LOGFILE option as follows:

```
SQL> ALTER DATABASE RECOVER MANAGED STANDBY DATABASE USING CURRENT
LOGFILE DISCONNECT FROM SESSION;

Database altered.
```

From the standby alert logfile, you will see the following lines:

```
Sun Aug 05 15:31:21 2012

ALTER DATABASE RECOVER MANAGED STANDBY DATABASE USING CURRENT
LOGFILE DISCONNECT FROM SESSION

Attempt to start background Managed Standby Recovery process
(INDIA)

Sun Aug 05 15:31:21 2012
```

 Note that stopping a Redo Apply service in the real-time mode is not different from stopping the standard Redo Apply.

What just happened?

We've seen how to start, stop, and monitor the Redo Apply service on the physical standby database. Also, the method to start Redo Apply in the real-time mode is covered. These are important tasks of an Oracle database administrator managing a Data Guard environment.

Verifying synchronization between the primary and standby databases

We must now ensure that the standby database is synchronized with the primary database after starting Redo Apply.

Time for action – verifying synchronization between the primary and standby databases

By using the following steps, you can control whether the standby database is synchronized with primary:

1. On the standby database, query the V$ARCHIVED_LOG view for the archived and applied sequences.

   For the last archived sequence, use the following:
   ```
   SQL> SELECT MAX(SEQUENCE#) FROM V$ARCHIVED_LOG;

   MAX(SEQUENCE#)

   -------------

               145
   ```

   For the last applied sequence, use the following:
   ```
   SQL> SELECT MAX(SEQUENCE#) FROM V$ARCHIVED_LOG WHERE
   APPLIED='YES';

   MAX(SEQUENCE#)

   -------------

               144
   ```

   From the preceding two queries, we see that the latest sequence, 145, is being archived or written into the standby redo logfiles. There's expected to be a lag of one sequence between archived and applied columns.

2. Check the status of the latest log sequence.
   ```
   SQL> SELECT SEQUENCE#,APPLIED FROM V$ARCHIVED_LOG ORDER BY
   SEQUENCE#;


    SEQUENCE# APPLIED

   ---------- ---------

          140 YES
          141 YES
          142 YES
          143 YES
          144 YES
          145 IN-MEMORY
   ```

   The log sequence 145 is still being shipped.

3. On the primary database query for the last archived logfile, perform a couple of log switches and then monitor if those archives are transported and applied.

```
SQL> SELECT MAX(SEQUENCE#) FROM V$ARCHIVED_LOG;

MAX(SEQUENCE#)
--------------
           145
```

Perform log switches several times and check.

```
SQL> alter system switch logfile;

System altered.


SQL> SELECT MAX(SEQUENCE#) FROM V$ARCHIVED_LOG;

MAX(SEQUENCE#)
--------------
           148
```

4. On the standby query for new archived logfiles and applied archived logfiles, query if the new archive log sequences are applied on standby.

```
SQL> SELECT SEQUENCE#,APPLIED FROM V$ARCHIVED_LOG ORDER BY
SEQUENCE#;

 SEQUENCE# APPLIED
---------- ---------
       143 YES
       144 YES
       145 YES
       146 YES
       147 YES
       148 YES
```

The APPLIED column on standby will be very helpful to determine which sequence is generated and which sequences are applied. In the previous scenario, the archives generated on primary and archives applied on standby have the same sequence number; hence, standby is synchronized with the primary database.

The value of the APPLIED column for the most recently received logfile will be IN-MEMORY, or YES if that logfile has been applied.

What just happened?

It's very important to know methods to verify synchronization between primary and standby databases. We've now seen one of these methods.

Time for action – testing real-time apply

If real-time apply is enabled, the apply services can apply redo data without waiting for the current standby redo logfile to be archived. This allows faster role transitions because you avoid waiting for a redo log to be transported to the standby database and then applied. In this example, we'll see how changes are transferred and applied to the standby database. The redo log that includes changes is not archived on primary.

1. In order to use real-time apply, the redo transport service from primary to standby must use `LGWR`. Run the following query on the primary database and check the log archive destination configuration.

   ```
   SQL> show parameter log_archive_dest_2

   NAME                   TYPE        VALUE
   --------------------   --------    ----------
   log_archive_dest_2     string      SERVICE=INDIA LGWR ASYNC VALID_FOR
   =(ONLINE_LOGFILES,PRIMARY_ROLE)              DB_UNIQUE_
   NAME=INDIA_UN
   ```

2. In the standby database, start Redo Apply using the `USING CURRENT LOGFILE` option.

   ```
   SQL> ALTER DATABASE RECOVER MANAGED STANDBY DATABASE USING CURRENT
   LOGFILE DISCONNECT FROM SESSION;

   Database altered.
   ```

3. Check the current status of processes related to Data Guard in the physical standby database. You need to verify that the status of the `MRP0` process is `APPLYING LOG`:

   ```
   SQL> SELECT THREAD#,SEQUENCE#,PROCESS,CLIENT_
   PROCESS,STATUS,BLOCK#,BLOCKS FROM V$MANAGED_STANDBY;
   ```

THREAD#	SEQUENCE#	PROCESS	CLIENT_P	STATUS	BLOCK#	BLOCKS
0	0	ARCH	ARCH	CONNECTED	0	0
0	0	ARCH	ARCH	CONNECTED	0	0
0	0	ARCH	ARCH	CONNECTED	0	0
0	0	ARCH	ARCH	CONNECTED	0	0
1	149	ARCH	ARCH	CLOSING	61440	1244
0	0	RFS	N/A	IDLE	0	0

```
1        150      RFS      LGWR      IDLE           8823        1
1        150      MRP0     N/A       APPLYING_LOG   23          204800
```

4. Create a table in the primary database by selecting the data logs from another table.

```
SQL> create table packt.oracle as select * from scott.emp;
Table created.

SQL> select count(*) from packt.oracle;
COUNT(*)
----------
    81920
```

 No log switches have been performed on the primary database.

5. Now monitor the number of redo blocks for the current redo log, written on primary, sent to standby, and applied on standby.

The redo blocks for the primary database:

```
SQL> SELECT THREAD#,SEQUENCE#,PROCESS,CLIENT_
PROCESS,STATUS,BLOCK#,BLOCKS FROM V$MANAGED_STANDBY;
```

THREAD#	SEQUENCE#	PROCESS	CLIENT_P	STATUS	BLOCK#	BLOCKS
1	143	ARCH	ARCH	CLOSING	1	2
0	0	ARCH	ARCH	CONNECTED	0	0
0	0	ARCH	ARCH	CONNECTED	0	0
1	149	ARCH	ARCH	CLOSING	61440	1244
1	146	ARCH	ARCH	CLOSING	2049	1868
1	150	LNS	LNS	WRITING	9016	1

The redo blocks for the standby database:

```
SQL> SELECT THREAD#,SEQUENCE#,PROCESS,CLIENT_
PROCESS,STATUS,BLOCK#,BLOCKS FROM V$MANAGED_STANDBY;
```

THREAD#	SEQUENCE#	PROCESS	CLIENT_P	STATUS	BLOCK#	BLOCKS
0	0	ARCH	ARCH	CONNECTED	0	0
0	0	ARCH	ARCH	CONNECTED	0	0
0	0	ARCH	ARCH	CONNECTED	0	0

0	0	ARCH	ARCH	CONNECTED	0	0
1	149	ARCH	ARCH	CLOSING	61440	1244
0	0	RFS	N/A	IDLE	0	0
1	150	RFS	LGWR	IDLE	8910	1
1	150	MRP0	N/A	APPLYING_LOG	8910	204800

6. You can also check the apply lag on the standby database using the V$DATAGUARD_STATS view in terms of time. Run the following query on the standby database:

```
SQL>  SELECT name, value, datum_time, time_computed FROM
V$DATAGUARD_STATS  WHERE name like 'apply lag';
```

NAME	VALUE	DATUM_TIME	TIME_COMPUTED
apply lag	+00 00:00:00	08/05/2012 22:14:16	08/05/2012 22:14:18

The apply lag metric is zero, which means there's no lag. This value is calculated with the data periodically received from the primary database. The DATUM_TIME parameter shows when this data was last sent from primary to the standby database. The TIME_COMPUTED column shows when the apply lag value was calculated. Normally, the difference between these two values should be less than 30 seconds.

The following query to the V$STANDBY_EVENT_HISTOGRAM view shows the history of apply lag values since the standby instance was last started:

```
SQL> SELECT * FROM V$STANDBY_EVENT_HISTOGRAM WHERE NAME = 'apply
lag'  AND COUNT > 0;
```

NAME	TIME	UNIT	COUNT	LAST_TIME_UPDATED
apply lag	0	seconds	431	08/05/2012 22:14:21
apply lag	1	seconds	7	08/05/2012 22:13:31

7. On the physical standby database (which is read-only and in the real-time apply mode), query the row number for the table that we created on primary.

```
SQL> select count(*) from packt.oracle;

COUNT(*)

----------

    81920
```

We can see that the changes were applied on the standby database without waiting for a log switch either on the primary or standby database. This is achieved by the LGWR redo transport mode on primary and real-time Redo Apply mode on the standby database.

What just happened?

The recommended Redo Apply method, real-time apply, is verified and we've seen that the redo switch is not required to apply changes to the standby database in the real-time apply mode.

Have a go hero – checking the network latency effect on real-time apply

In order to check if network latency and bandwidth have any effect on real-time apply, run an insert operation on the primary and commit. Right after the commit, query the physical standby database to see if the changes are applied immediately. You may see some seconds of delay, which is most probably caused by network performance.

Summary

We have finished this chapter by describing Data Guard physical standby database creation, configuration, and controlling. We used the RMAN duplicate from the active database method, which is the easiest and most efficient way of creating a physical standby database. This method doesn't require a backup staging disk area in either primary or standby servers because it performs a direct copy from primary files to standby. This chapter also covered pre and post steps of creating a standby database with RMAN duplicate. We learned starting, stopping, and monitoring Redo Apply and the synchronization method of physical standby databases, including real-time apply. In the next chapter, we'll learn about building a Data Guard logical standby database environment.

3
Configuring Oracle Data Guard Logical Standby Database

The objective of this chapter is to show you how to create and manage a logical standby database environment. We've already learned what a logical standby database is and what are its highlights. Now it's time to study the installation and administration of the logical standby database with hands-on examples.

In this chapter we'll discuss the following topics:

- Features and working principles of the logical standby database
- The pre-installation steps for a logical standby database configuration
- Creating a logical standby database from a physical standby database
- Verification of the newly created logical standby database configuration
- Customizing the environment with selective replication, Database Guard settings and creating an independent database object on the logical standby database

Logical standby database characteristics

It's important to know the logical standby database properties well in order to decide if your business needs the physical or logical option. The different log apply modes make them distinct solutions for data replication, high availability, and disaster recovery. By using SQL Apply (the log apply method of logical standby databases), Data Guard mines the redo data (which was transferred from the primary database), builds the SQL statements (which will result in the same data change as in the primary database).

Finally executes these SQL statements on the logical standby database as shown in the following diagram:

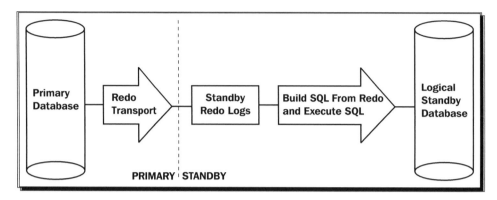

Maintaining this kind of standby database has its own pros and cons. Now let's see what they are.

Not everything must be duplicated

Depending on your conditions, there may be cases where you don't want all the data in your primary database to be replicated. This is not possible with a physical standby database; however, the logical standby database offers to skip replication of some tables or schemas.

Use for reporting at all times

It's possible to use a logical standby database anytime to offload reporting jobs from the primary database because a logical standby database is always open for user connections. This is also available with the Oracle version 11*g* physical standby feature of Active Data Guard but it requires an additional license.

Independent standby database objects

A logical standby database may contain additional schemas and objects that do not exist on the primary database. This feature also relies on the fact that the logical standby database is a read/write accessible database. We can use this feature particularly for the reporting jobs running on the standby database. It's possible to create indexes and materialized views on the standby database, which can be expensive to maintain on the primary database. Also, many reporting tools require us to create global temporary tables. These reporting tools may run on a logical standby database but not on an Active Data Guard standby, because Active Data Guard allows only read operations on the standby database.

Protecting writes on replicated standby tables

The replicated data on a standby database normally needs to be non-modifiable in order to provide data consistency. Logical standby database is capable of guaranteeing this with the use of Database Guard settings. It's also possible to configure a logical standby database in order to allow users to create new objects and modify the data on these non-replicated objects or not allow any modification on the standby database.

Limitation for specific data types and objects

There are specific Oracle database objects and data types that are not supported for replication in a logical standby database configuration. Updates on the following objects will not be replicated to a logical standby:

- Tables containing LOB columns stored as `SecureFiles` (unless the compatibility level is set to 11.2 or higher)
- Tables with virtual columns

We should also keep in mind that changes on the tables or sequences owned by `SYS` are not applied by SQL Apply, because `SYS` organizes its own structure on the logical standby database. We should be careful so as to not put any user data under `SYS` objects or create any object under the `SYS` schema in the primary database manually.

Another important point is redo will not be generated for DML on Global Temporary Tables. Hence, they're out of the replication scope.

The following data types are also not supported in a logical standby database configuration. If a table contains a column with one of these data types, the entire table will be skipped by SQL Apply:

- `BFILE`
- Collections (including `VARRAYS` and nested tables)
- Multimedia data types (including spatial, image, and Oracle text)
- `ROWID` and `UROWID`
- User-defined data types

And last but not least, DDL statements for materialized views and database links are skipped by SQL Apply. Therefore, these objects must be handled manually on the logical standby database, if necessary.

High availability and disaster recovery considerations

A logical standby database can be used for switchover or failover just like the physical standby database configuration. We can also configure fast-start failover with the logical standby environment. These properties make the logical standby database an appropriate solution for high availability and disaster recovery. However, the following considerations are very important if you use the logical standby database for high availability and disaster recovery:

◆ There is no guarantee that all primary data will be present in the logical standby database. We should be aware of the unsupported objects that will not be replicated. If there are important tables on your primary database, which will not be replicated because of the unsupported data type, you should consider the physical standby database for these purposes.

◆ Once we failover to a logical standby database, all other standby databases in the configuration must be recreated. This is not the same on physical standby configuration. Physical standby databases are able to send redo to other standby databases in the configuration after a switchover or failover. If you consider using more than one standby, using a physical standby for disaster recovery will be more effective.

◆ Physical standby offers higher recovery performance than the logical standby because it consumes less memory, CPU, and I/O resource on the apply process. If the primary database has high redo generation rate, you can consider using a physical standby for the purposes in question.

◆ The management of a logical standby configuration is more complex than that of physical. In a physical standby database we start Redo Apply and it's guaranteed that all the changes on the data will be replicated to standby. Logical standby will require more manual administrator interferences and they need to be consistently synchronized and work with optimum performance.

Preparation for the configuration

Now it's time to get our hands dirty in the process of creating a logical standby database. First we'll start preparing the primary database for the configuration. Then we'll convert a physical standby database into a logical standby database. This is the method of creating logical standby Data Guard configuration.

You can use the physical standby database that we created together in *Chapter 2, Configuring Oracle Data Guard Physical Standby Database* for this purpose. However, we'll need a physical standby in the following chapters to study on. So, it would be better to create a separate physical standby database with one of the mentioned methods to use in the logical standby configuration.

There are some prerequisites that we need to complete before starting the configuration. One of them is checking the primary database for specifying any tables that will be skipped by SQL Apply because of the unsupported data types. It doesn't make sense to build a configuration where you're not sure which objects will and will not be replicated.

The other important control is ensuring the objects that will be replicated and maintained by SQL Apply are uniquely identified. As the logical standby is actually a standalone database, synchronizing it with SQL statements might result in ROWIDs being different on primary and standby databases. Thus, primary ROWID cannot be used to identify the corresponding row in the logical standby database. SQL Apply needs another unique identifier to apply changes, which are the primary keys, non-null unique-constraint/index, or all columns of bounded size, respectively depending on their existence.

Time for action – checking for the unsupported data types

In order to be aware of what will and will not be replicated, we should check which primary database tables are not supported for the logical standby database.

1. Run the following query on the primary database to see the unsupported table names:

```
SQL> SELECT * FROM DBA_LOGSTDBY_UNSUPPORTED_TABLE ORDER BY
OWNER, TABLE_NAME;

OWNER        TABLE_NAME
----------   -------------------------------
IX           AQ$_ORDERS_QUEUETABLE_G
IX           AQ$_ORDERS_QUEUETABLE_H
IX           AQ$_ORDERS_QUEUETABLE_I
IX           AQ$_ORDERS_QUEUETABLE_L
IX           AQ$_ORDERS_QUEUETABLE_S
IX           AQ$_ORDERS_QUEUETABLE_T
IX           AQ$_STREAMS_QUEUE_TABLE_C
IX           AQ$_STREAMS_QUEUE_TABLE_G
IX           AQ$_STREAMS_QUEUE_TABLE_H
IX           AQ$_STREAMS_QUEUE_TABLE_I
IX           AQ$_STREAMS_QUEUE_TABLE_L
IX           AQ$_STREAMS_QUEUE_TABLE_S
IX           AQ$_STREAMS_QUEUE_TABLE_T
IX           ORDERS_QUEUETABLE
IX           STREAMS_QUEUE_TABLE
OE           CATEGORIES_TAB
OE           CUSTOMERS
OE           PURCHASEORDER
```

```
OE          WAREHOUSES
PM          ONLINE_MEDIA
PM          PRINT_MEDIA
SH          DIMENSION_EXCEPTIONS

22 rows selected.
```

As mentioned earlier, we use a newly created 11*g* release 2 database, which only includes built-in example schemas. The unsupported tables are from the IX, OE, PM, and SH schemas. Now let's check the reasons for which these tables are on the unsupported list.

2. Run the following query for one of the unsupported tables to check the reason. We're now running STREAMS_QUEUE_TABLE under the IX schema:

```
SQL> SELECT DISTINCT(ATTRIBUTES)  FROM DBA_LOGSTDBY_UNSUPPORTED
WHERE OWNER='IX' and TABLE_NAME = 'STREAMS_QUEUE_TABLE';

ATTRIBUTES
------------------
AQ queue table
```

We've only queried the ATTRIBUTES column of the DBA_LOGSTDBY_ UNSUPPORTED view for a specific table name. The ATTRIBUTES column displays the reason the table is not supported by SQL Apply. If the structure of the table is unsupported, the ATTRIBUTES column will show the description for that. In the example we can see that STREAMS_QUEUE_TABLE is unsupported because it is an AQ queue table.

3. If the structure of the table is supported but some columns in the table have unsupported data types, the ATTRIBUTE column will be NULL. Let's check which columns of which tables have ATTRIBUTE value NULL, in other words which tables have unsupported data types on specific columns.

```
SQL> SELECT OWNER, TABLE_NAME, COLUMN_NAME,DATA_TYPE FROM DBA_
LOGSTDBY_UNSUPPORTED  WHERE ATTRIBUTES IS NULL;
```

OWNER	TABLE_NAME	COLUMN_NAME	DATA_TYPE
PM	ONLINE_MEDIA	PRODUCT_PHOTO_SIGNATURE	OBJECT
PM	ONLINE_MEDIA	PRODUCT_THUMBNAIL	OBJECT
PM	ONLINE_MEDIA	PRODUCT_VIDEO	OBJECT
PM	ONLINE_MEDIA	PRODUCT_AUDIO	OBJECT
PM	ONLINE_MEDIA	PRODUCT_TESTIMONIALS	OBJECT
PM	ONLINE_MEDIA	PRODUCT_PHOTO	OBJECT
PM	PRINT_MEDIA	AD_HEADER	OBJECT

```
PM      PRINT_MEDIA          AD_GRAPHIC           BFILE
OE      CUSTOMERS            CUST_ADDRESS         OBJECT
OE      CUSTOMERS            PHONE_NUMBERS        VARRAY
OE      CUSTOMERS            CUST_GEO_LOCATION    OBJECT
OE      WAREHOUSES           WH_GEO_LOCATION      OBJECT
SH      DIMENSION_EXCEPTIONS BAD_ROWID            ROWID

13 rows selected.
```

We can see that 5 tables have unsupported columns and will be ignored by SQL Apply like the others, because of their table structure.

Keep in mind that the changes on the unsupported tables will still be sent by the redo transport service; however, SQL Apply will ignore the changes on the unsupported tables. Another point is the unsupported tables will exist on the logical standby database, because a logical standby is converted from a physical standby database, which is an exact copy of the primary. These tables will exist but will not be updated by SQL Apply on the logical standby database.

What just happened?

We've seen how to query unsupported data for logical standby in the existing database. This information is important in the decision of using logical standby databases.

Now let's search for any table row uniqueness problem in the primary database and how to fix the issue if it exists.

Time for action – searching for and fixing any table row uniqueness problem

1. In order to check for any table row uniqueness, we can run the following query on the primary database:

```
SQL> SELECT * FROM DBA_LOGSTDBY_NOT_UNIQUE;

OWNER                            TABLE_NAME                      B
------------------------------   -----------------------------   -
SCOTT                            BONUS                           N
SCOTT                            SALGRADE                        N
SH                               SALES                           N
SH                               COSTS                           N
SH                               SUPPLEMENTARY_DEMOGRAPHICS      N
```

This query was run on a newly created 11*g* release 2 database, which only includes built-in example schemas. The output shows that several tables from SCOTT and SH schemas have row uniqueness problem.

The BAD_COLUMN column has two values, which are Y and N. If you see the rows with BAD_COLUMN=Y, it means that the table column is defined using an unbounded data type, such as LONG or BLOB. If two rows contain the same data except in their LOB columns, the replication will not work properly for this table. If the application ensures the rows are unique, we should consider adding a disabled primary key RELY constraint to these tables. When RELY is used, the system will assume that rows are unique and not validate them on every modification to the table. This method will avoid the overhead of maintaining a primary key on the primary database. However, if there's no such uniqueness, we must add a unique-constraint/index to the columns on the primary database.

BAD_COLUMN=N means that there is enough column information to maintain the table in the logical standby database; however, the transport and apply services will run more efficiently if you add a primary key to the table. We should again consider adding a disabled RELY constraint to these tables.

2. Let's add a disabled primary key RELY constraint to the BONUS table in the SCOTT schema. First we check the columns of the table using the following query:

```
SQL> DESC SCOTT.BONUS
 Name              Null?     Type
 ---------------   --------  ----------------------------
 ENAME                       VARCHAR2(10)
 JOB                         VARCHAR2(9)
 SAL                         NUMBER
 COMM                        NUMBER
```

3. Now we add the disabled RELY constraint to the ENAME column of the table:

```
SQL> ALTER TABLE SCOTT.BONUS ADD PRIMARY KEY (ENAME) RELY DISABLE;

Table altered.
```

4. We can check the DBA_LOGSTDBY_NOT_UNIQUE view again to see if the BONUS table has disappeared from the list using the following query:

```
SQL> SELECT * FROM DBA_LOGSTDBY_NOT_UNIQUE;
```

OWNER	TABLE_NAME	B
SCOTT	SALGRADE	N
SH	SALES	N
SH	COSTS	N
SH	SUPPLEMENTARY_DEMOGRAPHICS	N

5. We should add disabled RELY constraints to the rest of the tables above. Now we're ready for the next step, which is creating the logical standby database.

What just happened?

We've just seen the prerequisite steps to create a logical standby database configuration. The first step was checking the unsupported tables that will not be replicated, in order to be aware which data will be missed on the logical standby and to decide whether to use the logical option or not. The next step is searching for and fixing any table row uniqueness problem, for properly working redo transport and SQL Apply services.

Creating a logical standby database

As mentioned, a physical standby database is needed to create a logical standby database. It is assumed that we have a Data Guard configuration with a primary and one or more physical standby databases, which are synchronized with the primary. In order to create a logical standby database, we should first check the primary and the physical standby databases and make them ready for a logical standby conversion. These configurations are as follows:

- Stopping the media recovery on the standby
- Configuring primary database initialization parameters to be ready for a logical standby role transition
- Building the LogMiner dictionary on the primary
- If standby is RAC, converting it to a single instance temporarily

After completing these tasks, we continue the process of converting the physical standby into a logical standby with the following tasks:

- Recovering the standby to the SCN that the LogMiner dictionary was built with
- Re-enabling RAC on the standby if it exists
- Modifying the archival initialization parameters for the standby
- Opening the database with resetlogs
- Starting SQL Apply on the standby

It's important to complete all these steps for a successful logical standby database configuration.

If Data Guard broker is used, it's advised to remove the physical standby database from the broker configuration before starting the logical standby conversion process. If you don't, broker will still show the standby database as a physical standby even if you convert it to a logical standby database and you'll struggle with this problem later on.

Time for action – making a physical standby database environment ready for conversion

You can perform the following steps to make a physical standby database environment ready for conversion:

1. Stop the media recovery on the physical standby with the following statement:

    ```
    SQL> ALTER DATABASE RECOVER MANAGED STANDBY DATABASE CANCEL;

    Database altered.
    ```

2. In order to prepare the primary database for possible switchovers with the logical standby in future, we will make some changes on the archival initialization parameters. This step is optional and if you don't plan any switchovers between the primary and logical standby in the future, you can skip this step. Run the following statements on the primary database to change the parameters:

    ```
    SQL> ALTER SYSTEM SET LOG_ARCHIVE_DEST_1='LOCATION=/u01/app/
    oracle/archive VALID_FOR=(ONLINE_LOGFILES,ALL_ROLES) DB_UNIQUE_
    NAME=TURKEY_UN' SCOPE=BOTH;

    System altered.

    SQL> ALTER SYSTEM SET LOG_ARCHIVE_DEST_3='LOCATION=/u01/app/
    oracle/archive_std VALID_FOR=(STANDBY_LOGFILES,STANDBY_ROLE) DB_
    UNIQUE_NAME=TURKEY_UN' SCOPE=BOTH;

    System altered.
    ```

    In this configuration LOG_ARCHIVE_DEST_1 will archive the online logfiles to the archived logfiles even if the database is primary or logical standby (ALL_ROLES option). After a switchover when the database role is logical standby, this setting will archive the local online redo logfiles and not the standby redo logs. It will be filled with the redo transferred from primary.

The `LOG_ARCHIVE_DEST_3` parameter (not set in physical standby Data Guard configuration) will be omitted when the database is primary (`STANDBY_ROLE` option). If the database role is logical standby, this parameter will archive the standby redo logs that contain redo generated and sent by the primary database.

There is already `LOG_ARCHIVE_DEST_2` defined on the primary database that sends redo to the standby. We are not going to change this parameter. The value of this parameter should resemble the following:

```
SERVICE=INDIA LGWR ASYNC VALID_FOR=(ONLINE_LOGFILES,PRIMARY_ROLE)
DB_UNIQUE_NAME=INDIA_UN
```

3. Execute the following statement on the primary database to make it ready to support a logical standby configuration. This package enables supplementary logging on the primary database, which ensures that the updates contain enough information to identify each modified row. It also builds the LogMiner dictionary and identifies the SCN that SQL Apply has to start mining redo.

```
SQL> EXECUTE DBMS_LOGSTDBY.BUILD;

PL/SQL procedure successfully completed.
```

 If the database version is 11gR2, the supplemental logging information is automatically propagated to any existing physical standby database in the configuration. In earlier releases, we must enable supplemental logging on the physical standby database, if we're going to switchover to a physical standby database. Otherwise, after the switchover, the new primary database will not be able to properly feed the logical standby database with redo.

4. If the physical standby is RAC, you must convert it to a single instance before the logical database conversion. Use the following statements for this purpose:

```
SQL> ALTER SYSTEM SET CLUSTER_DATABASE=FALSE SCOPE=SPFILE;
SQL> SHUTDOWN ABORT;
SQL> STARTUP MOUNT EXCLUSIVE;
```

What just happened?

We're now ready to continue with the conversion of the standby database from physical to logical.

Time for action – converting a physical standby database into a logical standby database

1. Execute the following special recovery command on the standby database in order to recover it until the SCN that the dictionary was built:

```
SQL> ALTER DATABASE RECOVER TO LOGICAL STANDBY ORCL2;

Database altered.
```

2. At the same time, if you check the standby database alert log you'll see the following lines:

```
Media Recovery Log /u01/app/oracle2/archive/1_106_791552282.arc
Media Recovery Log /u01/app/oracle2/archive/1_107_791552282.arc
Incomplete Recovery applied until change 1873735
Media Recovery Complete (INDIA)
...
RESETLOGS after incomplete recovery UNTIL CHANGE 1873735
Resetting resetlogs activation ID 1319360408 (0x4ea3d798)
standby became primary SCN: 1873733
...
RECOVER TO LOGICAL STANDBY: Complete - Database shutdown required
after NID finishes
*** DBNEWID utility started ***
DBID will be changed from 1319333016 to new DBID of 773141456 for
database ORCL
DBNAME will be changed from ORCL to new DBNAME of ORCL2
Starting datafile conversion
Datafile conversion complete
Database name changed to ORCL2.
Modify parameter file and generate a new password file before
restarting.
Database ID for database ORCL2 changed to 773141456.
All previous backups and archived redo logs for this database are
unusable.
Database has been shutdown, open with RESETLOGS option.
Succesfully changed database name and ID.
*** DBNEWID utility finished succesfully ***
Completed: ALTER DATABASE RECOVER TO LOGICAL STANDBY ORCL2
```

We can see that the MRP applied the changes until a specific SCN. This SCN is the point at which the LogMiner dictionary was built. Then the standby database was activated and became the primary database. The rest of the lines show the process of changing the DB_NAME of the database. If you look at the recovery command, you'll see that we specified the name ORCL2 at the end. The database name needs to be changed for the physical standby database to become a logical standby and ORCL2 will be the new name of the standby database. All of these changes were applied to the database by the recovery command we ran.

In the alert log, we can see the following line:

```
modify parameter file and generate a new
password file before restarting.
```

If spfile is being used, the DB_NAME parameter will be changed automatically after this command. If pfile is in use, we need to manually change the DB_NAME to the new value in the init.ora file.

Prior to 11*g* it was necessary to create a new password file, but it's not required in 11*g*. So we can ignore this line of the alert.log.

3. If the standby database is RAC, we can enable the cluster again using the following query:

```
SQL> ALTER SYSTEM SET CLUSTER_DATABASE=TRUE SCOPE=SPFILE;
SQL> SHUTDOWN;
SQL> STARTUP MOUNT;
```

4. There are two kinds of archived redo logfiles on the logical standby databases. The first one is created from the online redo logs and the second is created from the standby redo logs. We'll create separate destinations for these archived logfiles using the following query:

```
SQL> ALTER SYSTEM SET LOG_ARCHIVE_DEST_1='LOCATION=/u01/app/
oracle/archive VALID_FOR=(ONLINE_LOGFILES,ALL_ROLES) DB_UNIQUE_
NAME=INDIA_UN';

System altered.

SQL> ALTER SYSTEM SET LOG_ARCHIVE_DEST_2='SERVICE=TURKEY ASYNC
VALID_FOR=(ONLINE_LOGFILES,PRIMARY_ROLE) DB_UNIQUE_NAME=TURKEY_
UN';

System altered.
```

```
SQL> ALTER SYSTEM SET LOG_ARCHIVE_DEST_3='LOCATION=/u01/app/
oracle/archive_std VALID_FOR=(STANDBY_LOGFILES,STANDBY_ROLE) DB_
UNIQUE_NAME=INDIA_UN';
```

```
System altered.
```

Here, the first destination will be used for archiving the online redo logs of the
logical standby database. The second destination was already set in physical standby
setup and was defined in order to be used in a switchover (PRIMARY_ROLE option
is used). The last destination, LOG_ARCHIVE_DEST_3 will be used for archiving
the standby redo logs that contains the redo generated and transferred from the
primary database.

5. We used specific and different destinations for the archived logs for a better
    understanding in this example. However, using fast recovery area for this purpose
    with the LOCATION=USE_DB_RECOVERY_FILE_DEST option is a good practice.
    In Oracle 10g, the logical standby database was not supported to keep the foreign
    archived logfiles (archived logs that were generated from standby redo logs) in
    the **flash recovery area** (**FRA**). In 11g, this is supported. In order to use FRA for
    archiving, you should first enable FRA by setting the following parameters:

    ```
    SQL> ALTER SYSTEM SET DB_RECOVERY_FILE_DEST_SIZE=10G;
    SQL> ALTER SYSTEM SET DB_RECOVERY_FILE_DEST='/U01/APP/ORACLE/FRA';
    ```

6. Then set LOG_ARCHIVE_DEST_1 as follows:

    ```
    SQL> ALTER SYSTEM SET LOG_ARCHIVE_DEST_1='LOCATION=USE_DB_
    RECOVERY_FILE_DEST';
    ```

7. LOG_ARCHIVE_DEST_1 will be enough to archive both online and standby logfiles
    and we will not need LOG_ARCHIVE_DEST_3 in this case. The directory structure
    will be automatically created as follows:

    ```
    /u01/app/oracle2/fra/INDIA_UN/foreign_archivelog à for the files
    archived from standby logs
    ```

    ```
    /u01/app/oracle2/fra/INDIA_UN/archivelog à for the files archived
    from online logs
    ```

8. Now restart the standby database and open it with the resetlogs option as shown
    in the following query:

    ```
    SQL> SHUTDOWN IMMEDIATE;
    SQL> STARTUP MOUNT;
    SQL> ALTER DATABASE OPEN RESETLOGS;
    ```

    ```
    Database altered.
    ```

    The database is now read/write opened for user connections. We only need to start
    SQL Apply to finish the logical standby configuration.

9. Start SQL Apply on the logical standby database by executing the following statement:

```
SQL> ALTER DATABASE START LOGICAL STANDBY APPLY IMMEDIATE;

Database altered.
```

Let's check what happened behind when we executed this statement, by reading the alert logfile for the standby database as follows:

```
alter database start logical standby apply immediate
LOGSTDBY: Creating new session for dbid 1319333016 starting at scn
0x0000.00000000
LOGSTDBY: Created session of id 1

...

LSP0 started with pid=33, OS id=15629
Completed: alter database start logical standby apply immediate
LOGMINER: Parameters summary for session# = 1
LOGMINER: Number of processes = 3, Transaction Chunk Size = 201
LOGMINER: Memory Size = 30M, Checkpoint interval = 150M
LOGMINER: SpillScn 0, ResetLogScn 0
```

When the statement executed, a new session was created for the SQL Apply, and then the LSP0 process was started, which is the Logical Standby Coordinator Process responsible for managing the LogMiner and Apply processes. Along with LSP0, miner processes were also started.

```
LOGMINER: Begin mining logfile during dictionary load for session 1
thread 1 sequence 105, /u01/app/oracle/archive_std/1_105_791552282.arc
Thread 1 advanced to log sequence 3 (LGWR switch)
  Current log# 3 seq# 3 mem# 0: /u01/app/oracle2/datafile/ORCL/redo03.log
Archived Log entry 2 added for thread 1 sequence 2 ID 0x2e14f3f9 dest 1
LOGMINER: End mining logfiles during dictionary load for session 1
```

At this point, we can see that SQL Apply mines the redo in order to find the dictionary and build it on the standby. If it's not able to find the necessary archived log sequences, it requests them from the primary database.

```
RFS LogMiner: Registered logfile [/u01/app/oracle/archive_
std/1_106_791552282.arc] to LogMiner session id [1]

...
```

```
LOGMINER: Begin mining logfile for session 1 thread 1 sequence 106, /u01/
app/oracle/archive_std/1_106_791552282.arc
LOGMINER: End   mining logfile for session 1 thread 1 sequence 106, /u01/
app/oracle/archive_std/1_106_791552282.arc
```

Now the configuration is over and logical standby starts the apply processes and applies all the logs to be synchronized with the primary database.

What just happened?

We have finished all the required steps to create a logical standby database. Now it's time to verify if the logical standby services are working properly.

Verifying the logical standby database

There are two services that we need to check for the verification of the logical standby configuration, which are the redo transport service and the SQL Apply service. There are several ways to check the status of these services. You can use alert log and trace files (whenever necessary) or you can query the views of the logical standby database that contains information about the status of the Data Guard services. Another way for controlling is modifying the primary database tables and querying the same tables on the logical standby. We'll now query the most useful views to gather information about the configuration and service status.

Time for action – checking the redo transport service status

The following steps can be performed to check the redo transport service status:

1. The first query to be executed to be sure that the redo transport service is working properly will be the V$DATAGUARD_STATS view.

   ```
   SQL> SELECT NAME, VALUE, TIME_COMPUTED FROM V$DATAGUARD_STATS
   WHERE NAME='TRANSPORT LAG';


   NAME                    VALUE                TIME_COMPUTED
   --------------------    --------------------    ----------------------
   transport lag           +00 00:00:00         08/27/2012 18:06:30
   ```

   The TIME_COMPUTED value has to be up-to-date. We can see that there is no redo transport lag in our logical standby configuration. We'll see a time value if there is a problem with the redo transport. Also, if there is an excessive redo generation on the primary database, this value may increase because the redo transport may not catch up with the redo generation. The lag must be zero again when the standby synchronized at the end.

2. By executing the following SQL query on the logical standby, we can check logs with which sequences are being transferred from primary and also which sequences are being archived from the local database online redo logs.

```
SQL> SELECT PROCESS, STATUS, THREAD#, SEQUENCE#, BLOCK#, BLOCKS
FROM V$MANAGED_STANDBY;
```

PROCESS	STATUS	THREAD#	SEQUENCE#	BLOCK#	BLOCKS
ARCH	CLOSING	1	90	90112	1026
ARCH	CONNECTED	0	0	0	0
ARCH	CLOSING	1	91	90112	1026
ARCH	CLOSING	1	92	90112	1018
RFS	IDLE	0	0	0	0
RFS	RECIEVING	1	114	6828	1
RFS	IDLE	0	0	0	0
RFS	IDLE	0	0	0	0

The primary database is currently sending redo to the logical standby. We can see that the RFS process, which is responsible for redo transportation on standby databases, is currently receiving the redo with sequence number 114. It's also obvious that the ARCH processes are archiving the online redo logs of the logical standby database and the last archived log has the sequence number 92.

 Don't forget that the sequences being received by RFS and the sequences being archived from the online redo logs by ARCH have no relationships. For example, the log sequence 90 archived from the online redo log of the logical standby database does not contain the same redo data with the sequence 90, which is received from the primary database.

3. On the other hand, we can use the following query to check which sequences were received from the primary database and if they were applied or not:

```
SQL>  SELECT FILE_NAME, SEQUENCE# as SEQ#, DICT_BEGIN AS BEG,
DICT_END AS END,APPLIED FROM DBA_LOGSTDBY_LOG ORDER BY SEQUENCE#;
```

FILE_NAME	SEQ#	BEG	END	APPLIED
/u01/app/oracle2/archive_std/1_105_791552282.arc	105	YES	YES	YES
/u01/app/oracle2/archive_std/1_106_791552282.arc	106	NO	NO	YES
/u01/app/oracle2/archive_std/1_107_791552282.arc	107	NO	NO	YES

```
/u01/app/oracle2/archive_std/1_108_791552282.arc  108 NO  NO  YES
/u01/app/oracle2/archive_std/1_109_791552282.arc  109 NO  NO  YES
/u01/app/oracle2/archive_std/1_110_791552282.arc  110 NO  NO  YES
...
```

The YES value of the DICT_BEGIN and DICT_END columns show by the archived log sequences that the LogMiner dictionary build was in place. The APPLIED column shows whether the archived log sequence was applied by SQL Apply or not.

What just happened?

We've verified that redo transport service of Data Guard, the logical standby configuration, is running healthfully.

Now let's see how we check SQL Apply service to see if it's running properly. It's very important to verify that changes are being applied on the standby database.

Time for action – checking the SQL Apply service status

The following steps can be performed to check the SQL Apply service status:

1. Use the following query on the logical standby database, to check the general SQL Apply status:

   ```
   SQL> SELECT * FROM V$LOGSTDBY_STATE;

      PRIMARY_DBID SESSION_ID REALTIME_APPLY  STATE
   -------------- ---------- --------------- ---------------
        1319333016          1 Y              APPLYING
   ```

   At the STATE column, we can see INITIALIZING, WAITING FOR DICTIONARY LOGS, LOADING DICTIONARY, WAITING ON GAP, APPLYING, and IDLE values, which describe the status of the SQL Apply clearly with their names.

2. The DBA_LOGSTDBY_LOG view, that we have queried in the Checking the Redo Transport Service Status action, will be very helpful to find the last applied archived log sequence and to check if there are archived log sequences that were received but not applied. Another view V$LOGSTDBY_PROCESS is helpful to control the status of the processes responsible for SQL Apply.

   ```
   SQL> SELECT TYPE, STATUS_CODE, STATUS FROM V$LOGSTDBY_PROCESS;

   TYPE         STATUS_CODE STATUS
   ----------- ----------- ------------------------------------
   COORDINATOR       16116 ORA-16116: no work available
   ```

```
ANALYZER              16116 ORA-16116: no work available
APPLIER               16123 ORA-16123: transaction 11 22 786 is
                                       waiting for commit approval
APPLIER               16117 ORA-16117: processing
APPLIER               16117 ORA-16117: processing
APPLIER               16117 ORA-16117: processing
APPLIER               16123 ORA-16123: transaction 11 25 786 is
                                       waiting for commit approval
READER                16127 ORA-16127: stalled waiting for additional
                                       transactions to be applied
BUILDER               16116 ORA-16116: no work available
PREPARER              16117 ORA-16117: processing
```

Output shows all the processes in the SQL Apply and their status. The READER, PREPARER, and BUILDER processes are responsible for the mining of the redo. On the other side, COORDINATOR, ANALYZER, and APPLIER processes work together to apply the changes to the database. We can see that the READER process is waiting for the transactions to be applied, so that memory will become available and it will read more redo. On the other side, some APPLIER processes apply redo and some wait for commit approval to continue applying redo as shown in the following diagram:

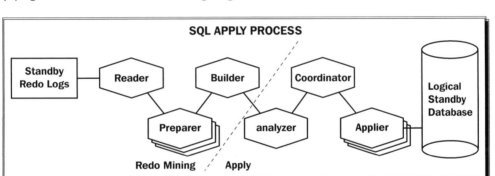

What just happened?

We have seen several queries to gather information about the logical standby configuration. We have verified that the newly created logical standby is synchronized with the primary and everything works fine.

Redo transport and SQL Apply, which are the two main services of logical standby, can be monitored at any time using the mentioned methods.

Have a go hero – check the services in a broken configuration

Now stop the listener on the logical standby site and run some operation on the primary database. New archived logs will be created but primary would not send these logs to standby. This will cause a gap between primary and standby. In the case of a gap, query redo transport and SQL Apply services with the same queries. Start the listener and continue checking the status.

Customization and management in a logical standby database

After the initial configuration of a logical standby database, we should make customizations to benefit from the standby at the highest level. Let's see what kind of customizations we are able to do and how we manage a logical standby database environment.

Selective replication in a logical standby database

In principle, we cannot directly specify what to replicate to a logical standby database, but we can specify tables for SQL Apply to `skip`. When this feature is used, the redo data about the tables specified in the `skip` rules is still transferred to the standby database, but at the mining stage SQL Apply will omit the relevant redo on the logical standby. We use `DBMS_LOGSTDBY.SKIP` for this purpose.

Time for action – working with skip rules on a logical standby database

We are now going to create some skip rules on the logical standby database in order to skip replication of DDL or DML operations on some tables. Then we'll see how to query the existing skip rules and finally the method for disabling the rules.

1. We need to create skip rules for tables and schemas, but first we need to stop SQL Apply using the following query:

   ```
   SQL> ALTER DATABASE STOP LOGICAL STANDBY APPLY;
   ```

2. Then, the following statement will create a `skip` rule to skip changes caused by DML statements on the EMP table of the SCOTT schema. Execute the following statement on the logical standby database:

   ```
   SQL> EXECUTE DBMS_LOGSTDBY.SKIP(STMT => 'DML', SCHEMA_NAME =>
   'SCOTT', OBJECT_NAME => 'EMP');

   PL/SQL procedure successfully completed.
   ```

3. If we also want skip DDL statements encountered for this table, the following statement will create another `skip` rule:

```
SQL> EXECUTE DBMS_LOGSTDBY.SKIP(STMT => 'SCHEMA_DDL',
SCHEMA_NAME => 'SCOTT', OBJECT_NAME => 'EMP');
```

4. The next rule will disable DML replication for a complete schema. Execute the following statement to skip all DML changes to the HR schema:

```
SQL> EXECUTE DBMS_LOGSTDBY.SKIP(STMT => 'DML', SCHEMA_NAME =>
'HR', OBJECT_NAME => '%');
```

 The wildcard character in the previous code can also be used in different ways such as `TMP_%`, which refers to the tables with the prefix `TMP_`.

5. The following example is disabling some statements to run on the logical standby database. The `CREATE/DROP DIRECTORY` commands will not be executed by SQL Apply:

```
SQL> EXECUTE DBMS_LOGSTDBY.SKIP(STMT => 'DIRECTORY');
```

6. Specify a procedure for DDL statements. Suppose we have different directory structures on primary and logical standby database servers. When we add a new datafile on primary under `/u01/app/oracle/datafile/ORCL`, we want the logical standby database to create the datafile under `/datafile/ORCL`. We can use the `DBMS_LOGSTDBY.SKIP` procedure with the `PROC_NAME` parameter for this goal. Let's create a rule for this purpose. First we'll create a procedure to replace datafile names. Run the following create procedure statement on the logical standby with `sys` user:

```
SQL> create or replace procedure sys.change_ts_ddl (
 2        old_stmt   in   varchar2
 3      , stmt_typ   in   varchar2
 4      , schema     in   varchar2
 5      , name       in   varchar2
 6      , xidusn     in   number
 7      , xidslt     in   number
 8      , xidsqn     in   number
 9      , action     out number
10      , new_stmt   out varchar2
11  ) as
12  begin
13  new_stmt := replace(old_stmt,
'/u01/app/oracle2/datafile/ORCL','/datafile/ORCL');
14  action := dbms_logstdby.skip_action_replace;
15
```

```
16    exception
17       when others then
18          action := dbms_logstdby.skip_action_error;
19          new_stmt := null;
20
21  end change_ts_ddl;
22  /
```

7. Now create a rule to invoke this procedure before running the replicated tablespace DDL commands on the logical standby database using the following query:

```
SQL> EXECUTE DBMS_LOGSTDBY.SKIP(STMT => 'TABLESPACE', PROC_NAME =>
'SYS.CHANGE_TS_DDL');

PL/SQL procedure successfully completed.
```

8. Create and alter the tablespace commands executed on the primary database. They will now be modified on the logical standby database before being executed. The path of the datafiles in the statements will change from /u01/app/oracle2/ datafile/ORCL value to /datafile/ORCL. Now let's add a datafile on the primary database as follows:

```
SQL> ALTER TABLESPACE SYSTEM ADD DATAFILE '/U01/APP/ORACLE/
DATAFILE/ORCL/SYSTEM02.DBF' SIZE 1G;

Tablespace altered.
```

9. Start SQL Apply on the logical standby as follows:

```
SQL> ALTER DATABASE START LOGICAL STANDBY APPLY IMMEDIATE;

Database altered.
```

10. On the alert logfile of the logical standby database, we'll see the following line, which states that the procedure worked as planned:

```
Completed: alter tablespace system add datafile
'/datafile/ORCL/system02.dbf' size 1G
```

11. If something goes wrong and the database cannot execute the procedure, SQL Apply will stop and you'll see the related error outputs on the alert log. For example, if there are missing arguments in the procedure, the following errors will be written into the alert logfile:

```
krvxerpt: Errors detected in process 42, role Apply Slave.

dglspc: unhandled failure calling user procedure 604

...

PLS-00306: wrong number or types of arguments in call to 'CHANGE_
TS_DDL'
```

```
ORA-06550: line 1, column 443:

PL/SQL: Statement ignored

ORA-06550: line , column :

LOGSTDBY Analyzer process AS00 server id=0 pid=41 OS id=13178
stopped

LOGSTDBY Apply process AS03 server id=3 pid=44 OS id=13184 stopped

LOGSTDBY Apply process AS04 server id=4 pid=45 OS id=13186 stopped

LOGSTDBY Apply process AS02 server id=2 pid=43 OS id=13182 stopped

LOGSTDBY Apply process AS05 server id=5 pid=46 OS id=13188 stopped

LOGMINER: session#=1, reader MS00 pid=37 OS id=13172 sid=145
stopped

LOGMINER: session#=1, preparer MS02 pid=40 OS id=13176 sid=178
stopped

LOGMINER: session#=1, builder MS01 pid=38 OS id=13174 sid=156
stopped
```

12. Now, we query the rules. Let's check what rules we have created, which data will not be replicated, and what procedures were defined for what kind of SQL statements on the logical standby database. We'll use the DBA_LOGSTDBY_SKIP view to gather this information. Run the following query on the logical standby database:

```
SQL> SELECT OWNER, NAME,STATEMENT_OPT, PROC  FROM DBA_LOGSTDBY_
SKIP  WHERE STATEMENT_OPT <> 'INTERNAL SCHEMA';
```

OWNER	NAME	STATEMENT_OPT	PROC
		DIRECTORY	
SCOTT	EMP	DML	
SCOTT	EMP	SCHEMA_DDL	
HR	%	DML	
		TABLESPACE	SYS.CHANGE_TS_DDL

We can see all the rules we created in this output. The first rule disables running the directory DDL commands on the logical standby database. The DML and DDL statements on the EMP table of the SCOTT schema will be skipped by SQL Apply. Also all the tables of the HR schema are out of replication scope in terms of DML operations. At the last line of the output, we can see the rule we created, which defines a procedure for the DDL operations on the logical standby database. The SYS.CHANGE_TS_DDL procedure will be executed prior to the replicated tablespace DDL commands on the logical standby databse. This procedure will change the directory of the datafiles.

13. Disable a skip rule. We may want to re-enable replication for a table or schema in the logical standby database. In this case we will use DBMS_LOGSTDBY.UNSKIP procedure to remove the skip rule for that table or schema. However, prior to this we need the current state of the table and its data on the logical standby database to start the replication again. For this purpose we will use the DBMS_LOGSTDBY.INSTANTIATE_TABLE procedure. This procedure will drop and recreate the table if it still exists on the logical standby database. The current data will be imported but associated indexes and constraints will not be replicated. First, we stop SQL Apply as follows:

```
SQL> ALTER DATABASE STOP LOGICAL STANDBY APPLY;
```

14. We need a database link to connect to the primary database to read and lock the table in the primary database. The link must connect to the primary database with a user who has privileges to read and lock the table, as well as the SELECT_CATALOG_ROLE procedure. Let's create this database link on the logical standby database as follows:

```
SQL> CREATE PUBLIC DATABASE LINK INSTANTIATE_TABLE_LINK CONNECT TO
SYSTEM IDENTIFIED BY ORACLE USING 'TURKEY';

Database link created.
```

15. Then execute the INSTANTIATE_TABLE procedure as follows:

```
SQL> EXECUTE DBMS_LOGSTDBY.INSTANTIATE_TABLE (SCHEMA_NAME =>
'SCOTT', TABLE_NAME => 'EMP', DBLINK => 'INSTANTIATE_TABLE_LINK');

PL/SQL procedure successfully completed.
```

This procedure uses Data Pump on the background. It locks the table on the primary for a moment and records that SCN. Then the drop table, create table and export/import operations are performed. After the procedure is completed, logical standby uses the SCN value for consistent replication of the table. You'll see the following lines in the alert log of the logical standby database, which indicates the use of Data Pump import:

```
DM00 started with pid=36, OS id=12415, job SYS.SYS_IMPORT_TABLE_01
DW00 started with pid=37, OS id=12426, wid=1, job SYS.SYS_IMPORT_
TABLE_01
```

16. Now we must delete the DML and DDL skip rules of SCOTT.EMP table from the logical standby database using DBMS_LOGSTDBY.UNSKIP as follows:

```
SQL> EXECUTE DBMS_LOGSTDBY.UNSKIP(STMT => 'DML', SCHEMA_NAME =>
'SCOTT', OBJECT_NAME => 'EMP');

PL/SQL procedure successfully completed.
```

```
SQL> EXECUTE DBMS_LOGSTDBY.UNSKIP(STMT => 'SCHEMA_DDL', SCHEMA_
NAME => 'SCOTT', OBJECT_NAME => 'EMP');

PL/SQL procedure successfully completed.
```

17. We're ready to start the SQL Apply again as follows:

```
SQL> ALTER DATABASE START LOGICAL STANDBY APPLY IMMEDIATE;
```

What just happened?

Now you know how to disable replication for a table or schema in a logical standby database configuration. You have learned how to use the DBMS_LOGSTDBY.SKIP procedure for this purpose. We also mentioned how to specify a procedure to run before DDL statements with an example of automatically changing the datafile directory structures for the tablespace DDL commands on the logical standby database. Then we saw how to query and disable the skip rules. The DBMS_LOGSTDBY.INSTANTIATE_TABLE procedure is used to re-build the table on the standby and the DBMS_LOGSTDBY.UNSKIP procedure removes the skip rule for the specified table or schema.

Database Guard settings for the logical standby database

In order to control user modification to tables on the logical standby database we will use the Database Guard setting. Database Guard offers the following three options:

- **ALL:** This setting will prevent all database users except SYS from modifying any table in the logical standby database. This is the default mode of a logical standby database.

- **STANDBY:** In standby mode, users may modify the database tables, which are out of the replication scope. The tables maintained by SQL Apply are still not modifiable by users except SYS.

- **NONE:** Users are free to modify any tables that they have necessary privileges for. This is the mode of a primary database.

 Note that we can set the Database Guard to ALL in a primary database to keep it read-only for a while without a shutdown.

Time for action – changing the Database Guard setting

As we mentioned before, the default Database Guard mode for a logical standby database is set to ALL. Let's try to insert data into the HR.REGIONS table, which is out of the replication scope because of the skip rule we created.

1. Connect the logical standby database with SYS user. Check the Database Guard mode and skip rules with the following query:

```
SQL> SELECT GUARD_STATUS FROM V$DATABASE;

GUARD_S
-------
ALL

SQL> SELECT OWNER, NAME,STATEMENT_OPT, PROC  FROM DBA_LOGSTDBY_
SKIP  WHERE STATEMENT_OPT <> 'INTERNAL SCHEMA';

OWNER     NAME          STATEMENT_OPT    PROC
--------  ------------  ---------------  ------------------
                        DIRECTORY
HR        %             DML
                        TABLESPACE       SYS.CHANGE_TS_DDL
```

Database Guard mode is ALL and all HR tables are skipped by SQL Apply.

2. Now connect with the HR user and insert a row to the REGIONS table:

```
SQL> CONN HR/HR
Connected.
SQL> INSERT INTO HR.REGIONS VALUES (10,'TEST');
insert into hr.regions values (10,'test')
                *
ERROR at line 1:
ORA-16224: Database Guard is enabled
```

It's not possible to insert into a table, which is not part of the replication because the database guard mode is ALL.

3. Let's change the mode to STANDBY and try to insert in the table again using the following query:

```
SQL> ALTER DATABASE GUARD STANDBY;

Database altered.
```

```
SQL> CONN HR/HR
Connected.

SQL> INSERT INTO HR.REGIONS VALUES (10,'TEST');

1 row created.
```

We're now able to modify the tables with skip rules.

4. Let's try to modify a table that is not skipped by SQL Apply:

```
SQL> CONN SCOTT/TIGER
Connected.
SQL> INSERT INTO DEPT VALUES (50,'TEST','TEST');
insert into dept values (50,'test','test')
                *
ERROR at line 1:
ORA-16224: Database Guard is enabled
```

What just happened?

We're now ready to change the logical standby database settings in order to let users modify non-replicated standby tables, all standby tables, or make the standby completely protected to user modification.

If only specific users need to modify standby tables, session-based disabling of database guard is more sensible.

Disabling database guard for a session

If specific users on the logical standby need to modify tables and you do not want other users to have this opportunity, users can disable the Database Guard in their current sessions only and you can keep the logical standby on ALL or STANDBY mode. Execute the following statement to disable Database Guard for the current session:

```
SQL> ALTER SESSION DISABLE GUARD;

Session altered.
```

The user must be granted the alter database privilege in order to disable Database Guard in its session.

Have a go hero – testing the NONE Database Guard mode

Now set your Database Guard mode to NONE and try to insert into the table SCOTT.DEPT with the user Scott again. You should be able to modify all tables, which are also being modified with SQL Apply. Also, think about using the Database Guard mode as NONE. How could you control the accuracy of the data for the replicated tables when the users are free to modify them?

Creating objects on the logical standby database

With a proper configuration, users are free to create database objects on the logical standby databases. However, we need to know some characteristics of the standby objects that are not handled by SQL Apply.

Creating and re-creating tables

In order to create a standalone table on the logical standby database, the Database Guard mode must be STANDBY or NONE. One other way is to disable Database Guard for the current session and creating the table, which works even when the Database Guard is ALL.

On the other hand, if we somehow lose a table on the logical standby, which is inside the scope of replication and we want to create it again with the up-to-date data, it's possible to use the built-in DBMS_LOGSTDBY.INSTANTIATE_TABLE procedure.

Creating scheduler jobs

The logical standby database supports the replication of the jobs created with the DBMS_JOB package. These jobs will be created but will not run on the standby database. However, in case of failover or switchover, jobs will automatically start running on the new primary database.

The scheduler jobs created with DBMS_SCHEDULER are not replicated to the logical standby. However, in 11g there is a new attribute called database_role for this package, which makes scheduler jobs possible to be run on logical standby. By default, this attribute equals to the database_role value of the v$database view. You can create a job on the logical standby database and if you don't specify the value for the database_role attribute, the job will be run as long as the database role is logical standby.

Again if you don't specify the value for the database_role attribute, the scheduler jobs created on the primary database will be run on the database as long as the role is primary and will not be replicated to logical standby. If you want to keep the job running after a switchover or failover on the new primary, you must create the same scheduler job on the logical standby with the database_role attribute as Primary.

If you plan to create a scheduler job on the logical standby database with `database_role` `Standby`, you should also create one in the primary database with `database_role` `Standby`. So that, when a switchover is performed, the job will still be running on the new standby.

Creating materialized views

When we create a logical standby database, all materialized views and materialized view logs on the primary database also exist on the logical standby. However, SQL Apply skips DDL statements related to materialized views and logs. So the newly created, altered or dropped materialized views and logs on the primary database will not be handled on the logical standby.

If we need to have any materialized view (existing on the primary or not) on the logical standby we are able to create it. The MVs created on the standby can be refreshed using a fast, complete, or forced refresh. Refreshes may be on-commit, which will be triggered by SQL Apply or on-demand with scheduling or manual execution.

Time for action – creating objects on the logical standby database

Now let's try to create some objects on the logical standby database. First we will create a test table with the HR user. The Database Guard mode is ALL, which is the default.

1. Connect the logical standby database with SYS user and execute the following query:

```
SQL> SELECT GUARD_STATUS FROM V$DATABASE;

GUARD_S
-------
ALL

SQL> CONN SCOTT/TIGER
Connected.
SQL> CREATE TABLE TEST (A NUMBER);
create table test (a number)
*
ERROR at line 1:
ORA-01031: insufficient privileges
```

The error message specifies a privilege problem but this is not due to the lack of `create table` privilege for the `HR` user. We receive this error because the Database Guard mode does not allow for creation of the table. Let's change it and try again.

2. Connect with the `SYS` user using the following query:

```
SQL> ALTER DATABASE GUARD STANDBY;
Database altered.

SQL> CONN SCOTT/TIGER
Connected.

SQL> CREATE TABLE TEST (A NUMBER);
Table created.

SQL> INSERT INTO TEST VALUES (1);
1 row created.

SQL> COMMIT;
Commit complete.
```

We're able to create a table when the Database Guard mode is `STANDBY` or `NONE`. What about an index? There is no doubt that we can create an index for the test table, which is a standalone standby object not maintained by SQL Apply.

3. Let's try to create an index on a table that is being replicated.

```
SQL> CONN SCOTT/TIGER
Connected.
SQL> CREATE INDEX TESTIDX ON DEPT (LOC);
create index testidx on dept (loc)
                       *
ERROR at line 1:
ORA-16224: Database Guard is enabled
```

The Database Guard mode is `STANDBY` and we are not able to create an index on a standby table handled by SQL Apply.

4. We should disable the Database Guard in session and try again. In order to disable Database Guard, the user needs the `Alter Database` privilege as shown in the following query:

```
SQL> GRANT ALTER DATABASE TO SCOTT;
Grant succeeded.

SQL> CONN SCOTT/TIGER
Connected.
```

```
SQL> ALTER SESSION DISABLE GUARD;
Session altered.

SQL> CREATE INDEX TESTIDX ON DEPT (LOC);
Index created.
```

If an index is being created on a table that is handled by SQL Apply, we need to disable Database Guard for that session.

5. Let's try if the same applies to the materialized views. Suppose a materialized view for a query on the EMP and DEPT tables of the user SCOTT was created on the primary database. As MV DDLs are not replicated with SQL Apply and we need the MV on the standby, we need to create it in the physical standby database. Let's create the MV using the following query:

```
SQL> CONN SCOTT/TIGER
Connected.
SQL> CREATE MATERIALIZED VIEW SCOTT.EMPDEPT  REFRESH ON DEMAND
ENABLE QUERY REWRITE AS SELECT E.ENAME, D.DNAME FROM SCOTT.EMP E,
SCOTT.DEPT D WHERE E.DEPTNO=D.DEPTNO;
Materialized view created.
```

We are able to create a materialized view without disabling Database Guard for that session.

6. Now we will create a scheduler job to refresh the MV periodically on the logical standby databse:

```
SQL> GRANT CREATE JOB TO SCOTT;
GRANT SUCCEEDED.

SQL> CONN SCOTT/TIGER
CONNECTED.

SQL> BEGIN
  2    DBMS_SCHEDULER.CREATE_JOB (
  3    JOB_NAME => 'REFRESH_EMPDEPT_MV' ,
  4    JOB_TYPE => 'PLSQL_BLOCK',
  5    JOB_ACTION => 'BEGIN DBMS_MVIEW.REFRESH (LIST =>''SCOTT.
EMPDEPT'', METHOD => ''C''); END; ',
  6    START_DATE => SYSDATE,
  7    REPEAT_INTERVAL => 'FREQ=MONTHLY;BYMONTHDAY=1;BYHOUR=0',
  8    END_DATE => NULL,
  9    ENABLED => TRUE,
 10    END;
 11    /

PL/SQL procedure successfully completed.
```

We didn't specify a value for the DATABASE_ROLE attribute, so it will have the default, which is the current role of the database, STANDBY. This job will run as long as this database role is logical standby.

We assume that MV exists on primary and a scheduler job is also running for the refresh of the MV on the primary database (with the DATABASE_ROLE attribute of PRIMARY). We also created the MV and a job for its refresh on the logical standby now. But what happens if we perform a switchover? Both scheduler jobs on the primary and standby will not run because of their DATABASE_ROLE attribute. So let's create one more scheduler job on standby and primary to be ready for switchover and failover.

7. On the standby database, enter the following set of statements:

```
SQL> CONN SCOTT/TIGER
CONNECTED.

SQL> BEGIN
  2   DBMS_SCHEDULER.CREATE_JOB (
  3   JOB_NAME => 'REFRESH_EMPDEPT_MV_PRIMARY' ,
  4   JOB_TYPE => 'PLSQL_BLOCK',
  5   JOB_ACTION => 'BEGIN DBMS_MVIEW.REFRESH (LIST =>''SCOTT.
EMPDEPT'', METHOD => ''C''); END; ',
  6   START_DATE => SYSDATE,
  7   REPEAT_INTERVAL => 'FREQ=MONTHLY;BYMONTHDAY=1;BYHOUR=0',
  8   END_DATE => NULL,
  9   ENABLED => TRUE);
 10   END;
 11   /

PL/SQL procedure successfully completed.

SQL> BEGIN
DBMS_SCHEDULER.SET_ATTRIBUTE
(NAME => 'REFRESH_EMPDEPT_MV_PRIMARY',
ATTRIBUTE => 'DATABASE_ROLE',
VALUE => 'PRIMARY');
END;
/

PL/SQL procedure successfully completed.
```

8. Now do the same for the primary database. Create a job with the name REFRESH_EMPDEPT_MV_STANDBY and set the DATABASE_ROLE attribute to STANDBY.

What just happened?

The most important feature of the logical standby database is its ability to access the standby and run reports with the flexibility of creating index, temporary tables, and materialized views on it. By creating these objects, you can achieve more performance on the reports. Also some reporting tools that require creating temporary objects can run on logical standby databases. In this section we have studied the methods, limitations, and considerations of creating database objects on the logical standby and tried to implement some of them. This information will help you customize the logical standby for your own needs.

Have a go hero – skip, disable guard, insert, instantiate, and disable skip

In order to revise what we saw in this chapter, execute the following exercise:

You will do some application tests and you'll do so on the logical standby database. The table SCOTT.SALGRADE will be modified in this test and when the test finishes, you want to revert all the changes to the table and configure the replication once again.

1. Disable replication for the table SCOTT.SALGRADE by creating a skip rule with DBMS_LOGSTDBY.SKIP.

2. To simulate the test, insert rows into this table on the logical standby after disabling Database Guard.

3. Reverse changes made to the table by restoring it from primary. Use the DBMS_LOGSTDBY.INSTANTIATE_TABLE procedure.

4. Remove the skip rule with the DBMS_LOGSTDBY.UNSKIP procedure.

5. Insert into the table SCOTT.SALGRADE on primary and check if the insert was replicated to standby.

Automatic deletion of archived logs

The two types of archived redo logfiles on the logical standby database need to be deleted as they become unnecessary depending on our data retention specifications. The archived logs containing redo that were sent from the primary database are called foreign archived logs and the archived log produced by the logical standby itself, containing the changes on the standby database are called local archived logs. Oracle handles this deletion process automatically while offering some customization.

Deletion of the foreign archived logs

It's possible to keep foreign archived logs on the fast recovery area defined by DB_RECOVERY_FILE_DEST or on another directory or ASM disk group outside the fast recovery area. The Archivelog deletion policy differs depending on whether the foreign archived logs are in FRA or not.

Files inside the fast recovery area

If we specified the log archive destination for the standby logfiles as `LOCATION=USE_DB_RECOVERY_FILE_DEST`, the foreign archive logs will be kept in FRA. A foreign archived log in FRA is automatically deleted by the logical standby database if all the redo it contains were applied and then the retention time period specified by `DB_FLASHBACK_RETENTION_TARGET` passes. The default value for this parameter is 1440 minutes, which is one day. This value is also valid if we did not specify any value for this parameter.

Files outside the fast recovery area

By default, even if we keep the foreign archived log outside the FRA, logical standby handles the automatic deletion of these files. The retention time value for the applied foreign archived logs can be defined with the following syntax:

```
SQL> EXECUTE DBMS_LOGSTDBY.APPLY_SET
('LOG_AUTO_DEL_RETENTION_TARGET','4320');
```

The default value for `LOG_AUTO_DEL_RETENTION_TARGET` is the `DB_FLASHBACK_RETENTION_TARGET` initialization parameter value in the logical standby database.

If we don't want the logical standby database to automatically delete the foreign archived logs, we can use the following procedure:

```
SQL> EXECUTE DBMS_LOGSTDBY.APPLY_SET('LOG_AUTO_DELETE', 'FALSE');
```

When we disable automatic deletion of foreign archived logs, the `DBA_LOGMNR_PURGED_LOG` view will help us identify the logs, which are ready to be deleted depending on the retention policy. In order to refresh this view use the following statement:

```
SQL> EXECUTE DBMS_LOGSTDBY.PURGE_SESSION;

PL/SQL procedure successfully completed.

SQL> SELECT * FROM DBA_LOGMNR_PURGED_LOG;

FILE_NAME
--------------------------------------------------
/u01/app/oracle2/archive_std/1_455_791552282.arc
/u01/app/oracle2/archive_std/1_456_791552282.arc
/u01/app/oracle2/archive_std/1_457_791552282.arc
/u01/app/oracle2/archive_std/1_458_791552282.arc
/u01/app/oracle2/archive_std/1_459_791552282.arc

5 rows selected.
```

We can now manually delete these files from the filesystem.

Deletion of the local archived logs

Local archived logs that were generated from online redo logs of the standby database are created in the same way within the primary databases. Unlike foreign archived logs, logical standby databases do not delete these archived logs automatically unless they're kept in the fast recovery area.

You can use RMAN to handle the deletion of the local archived logs. If a backup strategy is used to backup the logical standby database, we should consider the deletion of the local archived logs in this strategy as we do on the primary databases.

Summary

In this chapter we have created a logical standby database using an existing physical standby database and verified redo transport and SQL Apply services. Then we practiced several customizations on the logical standby database.

Installing a robust Data Guard logical standby configuration and customizing the environment to achieve the best performance and effectiveness are the main role of the Database Administrator. The logical standby database offers many more customization possibilities when compared with the physical standby database. This fact makes its success more dependent on the configuration and customization.

The following chapter will show you how the Data Guard broker is configured and used to monitor and manage the Data Guard environment.

4
Oracle Data Guard Broker

This chapter covers the implementation and management of the Data Guard administration framework Data Guard broker.

The following topics will be discussed in this chapter:

◆ Implementing the Data Guard broker

◆ Monitoring and managing using Data Guard broker

◆ Troubleshooting the Data Guard broker

◆ Configuring a fast-start failover

Introduction to Data Guard broker

The Data Guard broker is a utility provided with the Oracle database server of the Enterprise edition. It includes the functionality to manage standby databases. It is also an integral part of Data Guard and of Oracle's Database Enterprise Manager. Broker interfaces are instinctive and easy, allowing for centralized control of the Data Guard configuration that makes the Data Guard an enhanced high availability and disaster protection solution. The Data Guard broker makes it easy to maintain and administer several standby databases. It maintains its own configuration files and runs a background process **Data Guard Monitor Process** (**DMON**) on both primary and standby database servers.

The Oracle Data Guard broker was introduced in the 9*i* Release 2, but the Oracle Database 11*g* version introduced several enhancements to the Data Guard broker feature so that a DBA could easily manage a complex and multidatabase disaster recovery environment.

The Data Guard broker consolidates the setup, upkeep, and monitoring of Data Guard configurations. The Data Guard broker when used with the Enterprise Manager becomes a powerful tool, offering configuration, monitoring, alerts, performance analysis, easy switchovers, and automatic failovers.

The Data Guard Monitor (DMON) process and configuration file resides on the server side. However the Oracle Data Guard broker can be managed by DGMGRL or OEM from the client side as well. The Data Guard broker can be configured on existing or new standby databases and on either physical or logical standby databases.

The Data Guard broker is an additional utility of the standby database that makes the maintenance and administration of several standby databases at once much easier. The Data Guard broker uses its own background process (DMON) on each primary and standby database and its own configuration file for interaction. The DMON process is started if you set the initialization parameter DG_BROKER_START to TRUE. This parameter is a dynamic parameter, and you can set it to TRUE or FALSE without any database bounce. To create and maintain the configuration files, you need to create a Data Guard configuration using either the Data Guard wizard from Cloud Control or you need to create it manually via the command-line DGMGRL.

The Data Guard broker framework facilitates the configuration and setup of Data Guard, monitors the redo log transport, and monitors the log apply services. It also helps in Data Guard operating tasks, such as switchovers, failovers, fast-start failovers, and reinstating the primary database. This can be better illustrated with the following diagram:

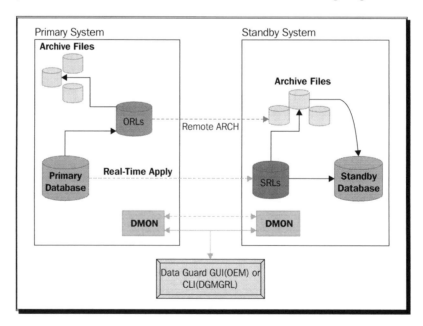

Data Guard broker features and benefits

The Data Guard broker can be configured on existing or new Data Guard configurations either with physical or with logical standby databases with a global configuration.

Centralized and simple management

The Data Guard broker provides a graphical user interface and command-line interface for the simple management and automation of management and operational tasks across multiple databases in a Data Guard configuration. The broker monitors all of the systems within a single Data Guard configuration. You can perform all management operations locally or remotely through the broker's easy-to-use interfaces, such as the Data Guard management pages in Oracle Enterprise Manager Cloud Control, that is, the broker's graphical user interface and the Data Guard command-line interface called DGMGRL.

Cloud Control integration

Integration with Enterprise Manager Cloud Control simplifies the management of standby databases by using graphical consoles. All operations are controlled through navigation when managed with Cloud Control. Role transitions (switchovers and failovers) can be performed, and redo transport and log apply services can be monitored using graphical consoles. In the case of any warning or error occurring in the Data Guard configuration, alerts can be received via e-mails. Enterprise Manager can perform Oracle Net Services configurations as they are required to support redo transport and log apply services.

To enable all the features required by Data Guard with Cloud Control, the following compatibility of Enterprise Manager with broker requirements should be met:

Database Version	Enterprise Manager Cloud / Grid Control
10.2.0.X	10.2.0.1 and above
11.1.0.X	10.2.0.5
11.2.0.X	10.2.0.5 with patches

Oracle Data Guard and RAC

Oracle Data Guard and RAC are the two products that combine in such a way that they enhance or emphasize each other's qualities. RAC refers to node or instance failures; it provides automatic instance recovery from failures, such as node failures, instance crashes, or service lost failures, that do not affect data. It also provides scalability along with high availability. On the other hand, Data Guard provides data protection through the use of transactional images in primary and standby databases. Data Guard enables recovery from site disasters or data corruptions.

In RAC, all the instances of nodes share the same data, including control files and datafiles, but the Data Guard data/control/redo logfiles are exclusive to primary and standby databases.

Use of Data Guard broker with RAC databases is supported by Oracle 10*g*.

Role transition with Data Guard broker

Performing role transitions with the broker helps avoid the need to perform tiresome tasks. To perform a switchover between a primary and standby database using SQL*Plus, you have to execute the commands step-by-step and check the synchronization and switchover status from both sites, the switchover status of both the sites, and the step-by-step commands from the primary and standby locations. The broker simplifies the performance of switchover and failover operations by gathering many tasks under a single command.

Data Guard fast-start failover

Fast-start failover was introduced to reduce unplanned downtime. Automatic database failover may occur because a primary database is down, due to designated health-check conditions, or due to the request of an application. **FSFO (fast-start failover)** is a feature of the broker that records information about the failover target, informs how long to wait after a failure before triggering another failover, and also records other FSFO-specific properties. When a fast-start failover is enabled, the Data Guard broker automatically fails over to a synchronized standby site in the event of a disaster at the primary site; it requires no intervention by the DBA. In addition to this, applications are automatically notified of the role transition. The disadvantage is that even though both the primary and standby databases' state is good, if there is any connectivity issue between the primary server and the observer server, failover will be initiated.

 Data Guard FSFO is being supported with the Maximum Availability mode from Version 10.2 and with the Maximum Performance mode from Version 11.1.

Recommendation

To sum up, the Data Guard broker can restart failed processes, manage CRS, automate switchovers/failovers, integrate with OEM so you can use GUI for management, and collect additional metrics for monitoring. On the other hand, one advantage of using SQL*Plus is that it requires you to have a full understanding of what's going on behind the scenes. We would recommend setting up a Data Guard configuration manually at least once, for the purpose of your own learning. You will have a better scope to learn. The broker has the advantage of providing shortcuts to the functions you might need to perform with your Data Guard configuration. If you use SQL*Plus to manage Data Guard, you'll likely develop scripts that are already duplicating some broker functionality.

For example, the first time that you create a standby and the first time you run a switchover, it would be good to do it with SQL*Plus and tail the alert log so that you can understand the parameters and see how it works. After you have successfully done a few switchovers manually, move to the Data Guard broker, and you will appreciate how much easier it is, how many errors it fixes, as well as understanding exactly what it is doing.

Data Guard broker components

We can divide the Data Guard broker components into two—client-side and server-side interfaces—as shown in the following diagram:

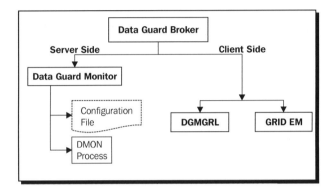

Oracle Data Guard broker server-side components

The components of the Data Guard broker are the Data Guard Monitor process and the configuration file, as shown in the following diagram:

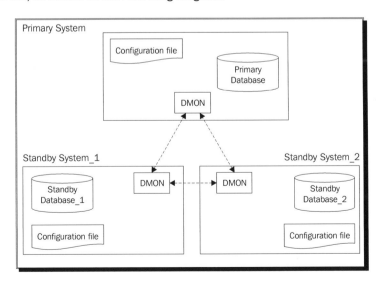

Data Guard Monitor process (DMON)

The DMON is installed as part of the Oracle database software and manifests as a background component when enabled. The DMON process on the primary database is the owner of the configuration. DMON controls all the databases by using configuration files. It maintains profiles of all the database objects in the configuration in the form of a binary configuration file. The configuration is maintained by the DMON process in all the standby databases of either a physical or a logical configuration. This two-way communication channel is used to pass requests between databases, to monitor the health of all the databases in the broker configuration using Oracle Net Services. DMON runs for every database instance that is managed by the broker. Whenever a broker command is issued, the following steps will occur:

1. The request will be processed on the primary database.

2. The DMON process coordinates with all the standby databases of the Data Guard configuration.

3. It then updates the changes, properties, and configuration in its configuration file.

4. The DMON process contacts and updates the configuration file of each database in the setup.

The following diagram illustrates the DMON process:

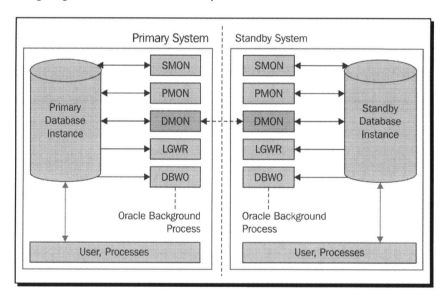

Configuration file

The configuration file is a server-side component. Database profiles are stored in a configuration file that holds all the settings needed by Data Guard. This file holds the configuration information of all the databases that are part of the configuration, and the state of each database in the configuration. The broker configuration files in Oracle 11gR2 can now reside on disks having any sector size (physical block size) up to 4KB. The component coordinate database state transitions and updates database properties dynamically with the broker. The broker propagates the changes to all the databases and their server parameter files in the configuration. Oracle uses two configuration files to store the last-known good configuration settings during the modification of the configuration properties or state by the DMON process.

Oracle Data Guard broker client-side components

The Data Guard broker client-side components are the broker command-line interface (DGMGRL) and the Enterprise Manager Cloud Control client. Both utilities are used to manage Data Guard configurations consisting of primary and standby databases.

DGMGRL utility

Using DGMGRL, you can change property values directly by using the command-line utility. It includes commands to create an observer process that monitors the whole configuration, including the primary and standby, to evaluate if a failover is necessary, and to initiate FSFO. It's also possible to add new standby databases to the configuration. Instead of managing primary and standby databases with various SQL*Plus statements, the broker provides a single, unified interface.

The Data Guard broker's parameter values must be changed by using broker interfaces. If the broker is active and you perform any parameter changes or role transitions by using SQL*Plus, it can create inconsistency in the configuration.

> From the command utility DGMGRL, you can obtain a list of all of the commands supported with the `help` command as follows:
>
> `DGMGRL> help`

Enterprise Manager Cloud Control client

As we have discussed, in the Cloud Control integration, it's the graphical interface that we can use to manage Data Guard configurations. It's possible to perform all of the operations supported by DGMGRL by using the Enterprise Manager Cloud Control interface.

Implementation of Oracle Data Guard broker

We will cover the initial setup and connection methods of the Data Guard broker and basic monitoring using the broker in this section.

Time for action – initial setup of Data Guard broker

We will now see the initial setup of the Data Guard broker in an existing Data Guard configuration.

1. Ensure that both the primary and standby databases are up and running as shown in the following query:

```
SQL> select db_unique_name,open_mode,database_role from
v$database;
DB_UNIQUE_NA OPEN_MODE            DATABASE_ROLE
------------ -------------------- -----------------
turkey_un    READ WRITE           PRIMARY

SQL>  select db_unique_name,open_mode,database_role from
v$database;
DB_UNIQUE_NA OPEN_MODE            DATABASE_ROLE
------------ -------------------- -----------------
india_un     READ ONLY WITH APPLY PHYSICAL STANDBY
```

2. Ensure that both the primary and standby databases are using server parameter files, so that the broker can form a healthy relationship between the broker properties and parameter values as follows:

```
SQL> show parameter spfile
NAME         TYPE        VALUE
----------- ----------- ------------------------------
spfile       string      /u01/home/oracle/product/11.2.0/
                         db_1/dbs/spfileTURKEY.ora
```

3. This step is optional. Set the configuration file location parameters on both the primary and standby databases. The default location of the broker configuration file in Windows is $ORACLE_HOME/dbs in Unix and %ORACLE_HOME%\database. If you want to keep them in a non-default location, change the parameters as shown. If you don't set these parameters, the files will automatically be created under the default locations in the following steps. The following commands are used to change the parameters:

```
ALTER SYSTEM SET dg_broker_config_file1 = '\u01\app\oracle\broker_
turkey01.dat' scope=both sid='*';

ALTER SYSTEM SET dg_broker_config_file2 = '\u01\app\oracle\broker_
turkey02.dat ' scope=both sid='*';
```

Or in an ASM filesystem, use the following command:

```
ALTER SYSTEM SET dg_broker_config_file1 = '+DATA_AREA/turkey/
broker_turkey01.dat' scope=both sid='*';

ALTER SYSTEM SET dg_broker_config_file2 = '+DATA_AREA/turkey/
broker_turkey02.dat' scope=both sid='*';
```

> In RAC databases, set the broker configuration file location to
> a shared location and use the same value on all the instances.

4. Start the DMON process on both the primary and standby databases by setting the
DG_BROKER_START parameter as follows:

```
SQL> alter system set dg_broker_start=TRUE scope=both;
System altered.
```

5. For UNIX systems, you can now check the existence of the DMON process using
the ps command as follows:

```
$ps -ef|grep dmon
oracle    27335     1  0 02:39 ?         00:00:00 ora_dmon_TURKEY
```

6. In the alert logfile, you will see the following:

```
Thu Aug 30 02:39:11 2012
DMON started with pid=35, OS id=27335
Thu Aug 30 02:39:11 2012
ALTER SYSTEM SET dg_broker_start=TRUE SCOPE=BOTH;
Starting Data Guard Broker (DMON)
```

7. If you monitor the DMON logfile, you'll see the error ORA-27037/ORA-16572 as
shown in the following command line. This is expected behavior. These errors will
be freed after creating the configuration using the broker utility DGMGRL:

```
2012-08-30 02:39:14.332   DMON: cannot open configuration file
"/u01/home/oracle/product/11.2.0/db_1/dbs/dr1turkey_un.dat",
retrying
2012-08-30 02:39:15.341   DMON: cannot open configuration file "/
u01/home/oracle/product/11.2.0/db_1/dbs/dr1turkey_un.dat"
2012-08-30 02:39:15.341   ORA-27037: unable to obtain file status
2012-08-30 02:39:15.341   inux-x86_64 Error: 2: No such file or
directory
2012-08-30 02:39:15.342   Additional information: 3
2012-08-30 02:39:15.342   DMON: Error opening "/u01/home/oracle/
product/11.2.0/db_1/dbs/dr1turkey_un.dat", error = ORA-16572
```

8. The configuration files will be created under the specified location or in the default directory automatically. The Data Guard broker will maintain two copies of its configuration files as follows:

```
SQL> show parameter DG_BROKER_CONFIG_FILE
NAME                    TYPE    VALUE
--------------------- ------- ----------------------------
dg_broker_config_file1  string  /u01/home/oracle/product/11.2.0/
                                db_1/dbs/dr1turkey_un.dat
dg_broker_config_file2  string  /u01/home/oracle/product/11.2.0/
                                db_1/dbs/dr2turkey_un.dat
```

9. Connect DGMGRL on the primary system and create the configuration as follows:

```
[oracle@oracle-primary ~]$ dgmgrl
DGMGRL for Linux: Version 11.2.0.1.0 - 64bit Production
Copyright (c) 2000, 2009, Oracle. All rights reserved.
Welcome to DGMGRL, type "help" for information.
DGMGRL> connect sys/free2go
Connected.
```

10. You will need to specify a configuration name and the unique name of the primary database. The configuration name can be anything, but the name of the primary database must be DB_UNIQUE_NAME as shown in the following query:

```
SQL> show parameter db_unique_name
NAME              TYPE        VALUE
---------------- ----------- ----------------------------
db_unique_name    string      turkey_un

DGMGRL> CREATE CONFIGURATION 'PACKT' AS PRIMARY DATABASE IS
'turkey_un' CONNECT IDENTIFIER IS TURKEY;
Configuration "PACKT" created with primary database "turkey_un"
```

In the previous command, TURKEY_UN refers to DB_UNIQUE_NAME and TURKEY refers to Oracle Net Services name. The primary database will be added to the configuration and the metadata will be updated in the broker configuration file.

11. Add a standby database to the Data Guard broker configuration as follows:

```
SQL> show parameter db_unique_name
NAME              TYPE        VALUE
---------------- ----------- ----------------------------
db_unique_name    string      india_un

DGMGRL> ADD DATABASE 'INDIA_UN' AS CONNECT IDENTIFIER IS 'INDIA';
Database "INDIA_UN" added
```

12. Enable the Data Guard broker configuration. After adding the standby database to the broker, the configuration will be disabled by default, as follows:

```
DGMGRL> show configuration;
Configuration - PACKT
  Protection Mode: MaxPerformance
  Databases:
    turkey_un - Primary database
    INDIA_UN  - Physical standby database
Fast-Start Failover: DISABLED
Configuration Status:
DISABLED

DGMGRL> enable configuration;
Enabled.

DGMGRL> show configuration;
Configuration - PACKT
  Protection Mode: MaxPerformance
  Databases:
    turkey_un - Primary database
    INDIA_UN  - Physical standby database
Fast-Start Failover: DISABLED
Configuration Status:
SUCCESS
```

What just happened?

We have seen the configuration of the Data Guard broker and how to add existing databases to the broker configuration.

Time for action – connecting to Data Guard broker

You can connect the DGMGRL interface locally by specifying only the username with the password, or just using / if OS authentication is possible. If you are connecting from a remote machine, you must use Oracle Net Services name to connect the Data Guard broker. Use the following steps to see some examples of broker connections:

1. To connect from either a primary or a standby database server with OS authentication enabled, you can connect using / as follows:

```
[oracle@oracle-primary ~]$ dgmgrl /
DGMGRL for Linux: Version 11.2.0.1.0 - 64bit Production
```

```
Copyright (c) 2000, 2009, Oracle. All rights reserved.
Welcome to DGMGRL, type "help" for information.
Connected.
DGMGRL>
```

2. In order to connect to the broker CLI database, authentication is required. Add the following line to the `sqlnet.ora` file to gain authentication:

```
[oracle@oracle-primary admin]$ cat sqlnet.ora|grep SQLNET
SQLNET.AUTHENTICATION_SERVICES = (NONE)
```

3. Connecting with OS authentication will not be possible as shown in the following command line:

```
[oracle@oracle-primary]$ dgmgrl /
DGMGRL for Linux: Version 11.2.0.1.0 - 64bit Production
Copyright (c) 2000, 2009, Oracle. All rights reserved.
Welcome to DGMGRL, type "help" for information.
ORA-01031: insufficient privileges
```

4. Connect using database user `SYS` login credentials as follows:

```
[oracle@oracle-primary]$ dgmgrl sys/free2go
DGMGRL for Linux: Version 11.2.0.1.0 - 64bit Production
Copyright (c) 2000, 2009, Oracle. All rights reserved.
Welcome to DGMGRL, type "help" for information.
Connected.
```

5. Try connecting it from the primary to the standby database, and vice versa, using the Oracle Net Services name as follows:

```
[oracle@oracle-stby ~]$ dgmgrl sys/free2go@turkey
DGMGRL for Linux: Version 11.2.0.1.0 - 64bit Production
Copyright (c) 2000, 2009, Oracle. All rights reserved.
Welcome to DGMGRL, type "help" for information.
Connected.
```

6. You can also include DGMGRL commands in the connection string. The following command will connect to the broker and show us the output of the `show database 'turkey_un'` statement:

```
[oracle@oracle-primary ~]$ dgmgrl sys/free2go "show database
'turkey_un'"
DGMGRL for Linux: Version 11.2.0.1.0 - 64bit Production
Copyright (c) 2000, 2009, Oracle. All rights reserved.
Welcome to DGMGRL, type "help" for information.
```

```
Connected.
Database - turkey_un
  Role:             PRIMARY
  Intended State:   TRANSPORT-ON
  Instance(s):
    TURKEY
Database Status:
SUCCESS
```

7. When the `SILENT` keyword is used, it will suppress the introduction lines of DGMGR as follows:

```
[oracle@oracle-primary]$ dgmgrl -silent sys/free2go@turkey  "show
configuration verbose"
Configuration - PACKT
  Protection Mode: MaxPerformance
  Databases:
    turkey_un - Primary database
    INDIA_UN  - Physical standby database
Fast-Start Failover: DISABLED
Configuration Status:
SUCCESS
```

8. Exit the broker command-line interface with the `EXIT` command as follows:

```
DGMGRL> exit
[oracle@oracle-primary ~]$
```

What just happened?

We have seen how to connect to the command line utility DGMGRL using different approaches, after the configuration of the Data Guard broker.

Time for action – basic monitoring with Data Guard broker

Now we'll see how to perform basic Data Guard monitoring using the broker interface DGMGRL.

1. Check the configuration status with the following command. It provides the overall health status of the Data Guard configuration. If the `Configuration Status` resulted to `SUCCESS`, it means that the Data Guard configuration is working properly. Output can also be `WARNING` or `ERROR` as follows:

```
DGMGRL> show configuration;
Configuration - PACKT
```

```
        Protection Mode: MaxPerformance
      Databases:
         turkey_un - Primary database
             Error: ORA-16778: redo transport error for one or more
      databases
          INDIA_UN  - Physical standby database
             Error: ORA-01031: insufficient privileges
      Fast-Start Failover: DISABLED
      Configuration Status:
      ERROR
```

2. Check the database status to find out if there are any warnings or errors in the databases of the Data Guard configuration. Use the following command from the DGMGRL utility:

```
DGMGRL> show database turkey_un;

Database - turkey_un

   Role:           PRIMARY
   Intended State:  TRANSPORT-ON
   Instance(s):
     TURKEY
        Error: ORA-16737: the redo transport service for standby
   database "INDIA_UN" has an error
Database Status:

ERROR
```

3. Check the redo transport status. `LogXptStatus` is the database property that returns an output containing the status of the redo transport services to each of the enabled standby databases. This property is applicable to the primary database as shown in the following command line:

```
DGMGRL> show database turkey_un 'LogXptStatus';

LOG TRANSPORT STATUS

PRIMARY_INSTANCE_NAME STANDBY_DATABASE_NAME                STATUS

TURKEY                INDIA_UN ORA-01031: insufficient privileges
```

4. Check `Status Report`. This is the database property that returns a list of errors or warnings about the status of the database. In RAC databases, it includes the status of all the running instances as follows:

```
DGMGRL> show database turkey_un 'StatusReport';

STATUS REPORT

INSTANCE_NAME    SEVERITY ERROR_TEXT
```

```
TURKEY       ERROR ORA-16737: the redo transport service
for standby database "INDIA_UN" has an error
```

5. Check `Inconsistent Properties`. This will return an output that shows all the database properties whose values are contained in the broker configuration file and are inconsistent with the values in the database. In RAC databases, a database-specific property may be inconsistent only on some instances as shown in the following line:

```
DGMGRL>  show database turkey_un InconsistentProperties;

INCONSISTENT PROPERTIES

INSTANCE_NAME PROPERTY_NAME   MEMORY_VALUE SPFILE_VALUE BROKER_
VALUE

TURKEY        LogArchiveTrace 255          00
```

6. Check the `TopWaitEvents` property that specifies the top five events that waited for the most amount of time in the specified instance as follows:

```
DGMGRL> show instance 'TURKEY' 'TopWaitEvents';

TOP SYSTEM WAIT EVENTS

Event            Wait Time
rdbms ipc message          162825637
DIAG idle wait            15930581
SQL*Net message from client   15074233
jobq slave wait            12516954
Streams AQ: qmn slave idle wait  7973917
```

7. Gather the same information using SQL*Plus as from the `v$system_event` view follows:

```
SQL> select event,TIME_WAITED from v$system_event order by time_
waited desc;
EVENT                                        TIME_WAITED
----------------------------------------- -----------
rdbms ipc message                             162816106
DIAG idle wait                                 15929381
SQL*Net message from client                    15069275
jobq slave wait                                12516954
Streams AQ: qmn slave idle wait                 7973917
```

8. Check the `SendQEntries` database property. The following output shows all the logfiles of the primary database that were not successfully archived to standby databases as shown in the following command line:

```
DGMGRL> show database turkey_un 'SendQEntries';

PRIMARY_SEND_QUEUE

          STANDBY_NAME      STATUS      RESETLOGS_ID
THREAD               LOG_SEQ        TIME_GENERATED        TIME_
COMPLETED    FIRST_CHANGE#     NEXT_CHANGE#        SIZE (KBs)

          INDIA_UN     ARCHIVED          788992101
1                227  09/01/2012 01:48:13  09/01/2012 01:48:14
2107092        2107097                   1

          INDIA_UN     ARCHIVED          788992101
1                228  09/01/2012 01:48:14  09/01/2012 01:48:16
2107097        2107101                   2

          INDIA_UN     ARCHIVED          788992101
1                229  09/01/2012 01:48:16  09/01/2012 01:48:17
2107101        2107104                   1

                       CURRENT          788992101
1                230  09/01/2012 01:48:17
2107104                                  1
```

9. Check the `RecvQEntries` database property that reports on all the logfiles that were received by the standby database but not yet applied. If there are no rows, it means that all the logfiles have been applied as follows:

```
DGMGRL> show database 'INDIA_UN'  'RecvQEntries';

STANDBY_RECEIVE_QUEUE

          STATUS      RESETLOGS_ID            THREAD
LOG_SEQ        TIME_GENERATED        TIME_COMPLETED    FIRST_CHANGE#
NEXT_CHANGE#       SIZE (KBs)

          NOT_APPLIED          788992101            1
238  09/01/2012 01:55:31  09/01/2012 01:56:04          2107788
2107823              20

          NOT_APPLIED          788992101            1
239  09/01/2012 01:56:04  09/01/2012 01:56:05          2107823
2107826               1

          NOT_APPLIED          788992101            1
240  09/01/2012 01:56:05  09/01/2012 01:56:07          2107826
2107831               2

          NOT_APPLIED          788992101            1
241  09/01/2012 01:56:07  09/01/2012 01:56:07          2107831
2107834               1
```

To get the status of the database or configuration with the previous commands, you can connect DGMGRL from the primary or standby database servers or even from the observer system if it exists.

What just happened?

We have seen how to connect to the Data Guard broker configuration and check the configuration status, database status, status of the instance with properties, and property values using the DGMGRL command-line utility.

Management with Data Guard broker

When the Data Guard configuration is managed with the Data Guard broker, you must use DGMGRL or the Cloud Control interface to make changes. In this topic, we will discuss management scenarios with the Data Guard broker.

Enabling and disabling broker configuration

As we have seen, after the successful creation of the Data Guard broker configuration, the configuration will be in `disabled` status, and we have to enable it in order to monitor all the databases of the configuration. We must enable the configuration only from the primary database. After the configuration has been enabled from primary, it will communicate this information to standby and the Data Guard broker instance Slave Process (NSV0). We can also disable it later if we don't want the broker to manage the Data Guard configuration.

Time for action – disabling broker configuration

Broker management of the primary database and all of its standby databases can be disabled using the DISABLE CONFIGURATION command. After disabling the configuration, it won't be possible to fetch any information from the Data Guard broker by using DGMGRL.

1. Before disabling the configuration, let's check the status of the broker configuration, as follows:

```
DGMGRL> show configuration;
Configuration - PACKT
   Protection Mode: MaxPerformance
   Databases:
     turkey_un - Primary database
     INDIA_UN  - Physical standby database
```

```
Fast-Start Failover: DISABLED

Configuration Status:

SUCCESS
```

The current status of the configuration is SUCCESS.

2. Disable the configuration as follows:

```
DGMGRL> disable configuration;

Disabled.
```

3. Check the current configuration status as follows:

```
DGMGRL> show configuration;

Configuration - PACKT

  Protection Mode: MaxPerformance

  Databases:

    turkey_un - Primary database

    INDIA_UN  - Physical standby database

Fast-Start Failover: DISABLED

Configuration Status:

DISABLED
```

You can disable the configuration either from the primary or the standby database. On disabling the broker, databases will not be monitored by the broker. This command won't remove the broker configuration from the configuration file. You're still able to perform changes on the database properties. However, the changes will only be applicable once you enable the configuration again.

What just happened?

We've already seen how to enable configuration of the broker from the initial setup of the Data Guard broker implementation; now we have learned how to disable the Data Guard broker configuration.

Enabling and disabling a standby database

Using DGMGRL, it's possible to disable or enable the standby databases of a Data Guard configuration in order to stop broker management for that database.

Time for action – disabling and enabling database

Follow these steps to test disabling and enabling the standby database:

1. Check the status of the standby database as follows:

    ```
    DGMGRL> show database 'INDIA_UN';

    Database - INDIA_UN

      Role:              PHYSICAL STANDBY
      Intended State:    APPLY-ON
      Transport Lag:     0 seconds
      Apply Lag:         0 seconds
      Real Time Query:   ON
      Instance(s):
        INDIA

    Database Status:
    SUCCESS
    ```

2. Disable the database from the configuration as follows:

    ```
    DGMGRL> disable database 'INDIA_UN';
    Disabled.
    ```

3. Check the database status after disabling it from the configuration as follows:

    ```
    DGMGRL> show database 'INDIA_UN';

    Database - INDIA_UN

      Role:              PHYSICAL STANDBY
      Intended State:    APPLY-ON
      Transport Lag:     (unknown)
      Apply Lag:         (unknown)
      Real Time Query:   OFF
      Instance(s):
        INDIA

    Database Status:
    DISABLED
    ```

4. Physical standby information still exists in the configuration, but the database will be in a `DISABLED` state and won't be monitored by the broker. However, the configuration status will be `SUCCESS`.

5. Now enable the database to the broker configuration as follows:

```
DGMGRL> enable database 'INDIA_UN';
Enabled.
```

6. After enabling the database, the Data Guard broker instance slave process will be started at the standby database name mentioned in the command. Implicitly, a log switch will occur in order to synchronize the environments.

7. Check the final database status as follows:

```
DGMGRL> show database 'INDIA_UN';

Database - INDIA_UN

  Role:            PHYSICAL STANDBY
  Intended State: APPLY-ON
  Transport Lag:  0 seconds
  Apply Lag:      0 seconds
  Real Time Query: ON
  Instance(s):
    INDIA
Database Status:
SUCCESS
```

Now the database is enabled and is part of the broker configuration again.

What just happened?

We've learned how to disable and enable Data Guard broker management completely, and how to disable and enable only a standby database of the configuration.

Changing configuration and database properties using broker

After the creation of the Data Guard configuration using DGMGRL, you can edit the configuration or single database properties. The following command is an example of a configuration change that changes the fast-start failover threshold value to 60 seconds. This command can be run either from the primary or the standby database:

```
DGMGRL> show configuration 'FastStartFailoverThreshold';
  FastStartFailoverThreshold = '30'
DGMGRL> edit configuration set property FastStartFailoverThreshold=60;
Property "faststartfailoverthreshold" updated
DGMGRL> show configuration 'FastStartFailoverThreshold';
  FastStartFailoverThreshold = '60'
```

These changes will be updated in all the configuration files.

On the other hand, database property changes are specific to either the primary or a standby database. It won't perform changes in the rest of the configuration. In case it's a clustered database, these changes will be applicable for all of the instances of that database. An example to change the archive log tracing level to `10` in the standby database only is as follows:

```
DGMGRL> show database 'INDIA_UN' 'LogArchiveTrace';

  LogArchiveTrace = '0'

DGMGRL>  edit database 'INDIA_UN' SET PROPERTY LogArchiveTrace=10;

Property "logarchivetrace" updated

DGMGRL> show database 'INDIA_UN' 'LogArchiveTrace';

  LogArchiveTrace = '10'
```

Have a go hero – more examples on property changes

Now it's your turn to try changing some database properties. You can practice with the following parameters by monitoring, changing, and restoring their values as follows:

```
DGMGRL> EDIT DATABASE 'INDIA_UN' SET PROPERTY 'LogArchiveFormat'=
'log_%t_%s_%r_%d.arc';
DGMGRL> EDIT DATABASE 'INDIA_UN' SET PROPERTY LogXptMode=SYNC;

DGMGRL> EDIT DATABASE 'INDIA_UN' SET PROPERTY LogShipping=OFF;

DGMGRL> EDIT DATABASE 'INDIA_UN' SET PROPERTY NetTimeout=30;

DGMGRL> EDIT DATABASE 'INDIA_UN' SET PROPERTY 'ReopenSecs'=400;

DGMGRL> EDIT DATABASE 'INDIA_UN' SET PROPERTY ArchiveLagTarget=800;

DGMGRL> EDIT DATABASE 'INDIA_UN' SET PROPERTY 'DbFileNameConvert' =
'/u01/app/oracle/oradata/orcl/, /u02/app/oracle/oradata/orcl/';

DGMGRL> EDIT DATABASE 'INDIA_UN' SET PROPERTY DelayMins='540';
```

Time for action – changing the database name

Follow these steps to change DB_UNIQUE_NAME of a database in the Data Guard broker configuration.

1. Prior to changing the database name, disable the database from the configuration as follows:

```
DGMGRL> show database 'INDIA_UN';

Database - INDIA_UN

  Role:           PHYSICAL STANDBY
```

```
      Intended State:   APPLY-ON
      Transport Lag:    0 seconds
      Apply Lag:        0 seconds
      Real Time Query:  ON
      Instance(s):
         INDIA
   Database Status:
   SUCCESS
   DGMGRL> disable database 'INDIA_UN';
   Disabled.
```

2. Change the DB_UNIQUE_NAME value of the standby database as follows:

```
SQL> select db_unique_name,database_role from v$database;
DB_UNIQUE_NAM DATABASE_ROLE
------------- ----------------
india_un       PHYSICAL STANDBY
SQL> alter system set db_unique_name='INDIA_NEW' scope=spfile;
System altered.
```

DB_UNIQUE_NAME is a static parameter, so you must use scope with SPFILE. If you are using PFILE, edit PFILE and bounce the database.

3. Now shut down and start up the database and check for the new value of DB_UNIQUE_NAME as shown in the following query:

```
SQL> select db_unique_name,database_role from v$database;
DB_UNIQUE_NAM DATABASE_ROLE
------------- ----------------
INDIA_NEW      PHYSICAL STANDBY
```

4. Rename the database name in the Data Guard broker as follows:

```
DGMGRL> edit database 'INDIA_UN' rename to 'INDIA_NEW';
Succeeded.
```

5. Enable the database as follows:

```
DGMGRL> enable database 'INDIA_NEW';
Enabled.
DGMGRL> show configuration;
Configuration - PACKT
   Protection Mode: MaxPerformance
   Databases:
```

```
     TURKEY_UN - Primary database
     INDIA_NEW - Physical standby database
Fast-Start Failover: DISABLED
Configuration Status:
SUCCESS
```

 After making changes in the database name, perform a couple of log switches and check for synchronization between both sites and also check the configuration status.

What just happened?

We've changed the database unique name of the standby database that is managed with the Data Guard broker.

Changing the state of the database

In order to perform state changes in databases, you must use Data Guard broker interfaces when these are managed with the databases.

For example, use the following command in order to turn off redo transport to all remote destinations on the primary database:

```
DGMGRL> edit database 'TURKEY_UN' SET STATE="LOG-TRANSPORT-OFF";
Succeeded.
```

To stop and start redo transport services to specific standby databases, use the following command:

```
DGMGRL> edit database 'INDIA_UN' SET PROPERTY 'LogShipping'='OFF';
Property "LogShipping" updated
DGMGRL> SHOW DATABASE 'INDIA_UN' 'LogShipping';
  LogShipping = 'OFF'
DGMGRL> edit database 'INDIA_UN' SET PROPERTY 'LogShipping'='ON';
Property "LogShipping" updated
DGMGRL>  SHOW DATABASE 'INDIA_UN' 'LogShipping';
  LogShipping = 'ON'
```

Have a go hero – more examples on state changes

Now try changing the states of the standby database using the following parameters. Also monitor the broker logfile and alert logfile whenever changing the configuration to track the operations behind as shown in the following commands:

```
DGMGRL> EDIT DATABASE 'INDIA_UN' SET STATE='READ-ONLY';

DGMGRL> EDIT DATABASE 'INDIA_UN' SET STATE='OFFLINE';

DGMGRL> EDIT DATABASE 'INDIA_UN' SET STATE='APPLY-OFF';

DGMGRL> EDIT DATABASE 'INDIA_UN' SET STATE='TRANSPORT-OFF';

DGMGRL> EDIT DATABASE 'INDIA_UN' SET STATE='ONLINE' WITH APPLY
INSTANCE='INDIA_UN2';
```

Do not forget that some of the operations restart the instance.

Troubleshooting Data Guard broker

In this section, we will discuss the most common issues that may arise when Data Guard is managed with the broker. In the case of an outage or problem, we first consider gathering diagnostic information. We must refer to the alert logfile in the Automatic Diagnostic Repository destination starting from Oracle 11*g*. In earlier versions, the alert logfile is located in BACKGROUND_DUMP_DEST. The trace file drc<sid>.log for the Data Guard broker is also located in the ADR destination.

The v$diag_info view can be used to list all the important ADR locations for the Oracle database instance as shown in the following code:

```
SQL> SELECT NAME,VALUE FROM V$DIAG_INFO;
NAME                       VALUE
-------------------------- -------------------------------------------
Diag Enabled               TRUE
ADR Base                   /u01/app/oracle
ADR Home                   /u01/app/oracle/diag/rdbms/turkey_un/TURKEY
..........
Default Trace File         /u01/app/oracle/diag/rdbms/turkey_un
   /TURKEY/trace/TURKEY_ora_16735.trc
Active Problem Count        0
Active Incident Count       0
```

Data Guard tracing

The LOG_ARCHIVE_TRACE parameter is used to trace redo transport and apply services on both the primary and standby databases. By default, the parameter is disabled and its value is 0. The Data Guard tracing levels are as follows. Depending on the required tracing value, the level can be changed online:

- 0: Disable archived log tracing (default)
- 1: Track archival of the redo logfile
- 2: Track the archival status of each archived log destination
- 4: Track archival operational phase
- 8: Track the archived log destination activity
- 16: Track the detailed archived log destination activity
- 32: Track archived log destination parameter modifications
- 64: Track the ARCn process state activity
- 128: Track FAL (fetch archived log) server related activities
- 256: Track RFS logical client
- 512: Track the LGWR redo shipping network activity
- 1024: Track the RFS Physical client
- 2048: Track RFS/ARCn Ping Heartbeat
- 4096: Track Real Time Apply
- 8192: Track Redo Apply (media recovery or physical standby)

If you want to turn on more than one tracing level, you can set LOG_ARCHIVE_TRACE to the sum of these levels. For example, setting it to 3 will turn on tracing archival of the redo logfile and the archival status of each archived log destination.

Most Common Data Guard broker issues

Now we will discuss some general Data Guard broker issues.

ORA-16797: database is not using a server parameter file

If you ever start an instance with PFILE instead of SPFILE, DMON will not be able to communicate with the databases. SPFILE is mandatory for communicating with remote destinations to fetch required information from the broker configuration file and server parameter files. This issue can eventually be identified from DGMGRL by retrieving configuration information as follows:

```
DGMGRL> show configuration;

Configuration - PACKT
```

```
Protection Mode: MaxPerformance
Databases:
  TURKEY_UN - Primary database
  INDIA_UN  - Physical standby database
    Error: ORA-16797: database is not using a server parameter file
Fast-Start Failover: DISABLED
Configuration Status:
ERROR
```

Create a new SPFILE on the standby system from PFILE, and bounce the standby database as follows:

```
SQL> create spfile from pfile;
File created.
SQL> shutdown immediate
SQL> startup mount
```

 After the creation of SPFILE from PFILE, in the next startup Oracle picks SPFILE even though PFILE exists.

```
DGMGRL> show configuration;
Configuration - PACKT
  Protection Mode: MaxPerformance
  Databases:
    TURKEY_UN - Primary database
    INDIA_UN  - Physical standby database
    UK_UN     - Physical standby database
Fast-Start Failover: DISABLED
Configuration Status:
SUCCESS
```

ORA-10458:standby database requires recovery

For a database to open, it must have consistency over all the data files. This can occur in case the recovery has been terminated in the previous sessions or the standby control file SCN is has not been synchronized with the data files as shown in the following query:

```
SQL> alter database open;
alter database open
*
```

```
ERROR at line 1:
ORA-10458: standby database requires recovery
ORA-01196: file 1 is inconsistent due to a failed media recovery
session
ORA-01110: data file 1: '/u02/app/oracle/oradata/orcl/system01.dbf'

DGMGRL>  show database 'INDIA_UN';
Database - INDIA_UN
  Role:              PHYSICAL STANDBY
  Intended State:   APPLY-ON
  Transport Lag:    (unknown)
  Apply Lag:        (unknown)
  Real Time Query:  OFF
  Instance(s):
    INDIA
  Database Warning(s):
    ORA-16770: Redo Apply not started since physical standby database
is opening
Database Status:
WARNING
```

Now the database status is in MOUNT. Either start Redo Apply from DGMGRL or bounce DMON so that DMON will initiate MRP to perform a recovery. Once enough number of archived logs are applied to provide consistency, you can open the database.

ORA-16737:the redo transport service for standby database "string" has an error

Usually, the ORA-16737 error occurs if there is any communication problem with the standby database. You can query the LogXptStatus property to see the error message and you can also review the Data Guard broker logfile as follows:

```
DGMGRL> show database TURKEY_UN  'LogXptStatus';

LOG TRANSPORT STATUS

PRIMARY_INSTANCE_NAME STANDBY_DATABASE_NAME              STATUS
            TURKEY              INDIA_UN ORA-12541: TNS:no listener


DGMGRL> show database 'INDIA_UN';

Database - INDIA_UN

  Role:              PHYSICAL STANDBY

  Intended State:   APPLY-ON

  Transport Lag:    (unknown)
```

```
 Apply Lag:        (unknown)
 Real Time Query: OFF
 Instance(s):
    INDIA
Database Status:
DGM-17016: failed to retrieve status for database "INDIA_UN"
ORA-12541: TNS:no listener
ORA-16625: cannot reach database "INDIA_UN"
```

Check the listener of the status and start the listener. Wait until the Oracle service is registered with the listener, or you can manually register it as follows:

```
SQL> alter system register;
```

Ensure that the service is registered with the listener.

ORA-16715:redo transport-related property string of standby database "string" is inconsistent

Usually, the ORA-16715 error occurs if there is any inconsistency between the initialization parameters and configuration file. By querying the database status from DGMGRL, we can see the parameter that is not consistent.

```
DGMGRL> show database 'TURKEY_UN';
Database - TURKEY_UN
  Role:            PRIMARY
  Intended State: TRANSPORT-ON
  Instance(s):
    TURKEY
      Warning: ORA-16715: redo transport-related property DelayMins of
standby database "INDIA_UN" is inconsistent
Database Status:
WARNING


SQL> select delay_mins,destination from v$archive_dest where dest_id=2;
DELAY_MINS DESTINATION
---------- ------------
        10 india
DGMGRL> show database 'TURKEY_UN' 'DelayMins';
  DelayMins = '0'
```

From the previous two queries, we can see that there is inconsistency between SPFILE and the configuration files. Either we have to edit the configuration file's property value to 10 or change the initialization parameter's value to 0.

ORA-12514:TNS:listener does not currently know of service requested in connect descriptor

One example of an ORA-12514 error is a post-switchover case. After performing a switchover using DGMGRL, Data Guard requires a shutdown and startup of both the primary and standby databases. This issue can occur if any necessary entry is missing in the listener.ora file. DGMGRL is unable to connect to the database after it has been stopped while performing the switchover.

Current listener description

The command for the current listener is as follows:

```
SID_LIST_LISTENER =
  (SID_LIST =
  (SID_DESC =
  (SID_NAME = PLSExtProc)
    (ORACLE_HOME = /u01/home/oracle/product/11.2.0/db_1)
    (PROGRAM = extproc)
  )
 (SID_DESC =
    (GLOBAL_DBNAME = india_un)
    (SID_NAME = INDIA)
    (ORACLE_HOME = /u01/home/oracle/product/11.2.0/db_1)
  )
 )
```

Add the correct entry of GLOBAL_DBNAME in the SID list description of the listener. This step is applicable for both the primary and standby databases.

Format GLOBAL_DBNAME=db_unique_name_DGMGRL.db_domain as follows:

```
SID_LIST_LISTENER =
  (SID_LIST =
  (SID_DESC =
  (SID_NAME = PLSExtProc)
```

```
      (ORACLE_HOME = /u01/home/oracle/product/11.2.0/db_1)
      (PROGRAM = extproc)
    )
  (SID_DESC =
      (GLOBAL_DBNAME = india_un_DGMGRL)
      (SID_NAME = INDIA)
      (ORACLE_HOME = /u01/home/oracle/product/11.2.0/db_1)
    )
  )
DGMGRL> show database 'TURKEY_UN' "StaticConnectIdentifier"
  StaticConnectIdentifier = '(DESCRIPTION=(ADDRESS=(PROTOCOL=IPC)
(KEY=EXTPROC1521))(CONNECT_DATA=(SERVICE_NAME=turkey_un_DGMGRL)(INSTANCE_
NAME=TURKEY)(SERVER=DEDICATED)))'
```

Oracle Data Guard fast-start failover

In Data Guard configurations, in case of any disasters in primary database systems or any corruptions or errors in the database that are not recoverable quickly, a failover can be performed manually on the standby database to convert it to a primary database and use it for production services. Another option is to automate the failover using the fast-start failover feature. A fast-start failover can be configured or managed either by DGMGRL or grid control.

If a fast-start failover is not configured and the production database is completely unavailable, and if you want to perform a failover on the standby database in such a case, you first have to understand the status of the standby database, whether all the archived logs or redo has been applied or not. Then you have to perform a failover manually. After the failover, you have to recreate a new standby database. These steps will increase the downtime of the system. Fast-start failover will be invoked automatically if the primary site is unavailable. Also, it'll recover the standby database, perform the failover, and reinstate the old primary database if possible.

Starting from 11*g*, you can implement a fast-start failover even in the Maximum Performance mode. It supports asynchronous redo transport.

The previously mentioned points can be illustrated in the following diagram:

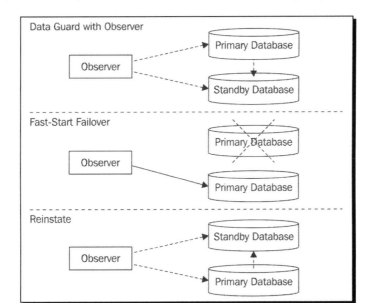

An observer is required to configure a fast-start failover. It should be configured in a location rather than on the primary and standby databases. It acts as a client and monitors both the primary and standby databases at all times. We must install either the Oracle Client Administrator software or the full Oracle Database software to the observer host.

Based on the `FastStartFailoverThreshold` value, observer automatically initiates the failover procedure. After performing the failover, the end users will connect to the database again and old connections will be redirected to the new primary database.

You can configure observer either in the primary or standby system, but for the best configuration of FSFO, the observer, primary, and standby databases should be on separate servers.

Time for action – configuring fast-start failover

The following steps will help you configure FSFO in a configuration managed by the Data Guard broker:

1. Check if Data Guard is in the Maximum Performance(11*g*Rx) or Maximum Availability mode using the following command:

```
DGMGRL> show configuration

Configuration - PACKT

  Protection Mode: MaxPerformance

  Databases:

    TURKEY_UN - Primary database

    INDIA_UN  - Physical standby database

Fast-Start Failover: DISABLED

Configuration Status:

SUCCESS
```

2. If your configuration is in the Maximum Availability mode, make sure that LogXptMode is set to synchronous redo transport.

3. Make sure you have configured a flashback database and fast recovery area. This is applicable on both the primary and standby databases and helpful in case you want to reinstate the old primary database or perform a flashback as shown in the following query:

```
SQL> select flashback_on from v$database;
FLASHBACK_ON
------------------
NO
```

4. We must set some parameters before turning on flashback. These parameters are DB_FLASHBACK_RETENTION_TARGET, DB_RECOVERY_FILE_DEST_SIZE, and DB_RECOVERY_FILE_DEST. The following query shows you how to set these parameters:

```
SQL> ALTER SYSTEM SET DB_FLASHBACK_RETENTION_TARGET=5760;
System altered.
SQL> ALTER SYSTEM SET DB_RECOVERY_FILE_DEST_SIZE=20G;
System altered.
SQL> ALTER SYSTEM SET DB_RECOVERY_FILE_DEST='/data/FLASHBACK';
System altered.
SQL> ALTER DATABASE FLASHBACK ON;
Database altered.
```

If you are using 11*g* ORACLE_HOME for observer, note that it is incompatible with 10*g* databases.

5. In the Oracle Net Services configuration, the listener.ora file needs to include a service with GLOBAL_DB_NAME , as follows, to enable the broker to automatically start the databases in the case of a switchover. This configuration is applicable on both servers. To set up the configuration, shut down the listener, make the changes, and restart the listener as follows:

```
(SID_LIST =
 (SID_DESC =
 (SID_NAME = PLSExtProc)
  (ORACLE_HOME = /u01/home/oracle/product/11.2.0/db_1)
  (PROGRAM = extproc)
 )
 (SID_DESC =
  (GLOBAL_DBNAME = turkey_un_DGMGRL)
  (SID_NAME = TURKEY)
  (ORACLE_HOME = /u01/home/oracle/product/11.2.0/db_1)
 )
)
```

6. Setting the FastStartFailoverTarget value is required if there are multiple standby databases available in the Data Guard configuration. Use the following commands for the same:

```
DGMGRL> edit database 'TURKEY_UN' SET PROPERTY
FastStartFailoverTarget='INDIA_UN';

Property "faststartfailovertarget" updated

DGMGRL> edit database 'INDIA_UN' SET PROPERTY
FastStartFailoverTarget='TURKEY_UN';

Property "faststartfailovertarget" updated
```

7. FSFO has two configuration properties. The FastStartFailoverLagLimit property refers to how much data loss is acceptable in terms of seconds. The FastStartFailoverThreshold property refers to the number of seconds for which the configuration will wait before initiating the failover process as follows:

```
DGMGRL> EDIT CONFIGURATION SET PROPERTY
FastStartFailoverLagLimit=30;

Property "faststartfailoverlaglimit" updated
```

```
DGMGRL> EDIT CONFIGURATION SET PROPERTY
FastStartFailoverThreshold=30;

Property "faststartfailoverthreshold" updated
```

 If you want to change the fast-start failover target property to a different standby database, you have to disable FSFO, and then after changing the property, you have to re-enable FSFO.

8. Enable fast-start failover as shown in the following command:

```
DGMGRL> enable fast_start failover;

Enabled.
```

9. Assuming Oracle software is installed on the observer host, start observer. The following command must be issued on the observer server:

```
$dgmgrl -logfile /tmp/obsvr.log sys/free2go@TURKEY "start
observer" &
```

The previous command statement is executed in the background because the `start observer` command doesn't return the DGMGRL prompt to the user.

10. Verify the FSFO configuration as follows:

```
DGMGRL> SHOW FAST_START FAILOVER;

Fast-Start Failover: ENABLED

    Threshold:          30 seconds

    Target:             INDIA_UN

    Observer:           oracle-ha

    Lag Limit:          30 seconds

    Shutdown Primary:   TRUE

    Auto-reinstate:     TRUE

Configurable Failover Conditions

    Health Conditions:

        Corrupted Controlfile          YES

        Corrupted Dictionary           YES

        Inaccessible Logfile            NO

        Stuck Archiver                  NO

        Datafile Offline               YES

    Oracle Error Conditions:
```

```
(none)

SQL> select DB_UNIQUE_NAME, FS_FAILOVER_STATUS, FS_FAILOVER_
CURRENT_TARGET from v$database;

DB_UNIQUE_NA FS_FAILOVER_STATUS       FS_FAILOVER_CURRENT_TARGET

------------ ---------------------    ----------------------------

turkey_un    TARGET UNDER LAG LIMIT INDIA_UN
```

The FS_FAILOVER_STATUS value will be in "TARGET UNDER LAG LIMIT" if it is in the Maximum Performance mode, and in case it is in the Maximum Availability mode, the value will be SYNCHRONIZED.

What just happened?

We've just seen how to configure a fast-start failover after setting the required parameters, and also verified the status of the configuration after starting the observer.

Troubleshooting observer configuration

After configuring the observer, sometimes the process may be dropped and you may see errors in the configuration as shown later. In such a case, FSFO may not be able to initiate a failover in the case of primary database failure as follows:

```
ORA-16824: multiple warnings, including fast-start failover-related
warnings, detected for the database
```

For any troubleshooting issue, first look at the configuration status as follows:

```
DGMGRL> show configuration;
Configuration - PACKT

  Protection Mode: MaxPerformance

  Databases:

    TURKEY_UN - Primary database

      Warning: ORA-16824: multiple warnings, including fast-start
failover-related warnings, detected for the database


    INDIA_UN  - (*) Physical standby database

      Warning: ORA-16824: multiple warnings, including fast-start
failover-related warnings, detected for the database

Fast-Start Failover: ENABLED

Configuration Status: WARNING
```

```
2012-09-09 19:01:15.111 00000000  1269603843 Operation HEALTH_CHECK
continuing with warning, status = ORA-16819
2012-09-09 19:01:15.112 00000000  1269603843 Operation HEALTH_CHECK
continuing with warning, status = ORA-16819
```

Check for the status report of the configuration as follows:

```
DGMGRL> show database 'TURKEY_UN'  'StatusReport';
STATUS REPORT
       INSTANCE_NAME    SEVERITY ERROR_TEXT
                 *      WARNING ORA-16819: fast-start failover observer
not started
```

As per the previous error, the observer is not running. The process may have been dropped or the observer system may have rebooted. Connect to the broker utility from the observer system using Oracle Net Services and start `observer` as follows:

```
$dgmgrl -logfile /tmp/obsvr.log sys/free2go@TURKEY "start observer" &
```

Check the configuration status as follows:

```
DGMGRL> SHOW FAST_START FAILOVER;
Fast-Start Failover: ENABLED
  Threshold:        30 seconds
  Target:           INDIA_UN
  Observer:         oracle-ha
  Lag Limit:        30 seconds
  Shutdown Primary: TRUE
  Auto-reinstate:   TRUE
Configurable Failover Conditions
  Health Conditions:
    Corrupted Controlfile          YES
    Corrupted Dictionary           YES
    Inaccessible Logfile           NO
    Stuck Archiver                 NO
    Datafile Offline               YES
  Oracle Error Conditions:
    (none)
```

Script to stop and start observer

To make the observer process highly available and running all the time, we may need to bounce the observer process when needed. So we can prepare a script and run it as a job regularly. It can be scheduled as an OS-level job. The following shell script example can be used on Linux/Unix systems:

```
# start and Stop Observer
export ORACLE_BASE=/u02/app/oracle
export ORACLE_HOME=/u01/home/oracle/product/11.2.0/db_1
export PATH=$ORACLE_HOME/bin:$PATH
dgmgrl << eof
connect sys/free2go@turkey
STOP OBSERVER;
START OBSERVER;
eof
```

Summary

In this chapter, we have learned the Data Guard broker architecture, the importance of using the Data Guard broker, and how to monitor and manage Data Guard using the broker, including how to troubleshoot with real-time issues and explained steps to configure a fast-start failover.

The next chapter will cover the configurations of Data Guard protection modes in detail.

5
Data Guard Protection Modes

Protection mode decision is crucial and database administrators need to work with IT managers and other responsible people to determine **RTO** *(***Recovery Time Objective***) and* **RPO** *(***Recovery Point Objective***) values and to select the most appropriate mode for their Data Guard configurations. After the decision is made, setting the data protection mode is a simple operation that can be performed by SQL*Plus,* **Data Guard command-line interface** *(***DGMGRL***) or Enterprise Manager Cloud Control.*

Data Guard offers three data protection modes, which meet different business requirements as mentioned in *Chapter 1*, *Getting Started*.

The following are the different modes:

- ◆ Maximum Protection
- ◆ Maximum Performance
- ◆ Maximum Availability

Let's look at the details of these protection modes and see how we can switch between the different modes.

The Maximum Protection mode

The Maximum Protection mode is referred to as the Guaranteed Zero Data Loss configuration. A primary database operating on the Maximum Protection mode doesn't provide an acknowledgment to the users that the commit is completed until transactions are successfully transferred to at least one standby destination. This setup requires the SYNC redo transport service using the LGWR attribute and guarantees that no data will be lost on the standby database in case of a primary database failure.

Of course, guaranteeing zero data loss comes at a cost. Because the primary database will always wait for an acknowledgment from standby destinations to continue its operation, there will be performance implications on the primary database. However, with 11*g*, the performance effect of using the SYNC redo transport service is less than the earlier releases. In the previous releases, the primary database doesn't send a redo to the standby database before completing the write to online redo logs. In 11*g*, the database writes redo to online redo logs and sends it to standby destinations simultaneously. This behavior reduces the time waited to complete a commit for a primary database.

Consider the following points before setting the Maximum Protection mode:

- Network bandwidth between sites is essential in this mode. If the bandwidth and latency of a network fails to satisfy real-time transport of redo generated by the primary database, there will be serious performance- and database-availability problems on the primary database.

- Using more than one standby database (preferably a physical standby one) for a Maximum Protection configuration is a good practice, which will increase the uptime of the primary database on standby and network failures. Also, the data protection will continue even if you lose the primary database and failover to one of the standby databases. It would be better to locate each standby database on different locations if possible.

- The primary database must be on the mount mode when changing the data protection mode from Maximum Performance to Maximum Protection.

- On all standby databases of the Data Guard configuration, the standby redo logs need to be created with the correct number and size before using the Maximum Performance mode. It's also a good practice to create standby redo logs in the primary database in order to be ready for a switchover.

- It wasn't possible to use a logical standby database with the Maximum Protection mode before 10*g*, because standby redo logs weren't supported by logical standby databases. Starting with 10*g*, we're able to use a logical standby with the Maximum Protection mode; however, we have to consider unsupported data types in such a case.

The Maximum Performance mode

This is the mode in which the primary database's availability is completely independent of the redo transport service. In other words, a primary database never waits for any acknowledgment from standby destinations to complete a transaction. Thus, we don't suffer from standby network-connection problems or standby availability-related performance problems and availability problems in the primary database.

This mode is the default protection mode and the log transport service must use the ASYNC mode with the LGWR or ARCH attribute. However, with 11*g*, ARCH transport is not recommended because it doesn't offer any advantage in terms of performance, and offers less data protection.

In the normal operation of the Maximum Performance configuration, the redo data, which is on the way from primary to standby, is at risk from primary database failures. The amount of data at risk is dependent to the bandwidth of the network.

The Maximum Availability mode

The Maximum Availability mode is the data protection mode that has the ability to run as a Maximum Protection or Maximum Performance mode depending on the accessibility of standby databases. In a normal operation where the standby is up and able to receive redo data synchronously, the primary database acts like the Maximum Protection mode and waits for acknowledgment from the standby database to complete transactions. However, the key point of the Maximum Availability mode is the behavior of the primary database when it's not able to receive acknowledgment from any standby database. It waits for a predefined period of time and if the connection cannot be established, the primary database continues its operation as a Maximum Performance mode database. The number of seconds that the primary waits before marking a standby inaccessible is defined with the NET_TIMEOUT attribute of the LOG_ARCHIVE_DEST_n parameter. The default value of this parameter is 30 seconds. In a Data Guard configuration with the Maximum Availability mode, the primary database does not stall for more than NET_TIMEOUT seconds if it's not able to access any standby database.

When the primary database is not able to connect to the standby database for NET_TIMEOUT seconds, it stops sending connection requests to the standby database and continues completing transactions. Then, the primary retries connecting to the standby immediately after every online log switch. We can use the REOPEN attribute to set the time (in seconds) for which the primary attempts to reconnect to the standby. When the connection is established, the missing archived redo logs will be sent to the standby by the ARCH process simultaneously with the online redo transport.

With its logic, the Maximum Availability mode provides zero data loss in a normal operation, and the primary database's availability is not at risk when there is no accessible standby database. On the other hand, what we sacrifice by using this mode will be the guaranteed zero data loss feature of the Maximum Availability mode and the performance independency of the primary database in the Maximum Protection mode. This mode uses the SYNC redo transport with the LGWR attribute as in the Maximum Protection mode, which has an impact on the response time of the primary database. So once again, the network bandwidth and latency are very important in this protection mode.

We can state that in a Maximum Availability mode Data Guard configuration, data is at risk only when two failures occur consecutively on the standby and primary databases.

Choosing the correct mode for your requirements

It's a very important decision to choose a protection mode. Every mode has its pros and cons. They all serve different requirements and require specific conditions. The following is a general guide to decide the correct mode:

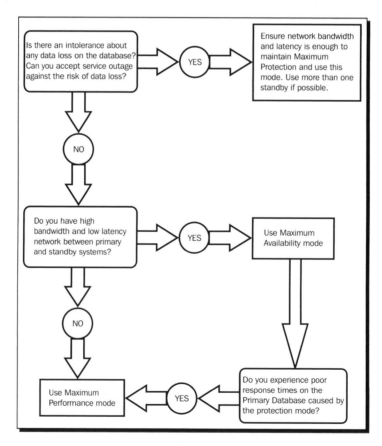

We've now learned the properties of the data protection modes and we're able to determine the correct mode according to our needs. Note that, if we decide to use the Maximum Protection or Maximum Availability modes but encounter performance problems, we should try to tune the database, server, disk, and network infrastructure before scaling down the data protection level.

Changing Data Guard protection mode

As mentioned earlier, changing the protection mode of Data Guard's configuration is not a challenging task, and it can be performed dynamically by using the SQL*Plus, DGMGRL or Enterprise Manager Cloud Control.

Let's see the examples of switching between protection modes using different interfaces.

Time for action – changing the protection mode with SQL*Plus

Now we'll convert Data Guard's configuration from Maximum Performance to Maximum Protection and then to the Maximum Availability mode using SQL*Plus commands. At the end, we'll convert it back to the Maximum Performance mode.

1. We have a physical standby configuration, which is in the Maximum Performance mode (by default) with `ASYNC` redo transport, without standby redo logs, and does not use Real-Time Apply. We'll try to convert it to the Maximum Protection mode. Let's execute the conversion command in the primary database without any change in the configuration as follows:

```
SQL> SELECT PROTECTION_MODE FROM V$DATABASE;

PROTECTION_MODE
--------------------
MAXIMUM PERFORMANCE

SQL> ALTER DATABASE SET STANDBY DATABASE TO MAXIMIZE
PROTECTION;
ALTER DATABASE SET STANDBY DATABASE TO MAXIMIZE PROTECTION

*
ERROR at line 1:
ORA-01126: database must be mounted in this instance and
not open in any instance
```

2. It's not possible to convert a standby in the Maximum Performance mode to the Maximum Protection and Maximum Availability modes when the primary database is open. We need to put the primary in a mount state in order to make this change. We can use use the following query:

```
SQL> SHUTDOWN IMMEDIATE
SQL> STARTUP MOUNT
SQL> ALTER DATABASE SET STANDBY DATABASE TO MAXIMIZE PROTECTION;

Database altered.

SQL> ALTER DATABASE OPEN;
alter database open
*
ERROR at line 1:
ORA-03113: end-of-file on communication channel
Process ID: 24904
Session ID: 113 Serial number: 3
```

3. We've restarted the primary database in the mount mode and changed the protection mode. However, when we tried to open it, we encountered an ORA-03113 error. We can see why the database raised this error in the alert logfile as follows:

```
LGWR: Destination LOG_ARCHIVE_DEST_2 is using asynchronous network I/O

LGWR: Minimum of 1 synchronous standby database required

Errors in file /u01/app/oracle2/diag/rdbms/TURKEY_UN/TURKEY/trace/ TURKEY_lgwr_24854.trc:

ORA-16072: a minimum of one standby database destination is required
```

4. The `LOG_ARCHIVE_DEST_2` parameter, which is used for the physical standby database log transport, is defined with the `ASYNC` attribute that is used for the Maximum Performance protection mode. In order to convert the database to Maximum Protection or Maximum Availability, we must change the `ASYNC` attribute to `SYNC` as follows:

```
SQL> ALTER SYSTEM SET LOG_ARCHIVE_DEST_2='SERVICE=INDIA
LGWR SYNC VALID_FOR=(ONLINE_LOGFILES,PRIMARY_ROLE)
DB_UNIQUE_NAME=INDIA_UN';

System altered.
```

We should also change the LOG_ARCHIVE_DEST_n parameter, which is "VALID_FOR = PRIMARY_ROLE", in the standby database to the SYNC redo transport mode. If we don't, the protection mode will not operate after a switchover because ASYNC cannot be used with the Maximum Protection mode. This step needs to be executed whenever changing the protection mode requires a redo transport mode change.

```
SQL> ALTER DATABASE OPEN;
alter database open
*
ERROR at line 1:
ORA-03113: end-of-file on communication channel
Process ID: 25062
Session ID: 113 Serial number: 3
```

5. We encountered the same error. Let's check the alert log again, shown as follows:

   ORA-16086: Redo data cannot be written to the standby redo log

   LGWR: Error 16086 verifying archivelog destination LOG_ARCHIVE_ DEST_2

   Destination LOG_ARCHIVE_DEST_2 is UNSYNCHRONIZED

   LGWR: Error 16086 disconnecting from destination LOG_ARCHIVE_ DEST_2 standby host 'INDIA'

   LGWR: Continuing...

   LGWR: Minimum of 1 applicable standby database required

   Errors in file /u01/app/oracle2/diag/rdbms/TURKEY_UN/TURKEY/trace/ TURKEY_lgwr_25020.trc:

   ORA-16072: a minimum of one standby database destination is required

6. In order to set Maximum Protection or Maximum Availability modes, we must create standby redo logfiles in the standby database. Stop Redo Apply, create standby redo logs and start Redo Apply again as Real-Time Apply on the standby database:

   ```
   SQL> ALTER DATABASE RECOVER MANAGED STANDBY DATABASE CANCEL;

   Database altered.

   SQL> alter database add standby logfile group 4 size 52428800;
   SQL> alter database add standby logfile group 5 size 52428800;
   SQL> alter database add standby logfile group 6 size 52428800;
   SQL> alter database add standby logfile group 7 size 52428800;
   ```

In *Chapter 2, Configuring Oracle Data Guard Physical Standby Database*, remember we mentioned that the standby redo log group number must be one more than that of the online redo log group number, and the size of standby redo logfiles must be the same as that of online redo logfiles.

```
SQL> ALTER DATABASE RECOVER MANAGED STANDBY DATABASE USING CURRENT
LOGFILE DISCONNECT FROM SESSION;

Database altered.
```

7. Start the primary database and query the data protection mode as follows:

```
SQL> STARTUP MOUNT
SQL> ALTER DATABASE OPEN;

Database altered.

SQL> SELECT PROTECTION_MODE FROM V$DATABASE;

PROTECTION_MODE
--------------------
MAXIMUM PROTECTION
```

8. We can see from the following code that the mode changes the information on the standby database alert log also:

Completed: ALTER DATABASE RECOVER MANAGED STANDBY DATABASE USING CURRENT LOGFILE DISCONNECT FROM SESSION

RFS[5]: Assigned to RFS process 1086

RFS[5]: Identified database type as 'physical standby': Client is LGWR SYNC pid 21839

Primary database is in MAXIMUM PROTECTION mode

Changing standby controlfile to MAXIMUM PROTECTION mode

9. Now try to shut down the standby database as shown in the following query:

```
SQL> SHUTDOWN IMMEDIATE
ORA-01154: database busy. Open, close, mount, and dismount not
allowed now
```

10. As you can see, it's not possible to shut down a standby database in the Maximum Protection mode if it's the only standby database alive. We'll see the following lines in the standby database alert log when we try to shut it down:

```
Attempt to shut down Standby Database

Standby Database operating in NO DATA LOSS mode

Detected primary database alive, shutdown primary first, shutdown
aborted
```

11. Now kill the SMON process to simulate a failure on the standby database server as follows:

```
$ ps -ef |grep smon_INDIA
oracle    7064    1  0 Sep16 ?          00:00:00 ora_smon_INDIA
$ kill -9 7064
```

12. The Oracle instance will be terminated in the standby database after the kill command. Now try modifying the primary database by inserting data into a table as shown in the following query:

```
SQL> INSERT INTO HR.REGIONS VALUES (102,'TEST');


1 row created.


SQL> COMMIT;
```

13. The commit statement will wait and not be executed. At this stage, the primary database will not accept any change because of the Maximum Protection mode's characteristic. Then the instance will be terminated by LGWR as shown in the following alert log lines:

```
Destination LOG_ARCHIVE_DEST_2 is UNSYNCHRONIZED

LGWR: All standby destinations have failed

**********************************************************

WARNING: All standby database destinations have failed

WARNING: Instance shutdown required to protect primary

**********************************************************

LGWR (ospid: 21839): terminating the instance due to error 16098

Instance terminated by LGWR, pid = 21839
```

Mount the standby database and start recovery at this stage.

14. Now let's try to change the data protection mode to Maximum Availability as shown in the following query:

```
SQL> ALTER DATABASE SET STANDBY DATABASE TO MAXIMIZE AVAILABILITY;

Database altered.
```

15. It's possible to perform this protection mode change without putting the primary database in the mount state. We can see the change in the standby database alert log as follows:

```
Primary database is in MAXIMUM AVAILABILITY mode

Changing standby controlfile to MAXIMUM AVAILABILITY mode

Standby controlfile consistent with primary
```

16. Try to shut down the standby database as shown in the following query:

```
SQL> SHUTDOWN IMMEDIATE
ORA-01109: database not open
Database dismounted.
ORACLE instance shut down.
```

17. It's possible to shut down the standby database in the Maximum Availability mode. It's also possible to modify the primary database when there is no standby alive, as shown in the following query:

```
SQL> INSERT INTO HR.REGIONS VALUES (102,'TEST');


1 row created.


SQL> COMMIT;


Commit complete.
```

18. In this step, we'll change the protection mode back to Maximum Performance. Don't forget to set the LOG_ARCHIVE_DEST_n attribute to ASYNC as shown in the following query:

```
SQL> ALTER DATABASE SET STANDBY DATABASE TO MAXIMIZE PERFORMANCE;

Database altered.

SQL> ALTER SYSTEM SET LOG_ARCHIVE_DEST_2='SERVICE=INDIA LGWR ASYNC
VALID_FOR=(ONLINE_LOGFILES,PRIMARY_ROLE) DB_UNIQUE_NAME=INDIA_UN';

System altered.
```

What just happened?

We've seen how to change the data protection mode of a Data Guard configuration using the SQL* Plus command line interface. If you didn't set up Data Guard broker or Cloud Control, this is the only way to change the protection mode.

Another way of performing protection mode changes in Data Guard is using Data Guard broker. If Data Guard broker was configured and being used, then it's recommended to use the broker in order to change the protection mode.

Time for action – changing the protection mode with Data Guard broker

Now execute the following steps in order to use Data Guard broker commands for changing the Data Guard protection mode:

1. We now have Maximum Performance as the default protection mode in our configuration. Let's check it through DGMGRL. We can connect the interface from the primary or standby as follows:

```
$ dgmgrl
DGMGRL for Linux: Version 11.2.0.1.0 - 64bit Production
Copyright (c) 2000, 2009, Oracle. All rights reserved.
Welcome to DGMGRL, type "help" for information.
DGMGRL> CONNECT /
DGMGRL> SHOW CONFIGURATION;
Configuration - PACKT
  Protection Mode: MaxPerformance
  Databases:
    TURKEY_UN - Primary database
    INDIA_UN  - Physical standby database
Fast-Start Failover: DISABLED
Configuration Status:
SUCCESS
```

2. Try to convert the configuration from Maximum Performance to the Maximum Availability mode as shown in the following command line:

```
DGMGRL> EDIT CONFIGURATION SET PROTECTION MODE AS MaxAvailability;
Error: ORA-16627: operation disallowed since no standby
databases would remain to support protection mode Failed.
```

Again, we should remember that we have to set the SYNC attribute of log_archive_dest_n before converting the protection mode from Maximum Performance to Maximum Availability and Maximum Protection.

3. Check and then change the log transport service attribute via DGMGRL, as shown in the following statements:

```
DGMGRL> SHOW DATABASE VERBOSE 'TURKEY_UN' LogXptMode;

  LogXptMode = 'ASYNC'

DGMGRL> SHOW DATABASE VERBOSE 'INDIA_UN' LogXptMode;

  LogXptMode = 'ASYNC'
```

4. The log transport service attribute should be changed for both the primary and standby databases as shown in the following command line:

For primary:

```
DGMGRL> EDIT DATABASE 'TURKEY_UN' SET PROPERTY LOGXPTMODE='SYNC';

Property "logxptmode" updated

DGMGRL> SHOW DATABASE VERBOSE 'TURKEY_UN' LogXptMode;

  LogXptMode = 'SYNC'
```

For standby:

```
DGMGRL> EDIT DATABASE 'INDIA_UN' SET PROPERTY LOGXPTMODE='SYNC';

Property "logxptmode" updated

DGMGRL> SHOW DATABASE VERBOSE 'INDIA_UN' LogXptMode;

  LogXptMode = 'SYNC'
```

5. Ensure that the standby redo logs exist and are created with the correct size on the standby database, as shown in the following query:

```
SQL> select group#,bytes from v$standby_log;

    GROUP#       BYTES
---------- ----------
         4    52428800
         5    52428800
         6    52428800
         7    52428800
```

6. Now change the protection mode to Maximum Availability as shown in the following command line:

```
DGMGRL> EDIT CONFIGURATION SET PROTECTION MODE AS MaxAvailability;

Succeeded.
```

7. Check the configuration status as follows:

```
DGMGRL> SHOW CONFIGURATION;
Configuration - PACKT
  Protection Mode: MaxAvailability
  Databases:
    TURKEY_UN - Primary database
    INDIA_UN  - Physical standby database
Fast-Start Failover: DISABLED
Configuration Status:
SUCCESS
```

The Protection status is changed to Maximum Availability. Ensure that the configuration status is SUCCESS.

What just happened?

We've successfully changed the protection mode from Maximum Performance to Maximum Availability using the DGMGRL command line interface.

Have a go hero - protection mode transitions with DGMGRL

Now change the Data Guard protection mode from Maximum Availability to Maximum Protection via DGMGRL. You should be able to make this change without restarting the primary database. Then try mode transition from Maximum Performance to Maximum Protection where you'll be prompted with the following warning:

```
ORA-16570: database needs restart
```

It's time to see how the protection mode can be changed with some clicks. Enterprise Manager Cloud Control offers great for monitoring and managing Data Guard environments. Changing the protection mode is also quite easy with this interface.

Time for action – changing the protection mode with Enterprise Manager Cloud Control

The following steps must be performed in order to change the protection modes of Data Guard's configuration using Enterprise Manager Cloud Control:

1. On the database's home page, click on **Availability** and then on **Data Guard Administration**.

2. In the Data Guard Administration page, we see the current protection mode of Data Guard. The mode is **Maximum Protection** and we'll change it to **Maximum Availability** by clicking on **Protection Mode** as shown in the following screenshot:

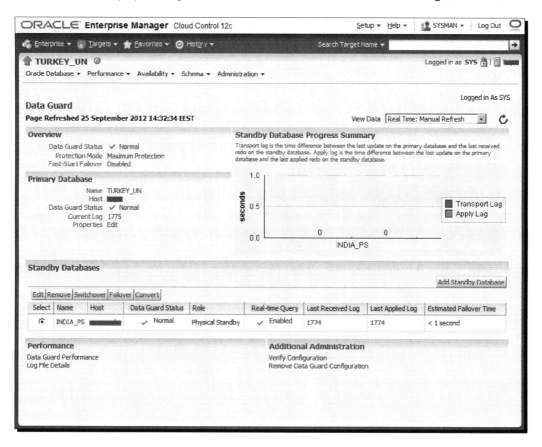

3. Next, we will see the **Change Protection Mode** page with options and their brief explanations. Select **Maximum Availability** and click on **Continue** as shown in the following screenshot:

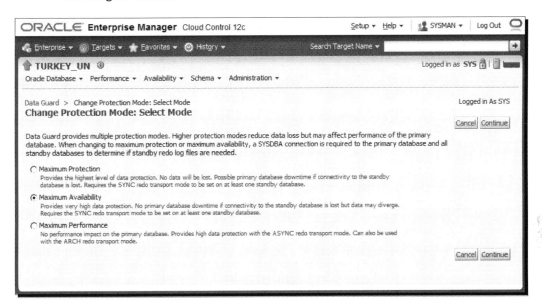

4. The next page will show you the standby databases in the Data Guard configuration. If there's more than one standby, we can select one or more to support the protection mode. Select the database and click on **Continue** as shown in the following screenshot:

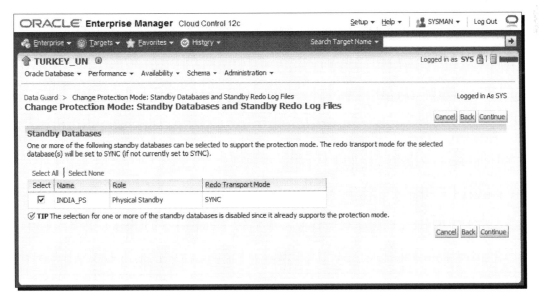

5. In the next page, we'll see a confirmation page; click on **Yes** to continue.

6. The protection mode will be changed to **Maximum Availability** and we'll see the following Data Guard Administration page showing the new protection mode of the configuration:

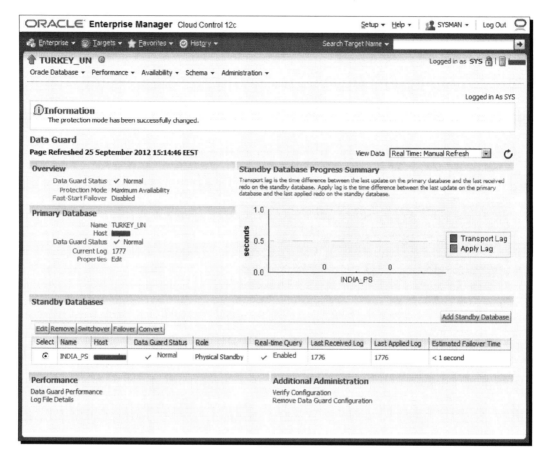

7. Now, let's change the protection mode to **Maximum Performance**, which requires a modification to LOG_ARCHIVE_DEST_n to convert the SYNC redo transport mode to ASYNC. Click on **Protection Mode** on the Data Guard Administration page, select **Maximum Performance**, and click on **Continue**.

8. We'll come up with a confirmation page, which indicates that the redo transport mode of SYNC will be changed to ASYNC. Click on **Yes** to continue as shown in the following screenshot:

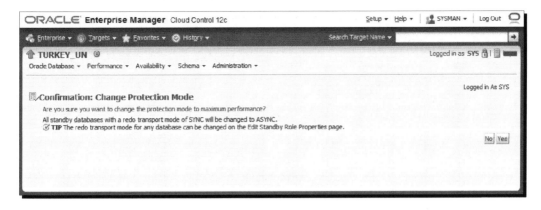

9. The protection mode will be changed in this step, and again we'll be directed to the Data Guard Administration page showing the new protection mode. If we check the primary database alert logfile during this stage, we can see the LOG_ARCHIVE_ DEST_n parameter showing the standby database that is changed to support the ASYNC redo transport.

10. Now let's change it back to the Maximum Protection mode. As we know, this operation will require you to restart the primary database. Let's see how Cloud Control handles this. When we repeat the same steps mentioned previously to change the protection mode and then click on **Continue** after selecting the standby database, we'll see the following page, which requires operating the system credentials for a user who can access the Oracle Home. This is the user that will be used to stop and mount the primary database. Enter a username and password or use a previously saved credential, if it exists. Click on **Continue** as shown in the following screenshot:

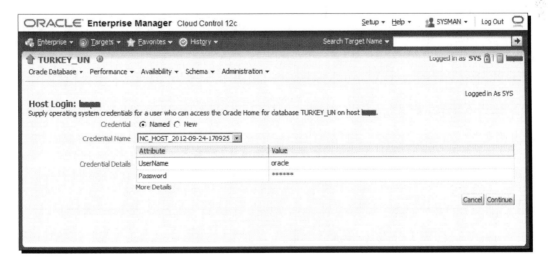

11. A confirmation screen will indicate that the primary database will be restarted. Click on **Yes** to continue, as shown in the following screenshot:

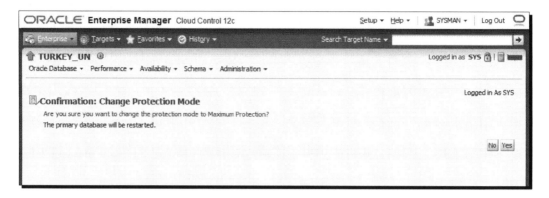

12. We will see the process of changing the protection mode in the following screen. This may take some time because it will include a restart of the primary database:

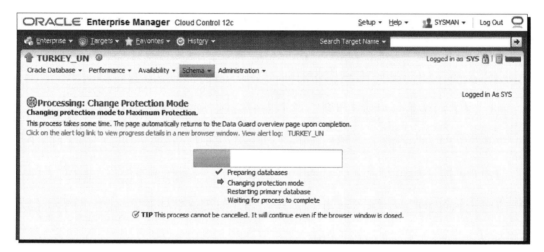

13. During this process, read the alert logfile of the primary database. You'll see the ALTER SYSTEM statement change the LOG_ARCHIVE_DEST_n parameter to the SYNC attribute. Then shutdown immediate and startup mount will be executed. After the instance starts, we can see that the following changes are applied automatically:

```
ALTER DATABASE SET STANDBY DATABASE TO MAXIMIZE PROTECTION;

ALTER SYSTEM SET log_archive_trace=0 SCOPE=BOTH SID='TURKEY';

ALTER SYSTEM SET log_archive_format='%t_%s_%r.arc' SCOPE=SPFILE
SID='TURKEY';
```

```
ALTER SYSTEM SET standby_file_management='MANUAL' SCOPE=BOTH
SID='*';
ALTER SYSTEM SET archive_lag_target=0 SCOPE=BOTH SID='*';
ALTER SYSTEM SET log_archive_max_processes=4 SCOPE=BOTH SID='*';
ALTER SYSTEM SET log_archive_min_succeed_dest=1 SCOPE=BOTH
SID='*';
```

These are the Cloud Control managed automatic changes. We should check the values and change the parameters again if necessary. For example, the LOG_ARCHIVE_MAX_PROCESSES value of 4 may not be sufficient for our Data Guard environment if there is an excessive redo generation rate. So we should set it to a higher value.

14. When the process is completed, you'll be directed to the Data Guard Administration page, which shows the new protection mode value as **Maximum Protection**, as shown in the following screenshot:

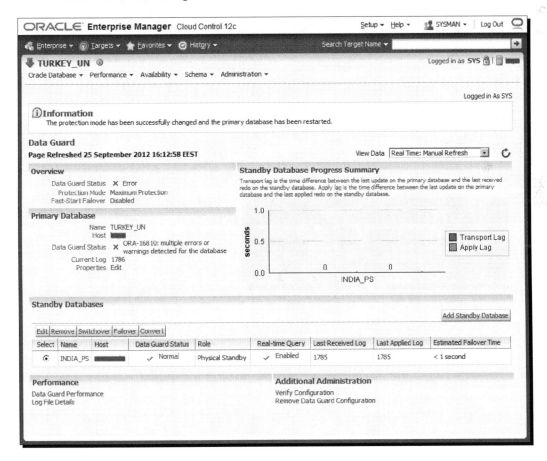

However, we see some errors and the status of the database is shown in the screenshot. If we examine the alert log, we can see that the primary database is mounted but not opened. Open the database manually with the `ALTER DATABASE OPEN` statement to complete the action.

What just happened?

Congratulations, all the Data Guard management interfaces are used to switch between protection modes and you're ready to perform all kind of mode-change operations. The SQL*Plus interface is the most administrator-controlled interface, but it also has the most number of manual options. Administration is simpler but less controlled with DGMGRL and Cloud Control.

Pop quiz – precautions for primary database availability issue in the Maximum Protection mode

Q1. The discouraging part of using the Maximum Protection mode is its effect on the primary database's performance and availability. Performance is affected by the latencies of the log transport and the apply services, which can be fixed by increasing the network, server, and disk performances. The primary database availability issue is caused by the inaccessibility of the standby database. What can we do to minimize the risk of the standby database's inaccessibility?

Summary

We've reached the end of this chapter and we have learned the details of the Data Guard protection modes and how to change the mode with all possible interfaces. The protection mode of the Data Guard configuration is an important consideration. Before designing the network, server, and disk infrastructure for the Data Guard installation, we should first decide the protection mode depending on the business requirements.

The next chapter will include information about role transitions in Data Guard. Also, details for performing switchover and failover operations will be covered for both physical and logical standby database configurations.

6

Data Guard Role Transitions

Switchover and failover are the role transition options in Data Guard. Physical and logical standby databases have different practices in this context. In this chapter we will cover the necessary steps to accomplish a successful switchover or failover in a physical or logical standby database environment.

Role transition considerations

In Data Guard, we can simply distinguish switchover and failover as planned and unplanned role transitions. A switchover is a planned role transition between the primary database and one of its standby databases. Switchover can be considered to reduce downtime during scheduled maintenance on the primary system or to test stability for future role transitions. Switchover guarantees no data loss. Using switchover, the primary database can transit to a standby role, and the standby database can transit to the primary role at any point of time. Switchover can be performed through Cloud Control, the Data Guard broker command-line interface, or by issuing SQL*Plus commands.

Once the standby database is configured and is functioning properly, you can test switchover. Switchover is used to reduce primary database downtime during any OS or hardware upgrades, which require an extended outage. A switchover allows the primary database to switch roles with its standby database. Once the maintenance on the primary server has been performed, you can switch the databases back to their original roles.

In the case of primary database failure, you need to perform failover to transit from the standby database role to the primary role. After a failover, the original primary database cannot participate in the Data Guard configuration without the use of flashback. So if the original primary database is still accessible, you should always consider a switchover first.

A failover is performed when the production database (all instances of an Oracle RAC production database) fails. By performing failover, one of the standby databases is transitioned to take over the production role, allowing business operations to continue. Once the failover is complete and applications have resumed, the administrative staff can turn its attention to resolving the problems with the failed system. Failover may or may not result in data loss depending on the Data Guard protection mode in effect at the time of the failover.

Switchover

A switchover is a planned role transition between the primary database and a standby database within the same Data Guard configuration. Switchover is used to reduce the downtime of production databases during any scheduled maintenance on the production server, to test the server capability or any changes at hardware level, or to check future role transitions. During switchover, there is no data loss and the role of each database changes from primary database to standby database and vice versa as shown in the following diagram:

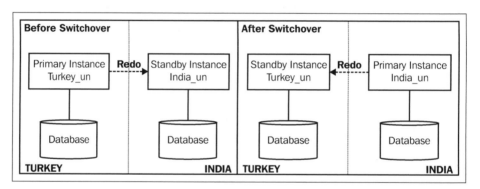

Data Guard switchover is also a good way to move databases to new hardware. We can perform RMAN backup and restore the database to the new server, but the disadvantage of using RMAN is that we have to open the database with `resetlogs`. Another alternative would be shutting down the database and copying all files onto the new server. But this method will take a lot of time depending on the size of the database, and also it's not easy to perform this method in the ASM framework.

Then what is the alternate solution to move the database to another server without OPEN RESETLOGS or the option of COLD backup?

Data Guard is a good choice in this situation. The following steps can be performed to move a database to new servers using Data Guard:

1. Implement Data Guard and create a standby database on the new hardware.

2. Test the new hardware using the standby database read-only (Active Data Guard) or the standby database read-write (snapshot standby) option.

3. Perform switchover in a planned maintenance window.

4. Decommission the old primary server hardware.

We always initiate switchover from the primary database. As stated before, switchover can be performed using SQL*Plus, the Data Guard broker, or Enterprise Manager Cloud Control. Whenever we initiate switchover, redo generation will be stopped immediately and no other operations will be allowed to be performed and the current log sequence will be archived, which is also known as **End of Redo (EOR)**. You can monitor the EOR status from v$archived_log. After switchover, we can see when and during which log sequence the switchover has been performed as seen in the following code:

```
SQL> select thread#,sequence#,END_OF_REDO,END_OF_REDO_TYPE from
v$archived_log;
    THREAD#   SEQUENCE# END END_OF_RED
---------- ---------- --- ----------
         1        337 NO
         1        337 NO
         1        338 YES SWITCHOVER
```

If it is an RAC database, redo will be archived from each of the active instances. Once again, the switchover process sends a flag to all of instances for the final redo to be generated by the log switch. If the Data Guard configuration has multiple standby databases, the primary database will be switched to one of the standby databases. In this case, the final online redo logs will be transferred from the primary database to all of the standby databases.

While the process of switchover is going on, restarting of primary and standby databases is expected behavior. Once switchover completes and it is properly configured, redo will automatically be transferred from the new primary database to the new standby database.

One last note about the change in switchover procedures of RAC databases in 11gR2:

- In versions before 11gR2, if the primary and standby were RAC databases, you had to shut down all of the primary instances except one and also shut down all of the standby instances except one. Once you perform switchover successfully, you can bring back the remaining cluster instances for both primary and standby databases.

- In the 11gR2 version, you still have to shut down all primary instances except one. However, it's not mandatory to close standby instances. We can perform switchover while all standby instances are in mount state.

Performing switchover with a physical standby database using SQL*Plus

Now we are going to perform switchover between the primary and standby databases. Performing the switchover operation is not a big deal if we have prepared the environment and verified our configuration. In order to do this, we must control the related initialization parameters on both the primary and standby databases and check the network bandwidth between primary and standby locations. If we are going to use the current standby as the future production database, we must check for the hardware resources of the server. The next exercise will show how we can prepare the Data Guard environment for a switchover.

Time for action – preliminary tests before performing switchover

In order to perform switchover, we have to prepare and verify both the primary and standby databases. Perform the following steps:

1. Check the standby redo logfile status on the primary database as follows:

```
SQL> select group#,member,type from v$logfile where
type='STANDBY';

    GROUP# MEMBER                                             TYPE
---------- ------------------------------------------------- -------
       ..   ........
        14 /u01/app/oracle/oradata/orcl/standby_redo05.log    STANDBY
        16 /u01/app/oracle/oradata/orcl/standby_redo06.log    STANDBY
6 rows selected.
```

Standby redo logfiles should have been created on the primary database; this is so that after performing switchover, the new standby database can receive redo using standby redo logfiles. This will help us save time in the post-configuration steps.

2. Verify the log archive destination on the standby database, which will be active after the switchover and will be used to transfer redo to the new standby database as follows:

```
SQL> show parameter log_archive_dest_2
NAME                 TYPE     VALUE
-------------------- ------   -----------------------------
log_archive_dest_2   string   SERVICE=TURKEY LGWR ASYNC VALID_FOR=
(ONLINE_LOGFILES,PRIMARY_ROLE) DB_UNIQUE_NAME=turkey_un'
```

3. Verify if the temporary files of the temporary tablespaces are created on the standby database. Compare the result of the following query from the primary and standby databases.

```
SQL>  select file_name,bytes/1024/1024 "Size
MB",maxbytes/1024/1024 "MaxSize MB",autoextensible from
dba_temp_files;

FILE_NAME                                   Size MB MaxSize MB AUT
------------------------------------------- ------- ---------- ---
/u02/app/oracle/oradata/orcl/temp01.dbf          20 32767.9844 YES
```

If temporary files don't exist on the standby database or the number and size of temporary files don't match in the primary and standby databases, create or modify the temporary files on the standby database properly.

> If you have created a standby database using the RMAN command DUPLICATE in Oracle 11gR2, the temporary files will be created by default.

4. Check if any offline datafiles exist on primary as well as standby. If they do exist, bring them online using the following code:

```
SQL> select name from v$datafile where status='OFFLINE';
```

5. Verify the status of the redo transport and apply services against any gap and synchronization issues as follows:

```
SQL> select db_unique_name, status, protection_mode,
synchronization_status, synchronized from v$archive_dest_status
where dest_id=2;

DB_UNIQUE_NAME STATUS  PROTECTION_MODE   SYNCHRONIZATION_STATUS SYN
-------------- ------- ----------------- ---------------------- ---
INDIA_UN        VALID  MAXIMUM PERFORMANCE CHECK CONFIGURATION   YES
```

6. In the previous output, you can ignore the synchronization status CHECK CONFIGURATION if the database is in Maximum Performance mode. If the configuration is either Maximum Protection or Availability, the status OK will be returned when there are no synchronization issues. Check the maximum archived log sequences on the primary and standby databases.

- From primary – to obtain the maximum number of archived log sequences for each instance, the following code can be used:

```
SQL> select thread#,max(sequence#) from v$archived_log group
by thread#;
```

```
THREAD# MAX(SEQUENCE#)
---------- --------------
         1            335
```

- From standby – to obtain the maximum number of archived log sequences for each instance, the following code can be used:

```
SQL> select thread#,max(sequence#) from v$archived_log where
applied='YES' group by thread#;

THREAD# MAX(SEQUENCE#)
---------- --------------
                     335
```

7. Now verify if the MRP process is running or not by running the following statement on the standby database:

```
SQL> select thread#,sequence#,process,status,client_process from
v$managed_standby where thread#=1;

THREAD#  SEQUENCE# PROCESS   STATUS        CLIENT_P
---------- ---------- --------- ------------ --------
         1        335 ARCH      CLOSING       ARCH
         1        333 ARCH      CLOSING       ARCH
         1        334 ARCH      CLOSING       ARCH
         1        336 MRP0      APPLYING_LOG N/A
         1        336 RFS       IDLE          LGWR
```

The current sequence 336 is being written into the standby redo logfiles and the MRP process is applying this sequence at the same time.

8. It's also possible to query the v$dataguard_stats view on the standby database to check the synchronization status:

```
SQL> select name,value,time_computed from v$dataguard_stats;

NAME                    VALUE           TIME_COMPUTED
---------------------- -------------- --------------------
transport lag          +00 00:00:00   10/10/2012 15:07:51
apply lag              +00 00:00:00   10/10/2012 15:07:51
apply finish time      +00 00:00:00   10/10/2012 15:07:51
estimated startup time            16  10/10/2012 15:07:51

SQL> !date
Wed Oct 10 15:07:52 IST 2012
```

9. Ensure that no backup jobs are running. Disable the RMAN and EXP/EXPDP backup jobs from CRONTAB if they exist.

10. If the primary and standby databases are monitored with EM Cloud/Grid Control and you're performing switchover using SQL*Plus or Data Guard broker, black out the database until the task is completed.

11. Set the JOB_QUEUE_PROCESSES parameter value to 0 so that no more jobs will be started. After the completion of switchover, reset it with the previous value.

```
SQL> alter system set JOB_QUEUE_PROCESSES=0 scope=both sid='*';
```

12. If the primary database is RAC, ensure all the remaining primary instances except one are shut down. If Active Data Guard is in use, disable it and ensure that all standby instances are in the mount state.

13. It's advisable to take a full backup of the database either from primary or standby.

What just happened?

We have just performed all the preliminary checks before performing switchover. Now we will explain how switchover will be performed, step by step, on primary and standby databases.

Time for action – switchover with a physical standby using SQL*Plus

Perform the following steps using the SQL*Plus connection for both the databases:

1. We have to check whether the primary database is ready for switchover to standby or not. Check the switchover status from the primary database by issuing the following command and verify that the status is either TO STANDBY or SESSIONS ACTIVE:

```
SQL> select switchover_status from v$database;
SWITCHOVER_STATUS
--------------------
TO STANDBY
```

The previous output shows that the primary database is ready to switch to the standby database role. The SESSIONS ACTIVE status indicates that some user sessions are still connected to the database. Such a case does not pose an obstacle for switchover. When output is SESSIONS ACTIVE, you have to perform switchover using the keyword WITH SESSION SHUTDOWN. This is so that those sessions will be terminated during the switchover.

2. Perform the switchover command from the primary database.

```
SQL> alter database commit to switchover to physical standby with
session shutdown;
Database altered.
```

3. This step covers what actually happens during switchover in detail. We need to monitor the alert logfile of both the primary and standby databases in parallel. The different types of logfiles are as follows:

- The switchover-related log from the primary alert logfile:

    ```
    Wed Oct 10 16:12:26 2012
    ```

    ```
    alter database commit to switchover to physical standby with
    session shutdown
    ```

    ```
    ALTER DATABASE COMMIT TO SWITCHOVER TO PHYSICAL STANDBY
    [Process Id: 23631] (TURKEY)
    ```

- Prior to switchover, the current log sequence number is 335. After performing switchover, all the transactions will be written to the online redo logfiles and the log switch will be forced on the primary database.

    ```
    Wed Oct 10 16:12:30 2012
    ```

    ```
    Archived Log entry 764 added for thread 1 sequence 336 ID
    0x4e7c64e3 dest 1:
    ```

    ```
    . . . . . .
    ```

    ```
    Waiting for potential switchover target to become
    synchronized...
    ```

    ```
    Wed Oct 10 16:12:47 2012
    ```

    ```
    Active, synchronized Physical Standby  switchover target has
    been
    ```

- The MRP status on the standby database alert log:

    ```
    Wed Oct 10 16:12:47 2012
    ```

    ```
    Media Recovery Log /u02/app/oracle/flash_recovery_area/
    INDIA_UN/archivelog/2012_10_10/o1_mf_1_337_87bn9793_.arc
    ```

    ```
    Media Recovery Waiting for thread 1 sequence 338
    ```

- The log sequence 337 is also switched and applied on standby. Now all the processes will be terminated and the redo thread of each respective thread will be closed; no further log switches can be performed. At the end, EOR will be generated as follows:

    ```
    ARCH: End-Of-Redo Branch archival of thread 1 sequence 338
    ```

    ```
    Archived Log entry 767 added for thread 1 sequence 338 ID
    0x4e7c64e3 dest 1:
    ```

    ```
    . . . . . . .
    ```

```
Backup controlfile written to trace file /u01/app/oracle/
diag/rdbms/turkey_un/TURKEY/trace/TURKEY_ora_23631.trc
```

```
Archivelog for thread 1 sequence 338 required for standby
recovery
```

```
Switchover: Primary controlfile converted to standby
controlfile succesfully.
```

❑ When EOR is generated, you can view the status of the sequence 338 from the primary database, as shown in the following code:

```
SQL> select thread#,sequence#,END_OF_REDO,END_OF_REDO_TYPE
from v$archived_log;
    THREAD#   SEQUENCE# END END_OF_RED
---------- ---------- --- ----------
          1        337 NO
          1        337 NO
          1        338 YES SWITCHOVER
```

❑ The sequence 338 including EOR will be applied on the standby database (INDIA) as shown in the following code:

```
Resetting standby activation ID 1316775139 (0x4e7c64e3)
```

```
Media Recovery End-Of-Redo indicator encountered
```

```
Media Recovery Applied until change 3085369
```

```
MRP0: Media Recovery Complete: End-Of-REDO (INDIA)
```

```
MRP0: Background Media Recovery process shutdown (INDIA)
```

❑ After performing recovery, the switchover process will be completed on the old primary database (TURKEY) as shown in the following code:

```
Wed Oct 10 16:12:58 2012
```

```
Switchover: Complete - Database shutdown required (TURKEY)
```

```
Completed: alter database commit to switchover to physical
standby with session shutdown
```

❑ During switchover command execution on the primary database, if you monitor the switchover status of the standby database closely, you can capture it as shown in the following code:

```
SQL> select switchover_status from v$database;
SWITCHOVER_STATUS
--------------------
NOT ALLOWED

SQL> /
SWITCHOVER_STATUS
--------------------
```

```
SWITCHOVER PENDING

SQL> /
SWITCHOVER_STATUS
--------------------
TO PRIMARY
```

4. Perform switchover from the standby database. By default the switchover status of the standby database will be NOT ALLOWED. After processing switchover from the primary database, during recovery the status will be changed to SWITCHOVER PENDING. Once End-of-Redo is applied on standby, the database will be ready to become primary as shown in the following code:

```
SQL> SELECT SWITCHOVER_STATUS FROM V$DATABASE;
SWITCHOVER_STATUS
--------------------
TO PRIMARY
```

5. Run the SWITCHOVER command on the standby database as shown in the following code:

```
SQL> ALTER DATABASE COMMIT TO SWITCHOVER TO PRIMARY WITH SESSION
SHUTDOWN;
Database altered.
```

On the alert logfile you will see the following:

```
Wed Oct 10 18:01:15 2012

ALTER DATABASE COMMIT TO SWITCHOVER TO PRIMARY WITH SESSION
SHUTDOWN

ALTER DATABASE SWITCHOVER TO PRIMARY (INDIA)

Maximum wait for role transition is 15 minutes.

. . . . . . . . . . . . .

SwitchOver after complete recovery through change 3085369

. . . . . . . . . . . . . .

Standby became primary SCN: 3085367

Switchover: Complete - Database mounted as primary
```

6. Now, from the new primary database (INDIA), you can check at what SCN the standby database role been changed, as shown in the following code:

```
SQL> select CURRENT_SCN,STANDBY_BECAME_PRIMARY_SCN from
v$database;
CURRENT_SCN STANDBY_BECAME_PRIMARY_SCN
----------- --------------------------
    3156173                    3085367
```

7. Change the open mode of the new primary to READ-WRITE. After successful switchover from standby to the primary database, the instance status will be MOUNTED as shown in the following code:

```
SQL> select db_unique_name,database_role,open_mode from
v$database;
DB_UNIQUE_NAME         DATABASE_ROLE     OPEN_MODE
-------------------    ---------------   -------------------

INDIA_UN               PRIMARY           MOUNTED
```

Open the database with the following statement:

```
SQL> alter database open;
Database altered.
```

8. Restart the new standby database and start Redo Apply. After switchover, the new standby instance will be in the NOMOUNT status.

```
SQL> select status from v$instance;
STATUS
-----------
STARTED
```

Now perform a clean shutdown with SHUTDOWN IMMEDIATE and then start up the new standby database in the READ ONLY mode if Active Data Guard will be used. Then start Redo Apply on the standby database (TURKEY)

```
SQL> alter database recover managed standby database using current
logfile disconnect from session;
Database altered.

SQL> select db_unique_name,open_mode from v$database;
DB_UNIQUE_NAME   OPEN_MODE
--------------   -------------------
turkey_un        READ ONLY WITH APPLY
```

If you have multiple standby databases in the Data Guard configuration, start Redo Apply on each standby database.

 After starting Redo Apply on another standby database, whenever EOR is applied on the standby database, the MRP process will be terminated immediately. Then you have to start Redo Apply again.

Performing switchover with a physical standby database using broker

Switchover can also be performed using the Data Guard broker. Managing switchover with the broker is very simple. In SQL*Plus, we have to manage commands from both the primary and standby databases. When using the broker, the SWITCHOVER command is executed from either the primary or the standby database.

Time for action – switchover with a physical standby using broker

1. If the primary database is RAC and you perform switchover with the broker, it will shut down all the remaining instances except one; and if there are any issues in terminating the instances, the switchover will exit without success. So ensure that all the primary instances are down except the one.

2. Even though the broker will verify the state of the both the primary and standby databases, it's recommended to check the database state manually as follows:

    ```
    DGMGRL> show configuration;

    Configuration - PACKT

      Protection Mode: MaxPerformance

      Databases:

        turkey_un - Primary database

        INDIA_UN  - Physical standby database

    Fast-Start Failover: DISABLED

    Configuration Status:

    SUCCESS
    ```

3. Now connect to the DGMGRL and issue the command as shown in the following screenshot:

    ```
    DGMGRL> switchover to 'INDIA_UN';
    Performing switchover NOW, please wait...
    New primary database "INDIA_UN" is opening...
    Operation requires shutdown of instance "TURKEY" on database "turkey_un"
    Shutting down instance "TURKEY"...
    ORA-01109: database not open

    Database dismounted.
    ORACLE instance shut down.
    Operation requires startup of instance "TURKEY" on database "turkey_un"
    Starting instance "TURKEY"...
    ORACLE instance started.
    Database mounted.
    Database opened.
    Switchover succeeded, new primary is "INDIA_UN"
    DGMGRL> exit
    ```

When performing a switchover, connect the database to the DGMGRL using a complete password such as `connect sys/******`, because DGMGRL doesn't support OS authentication.

4. After performing the switchover, the broker configuration file is updated regarding the role transition.

```
2012-10-11 13:08:31.463 02001000  1799321493 DMON: Switchover -
updated Seq.MIV to 1.0 (2.1.1799321493), writing metadata to "/
u01/home/oracle/product/11.2.0/db_1/dbs/dr2INDIA_UN.dat"

2012-10-11 13:08:31.477 02001000  1799321493 DMON: posting primary
instances for SWITCHOVER phase 3
```

5. After updating the configuration file, the broker configuration restarts the new primary database in read-write mode and the new standby database will be terminated and restarted with the previous configuration; that is, the `Read Only With Apply` mode.

6. Now, after performing the switchover, check the configuration status using DGMGRL as follows:

```
DGMGRL> show configuration;

Configuration - PACKT

  Protection Mode: MaxPerformance

  Databases:

    INDIA_UN  - Primary database

    turkey_un - Physical standby database

Fast-Start Failover: DISABLED

Configuration Status:

SUCCESS
```

What just happened?

We have discussed how to perform switchover from the primary database to the standby database and vice versa using SQL*Plus and also the Data Guard broker utility DGMGRL.

Performing switchover with a physical standby database using EM Cloud Control

As discussed at the beginning of this chapter, we can use the Enterprise Manager Cloud Control Data Guard administration interface to perform the switchover operation. This is an easy but less controlled way of performing a switchover. Let's see how we use Cloud Control in this context.

Time for action – switchover with a physical standby using EM Cloud Control

Assuming a Cloud Control installation and Data Guard integration is already set up, perform the following steps on the Cloud Control interface.

1. On the Data Guard Administration home page, click on **Switchover** as shown in the following screenshot:

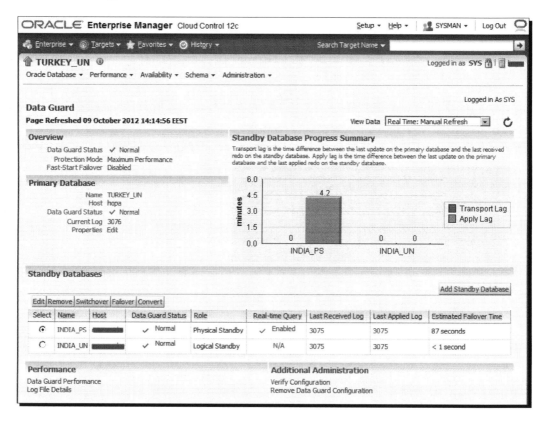

2. Enter credentials to connect the standby and primary hosts.

3. On the confirmation page, click on **Yes** to start the switchover. At the bottom of the screen, check **Swap Monitoring Settings** if you want the current Enterprise Manager monitoring settings (including metric thresholds) for the primary and standby databases to be swapped after the role change, as shown in the following screenshot:

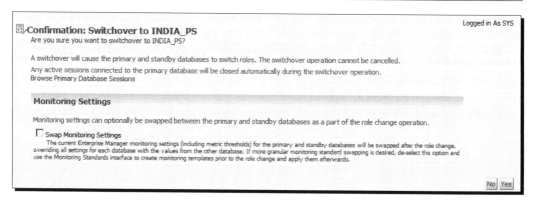

4. We'll see the switchover processing window on the next screen. A notification will appear, **Switchover completed successfully**, when the process is completed successfully. The following screenshot is the processing screen:

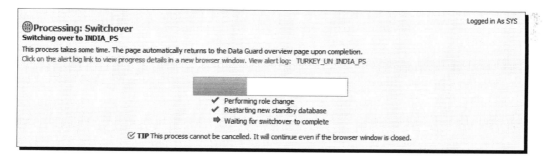

 Similarly, we can use the **Failover** button on the Data Guard Administration home page to initiate a failover.

Performing switchover with a logical standby database using SQL*Plus

So far we have explained the switchover procedure between primary and physical standby databases. In the same manner, we can perform a switchover between the primary database and the logical standby database. However, there are some differences in this operation.

For versions above 11g, there's no need to shut down either the primary or the logical standby database for a switchover.

Time for action – switchover with a logical standby database using SQL*Plus

Now we will see a step-by-step approach to perform a switchover between the primary and the logical standby database:

1. Check the switchover status of the primary database. Ensure that the status is either TO STANDBY or SESSIONS ACTIVE; if so, you are safe to perform a switchover as shown in the following code:

```
SQL> select switchover_status from v$database;
SWITCHOVER_STATUS
--------------------
TO STANDBY
```

 In case of RESOLVABLE GAP, wait until SQL was applied on the logical standby database; for other statuses, troubleshoot and fix the synchronization for the switchover process to be successful.

2. Prepare the primary database for switchover. Execute the following command from the primary database so that the current primary database will be accepted to perform a switchover to a logical standby database:

```
SQL> alter database prepare to switchover to logical standby;
Database altered.
```

On the primary alert log, issue the following command:

```
Fri Oct 12 08:50:50 2012
alter database prepare to switchover to logical standby
ALTER DATABASE PREPARE TO SWITCHOVER TO LOGICAL STANDBY (TURKEY)
Completed: alter database prepare to switchover to logical standby
```

3. After issuing the previous command, the switchover status will be PREPARING SWITCHOVER.

4. Prepare the logical standby database for switchover. After issuing the switchover initiation command from the primary database, you can execute the following code from the standby database:

```
SQL> alter database prepare to switchover to primary;
Database altered.
```

On the standby alert log, issue the following command:

```
Fri Oct 12 08:51:55 2012
alter database prepare to switchover to primary
ALTER DATABASE SWITCHOVER TO PRIMARY (INDIA)
ALTER DATABASE PREPARE TO SWITCHOVER TO PRIMARY (INDIA)
```

5. Perform the switchover from the primary database. After performing step 4, the switchover status in the current primary database will change from PREPARING SWITCHOVER to TO LOGICAL STANDBY. In this stage, both the databases wait for acknowledgment from each other. Now check the switchover status on the primary database as shown in the following lines:

```
SQL> select switchover_status from v$database;
SWITCHOVER_STATUS
--------------------
TO LOGICAL STANDBY
```

6. You must ensure that there are no active transactions during switchover. Therefore, clean up the transactions and proceed to switchover over. The SWITCHOVER command waits until this transaction is complete, as shown in the following code:

```
SQL> select addr,status,flag from v$transaction;
ADDR              STATUS             FLAG
---------------- ----------------- ----------
000000008EF5A950 ACTIVE                 7683

SQL> select username,status from v$session where username is not
null and username not in ('SYS','PUBLIC');
USERNAME   STATUS
---------- --------
PACKT      ACTIVE
```

7. Even after you perform the previous step, the session is still in the ACTIVE mode. Let's see what happens in the alert logfile when the switchover is issued, as follows:

```
SQL> alter database commit to switchover to logical standby;
```

On the primary alert logfile you will see the following:

```
Fri Oct 12 14:51:12 2012
alter database commit to switchover to logical standby
ALTER DATABASE COMMIT TO SWITCHOVER TO LOGICAL STANDBY (TURKEY)
.........
Fri Oct 12 14:52:25 2012
Waiting for transactions in flight at scn 0x0000.003337d6 to
complete
```

Perform commit from the user session as follows:

```
SQL> show user
USER is "PACKT"
SQL> commit;
Commit complete.
```

After performing commit from the user session, the switchover will be processed successfully and we'll see `Database altered` as the output on the session in which we ran the switchover statement, as shown in the following code:

```
SQL> alter database commit to switchover to logical standby;
Database altered.
```

On the primary alert logfile you can perform the following:

LOGSTDBY: Switchover complete (TURKEY)

LOGSTDBY: enabling scheduler job queue processes.

JOBQ: re-enabling CJQ0

Completed: alter database commit to switchover to logical standby

Note that during switchover, log apply services will be stopped on the logical standby database. Now check the latest status on the former primary database using the following code:

```
SQL> select db_unique_name,database_role,open_mode from
v$database;
DB_UNIQUE_NAME   DATABASE_ROLE      OPEN_MODE
---------------  -----------------  --------------------
turkey_un        LOGICAL STANDBY    READ WRITE
```

8. Perform the switchover from the logical standby database.

9. We have completed the required steps on the primary database. Now check the status on the current logical standby database (INDIA) and issue the following switchover command:

```
SQL> select switchover_status from v$database;
SWITCHOVER_STATUS
--------------------
TO PRIMARY
SQL> alter database commit to switchover to primary;

Database altered.
```

The switchover from the logical standby to the primary was successful, as can be seen in the following command-line output:

```
Fri Oct 12 15:04:43 2012
alter database commit to switchover to primary
ALTER DATABASE SWITCHOVER TO PRIMARY (INDIA)
ALTER DATABASE COMMIT TO SWITCHOVER TO PRIMARY (INDIA)
LOGSTDBY: Successful close of the current log stream:
LOGSTDBY:   primary:        [1316772835]
. . . . . . . . . . . .
Completed: alter database commit to switchover to primary
```

10. During switchover, there will be zero data loss and the session will still be in the ACTIVE mode. The following output shows that the session is still in the ACTIVE mode on the former primary database:

```
SQL> select sysdate from dual;
SYSDATE
-------------------
12-OCT-2012 15:10:10
SQL> show user
USER is "PACKT"
SQL>  select username,logon_time from v$session where username is
not null and username not in ('SYS','PUBLIC');
USERNAME   LOGON_TIME
---------- --------------------
PACKT      12-OCT-2012 14:44:06
```

11. Check the status of new primary database using the following code:

```
SQL>  select db_unique_name,database_role,open_mode from
v$database;
DB_UNIQUE_NAME  DATABASE_ROLE     OPEN_MODE
--------------- ----------------- --------------------
india_un        PRIMARY           READ WRITE
```

12. Start SQL Apply and monitor the logical standby database. Both the new primary database and the logical standby database are ready. Now start SQL Apply on the new logical standby database as follows:

```
SQL> !ps -ef|grep lsp
oracle   24824   8569  0 16:06 pts/1    00:00:00 /bin/bash -c ps
-ef|grep lsp
SQL> alter database start logical standby apply immediate;
Database altered.
```

```
SQL>  !ps -ef|grep lsp
oracle   24860    1  1 16:08 ?        00:00:01 ora_lsp0_TURKEY
oracle   24914  8569  0 16:09 pts/1   00:00:00 /bin/bash -c ps
-ef|grep lsp
```

On the standby alert logfile you will see the following:

```
Fri Oct 12 16:08:01 2012
alter database start logical standby apply immediate
ALTER DATABASE START LOGICAL STANDBY APPLY (TURKEY)
with optional part IMMEDIATE
Attempt to start background Logical Standby process
Fri Oct 12 16:08:01 2012
LSP0 started with pid=35, OS id=24860
Completed: alter database start logical standby apply immediate
```

What just happened?

We've seen the step-by-step approach to perform a switchover between the primary and logical standby database using SQL*Plus. We've also monitored switchover transactions by tracking the alert logfile on both databases.

Pop quiz

Q1. You've prepared either the primary or the standby database to perform switchover and then you have decided not to perform switchover. Is it possible to cancel it?

Performing switchover with a logical standby database using broker

Managing any role transition or other administrative tasks of Data Guard with the broker is quite easy. Now we will see the step-by-step approach of a switchover between primary and logical standby databases using the DGMGRL utility.

Time for action – switchover with a logical standby using broker

Perform the following steps to change the roles of the primary and logical standby databases:

1. Check the configuration of Data Guard. In the broker's configuration, we have one primary database and one logical standby database already configured. Ensure that the status is SUCCESS before performing a switchover as shown in the following code:

```
DGMGRL> show configuration;
Configuration - PACKT
```

```
Protection Mode: MaxPerformance
Databases:
   INDIA_UN      - Primary database
   turkey_un     - Logical standby database
Fast-Start Failover: DISABLED
Configuration Status:
SUCCESS
```

2. Perform a switchover using the DGMGRL command. Before performing switchover, connect to the DGMGRL utility using the complete username and password of the SYS user instead of connecting with / as shown in the following code:

```
DGMGRL>  connect sys/*******
Connected.
```

Once authenticated, initiate the switchover with the following command as shown in the screenshot:

```
DGMGRL> switchover to 'turkey_un';
Performing switchover NOW, please wait...
Switchover succeeded, new primary is "turkey_un"
DGMGRL>
```

On the alert logfile you will see the following:

```
2012-10-12 17:24:03.052 02001000   1399597225 DMON: posting standby
instances for SWITCHOVER phase 5

2012-10-12 17:24:03.053                       INSV: Received
message for inter-instance publication

. . . . . . . . . . .

2012-10-12 17:23:05.766 02001000   1399597225 DMON: dispersing
message to standbys for SWITCHOVER phase BEGIN
```

3. Check the configuration of Data Guard once again. After performing a switchover, the broker will start SQL Apply on the new logical standby database as shown in the following code:

```
[oracle@oracle-ha dbs]$ ps -ef|grep lsp
oracle   14604    1  0 17:23 ?       00:00:02 ora_lsp0_INDIA
oracle   15232  6342  0 17:31 pts/1   00:00:00 grep lsp

DGMGRL> show configuration;
Configuration - PACKT
  Protection Mode: MaxPerformance
  Databases:
```

```
      turkey_un - Primary database
      INDIA_UN  - Logical standby database
Fast-Start Failover: DISABLED
Configuration Status:
SUCCESS
```

What just happened?

We have successfully completed the switchover operation in a logical standby Data Guard configuration using the Data Guard broker.

Failover

Failover is initiated when a serious problem exists on the primary database, making it inaccessible. This problem generally arises from hardware or software errors on the server or storage layer; also, a disaster may cause complete or partial loss of services. In such cases, we can convert a standby database role to primary by performing failover and continue providing it with production database service. Performing a Data Guard failover operation for production purposes is a serious consideration and needs a lot of caution. The following considerations are important in this context:

- ◆ Failover decision must be taken with regard to the service **Recovery Time Objective (RTO)** value.

- ◆ The standby database hardware must be powerful enough to sustain production load.

- ◆ Multiple standby databases are recommended; this is so that data protection continues after a failover operation.

- ◆ If the flashback database is not enabled on the primary database, after a failover it's not possible to include the old primary database into the Data Guard configuration again. This means we'll have to restore the database on the primary side. If flashback is enabled, it's possible to reinstate the failed primary database without a full restore operation. The following diagram explains the failover process:

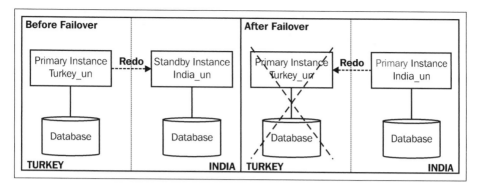

Before performing failover, ensure that all the available redo is being applied on the standby database for minimum data loss. Remember that it's also possible to guarantee a zero data loss failover by using the Maximum Protection mode. Also note that once the failover process is finished, the new primary database will be started in Maximum Performance mode even though your previous Data Guard protection mode is either Maximum Protection or Maximum Availability.

Failover can be performed manually with SQL*Plus, the Data Guard broker, Cloud Control, or automatically using the Fast Start failover with an observer. In automatic failover, the observer will monitor the state of the primary database and all the standby databases of the Data Guard configuration. Whenever the primary database is not accessible, the observer will wait according to the predefined parameter `FastStartFailoverThreshold` and then perform the failover to the standby database.

As stated before, if the flashback database is enabled and the standby database role is changed to primary by FSFO and if the observer reestablishes the connection to the failed primary database as well as reinstates it as a new standby database, the new primary database starts sending redo to the new standby database.

Performing failover with a physical standby database

Just as with the switchover operation, the failover operation can be performed on both the physical and logical standby databases. We'll now see both scenarios.

Time for action – failover with a physical standby database using SQL*Plus

Follow these steps to complete a failover on the physical standby Data Guard environment:

1. If you're able to mount a primary database, perform the following command to flush the redo from the primary online redo logfiles:

```
SQL> alter system flush redo to INDIA_UN;
```

Use `DB_UNIQUE_NAME` of the standby database so that redo will be sent to the respective standby database.

2. Check the status of both the primary and standby databases. With the primary database in the MOUNT state, check the maximum archive log sequence that has been generated as shown in the following code:

```
SQL> select max(sequence#) from v$archived_log;
MAX(SEQUENCE#)
-------------
          462
```

3. If the primary database is inaccessible, refer to the alert logfile for the latest log switch sequence or go to the archive log location and check the maximum sequence number as shown in the following command:

```
Fri Oct 12 22:20:30 2012

Thread 1 advanced to log sequence 462 (LGWR switch)

Current log# 1 seq# 462 mem# 0: /u01/app/oracle/oradata/orcl/
redo01.log

. . . . . . . . . .

Archived Log entry 1064 added for thread 1 sequence 462 ID
0x4eede1f7 dest 1:
```

Optionally, you can use the following:

```
[oracle@oracle-primary 2012_10_12]$ls -alrt

-rw-r----- 1 oracle oinstall  40261120 Oct 12 22:20 o1_
mf_1_461_87j11pq3_.arc

-rw-r----- 1 oracle oinstall  41197056 Oct 12 23:08 o1_
mf_1_462_87jodh9n_.arc
```

The maximum archive sequence generated is 462, which we can see by querying `v$archived_log`, the alert logfile, or the file systems.

4. Now check the maximum sequence applied on the standby database using the following code:.

```
SQL>  select max(sequence#) from v$archived_log where
applied='YES';
MAX(SEQUENCE#)
-------------
          449
```

There are 13 archive logs that are not applied on the standby database. If they're not shipped from primary, you should transfer those archived logfiles and register and apply them to the standby database. If shipped but not applied, you must start Redo Apply on the standby database.

If the primary server is completely unavailable, you have to perform recovery on the standby database until the maximum transported archive log sequence.

5. Initiate failover by stopping Redo Apply and running the `recover` command with the `finish force` option on the standby database as shown in the following command:

```
SQL> alter database recover managed standby database cancel;
Database altered.
SQL> alter database recover managed standby database finish force;
Database altered.
```

> The FINISH keyword is used for failover and recovers the current standby redo logfiles. The FORCE keyword is used to terminate RFS processes immediately so that failover will not wait for them to exit.

On the alert logfile you will see the following:

```
Terminal Recovery: log 10 reserved for thread 1 sequence 463
Recovery of Online Redo Log: Thread 1 Group 10 Seq 463 Reading mem
0
   Mem# 0: /u02/app/oracle/oradata/orcl/standby_redo01.log
Identified End-Of-Redo for thread 1 sequence 463
Incomplete Recovery applied until change 3476339 time 10/12/2012
23:08:22
Media Recovery Complete (INDIA)
Terminal Recovery: successful completion
```

> If the recovery command raises an error because of a possible gap, try to resolve it. If this is not possible, continue failover with the following command and proceed to step 5.
>
> ```
> SQL> alter database activate physical standby
> database;
> ```
>
> If the `recover` command completes successfully, continue with the next step.

6. Complete failover to the physical standby database by converting it from the standby role to primary as follows:

```
SQL> alter database commit to switchover to primary with session
shutdown;
Database altered.
```

On the alert logfile you will see the following:

```
Standby became primary SCN: 3476337
Fri Oct 12 23:34:36 2012
Setting recovery target incarnation to 3
Switchover: Complete - Database mounted as primary
Completed: alter database commit to switchover to primary
```

After that, perform the following code:

```
SQL> select db_unique_name,database_role,standby_became_primary_
scn from v$database;
DB_UNIQUE_NAME        DATABASE_ROLE     STANDBY_BECAME_PRIMARY_SCN
-------------------   ---------------   --------------------------
INDIA_UN              PRIMARY                           3476337
```

7. After performing failover, the new primary database will be in the MOUNT state. Shut down and start up the new primary database as shown in the following code:

```
SQL> SHUTDOWN IMMEDIATE;
SQL> STARTUP;
```

Have a go hero

We have just performed a failover to a physical standby database. Now go ahead and perform a failover to the logical standby database using SQL*Plus. In this case, after step 1 and 2, you just need to use the following command on the logical standby to perform a failover:

```
SQL> ALTER DATABASE ACTIVATE LOGICAL STANDBY DATABASE FINISH APPLY;
```

Performing failover with a logical standby database

Performing failover with a logical standby database has some disadvantages because of the following points:

- A logical standby database functions with SQL Apply instead of Redo Apply and there are limitations to accept the incoming DML from primary and also unsupported data types. So we can't guarantee that all the changes from the primary database have been successfully applied on the logical standby database.

- Once you perform failover, you have to recreate other standby databases for the configuration.

So it's not recommended to perform failover to the logical standby database if it's possible to perform failover to a physical standby. Also, depending on the RTO, RMAN restore and recovery is preferred over failover to a logical standby.

Time for action – failover with a logical standby using broker

Follow these steps to perform failover to a logical standby database using the Data Guard broker:

1. Check both the primary and logical standby databases' status. If the primary database is completely unavailable, you can check the configuration status from the logical standby database as shown in the following code:

```
DGMGRL> show configuration;
Configuration - PACKT
  Protection Mode: MaxPerformance
  Databases:
    turkey_un    - Primary database
    INDIA_UN     - Logical standby database
Fast-Start Failover: DISABLED
Configuration Status:
ORA-12514: TNS:listener does not currently know of service
requested in connect descriptor
ORA-16625: cannot reach database "turkey_UN"
DGM-17017: unable to determine configuration status
```

2. Perform the failover to the logical standby database. Connect to the DGMGRL utility of the logical standby database and issue the command shown in the following screenshot to perform failover:

```
DGMGRL> failover to 'INDIA_UN';
Performing failover NOW, please wait...
Failover succeeded, new primary is "INDIA_UN"
DGMGRL>
```

On the alert logfile, you will see the following:

```
2012-10-13 16:00:00.862                    Executing SQL [ALTER
DATABASE activate logical standby database finish apply]

2012-10-13 16:00:02.348                    SQL [ALTER DATABASE
activate logical standby database finish apply] Executed
successfully

2012-10-13 16:00:02.354                    RSM: refreshing
IncarnationTable internal property. New value is '2,3166193,796392
156,1*1,3166192,796392049,0#'

2012-10-13 16:00:02.366                    Database Resource
SetState succeeded
```

 During failover to a physical or logical standby database using broker, you can use the IMMEDIATE option to perform failover without waiting for applying any redo. You can use the following command:

DGMGRL> FAILOVER TO <DB_UNIQUE_NAME> IMMEDIATE

3. Check the status of the new primary database. After a successful failover, the new primary database will be in READ WRITE mode as shown in the following code:

```
SQL> select db_unique_name,database_role,open_mode from
v$database;
DB_UNIQUE_NAME        DATABASE_ROLE     OPEN_MODE
-------------------   ----------------  -------------------
india_un              PRIMARY           READ WRITE
DGMGRL> show configuration;
Configuration - PACKT
  Protection Mode: MaxPerformance
  Databases:
    INDIA_UN      - Primary database
    turkey_un     - Logical standby database (disabled)
       ORA-16661: the standby database needs to be reinstated
Fast-Start Failover: DISABLED
Configuration Status:
SUCCESS
```

What just happened?

We have discussed how to perform failover to a physical standby database and a logical standby database. To perform this, we have used both SQL*Plus and the Data Guard broker.

Summary

In this chapter, we focused on planned outages, unplanned outages, and how to perform role transitions against them. We've seen the key points and all the possible techniques to perform role transitions, which are SQL*Plus, the Data Guard broker, and Enterprise Manager 12*c* Cloud Control.

In the next chapter, we'll learn about configuring and using Active Data Guard and snapshot standby database. These are very important features of Data Guard. Also, some advanced topics such as cascading standby databases, advanced compression, cross platform configuration, and Data Guard tuning will be covered.

7

Active Data Guard, Snapshot Standby, and Advanced Techniques

Active Data Guard and snapshot standby databases are two very important new features of Oracle 11g. With Active Data Guard, it's possible to use a physical standby database read-only mode while the replication is ongoing. The snapshot standby feature is used to run a standby database in a read-write mode for testing purposes where all the changes made to the snapshot standby can be reverted. This chapter includes details of these features along with several other advanced techniques.

The following features will be covered in this chapter:

- ◆ Oracle Active Data Guard
- ◆ Using snapshot standby databases
- ◆ Cascade standby database and more options
- ◆ Oracle Advanced Compression
- ◆ Preparing the standby database on a cross-platform
- ◆ Data Guard tuning

Oracle Active Data Guard

Earlier versions of Oracle 11*g* standby databases have limitations as they can be used either for a recovery purpose or for a read-only purpose without recovery. From 11*g*R1 onwards, Oracle introduced more features, and standby databases can now work in recovery even in an open status. While recovery is in progress, real-time data can be accessible to the users just as production data is. Real time query can be used if Oracle Active Data Guard option has been purchased. Apart from that, some additional benefits of Active Data Guard are as follows:

♦ You can use applications on Active Data Guard and the additional processing from the production can be reduced so that both primary and standby databases can be utilized.

♦ If any ad-hoc jobs are running on Active Data Guard and if they don't meet the SLA provided by the STANDBY_MAX_DATA_DELAY parameter using triggers, they can immediately be redirected to the primary database.

♦ Automatic block recovery. If there are any corrupted blocks in the primary database, Active Data Guard will copy the good state of the block from standby and it will be recovered in the primary database.

♦ Active Data Guard can work in both ways to recover corrupted blocks.

♦ Zero data loss can be achieved.

♦ You can load off the EXPDP jobs to the standby database.

♦ You can schedule RMAN jobs from the standby with a real-time query.

♦ You can use Statspack from the standby database.

♦ You can monitor **Active Session History (ASH)** reports.

Why Active Data Guard?

Most of the customers choose the Active Data Guard license for both disaster protection and also for securing read-only access to the applications. Note that all the applications (for example, SAP) don't support Active Data Guard; further, we will discuss several top applications that support Active Data Guard. If we pick any live database, most of the query ratios will be of the read-only (select queries) operations and there will be few read and write (insert/update/delete/merge) transactions. I would like to highlight a sample example in order to differentiate between read-only and read-write operations in any business. There are no restrictions on the storage of data types, DML, or DDL operations. Reports can view the latest data from the standby as real-time apply is on. Moreover, you can simplify tuning and Active Data Guard that is certified with Exadata.

The following are the basic requirements and licenses that you must have in order to use Data Guard for a standby system:

- Server hardware
- Power systems
- An operating system (Linux/Unix, Windows) license
- Oracle Enterprise Edition license

These all are the necessary requirements needed to build a standby system. You must have already made lot of effort to configure a standby database for high availability; thus it is worth to add an additional license of Active Data Guard. Of course you can question, why should I choose Active Data Guard and what benefits can we gain from this additional costly step?

In any business, as we discussed earlier, most of the operations are not transactional (Select statements). For read-only queries, if 1000 user sessions are concurrently accessing the production database and the resources are allocated to the user sessions, then the users can either perform a physical or logical I/O depending on the data being cached into a buffer cache. Even though you have a standby database performing all of the previous transactions/operations from a production database, it can have additional disadvantages as follows:

- Load average
- CPU busy
- Swapping/paging
- System calls

The following diagram illustrates a database without Active Data Guard:

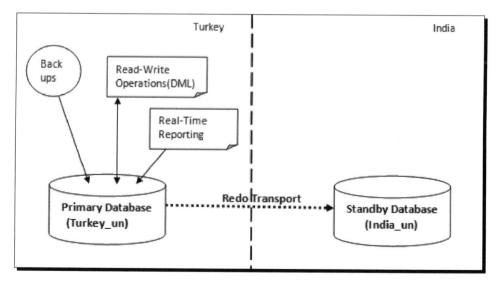

Apart from read-only and read-write operations on the database, there may be other scheduled backup jobs configured on the database such as EXPDP, RMAN backup jobs, and gathering of statistics on a daily or round-robin basis. In the previous diagram, the standby site is just performing recovery, and there will be no load until and unless a switchover takes place in case of disaster recovery. Active Data Guard is not limited to simply reporting; you can use the OLTP query workload with the required modifications on the applications. Overall, it's a simple administration process because no tasks are required to detect and resolve the data conflicts, and no troubleshooting is necessary for any trail errors. Of course, you may need to adjust the settings and tune the old standby database in case the primary database is unavailable. Oracle Active Data Guard can be configured from a primary standalone to a standalone database or from an RAC primary to a standby standalone database or from an RAC primary to RAC standby databases also. In order to maintain business continuity in case of disaster recovery, we can implement Active Data Guard with fast-start failover. By implementing Active Data Guard, it can enable the flexible use of resources for multiple purposes. The following diagram illustrates the discussed points:

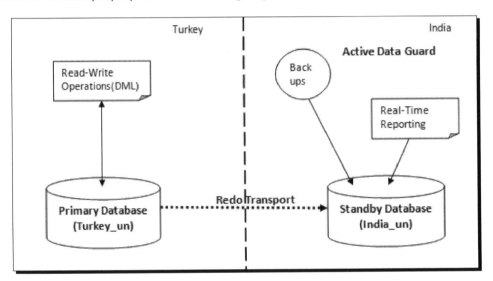

The previous diagram explains how to eliminate contention between read-only and read-write operations. Now we will discuss what are the jobs that can be moved from the primary database if Active Data Guard is enabled and how to offload these operations to a physical standby database(s) to avoid additional processing from the production database. In this chapter, we have explained with examples how to use ASH reports with Active Data Guard and other options. It can be further understood with the help of the following diagram:

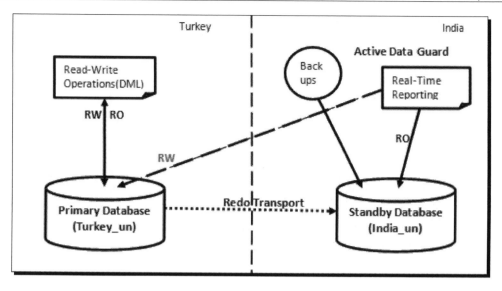

Even though applications are used from a standby system, they can connect to a primary database anytime whenever read-write operations are required.

Oracle Data Guard license

Before you implement and use Active Data Guard, it is necessary to understand the licensing involved with this feature. If you are implementing Active Data Guard, then both the primary and standby servers must be licensed. For the licensing prices, you must always visit Oracle Technology price list for the Active Data Guard. The price may vary depending on the license of the named user or processor license. If licensing is done by the processor, the licenses may not match due to variance in core factors between the times the respective programs were licensed. For any future reference, you can check for the latest updates on `http://www.oracle.com/in/corporate/pricing/index.html`.

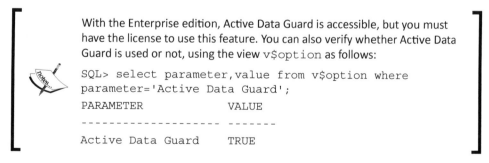

With the Enterprise edition, Active Data Guard is accessible, but you must have the license to use this feature. You can also verify whether Active Data Guard is used or not, using the view `v$option` as follows:

```
SQL> select parameter,value from v$option where
parameter='Active Data Guard';
PARAMETER               VALUE
-------------------- -------
Active Data Guard    TRUE
```

Enabling Active Data Guard

Enabling Active Data Guard is not a challenging task; it requires minimal effort. Here we are not making any changes at the database level, we are just enhancing the option of the Enterprise edition by enabling Active Data Guard. There are no changes to be made to the primary database, and we just need to ensure that redo transport is an LGWR process so that real-time data can be viewed by the users.

Time for action – enabling Active Data Guard if Redo Apply is running using SQL *PLUS

1. If you have previously upgraded your database from Version 10gRx to 11gRx, then in order to use Active Data Guard the compatible parameter must at least be set to 11.0.0 as shown in the following query:

```
SQL> show parameter compatible
NAME                                 TYPE        VALUE
------------------------------------ ----------- --------------------
compatible                           string      11.2.0.0.0
```

2. If you are using Active Data Guard for the first time, your standby database will definitely be in the MOUNT status and MRP will be in progress; hence, cancel MRP. After cancelling MRP, make sure MRP is not running any more either through the OS level grep commands or the v$managed_standby view as shown in the following query:

```
SQL> select db_unique_name,open_mode from v$database;
DB_UNIQUE_NA OPEN_MODE
------------ --------------------
INDIA_UN     MOUNTED
SQL> alter database recover managed standby database cancel;
Database altered.
SQL> !ps -ef|grep mrp
oracle   27188  5882  0 11:56 pts/1     00:00:00 /bin/bash -c ps
-ef|grep mrp
oracle   27190 27188  0 11:56 pts/1     00:00:00 grep mrp
```

3. Open the database in the Read-Only mode to enable Active Data Guard as follows:

```
SQL> alter database open ;
Database altered.
SQL>
SQL> select db_unique_name,open_mode from v$database;
```

```
DB_UNIQUE_NA OPEN_MODE
------------ --------------------
INDIA_UN      READ ONLY
Now restart Redo Apply
SQL> alter database recover managed standby database using current
logfile disconnect from session;
Database altered.
```

4. Verify whether redo-apply is enabled or not using the following query:

```
SQL> select process,status,sequence# from v$managed_standby where
process like '%MRP%';
PROCESS    STATUS         SEQUENCE#
--------- ------------- ----------
MRP0       APPLYING_LOG       522
```

Time for action – enabling Active Data Guard if the standby database is shut down

1. If the standby database is completely shut down, use the following steps to enable Active Data Guard. Now start the database normally as follows:

```
[oracle@oracle-stby ~]$ sqlplus / as sysdba
SQL*Plus: Release 11.2.0.1.0 Production on Tue Nov 6 12:13:27 2012
Copyright (c) 1982, 2009, Oracle.  All rights reserved.
Connected to an idle instance.
SQL> startup
ORACLE instance started.
Total System Global Area  818401280 bytes
Fixed Size                  2217792 bytes
Variable Size             528484544 bytes
Database Buffers          285212672 bytes
Redo Buffers                2486272 bytes
Database mounted.
Database opened.
SQL>
```

2. Once the database is opened successfully, by default it will be in the `Read Only` mode because it's a standby control file. Now start Redo Apply as follows:

```
SQL> select db_unique_name,open_mode from v$database;
DB_UNIQUE_NAME   OPEN_MODE
--------------- --------------------
INDIA_UN         READ ONLY
SQL>
SQL> alter database recover managed standby database using current
logfile disconnect from session;
Database altered.
SQL>
```

Time for action – enabling Active Data Guard using broker

If Data Guard is managed using a broker, it is always simple and even easier to manage it from Oracle 11*g*R2. When both broker and MRP are running on the standby, you can open the database at any time for reporting purposes.

1. Check the configuration and state of the database as follows:

```
DGMGRL> show configuration;

Configuration - PACKT

  Protection Mode: MaxPerformance

  Databases:

    turkey_un - Primary database

    INDIA_UN  - Physical standby database

Fast-Start Failover: DISABLED

Configuration Status:

SUCCESS

DGMGRL>


SQL> select db_unique_name,open_mode from v$database;

DB_UNIQUE_NAME   OPEN_MODE
--------------- --------------------
INDIA_UN         MOUNTED

SQL>
SQL> !ps -ef|grep mrp
oracle    4686    1  0 16:31 ?        00:00:00 ora_mrp0_INDIA
```

```
oracle    4815  3948  0 16:35 pts/1    00:00:00 /bin/bash -c ps
-ef|grep mrp
```

Open Database for the use of Active Data Guard

```
SQL> alter database open read only;
```

Database altered.

```
SQL>
```

```
DGMGRL> show configuration;
```

Configuration - PACKT

  Protection Mode: MaxPerformance

  Databases:

    turkey_un - Primary database

    INDIA_UN - Physical standby database

Fast-Start Failover: DISABLED

Configuration Status:

SUCCESS

```
DGMGRL>
```

From the previous command, it looks as if the database is opened successfully; internally it will perform the following three operations:

- **Completed:** ALTER DATABASE RECOVER MANAGED STANDBY DATABASE CANCEL
- **Completed:** ALTER DATABASE OPEN READ-ONLY
- **Completed:** ALTER DATABASE RECOVER MANAGED STANDBY DATABASE THROUGH ALL SWITCHOVER DISCONNECT USING CURRENT LOGFILE

> If you are using Oracle 11*g*R1 with Data Guard broker, then use a combination of Data Guard broker and SQL *Plus to enable Active Data Guard using the following commands:
>
> DGMGRL> edit database 'INDIA_UN' SET STATE='APPLY-OFF';
>
> SQL> alter database open read only;
>
> DGMGRL> edit database 'INDIA_UN' SET STATE='APPLY-ON';

What just happened?

We've just revised how to enable Active Data Guard using SQL *Plus and also using Data Guard broker.

After performing the previous steps to enable Active Data Guard, we will see how to find out whether the Active Data Guard feature is enabled or not. There is no direct column in any view/tables to find out whether the Active Data Guard feature is enabled or not. But if we merge two columns of two tables and if both the processes are running, then it is for reporting purpose as shown in the following query:

SQL> select 'YES' Active_DataGuard from v$managed_standby ms, v$database db where ms.process like '%MRP%' and db.open_mode like '%READ ONLY%';

ACTIVE_DATAGUARD

YES

Monitoring Active Data Guard

We have successfully enabled Active Data Guard on a standby database; no further steps need to be performed on the primary database if real-time apply is running. There are several ways to find whether Active Data Guard is enabled or not.

From primary

To determine if Active Data Guard is enabled from the primary, `v$archive_dest_status` describes the status of all local and remote destinations, including several options such as database role and recovery mode, as follows:

```
SQL> select dest_name,status,database_mode,recovery_mode from
v$archive_dest_status where dest_id=2;
DEST_NAME               STATUS    DATABASE_MODE   RECOVERY_MODE
---------------------   --------- --------------- --------------------
LOG_ARCHIVE_DEST_2      VALID     OPEN_READ-ONLY  MANAGED REAL TIME APPLY
```

From standby

Using the standby database you can check whether the standby database is Mount status Read Only, or READ ONLY WITH APPLY by using v$database as follows:

```
SQL> select open_mode from v$database;
OPEN_MODE
--------------------
READ ONLY WITH APPLY
```

By using a custom query you can merge the views as follows:

```
SQL>  select 'YES' Active_DataGuard from v$managed_standby ms,
v$database db where ms.process like '%MRP%' and db.open_mode like
'%READ ONLY%';
ACTIVE_DATAGUARD
--------------------
YES
SQL> SELECT * FROM V$STANDBY_EVENT_HISTOGRAM WHERE NAME = 'apply lag'
AND COUNT > 0;
NAME            TIME UNIT             COUNT LAST_TIME_UPDATED
---------- ---------- ---------------- ---------- --------------------
apply lag          0 seconds          5787 11/06/2012 23:01:28
apply lag          1 seconds            98 11/06/2012 23:01:09
apply lag          2 seconds             8 11/06/2012 22:45:06
apply lag          3 seconds             6 11/06/2012 22:45:37
apply lag          4 seconds             4 11/06/2012 22:43:03
apply lag          5 seconds             4 11/06/2012 22:45:43
```

The v$standby_event_histogram view is accessible only if the database is OPEN with READ-ONLY mode and real-time apply is on, that is Active Data Guard. However, this view is also accessible from MOUNT but it returns no information.

Active Data Guard with applications

Active Data Guard has limitations with several applications; your application may or may not be compatible with Active Data Guard to use its features. Before purchasing the license, you should check the compatibility of the applications. Here we will discuss briefly some of the top applications that are used for business and how it works with Active Data Guard.

Active Data Guard with PeopleSoft

From PeopleSoft Version 8.51, reports can be executed in the Active Data Guard database instead of running in the production/primary OLTP database. Specific to PeopleSoft applications, it uses reporting tools such as NVisions. These job queries select against the database and retrieve the results into an Excel spreadsheet as per the user's formatting. Internally it calls a number of batch jobs and some of the queries may use hints such as parallel if they create any SQL profiles and these can cause much load on production. All NVision reports are pure `select` queries. Only the tree performance tuning parameters/settings that are enabled will have DML statements on Treeselector tables otherwise any NVisions report on `PS_LEDGER`, `PS_LEDGER_BUDG` is always pure select process. NVisions are reports that can run on FIN, HR, or EPM(DWH). If you enable Active Data Guard on a standby database, components such as the PSQUERY viewer, the TREE viewer, QAS, G&R, and the XMLP viewer should always run on the standby system. To enhance this feature you must perform configuration changes in both the process scheduler server and the application server. The following diagram explains Active Data Guard with PeopleSoft:

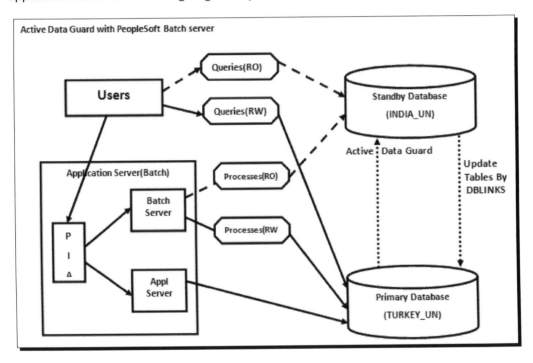

If you perform changes in the component's properties of the application designer, you can run more components on the standby system; even the process scheduler definitions can be configured on the standby system by setting the read-only option in it. With the option of Active Data Guard, database links and remote synonyms that are defined by scripts from PeopleTools can run batch programs on a standby system.

Time for action – Active Data Guard with PeopleSoft

PeopleSoft with Active Data Guard require DB links because they will update the processes' tables using DB links so that remote synonyms are required to give access to the standby system. But a very detailed analysis is required if you consider implementing Active Data Guard. Perform the following steps to implement Active Data Guard with PeopleSoft:

1. Create a standby database and enable Active Data Guard.

2. Add a new database service for accessing Active Data Guard on the primary database in case there is any maintenance on the standby server.

3. Confirm that Oracle Net Services is configured between the Active Guard database and the application servers; also ensure that the Oracle net configuration points to the database service instead of a specific instance and includes both the primary and standby listeners, so that PeopleSoft can connect to any of the services that are not started or running also.

4. In PeopleSoft, we do not have much control to use any custom scripts, and we must always go for the derived scripts from PeopleSoft. To enhance this Active Data Guard feature with PeopleSoft, ensure that the following scripts are available:

    `psadmin.sql($PS_HOME/scripts/unix)`

    `createlocalsynonyms.sql($PS_HOME/scripts)`

    `createremotesynonyms.sql($PS_HOME/scripts)`

    `createdblinktoprimarydb.sql($PS_HOME/scripts)`

5. Create a secondary access ID as `ACCESS_ID` on the primary database using the script `psadmin.sql`. `ACCESS_ID` is the RDBMS ID with which PeopleSoft applications are connected to the database so that it will create an owner `ACCESSID` besides the default user `SYSADM`.

6. Insert the corresponding database name and username in the table `PSDBOWNER` and perform a commit after the insert.

7. From the application designer, add a new `SYMBOLICID` for `ACCESSID`.

8. Create a dedicated application user attached to the secondary `SYMBOLICID` attribute.

9. Create a database link to the primary database using the following query:

    ```
    SQL> create database link Prim_ADG connect to sysadm identified by
    password using 'TURKEY_UN';
    ```

10. Create a local synonym using the derived script `createlocalsynonyms.sql`.

11. Create a remote synonym using the derived script `createremotesynonyms.sql`.

12. Confirm that the standby system is able to synchronize it all the time without any delay and also check for the newly created database link.

13. Now configure the batch server on both the primary and standby systems.

14. Modify the `psprcs.cfg` file with `StandbyDBname`, `StandbyDBType`, `StandbyUserId`, and `StandbyUserPsswd`.

15. After modifying the `PRCSDOM` batch server, reconfigure it using the `$PS_HOME/appserv/psadmin` script.

16. Now start the batch server `PRCSDOM` after all the modifications and confirm the standby connections using `v$session`.

17. By setting `DDDAUDIT` to read-only, you can perform the tests.

> The earlier discussed steps are specific to how to configure the batch server. Of course you can configure an application server on Active Data Guard but the configuration is different.

Active Data Guard with EBS

Active Data Guard can be implemented on EBS but there are some limitations specific to EBS R12; you should meet software and patches requirements, as discussed in the following table:

Oracle products	Minimum version	Additional patches
Oracle EE 11*g*R1	> = 11.1.0.7	Recording ADG violations: <patch 10070167> patch `10134846`
Oracle EE 11*g*R2	>=11.2.0.2	Included in a patch set; no additional patches required
Oracle EBS	>=12.1.3	Infrastructure patch `9434627` `9434627:R12.FND.B`
		Enabling patch `9505793` `9505793:R12.FND.B`
		and patch `9526837` `9526837:R12.FND.B.`

If you want to use concurrent manager reporting, you must use parallel concurrent processing with new processing nodes that are set up to handle Active Data Guard reports. Ensure that there is no network latency between the primary and standby systems. In Active Data Guard, the concurrent manager connects to the primary database and only the reports will be connected to the Active Data Guard database. However, no DMLs are allowed on Active Data Guard; DML will be executed via database links to the primary database. Hence, it is applicable to both the user and the dictionary DML.

In brief, first clone an application tier to set up parallel concurrent processing and then register the node for batch processing only. Now start the application and register a new concurrent manager, assigning it the node co-located with Active Data Guard. To ensure that this manager only handles reports for meeting the requirements of Active Data Guard, use the exclude/include rules. Customers may use Active Data Guard instances to execute SQL that does not require a write activity. In terms of the use of E-Business Suite with Active Data Guard, if the concurrent program is not on the list of supported reports, then it is not certified by Oracle Development and is considered a customization. For more configuration limitations over Active Data Guard, refer to the installation documents.

Active Data Guard with TopLink

Oracle TopLink is a part of Oracle Fusion Middleware; it's an advanced framework that provides development tools and runtime capabilities so that the development and maintenance efforts are reduced, thereby increasing the application functionality. It can successfully transform object-oriented data into relation data or Extensible Markup Language(XML). TopLink can address the difference between Java objects and data sources. Its engine has a great mechanism to use read pool for all non-transitional transactions and write pool for the actual transactions. The same concept can be implemented with Active Data Guard by processing read-only operations to a standby database and read-write transactions to a primary database; the high-level steps are as follows:

- TopLink can read objects using the read-only database connection and it uses a locking mechanism so that users have the option to choose and update the object later. It can detect a conflict.

- Once an object is processed to higher application layers, it will be converted into the HTML format and some of the attributes will be hidden, and they will be visible once the form is submitted.

- In the next level that the object will be passed to, the application server acts as the TopLink object and along with its changes, it will be saved in the database through the read-write connection pool.

- After the commit of the UPDATE statement, the redo data will of course be transported to the physical standby database and it will be applied to the same.

Active Data Guard with Oracle BI

Oracle Business Intelligence Suite EE Plus is an element of Enterprise BI products. From 11*g* onwards, OBIEE is based on the web service oriented, unified architecture. OBIEE 11*g* delivers ad hoc queries and analysis, OLAP, and its functionality. It can access multiple enterprise sources including Oracle and also non-Oracle data, and it has advanced enterprise reporting and publishing features.

OBIEE 10.1.3.4 has been certified with Oracle Active Data Guard 11*g*. The OBIEE server is mostly related to the read-only application server and the read-only operations that we can run on the Active Data Guard standby database with some configuration changes. Hence, we can share the load with the standby database and avoid many read-only operations on the primary database. By enabling Active Data Guard, scalability can be enhanced significantly. To improve query performance, OBIEE has the mechanism to create temporary tables; so we have to disable OBIEE from creating temporary tables and from modifying scripts to use the primary connection pool explicitly for any DML statements. The high-level steps to use OBIEE with Active Data Guard are as follows:

- Create a database connection to the Active standby database
- Disable temporary table creation
- Using the OBIEE server administrator tool, create a write-back connection pool that points to the primary database for any DML transactions
- To monitor the queries and their elapsed time, the OBIEE server has been provided with the Usage Tracking functionality and you can mention the OBIEE server to write in tables using the primary connection to modify NQSConfig.INI file of your SA_HOME\config directory.
- OBIEE has another feature known as **Event Polling**, which has the mechanism to notify the cache system to invalidate the outdated data cache

Thus, OBIEE with Oracle 11*g* Active Data Guard provides high-scalable solutions, and with proper configurations, the OBIEE repository can adapt OBIEE for read-only requirements of an Active Data Guard standby database.

Active Data Guard with SAP

Many DBAs seem to have the misconception that Active Data Guard can be configured for SAP systems. They must be aware of the fact that Active Data Guard cannot be used to run any SAP system against the standby database for any reporting purpose. Active Data Guard allows only read-only access to the standby database. But SAP systems are never read-only. Therefore this would not work. Of course, you can run any administrative task against the standby server that is read-only. Since you cannot start a SAP system against an Active Data Guard standby system, you are limited to pure Oracle-related administration tasks.

Active Data Guard features

In the license of Active Data guard, apart from read-only operations we have some more features and a couple of examples that we are going to discuss on how to use Active Data Guard more than just named `Read-Only`. Most of the tasks that run on the standby and primary database will be used only if DML operations are required. Also, we can offload operations to physical standby databases and hence we can put more additional processing on production databases, thereby we can eliminate the contention between read-only and read-write operations.

EXPDP from standby database using NETWORK_LINK (ADG)

In the previous section, we created database links on the primary database and we created remote synonyms to be used by the physical standby database. In this procedure we will be performing all the operations in the standby database only in the case of creating or updating master tables after which it routes transactions to the primary database via database links.

Apart from application usage, we can use Active Data Guard even for fully exporting the database. For a huge OLTP transactional database of size 600 GB to 700 GB, the elapsed ETA to export a full backup is around 5 hours to 6 hours using high parallelism of 32. During the export job, it is always expected to have a high load average that can cause much CPU busy depending on the hardware configurations. Hence, for almost 5-6 hours there will be huge activity both on the database and also at the server level because CPU cores are serving the EXPDP job. If you want to use EXPDP from a standby database, you must schedule the job from the primary database because it has to create a master table, and all the database reads will be performed from the standby database so that disk I/Os can be reduced on the primary database.

Time for action – exporting a database backup from Active Data Guard

In order to export a database backup from Active Data Guard, perform the following steps:

1. Ensure that your standby database is in the `Read Only` mode and the `MRP` process should not be running, as shown in the following query:

```
SQL> select open_mode from v$database;
OPEN_MODE
--------------------
READ ONLY
```

2. Create a directory in the primary database logically and create the same directory name physically at the OS level as follows:

```
SQL> create directory expdp_india as '/u02/backups/expdp';
Directory created.
SQL>
```

3. Create a database link from the primary database so that TNS string should point to the standby database, as shown in the following query:

```
SQL> create public database link exp_turkey connect to system
identified by "free2go" using 'india';
Database link created.
SQL>
```

4. Now execute EXPDP from the primary database as follows and ensure that you have proper roles and privileges to export the backups:

```
[oracle@oracle-primary ~]$ expdp system/free2go directory=EXPDP_
INDIA network_link=exp_turkey tables=packt.oracle dumpfile=Sample_
Standby.dmp logfile=FULL_standby.log

Export: Release 11.2.0.1.0 - Production on Wed Nov 7 15:55:28 2012

. . . . . . . . . . . . . . . . . . . . . . .
Starting "SYSTEM"."SYS_EXPORT_TABLE_02":  system/********
directory=EXPDP_INDIA network_link=exp_turkey tables=packt.oracle
dumpfile=Sample_Standby.dmp logfile=FULL_standby.log

Estimate in progress using BLOCKS method...

Dump file set for SYSTEM.SYS_EXPORT_TABLE_02 is:

  /u02/backups/expdp/Sample_Standby.dmp

Job "SYSTEM"."SYS_EXPORT_TABLE_02" successfully completed at
15:55:41

[oracle@oracle-primary ~]$
```

What just happened?

We've just revised how to perform a logical backup of a database with the method of export (EXPDP) by reading data of a standby database to reduce the number of I/Os from the primary database.

Time for action – using the ASH report from the standby database

From 11*g*R2 onwards, the Active Session History report can be created to monitor the performance of a standby database from the standby system. To use this feature, ensure that the database is up-and-running in the `Read-Only` mode and the session history has retained the memory. Then, you can perform the following steps:

1. Generate an ASH report using the `ashrpt.sql` script. Before using this report you must know what parameters we have to pass while the report is running, for example, duration between two dates and times. Use the `ashrpt.sql` script as follows:

```
SQL> @?/rdbms/admin/ashrpt.sql

Current Instance

~~~~~~~~~~~~~~~~~

   DB Id     DB Name       Inst Num Instance

----------- ------------- -------- ------------

 1316772835 ORCL                 1 INDIA
```

You are running ASH report on a Standby database. To generate the report

over data sampled on the Primary database, enter 'P'.

Defaults to 'S' - data sampled in the Standby database.

Enter value for stdbyflag: S

Using Primary (P) or Standby (S): S

   Once you initiate the ASH report, you can choose the text or HTML option for the report. The default mode of the ASH report is HTML. In the second phase you have the option to choose the instance type, so select the instance type as `Standby`.

2. Now you have to specify the timeframe to generate the ASH report. Specific to this report, you can choose `Sysdate-10`. Hence, from the current date and time it will get the session history report for the past 10 minutes as follows:

```
Enter begin time for report:

--      Valid input formats:
--        To specify absolute begin time:
--          [MM/DD[/YY]] HH24:MI[:SS]
--          Examples: 02/23/03 14:30:15
--                    02/23 14:30:15
--                    14:30:15
--                    14:30
--        To specify relative begin time: (start with '-' sign)
--          -[HH24:]MI
--          Examples: -1:15   (SYSDATE - 1 Hr 15 Mins)
--                    -25     (SYSDATE - 25 Mins)
Defaults to -15 mins
Enter value for begin_time: -10
Report begin time specified: -10
```

3. You can mention the report name or it will be created using the default name, which uses the time and interval of the selection as shown in the following code:

```
</table><p />
<br /><a class="awr" href="#top">Back to Top</a><p />
<p />
End of Report
</body></html>
Report written to ashrpt_1_1107_1557.html
SQL>
```

This report will be generated from the default directory where you been logged into the SQL *Plus session. Now you can save or open in any browser to view the statistics.

A sample ASH report output of a standby database is shown in the following screenshot:

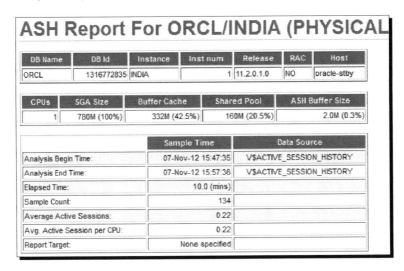

You can see the wait events **Standby redo I/O** and **RFS write** that are related to a standby database, as shown in the following screenshot:

Top User Events

Event	Event Class	% Event	Avg Active Sessions
Standby redo I/O	System I/O	33.33	0.00
CPU + Wait for CPU	CPU	11.11	0.00
RFS write	System I/O	11.11	0.00
db file sequential read	User I/O	11.11	0.00

What just happened?

We've just revised how to generate an active session history report from a standby database; this report helps us to find out the top wait events with the standby database and also to find any sort of issue either with the database or with redo being written.

Have a go hero – running Statspack from a standby database

You can add a standby instance in Statspack to create reports specifically related to a standby database. The high-level steps are as follows:

1. Ensure Statspack is already installed using @?/rdbms/admin/sbcreate.sql.

2. The database must not shut down between two snapshot times to gather reports. For that, use the script @?/rdbms/admin/sbreport.sql.

Using a snapshot standby database

The snapshot concept was introduced from the 11*g* Version, which allows the use of a physical standby database in the read-write mode for a short period of time. You can convert a physical standby to a snapshot standby by using either traditional SQL *Plus or using the Data Guard broker and grid control at any time. Even if you convert it to a snapshot standby, it will still receive data continuously from the production database archive, so that in the next conversion from a snapshot to a physical standby it will be used for recovery. In case you have performed recovery at any point in time, the new incarnation will be started. Even though a new incarnation has started, the snapshot standby database will still continue accepting redo from the primary database. If your standby database is clustered and has more than one node, then shut down all the auxiliary RAC instances of the standby prior to performing a snapshot. Note that you should not put a standby database in the snapshot mode for a long time; it results in huge archive logs between the production database and the standby database and in case of critical databases it can have a serious impact.

Time for action – converting to a snapshot standby database

Perform the following steps to convert a physical standby database to a snapshot standby database:

1. To convert a physical standby database to a snapshot standby database, flashback should be enabled and the database should be brought to the MOUNT status after cancelling recovery as follows:

```
SQL> select open_mode,database_role,flashback_on from v$database;
OPEN_MODE              DATABASE_ROLE     FLASHBACK_ON
-------------------    ----------------  ------------------
MOUNTED                PHYSICAL STANDBY  YES
```

2. Now process the following command to convert the physical standby database to a snapshot standby database:

```
SQL> ALTER DATABASE CONVERT TO SNAPSHOT STANDBY;

Database altered.

SQL>

Wed Nov 07 20:10:27 2012

ALTER DATABASE CONVERT TO SNAPSHOT STANDBY

Created guaranteed restore point SNAPSHOT_STANDBY_
REQUIRED_11/07/2012 20:10:27

. . . . . . . .

Standby became primary SCN: 3938237

Wed Nov 07 20:10:29 2012

Setting recovery target incarnation to 3

CONVERT TO SNAPSHOT STANDBY: Complete - Database mounted as
snapshot standby

Completed: ALTER DATABASE CONVERT TO SNAPSHOT STANDBY
```

3. Internally, a standby database creates a restore point so that we can convert the snapshot standby database to a physical standby database at any time, and the standby database will be converted as a primary with a new incarnation as follows:

```
SQL> select open_mode,database_role,resetlogs_change#,prior_
resetlogs_change# from v$database;
OPEN_MODE   DATABASE_ROLE   RESETLOGS_CHANGE# PRIOR_RESETLOGS_CHANGE#
----------  --------------- ---------------- --------------------

MOUNTED     SNAPSHOT STANDBY      3938240                   945184
```

4. After successful conversion, you can now validate the snapshot standby database as follows:

```
SQL> select name,restore_point_time from v$restore_point;
NAME                                          RESTORE_POINT_TIME
-------------------------------------------   ---------------- ---
SNAPSHOT_STANDBY_REQUIRED_11/07/2012 20:10:27 08.10.27.000000000 PM
```

Even though the old standby database is converted to a snapshot standby database, the archives will be received from the primary database whenever log switch occurs, and note that the database will be in the MOUNT status after conversion as follows:

```
Wed Nov 07 21:07:27 2012
RFS[5]: Selected log 11 for thread 1 sequence 619 dbid 1316772835 branch 788992101
Wed Nov 07 21:07:27 2012
Archived Log entry 14 added for thread 1 sequence 618 ID 0x4eede1f7 dest 1:
```

You have to explicitly open the database so that it will be ready for read and write purposes.

What just happened?

We've just revised how to convert a database from a physical standby to a snapshot standby using the SQL* Plus command using a step-by-step approach.

Time for action – converting to a physical standby database

To convert from the snapshot mode to a physical standby, the procedure is the same as discussed earlier. Perform the following steps:

1. For validation, perform some DML transactions to verify the number of rows of any table before and after the conversion, as shown in the following query:

    ```
    SQL> select open_mode from v$database;
    OPEN_MODE
    --------------------
    READ WRITE
    SQL> conn packt/packt;
    Connected.
    SQL> select count(*) from packt.oracle;
    COUNT(*)
    ----------
    41943040
    SQL> insert into oracle select * from oracle where sal > 4500;
    2097152 rows created.
    SQL> commit;
    Commit complete.
    SQL> select count(*) from packt.oracle;
      COUNT(*)
    ----------
      44040192
    ```

2. Shut down the database and put it in the MOUNT status to initiate the conversion as follows:

```
SQL> alter database convert to physical standby;
Database altered.
SQL>
```

The following output will be visible:

```
Wed Nov 07 22:28:12 2012

alter database convert to physical standby

ALTER DATABASE CONVERT TO PHYSICAL STANDBY (INDIA)

krsv_proc_kill: Killing 2 processes (all RFS)

Flashback Restore Start

Wed Nov 07 22:30:23 2012

Flashback Restore Complete
```

3. After successful conversion, the instance will be brought to the STARTED status, and you have to perform complete shutdown and startup in the Read Only mode with the recovery mode as the standby database for the purpose of reporting, as shown in the following query:

```
SQL> select count(*) from packt.oracle;
  COUNT(*)
----------
  41943040
```

From step 1, the number of rows inserted are 2097152, and after performing a flashback to the restore point, all the newly inserted rows will be reverted.

> You can convert a physical standby database to snapshot standby database either a Maximum Performance or Maximum Availability mode. It's not supported with the Maximum Protection mode and the snapshot standby is never considered to perform switchover or failover.

What just happened?

We've just revised how to convert a database from a snapshot standby to a physical standby using the SQL* Plus command and we also verified how the new DMLs are reverted using the flashback restore point.

Have a go hero – convert the physical standby to a snapshot and vice versa using broker

We have converted the physical standby to a snapshot standby database for read and write purposes using traditional SQL *Plus. This procedure can also be accomplished using a broker. By using SQL *Plus, we have to bounce the database to the MOUNT status; if you are managing it using the broker, it will handle this automatically. Refer to the following screenshot for a better understanding:

```
DGMGRL> convert database 'INDIA_UN' to snapshot standby;
Converting database "INDIA_UN" to a Snapshot Standby database, please wait...
Database "INDIA_UN" converted successfully
DGMGRL> ▮
```

Cascade standby databases

The cascade standby database concept was introduced from Oracle 9*i* Release 2 onwards. In the latest versions and releases there are many changes in the cascade standby databases. The cascade standby database concept was introduced to reduce the load on your primary database and to transmit redo data from the primary to all standby databases, and the network bandwidth needs to be large enough to handle the load. If it is a huge OLTP then it will be more problematic to handle. The cascade standby databases are shown in the following diagram:

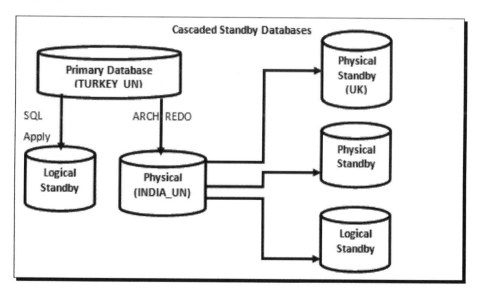

Limitations with cascade standby database

The limitations with a cascade standby database are as follows:

- Data cannot be transmitted to other standby databases from a logical standby or a snapshot standby database.
- Data Guard broker is not supported in a cascade standby database environment.
- Cascading is not supported in RAC on versions prior to 11.2.0.2.
- If you are using synchronous redo transport, they cannot cascade redo data in a Maximum Protection mode.
- If the primary database is transmitting redo to the standby redo logfiles and writing into standby redo logfiles once SRL is full and archived, then the respective archive sequence will be transmitted and applied to the cascade standby database(s). This will delay redo to the cascade database.

Time for action – cascade standby database

Perform the following steps for a cascade standby database:

1. Verify whether each destination's status is valid or not from `v$archive_dest` as follows:

```
ID STATUS      DB_MODE          TYPE RECOVERY_MODE
PROTECTION_MODE        SRLs ACTIVE    ARCHIVED_SEQ#
--- --------- --------------- ---- -----------------------  -------
------------- ---- ------ ---------------
  1 VALID     OPEN             ARCH IDLE                              MAXIMUM
PERFORMANCE     0      0          731
  2 VALID     OPEN_READ-ONLY   LGWR MANAGED REAL TIME APPLY MAXIMUM
PERFORMANCE     6      1          731
  3 VALID     OPEN_READ-ONLY   LGWR MANAGED REAL TIME APPLY MAXIMUM
PERFORMANCE     6      1          731
```

   All remote destinations are using real-time apply with read only for reporting purpose in the Maximum Performance mode. It is to ensure that the standby database has enough standby redo logfiles so that there would be no interruption while sending data to the cascade standby database.

2. Increase the `LOG_ARCHIVE_MAX_PROCESSES` parameter on the standby database so that more archive processes will run frequently to send data to all remote destinations in parallel as follows:

```
SQL> show parameter log_archive_max_processes
NAME                         TYPE         VALUE
---------------------------- ----------- ----------
log_archive_max_processes    integer      5
```

```
SQL> alter system set log_archive_max_processes=30;
System altered.
SQL> show parameter log_archive_max_processes
NAME                              TYPE        VALUE
--------------------------------- ----------- -----
log_archive_max_processes         integer     30

SQL>
```

3. Configure the parameter as follows from the primary, standby, and cascade databases according to the database type.

From the primary (TURKEY) database, you can configure as follows:

```
DB_UNIQUE_NAME=turkey_un
LOG_ARCHIVE_CONFIG=DG_CONFIG=(TURKEY_UN,INDIA_UN,UK_UN)
LOG_ARCHIVE_DEST_2=service=INDIA VALID_FOR=(ONLINE_
LOGFILES,PRIMARY_ROLE) DB_UNIQUE_NAME=INDIA_UN
FAL_SERVER='INDIA_UN'
```

From the standby (INDIA) database, you can configure as follows:

```
DB_UNIQUE_NAME=india_un
LOG_ARCHIVE_CONFIG=DG_CONFIG=(TURKEY_UN,INDIA_UN,UK_UN)
LOG_ARCHIVE_DEST_2=service=UK VALID_FOR=(STANDBY_LOGFILES,STANDBY_
ROLE) DB_UNIQUE_NAME=UK_UN
FAL_SERVER='UK_UN'
```

From the cascade standby (UK) database, you can configure as follows:

```
DB_UNIQUE_NAME=uk_un
LOG_ARCHIVE_CONFIG=DG_CONFIG=(TURKEY_UN,INDIA_UN,UK_UN)
```

Apart from these parameters, you can configure more destinations if your environment contains more standby databases that are either physical or logical.

4. Verify the physical standby and cascade standby databases.

Verify it from the primary (TURKEY) database as follows:

```
SQL> select db_unique_name,database_role from v$database;
DB_UNIQUE_NA DATABASE_ROLE
------------ ----------------
turkey_un    PRIMARY
```

ID	STATUS	DB_MODE	TYPE	PROTECTION_MODE
1	VALID	OPEN	ARCH	MAXIMUM PERFORMANCE
2	VALID	OPEN_READ-ONLY	LGWR	MAXIMUM PERFORMANCE

```
SQL> select max(sequence#) from v$archived_log;
MAX(SEQUENCE#)
- - - - - - - - - - - - -
            747
```

Verify it from the standby (INDIA) database as follows:

```
SQL> select db_unique_name,database_role from v$database;
DB_UNIQUE_NA DATABASE_ROLE
- - - - - - - - - - - -   - - - - - - - - - - - - - - - -
INDIA_UN     PHYSICAL STANDBY
SQL> select max(sequence#) from v$archived_log where
applied='YES';


MAX(SEQUENCE#)
- - - - - - - - - - - - -
            747
```

Verify it from the cascade standby (UK) database as follows:

```
SQL> select db_unique_name,database_role from v$database;
DB_UNIQUE_NA DATABASE_ROLE
- - - - - - - - - - - -   - - - - - - - - - - - - - - - -
uk_un        PHYSICAL STANDBY
 ID STATUS    DB_MODE          TYPE RECOVERY_MODE
SQL> select max(sequence#) from v$archived_log where
applied='YES';

 MAX(SEQUENCE#)
 - - - - - - - - - - - - -
            747
```

If we define a cascade physical standby database from a physical standby database, then initially the redo will be transmitted from the primary database to the physical standby database. Thus, once the standby redo logfile is archived, that archive will be transferred and applied on the cascade physical standby database. Hence, there is an expected delay in data between the primary database and the cascade standby database. From the earlier outputs, we know that the maximum sequence generated in the primary is 747 and an archive has been applied on the physical standby and also on the cascade physical standby database.

What just happened?

We've just explained the concept of a cascade standby database, the advantages associated with it, and also a step-by-step configuration of a cascade standby database.

Advanced compression in Data Guard

Oracle Database 11*g* Advanced Compression introduced several set of options. Oracle also introduced compression for network traffic. With the option of advanced compression, the primary database will send the redo data and may be transported in a compressed format to reduce network consumption on the standby database. In the earlier releases, redo has been compressed over the network using third-party utilities such as WAN accelerators and other tools. To use the compression feature of Oracle, you must have purchased the license of Oracle 11*g* advanced compression. By licensing this option, archive gaps can be resolved up to three times faster, thereby providing better protection, and network utilization can be controlled by reducing the redo transfer time. Compression is supported for all the redo transport modes such SYNC and ASYNC and for the transport methods such as ARCH and LGWR to resolve gaps of Data Guard. These are compatible with all the protection modes—Maximum Performance, Maximum Protection, and Maximum Availability.

Before implementing compression, ensure that sufficient CPU resources are available and the database redo rate is higher than the available network bandwidth to take advantage of compression. This feature can be used in 11*g*R1 by setting the undocumented parameter _ REDO_TRANSPORT_COMPRESS_ALL to TRUE along with the attribute COMPRESSION=ENABLE in LOG_ARCHIVE_DEST_n. From 11*g*R2 onwards, this parameter is no longer required.

Time for action – enabling advanced compression

Perform the following steps in order to enable advanced compression:

1. Check for the current settings of the remote destinations and options of compression as follows:

```
SQL>  select parameter,value from v$option where
parameter='Advanced Compression';
PARAMETER                        VALUE
------------------------         -----
Advanced Compression             TRUE


SQL> select dest_id,compression,db_unique_name from v$archive_dest
where dest_id=2;
   DEST_ID COMPRESSION      DB_UNIQUE_NAME
---------- ---------------  ----------------------------
         2 DISABLE          INDIA_UN
```

2. Enable compression by modifying the remote destination parameter as follows:

```
SQL> alter system set LOG_ARCHIVE_DEST_2='service=INDIA LGWR ASYNC
COMPRESSION=ENABLE VALID_FOR=(ONLINE_LOGFILES,PRIMARY_ROLE) DB_
UNIQUE_NAME=INDIA_UN';
System altered.
SQL> select dest_id,compression,db_unique_name from v$archive_dest
where dest_id=2;
    DEST_ID COMPRESSION     DB_UNIQUE_NAME
---------- ---------------- ------------------------------
          2 ENABLE          INDIA_UN
```

3. Perform a large number of DML transactions for testing purposes as follows:

```
SQL> conn packt/packt
Connected.
SQL> insert into oracle select * from oracle;
41943040 rows created.
SQL> commit;
Commit complete.
SQL>
```

4. Redo the size for the session of `Packt` as follows:

```
SQL> ;
  1  select v$session.sid, username, value redo_size
  2  from v$sesstat, v$statname, v$session
  3  where v$sesstat.STATISTIC# = v$statname.STATISTIC#
  4  and v$session.sid = v$sesstat.sid
  5  and name = 'redo size'
  6  and value > 0
  7  and username is not null
  8* order by value
SQL> /
       SID USERNAME                             REDO_SIZE
---------- ---------------------------- ----------
        48 packt                             2125379564
```

5. Advanced compression uses the mechanism of the `zlib` engine at level 1 as `gzip`. So you can verify it using the `gzip` command as follows:

```
[oracle@oracle-primary 2012_11_08]$ gzip -1 o1_
mf_1_753_89q187xv_.arc

[oracle@oracle-primary 2012_11_08]$ ls -ltr o1_mf_1_749_89q13d2*

-rw-r----- 1 oracle oinstall 8209301 Nov  8 15:37 o1_
mf_1_749_89q13d2z_.arc.gz
```

```
[oracle@oracle-primary 2012_11_08]$ gzip --list o1_
mf_1_749_89q13d2z_.arc.gz
         compressed         uncompressed  ratio uncompressed_name
            8209301            101288960  91.9% o1_
mf_1_749_89q13d2z_.arc
[oracle@oracle-primary 2012_11_08]$
```

In the previous output, after enabling compression, nine percent of the actual data has been compressed and transported to the standby database. Note that the compression ratio may vary.

What just happened?

We've just revised advanced compression with its brief introduction and also tested how compression of redo works in a Data Guard environment using a step-by-step approach.

Preparation of standby on a cross-platform Data Guard

Cross-platform Data Guard was introduced in Oracle 11g Release 1. We may have 32-bit primary and 64-bit standby database combinations on some platforms of 10g, but from 11g onwards it supports even heterogeneous platforms ranging from Linux/Unix to Windows or vice versa. Most of the customers choose this procedure for moving the database on a different OS. Migration is made simple by this procedure with the same incarnation of a database. Prior to moving the production to a heterogeneous platform, it is recommended to test the standby in the read-write mode for the capacity of the standby server.

Note that you must create a cross-platform standby database on the same database's release and patch set. You can have different hardware manufacturers, hardware configuration, processors, operating systems, and operating system versions. From 11g onwards you can configure Data Guard broker between the cross-platforms, and you can configure the cross-platform standby by using the Oracle grid manager also.

	Operating system	Operating system release	Database release	Database version
Primary database	Linux	Enterprise Linux Server release 5, 64 bit	11g	11.2.0.1.0 - 64 bit
Standby database	Windows	Windows 7, 64 bit	11g	11.2.0.1.0 - 64 bit

Time for action – creating a cross-platform Data Guard setup

In order to create a cross-platform Data Guard setup, perform the following steps:

1. Check certification by Oracle support for Oracle database versions of the operating systems on the website `https://support.oracle.com/ epmos/faces/CertifyHome?_adf.ctrl-state=dattfx3qm_9&_ afrLoop=878199589056576`.

Each Operating System, according to the 32/64 bit architecture, can be verified whether it is certified by Oracle or not. Oracle Database 11.2.0.1.0 is certified on Microsoft Windows x64 (64-bit) 7.

2. Determine the platform ID of both the primary and standby database as follows:

```
SQL> select platform_id, platform_name from v$database;
PLATFORM_ID PLATFORM_NAME
----------- -----------------------------
         13 Linux x86 64-bit
SQL>  select platform_id, platform_name from v$database;


PLATFORM_ID PLATFORM_NAME
----------- -----------------------------
         12 Microsoft Windows x86 64-bit
```

3. If the platform ID of both the primary and standby systems is different, check for the compatibility and supported Data Guard configuration from My Oracle Support note `Data Guard Support for Heterogeneous Primary and Physical Standbys in Same Data Guard Configuration [ID 413484.1]`.

4. Create `PFILE` and configure the listener with a static entry in the standby system, as we discussed in *Chapter 2, Configuring the Oracle Data Guard Physical Standby Database*. Add the following additional parameters mentioned in the standby database. It will be useful in case of a switchover too because the filesystem as well as the OS of the primary and standby systems are different.

Perform the following on the primary database:

```
db_file_name_convert='/u01/app/oracle/oradata/orcl','D:\APP\ADMIN\
ORADATA\INDIA'

log_file_name_convert='/u01/app/oracle/oradata/orcl','D:\APP\
ADMIN\ORADATA\INDIA'
```

Perform the following on the standby database:

```
db_file_name_convert='D:\APP\ADMIN\ORADATA\INDIA', '/u01/app/
oracle/oradata/orcl'

log_file_name_convert='D:\APP\ADMIN\ORADATA\INDIA', '/u01/app/
oracle/oradata/orcl'
```

5. Now create a service on Windows that is specific to a standby instance. This is applicable if your standby is on the Windows Operating System as shown in the following command line:

```
C:\Windows\system32>oradim -new -sid INDIA -INTPWD free2go
-startmode auto -pfile d:\app\admin\product\11.2.0\dbhome_1\
database\initINDIA.ora

Instance created.

C:\Windows\system32>
```

 To create a service in Windows, run the command prompt with Administrator privileges by right-clicking on the application.

6. Set the environment variables and a startup instance in the NOMOUNT status as follows:

```
C:\Windows\system32>set ORACLE_SID=INDIA

C:\Windows\system32>echo %ORACLE_SID%

INDIA

C:\Windows\system32>sqlplus / as sysdba

SQL*Plus: Release 11.2.0.1.0 Production on Fri Nov 9 08:50:32 2012

Copyright (c) 1982, 2010, Oracle.  All rights reserved.

Connected to an idle instance.

SQL> startup nomount

ORACLE instance started.

Total System Global Area   818401280 bytes
Fixed Size                   2180184 bytes
Variable Size              482347944 bytes
Database Buffers           331350016 bytes
Redo Buffers                 2523136 bytes

SQL>
```

7. Connect to the primary database with a standby auxiliary instance using the net service name as follows:

```
C:\Windows\system32>rman target sys/free2go@turkey auxiliary sys/
free2go@india

Recovery Manager: Release 11.2.0.1.0 - Production on Fri Nov 9
11:26:28 2012

Copyright (c) 1982, 2009, Oracle and/or its affiliates.  All
rights reserved.
```

connected to target database: ORCL (DBID=1316772835)

connected to auxiliary database: ORCL (not mounted)

RMAN>

Refer the following screenshot:

```
RMAN> duplicate target database for standby from active database nofilenamecheck;

Starting Duplicate Db at 09-NOV-12
using target database control file instead of recovery catalog
allocated channel: ORA_AUX_DISK_1
channel ORA_AUX_DISK_1: SID=19 device type=DISK

contents of Memory Script:
{
   backup as copy reuse
      targetfile '/u01/home/oracle/product/11.2.0/db_1/dbs/orapwTURKEY' auxiliary format
 'D:\app\admin\product\11.2.0\dbhome_1\DATABASE\PWDindia.ORA'   ;
}
executing Memory Script

Starting backup at 09-NOV-12
allocated channel: ORA_DISK_1
channel ORA_DISK_1: SID=53 device type=DISK
Finished backup at 09-NOV-12

contents of Memory Script:
```

8. After the successful duplication of a standby database, start MRP on the standby database and verify whether redo data is transferring into heterogeneous platforms as follows:

```
SQL> alter database recover managed standby database using current
logfile disconnect from session;
Database altered.
SQL>
```

The following output will appear:

```
MRP0 started with pid=20, OS id=3916

Serial Media Recovery started

Managed Standby Recovery starting Real Time Apply

. . . . . . . . . . . .

Media Recovery Log D:\APP\ADMIN\FLASH_RECOVERY_AREA\INDIA_UN\
ARCHIVELOG\2012_11_09\O1_MF_1_776_89S7S0KJ_.ARC

Media Recovery Waiting for thread 1 sequence 777 (in transit)
```

What just happened?

We've implemented Data Guard in *Chapter 2, Configuring the Oracle Data Guard Physical Standby Database* for the homogenous platforms of the Operating System. Here we have explained how to configure Data Guard on cross-platform environments ranging from Linux to Windows.

Data Guard tuning and wait events

Specific to standby database(s), we may have performance issues to read redo data and to transport over a network, redo write phase because of bad RAID configurations, Redo Apply phase because of huge redo, improper memory settings, or the issues can be with bugs. Here we will discuss some of them.

Network tuning

Standby databases will be placed geographically in different locations with WAN for high availability in case of a disaster. Even though you keep your standby database geographically far away, you should have reasonable bandwidth to avoid data lag between the primary and standby databases. It can be a bigger problem if you are using synchronous redo with AFFIRM. Consider the use of a high latency network to fulfill redo rate shipping as follows:

```
Required network bandwidth = ((Redo rate bytes per sec. /  0.7) * 8) /
1,000,000 = bandwidth in Mbps.
```

By using this formula according to the redo generation rate, you can estimate the required network bandwidth. You can get redo rate in bytes per second from DBA_HIST_SNAPSHOT or from the AWR/Statspack reports.

Network throughput can be increased by setting Oracle net parameters RECV_BUF_SIZE and SEND_BUF_SIZE equal to three times of Bandwidth Delay Product. To calculate Bandwidth Delay Product, the bandwidth of the link and the Network Round Trip time are required. RTT is measured by the complete two-way travel from the primary to standby database, including the standby and primary databases.

```
BDP = (Network speed * RTT) /8
```

By this calculation, the optimal send and receive buffer sizes can be estimated with the following formula:

```
Socket buffer size = 3 * (Bandwidth Speed) * (RTT)
```

Or you can also use the following:

```
Socket buffer size = 3 * (BDP)
```

If the value of the socket buffer size is 11718750 bytes, the socket buffer size can be set as the following in sqlnet.ora or at the Operating System level:

```
[oracle@oracle-primary admin]$ cat sqlnet.ora|grep BUF_SIZE
RECV_BUF_SIZE=11718750
SEND_BUF_SIZE=11718750
[oracle@oracle-primary admin]$
```

You can also configure to send and receive buffer sizes to the net service for connector descriptor in the client-side `sqlnet.ora` file as follows:

```
INDIA =
  (DESCRIPTION =
    (RECV_BUF_SIZE=11718750)
    (SEND_BUF_SIZE=11718750)
    (ADDRESS = (PROTOCOL = TCP)(HOST = 192.168.180.20)(PORT = 1521))
    (CONNECT_DATA =
      (SERVER = DEDICATED)
      (SERVICE_NAME = india_un)
    )
  )
```

If you are replicating data remotely either using database links for materialized views or Data Guard, the data will be transferred over the network in terms of data sized units (SDU); if a large amount of redo is being transmitted, you can increase the size of the SDU buffer to improve performance and network utilization. You can configure it in the `sqlnet.ora` file as `DEFAULT_SDU_SIZE`, which ranges from 512 bytes to 32767 bytes. The default SDU size of 2048 bytes is applicable for the client and dedicated server, where for the shared server the default SDU will be 32767 bytes.

On the standby databases, you can configure either in the `sqlnet.ora` or `listener.ora` file where we can specify buffer parameters for the address in description as follows:

```
SID_LIST_LISTENER =
  (SID_LIST =
    (SID_DESC =
    (SDU = 32767)
    (GLOBAL_DBNAME = india_un)
    (SID_NAME = INDIA)
    (ORACLE_HOME = /u01/home/oracle/product/11.2.0/db_1)
    )
  )
```

Redo transport and apply tuning

If you are using a redo transport type such as ARCH, consider increasing the number of LOG_ARCHIVE_MAX_PROCESSES parameters. The default value in 11*g*R2 is 4 and it can be controlled from 1 to 30, if you set this parameter with a higher value. According to the archive processes and the system configuration, all the ARCn processes work in parallel to resolve the archive gaps.

Choose the optimal value after several tests with an archive gap resolution as follows:

```
SQL> select * from V$PGASTAT where name='total PGA allocated';
NAME                          VALUE UNIT
-------------------- ----------- ------------
total PGA allocated   249153536 bytes
```

The following output can be extracted using the view `v$process`:

```
PROGRAM                         PGA_USED_MEM   PGA_MAX_MEM
------------------------------- ------------   -----------

oracle@oracle-stby (ARC2)          11270688      12050576

oracle@oracle-stby (ARC1)          11297656      12050576

oracle@oracle-stby (ARC4)          28942512      30924944

oracle@oracle-stby (ARC3)          28942512      30924944

oracle@oracle-stby (ARC0)          28942512      30924944
```

So every archive process is consuming nearly 30 MB of memory; this calculation is completely based on the memory management you have used. Consider the parameter value LOG_ARCHIVE_MAX_PROCESSES depending on the available resources.

If you are using synchronous redo transport with LGWR redo, consider decreasing the value of NET_TIMEOUT to avoid outages on the production database's performance; this value can be defined from one to 1200 according to 11gR2 and the default value is 30 seconds. Oracle recommends setting the value of NET_TIMEOUT to 10 seconds or less to avoid disconnection from the standby database.

Redo data is received from the primary to standby database and it will be applied by the background process MRP0. Redo Apply is a block-to-block physical replication of the primary database. It uses media recovery to read records from standby redo logfiles into memory and applies directly to the standby database. If you start MRP as alter database recover managed standby database disconnect from session, only one MRP process will be started to perform recovery. For huge OLTP databases, there are various possibilities for having a lot of redo to be applied on a standby database, with a single background process recovery being delayed. So we can initiate parallel recovery and it starts slave processes along with MRP background processes as follows:

```
SQL> alter database recover managed standby database using current
logfile disconnect from session parallel 5
SQL> !ps -ef|grep pr0
oracle   32243     1  0 19:33 ?        00:00:00 ora_pr00_INDIA
oracle   32245     1  0 19:33 ?        00:00:00 ora_pr01_INDIA
oracle   32247     1  0 19:33 ?        00:00:00 ora_pr02_INDIA
```

```
oracle    32249     1  0 19:34 ?        00:00:00 ora_pr03_INDIA
oracle    32251     1  0 19:34 ?        00:00:00 ora_pr04_INDIA
oracle    32253     1  0 19:34 ?        00:00:00 ora_pr05_INDIA
oracle    32292 31785  0 19:34 pts/2    00:00:00 /bin/bash -c ps
-ef|grep pr0
```

 In the previous example, we have explicitly mentioned parallelism with the number 5. We can also mention parallel without any specific value so that parallelism will be the default for the number of CPUs.

Data Guard wait events

Data Guard wait events are classified into primary-and standby-related wait events. According to the new releases, many of the wait events are introduced; some of them are as follows:

- Data Guard wait events on the primary database with an ARCH transport

    These wait events are specific to sending redo from the primary database to the standby database using ARCH with synchronous or asynchronous redo transport. There is an ARCH wait on ATTACH, an ARCH wait on SENDREQ, and an ARCH wait on DETACH.

- Data Guard wait events on the primary database with LGWR transport

    If you are using real-time apply with LGWR redo transport, the LNS process will be working with the standby RFS server in redo transport and the wait events can be LNS wait on ATTACH, LNS wait on SENDREQ, LNS wait on DETACH, LGWR wait on LNS, LNS wait on LGWR, and LGWR-LNS wait on a channel.

- Database wait events related to Data Guard

    These wait events are applicable even in a normal system and are related to I/O. They are log file sync, log file parallel write, and DB file sequential read.

- Data Guard wait events on a standby database

    These wait events will occur in case time is spent on I/O on the standby. They are RFS write, RFS random I/O, and RFS sequential I/O.

Use the following query to get the details about all wait events:

```
SQL> select event,total_waits,time_waited,total_timeouts from
v$system_event order by total_waits desc;
EVENT                                      TOTAL_WAITS TIME_WAITED
------------------------------------------ ----------- -----------
parallel recovery slave next change             260168      381493
control file sequential read                     67687        2373
parallel recovery change buffer free             60053       82981
parallel recovery read buffer free               18975       24964
SQL*Net vector data from client                  10534       79202
```

 For an in-depth analysis of the events discussed, use a load profile of AWR or a Statspack report or performance dynamic views, and the wait events can be varied from environment to environment depending on the configurations and settings.

Summary

In this chapter we have briefly discussed about the new feature of Oracle 11gRx and Active Data Guard and their compatibility with several applications. Then we learned how logical backups work and how to generate ASH reports with the ADG feature.

We also worked on how to prepare a cascade standby database, advanced compressions with Oracle Data Guard, and how to prepare Data Guard in cross-platform environments (ranging from Linux to Windows). In the next chapter we will discuss how to integrate Data Guard with GRID EM, RMAN, and RAC.

8
Integrating Data Guard with the Complete Oracle Environment

After preparing a Data Guard configuration by creating one or more standby databases, we should also integrate this configuration with the existing Oracle environment. This integration lets us benefit from Oracle Data Guard more effectively, makes it more robust and easily manageable, and also serves the purpose of Maximum Availability.

In this chapter, we'll discuss integrating the Data Guard configuration with the following Oracle software products:

- Oracle Enterprise Manager Cloud Control
- Recovery Manager (RMAN)
- Real Application Cluster (RAC)

Let's start with learning how we can incorporate Data Guard installations into an existing Enterprise Manager Cloud Control configuration.

The Oracle Enterprise Manager Cloud Control integration

The Oracle Enterprise Manager product family involves products to monitor and manage IT environments right from servers to applications and services. Cloud Control 12c (formerly named as Grid Control) is the comprehensive and integrated management solution of Oracle; it has been intended to control all IT infrastructure and cloud-based IT services.

From the database management perspective, Cloud Control offers unique properties to control the Oracle Database environment centrally. In addition to traditional database management features, Cloud Control has the following packs to address all kinds of administrative requirements. You can use these packs after purchasing the related license:

◆ Oracle Diagnostic Pack for Database

◆ Oracle Tuning Pack for Database

◆ Oracle Lifecycle Management Pack for Database

◆ Data Masking Pack

◆ Oracle Test Data Management Pack

◆ Exadata Management

Data Guard management does not require an extra pack, so it's a built-in feature in Cloud Control. We can monitor and manage Data Guard configurations using the **Availability** tab in the Database Management home page. However, in order to use Cloud Control's Data Guard management features, we first need to add the Data Guard configurations into Cloud Control properly. Let's see how we can accomplish this.

It has been assumed that an Enterprise Manager Cloud Control 12*c* server is already installed and ready to use. It has also been assumed that the EM agent software is installed on servers in the Data Guard configuration, so the hosts have been added as targets to the Cloud Control environment. Preparing this environment is out of the scope of this book; so if you don't have a Cloud Control environment but want to prepare it, please refer to the related documentation at `http://docs.oracle.com`.

Time for action – adding the Data Guard configuration into Cloud Control

1. We have a Data Guard configuration of one primary, one physical standby, and one logical standby database. The hosts in the Data Guard configuration were added as targets to Cloud Control. Now the first thing we need to do is add the databases as targets. Log in to the Cloud Control interface, and on the main page click on **Targets** and then **Databases**. See the following screenshot showing no database targets. Click on **Add** to create a database target.

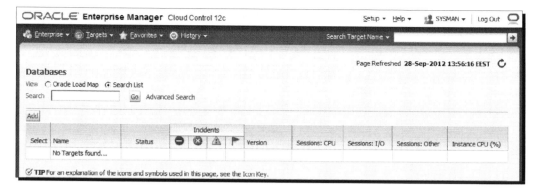

2. The next page will ask for the host that runs on the database. First add the primary database as the target, so type the hostname of the primary database server and click on **Continue**.

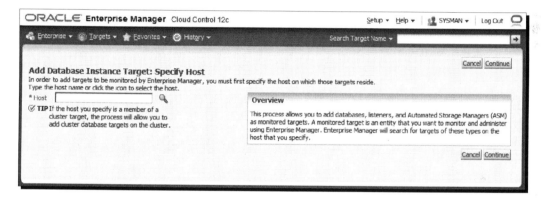

3. Cloud Control will discover all the databases running on the specified host, including ASM instances, if they exist. Select the primary database and click on the configure button that is shown with a wrench icon:

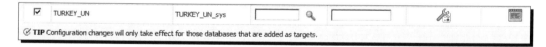

4. On the database configuration screen shown in the following screenshot, control the autofilled fields; type the password of the DBSNMP user and also the connect string for the database. We can click on **Test Connection** to check if Cloud Control is able to connect to the database. Click on **Next** to continue. A review screen will show up; check the information and click on **OK**.

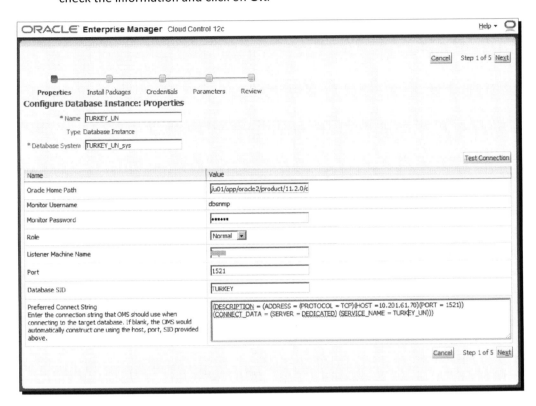

5. After completing the configuration of the database target, turn back to the screen showing the discovered databases. Click on **Finish** and then on the **Summary** page; then click on **Save**. The primary database will be added to the database target list.

 It may take a few minutes to gather information about the status of the database target. So at the beginning, there will be no information in some fields of the database management screens.

6. Repeat the same steps to add all the standby databases to the target database list. At the end, we'll be able to see all the databases of the Data Guard configuration as targets on the database targets screen:

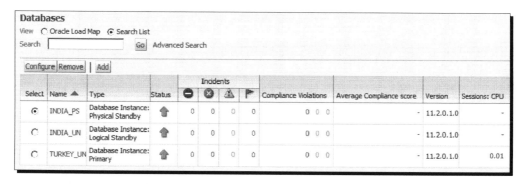

7. All the databases are listed, but Cloud Control is not aware yet that these databases are in the same Data Guard configuration. In order to complete the integration, click on the name of the primary database. On the database home screen, click on **Availability** and then click on **Add Standby Database**. We'll see a database login screen as shown in the following screenshot. We need to connect to the primary database as **SYSDBA** to add a standby database. So type the login information for the sys user and select the **SYSDBA** role. We can save this login information for logging in again in the future, and also set it as a preferred credential as shown in the following screenshot. Click on **Login** to continue.

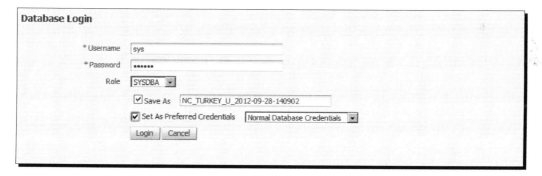

8. We'll see the **Add Standby Database** wizard screen. Besides adding an existing standby to Cloud Control, it's also possible to create a new standby database with this wizard. Now select the **Manage an existing standby database with Data Guard broker** option and click on **Continue**:

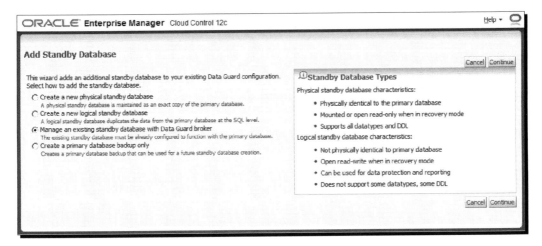

9. Now we can see the two standby databases. Select one of them and click on **Next**. If there is only one standby database, just click on **Next**:

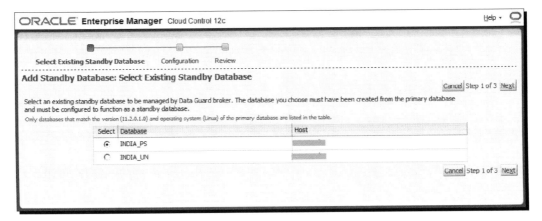

10. Enter the login credential in the next step and click on **Next**.

11. The next step will show the standby archive location and Data Guard connect identifier. If FRA is enabled, the standby archive location will be shown as USE_DB_ RECOVERY_FILE_DEST. In the connect identifier, it's possible to select the connect descriptor used by Enterprise Manager for the standby database or use an existing net service name, which is the same as the example used in our book. Click on **Next** to continue:

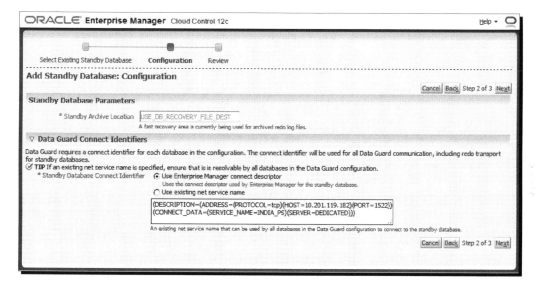

12. A review screen will show up. Check the information and click on **Finish** to complete integrating the standby database with the primary database.

> After this step, Enterprise Manager will execute several ALTER commands on the primary and standby databases. This is a reconfiguration of the Data Guard parameters in order to guarantee a properly integrated Data Guard environment. Check the primary and standby database alert logs to see the ALTER commands.

What just happened?

We've now completed integrating the existing Data Guard environment with Enterprise Manager Cloud Control, and we're able to benefit from the Data Guard monitoring and management properties of Cloud Control.

Have a go hero

Add the logical standby database, if it exists, with the same steps. Note that physical and logical standby databases have no difference when integrating with the primary database on Cloud Control.

Cloud Control Data Guard administration home page

We can access the Data Guard administration home page, shown in the following screenshot, by clicking on **Availability** and then on **Data Guard Administration** on the database home page of any of the databases in the Data Guard configuration. It's possible to monitor and manage Data Guard properties using this screen.

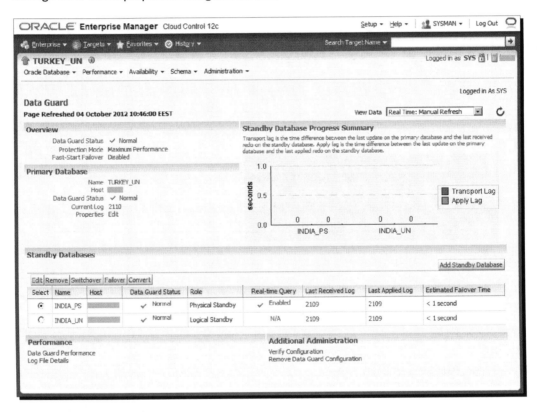

This screen provides general information about the status of Data Guard. We can see the member databases and roles of the Data Guard configuration, the protection mode, Active Data Guard, and the fast-start failover status, the transport and apply lags, if they exist, the last received and applied log sequences, and the estimated failover time on this screen. So it provides a lot of useful information at a single glance.

Whereas a lot of this information can also be gathered easily with other interfaces, it's very practical to access it all in one screen. The **Estimated Failover Time** information shows the approximate number of seconds required for the failover to this standby database. It is very useful to compare the current Data Guard status with **Recovery Time Objective** (**RTO**), which is the disaster recovery element specifying the duration of time within which a business process (database in our case) must be restored after a disaster.

Besides monitoring the Data Guard configuration, this screen also provides links to change the Data Guard properties, which is covered in the next section. We will use the **Data Guard Administration** interface of Cloud Control to modify the configuration.

Modifying the Data Guard configuration

The **Data Guard Administration** home page offers quick links to change a property when showing its current value. For example, in the **Overview** section, the **Protection Mode** field shows **Maximum Performance**; when we click on the **Maximum Performance** link, we can access the **Change Protection Mode** screen. Also, **Fast-Start Failover** shows **Disabled**, and when we click on **Disabled**, we see the **Fast-Start Failover: Configure** screen.

You can edit primary database properties by clicking on **Edit** in the **Primary Database** section. The screen will offer three tabs to change the properties:

- **General**: Using this tab, we can stop/start the redo transport services, view the alert logs of all the databases in the configuration, open the telnet session for the database hosts and disable/enable the Data Guard broker.

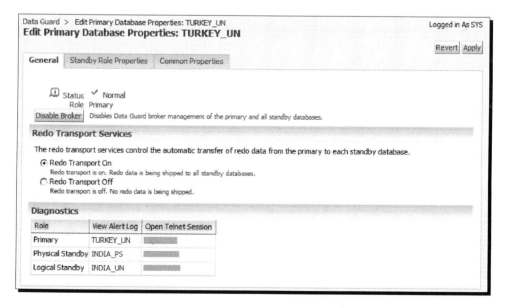

- ◆ **Standby Role Properties**: This tab enables us to set the standby role properties that will be valid after a role change. We can set the **Redo Transport Mode** field to **SYNC** or **ASYNC**, enable/disable redo compression, set the timeout and delay, choose an archive log location for the standby role, and specify the filename convert parameters.

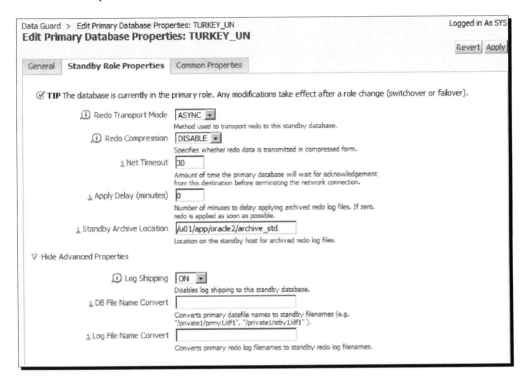

- ◆ **Common Properties**: In this tab, there are some properties that are not role-specific, such as the connect identifier, number of archiver processes, and level of tracing output generated by the Data Guard processes.

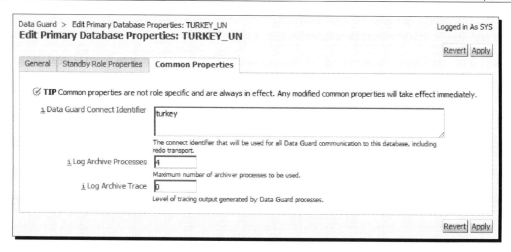

At the bottom of the **Data Guard Administration** home page, we have buttons to perform the following tasks:

- To edit the standby database properties, which offer similar options to the primary database

- To start a switchover or failover to a target standby

- To convert a physical standby into a snapshot standby database

- To add a new standby database to the Data Guard configuration

We can also enable/disable Active Data Guard using the link under **Real-time Query**. If we click on the sequence numbers of the last received and applied archive logs, we'll see the **Log File Details** screen that lists the log files that have not been received and those that have been received but not applied by the standby databases in the Data Guard configuration.

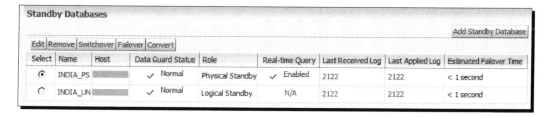

Now let's try changing a Data Guard property. The following section will show how to enable or disable the fast-start failover.

Time for action – enabling/disabling fast-start failover

1. The fast-start failover feature, which can be used for automated failovers in standby databases in the case of a primary database outage, can be enabled and disabled using Cloud Control. On the **Data Guard Administration** home page, in the **Overview** section click on **Disabled** in the **Fast-Start Failover** field. This will enable us to access the fast-start failover configuration page. At the top of the page, it's indicated that there's no specified **Observer** for the Data Guard configuration. Select the standby database that will be the fast-start failover target, and then click on **Configure Observer**.

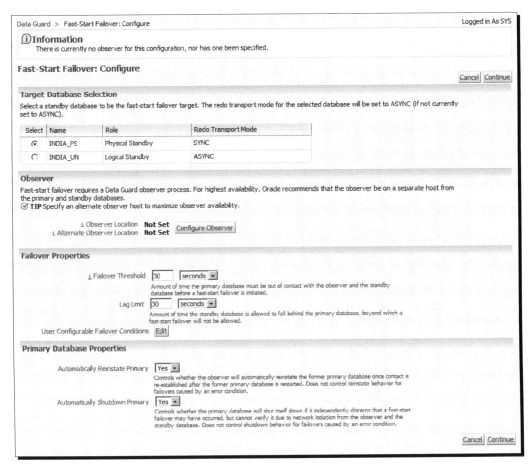

2. Fill the observer hostname and Oracle Home information for the primary and alternate observers. If a problem on the observer is detected, Enterprise Manager will restart it on the primary observer host and fall back to the alternate host when necessary. (We can optionally specify connect identifiers for the primary and standby databases.) If not, the observer will use the connect identifiers used in the Data Guard configuration. Click on **OK** to continue.

 Oracle recommends that the observer be on a separate host from the primary and standby database servers.

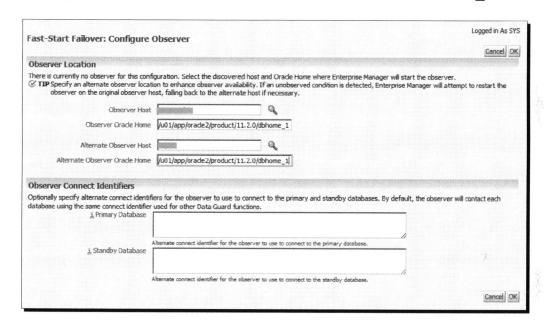

3. We'll return to the fast-start failover configuration page. At the bottom of the page, we'll see the **Failover Properties** and **Primary Database Properties** sections.

There are two properties in the **Failover Properties** section; they are set to 30 seconds by default, but can be changed. The **Failover Threshold** property is the amount of time that the primary database must be unreachable to initiate the failover, and **Lag Limit** is the maximum lag between the primary and standby databases, beyond which a fast-start failover will not be allowed. Now click on **Edit** next to **User Configurable Failover Conditions**. We're able to specify conditions that should cause a fast-start failover if detected on the primary database in this page. Click on **OK** to apply any changes and go back to the fast-start failover configuration page.

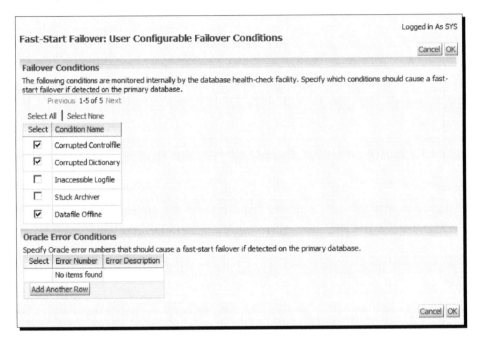

4. Check all the fast-start failover settings and click on **Continue**. The following steps will require OS credentials to connect primary and alternate observer hosts.

5. Now we must enable flashback logging on the primary and standby databases if it has not yet been enabled. We need to specify the **Flash Recovery Area** path, **Flash Recovery Area Size**, and **Flashback Retention Time** if flashback logging is not enabled. If it's enabled, we can see the current values. Specify the values and click on **Continue**.

6. The last page will request a confirmation about enabling flashback logging, starting the observer on the specified host, and enabling a fast-start failover. Click on **Yes** to continue.

7. We can see the progress as shown in the following screenshot. If it is accomplished successfully, we'll see the message, **The fast-start failover mode has been successfully changed**. Also, the fast-start failover status will show **Enabled to INDIA_PS** and the observer hostname will appear on the **Data Guard Administration** home page.

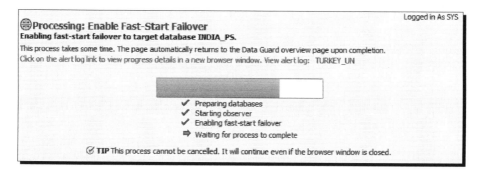

What just happened?

We've seen which properties of Data Guard can be changed with the Enterprise Manager Cloud Control interface. We've also examined the steps and options for enabling a fast-start failover using Cloud Control.

Have a go hero

Now enable and disable the real-time query (Active Data Guard) option on the physical standby database using Cloud Control. At the same time, check the standby alert log file to track the statements run on the database.

Monitoring Data Guard performance

Enterprise Manager Cloud Control offers a separate screen to monitor Data Guard performance. We can access this screen by clicking on **Availability** and then on **Data Guard Performance** on the database home page. Here's a screenshot of the **Data Guard Performance** page:

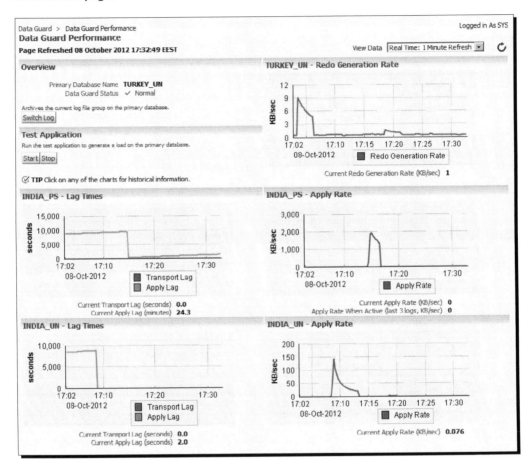

We will see the following information on the performance page:

- The redo generation rate of the primary database
- The lag times for all the standby databases
- The Redo Apply rate for all the standby databases

The redo generation rate of the primary database and the Redo Apply rates of the standby database are important information for Data Guard management. We can use this information to calculate how much time it takes for resynchronization when there's a lag. Also, we can use this information to calculate **Recovery Time Objective (RTO)** when a physical standby is opened as a snapshot standby or when we stop synchronization for maintenance operations.

> Note that the apply rate on this screen is not the Redo Apply capacity of the standby database. It shows the current state of Redo Apply. So if the load on the database is low, we'll see lower apply rates than its actual capacity. We can determine the Redo Apply capacity of a standby database when the Redo Apply process does not wait for a new redo to arrive. So we can achieve this by stopping Redo Apply for a while and starting it again or increasing the redo generation rate on the primary database to a higher value.
>
> On the **Data Guard Performance** screen, we can click on the charts to reach the historical information.

The **Data Guard Performance** screen of Cloud Control has another part named **Test Application**. We can see the **Start** and **Stop** buttons here. When we start a test application, it generates a load on the primary database. Then we can pause or stop it at any time. This is useful if you want to see the behavior of a low-load Data Guard configuration under heavy load.

Using Incident Manager to monitor Data Guard

Enterprise Manager Cloud Control 12*c* provides a centralized incident management console called **Incident Manager**. This console is an advanced interface to track, diagnose, and resolve default and user-defined incidents. Additionally, it provides features to help rectify the root causes of recurring incidents. Incident Manager also provides lifecycle operations for incidents. It's possible to assign the ownership of an incident to a specific user, set the priority for an incident, escalate it or suppress it for a later time, and track an incident's status.

From the Data Guard management perspective, Incident Manager can help administrators be informed about the issues related to Data Guard, and help track and resolve them. We can define thresholds to default Data Guard metrics and also create user-defined metrics using SQL statements. When the current state of a metric reaches its threshold, an incident is created automatically.

To access the default metrics of Data Guard on the database home page, perform the following steps:

1. Click on **Oracle Database**.

2. Click on **Monitoring**.

3. Click on **All Metrics**.

4. Expand the **Data Guard Failover**, **Data Guard Fast-Start Failover Observer**, **Data Guard Performance**, and **Data Guard Status** (only in the primary database) categories to see all the related metrics. The primary and standby databases have different metrics as we can see in the following screenshot:

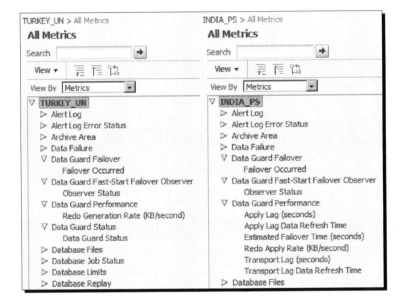

It's possible to define the thresholds of some of these metrics. We can define two values: the **Warning** and **Critical** thresholds. However, some of them are not editable because they're simple 0/1 controls such as **Observer Status** or **Failover Occurred**.

These metrics produce incidents; we can see the details of an incident on the Incident Manager page, which is accessible from the **Enterprise** menu, select **Monitoring**, and then **Incident Manager**. It's also possible to monitor incidents for a specific database by clicking on the **Oracle Database** menu and then going to **Monitoring | Incident Manager** on the database home page.

Time for action – setting the threshold and creating an incident for estimated failover time metric

Perform the following steps to set a threshold and create an estimated failover time metric:

1. Open the database home page for the standby database by navigating to **Targets | Databases** and then clicking on the name of the standby database.

2. Navigate to the metrics page by navigating to **Oracle Database | Monitoring | All Metrics**.

3. Expand the **Data Guard Performance** category and click on the **Estimated Failover Time** section:

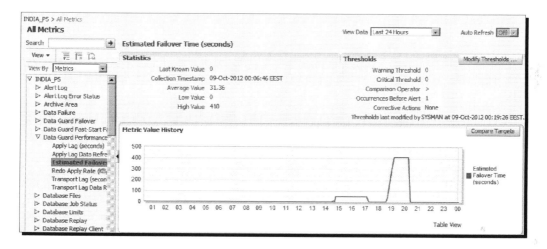

4. Click on **Modify Thresholds**. Enter 15 for **Warning Threshold** and 20 for **Critical Threshold**. Then click on **Save Thresholds**:

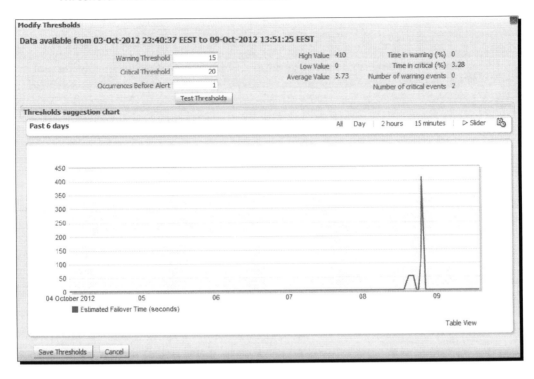

5. Navigate to the Data Guard Administration page by navigating to **Availability | Data Guard Administration**. Click on **Edit** to edit the standby database properties.

6. Stop the Redo Apply process by selecting **Apply Off** and click on **Apply**:

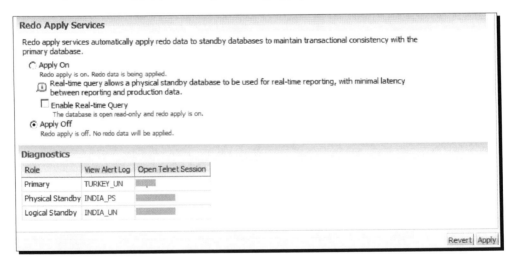

7. Navigate to the Data Guard performance page by navigating to **Availability | Data Guard Performance** and start the test application. After the test application is started, load will be generated on the primary database. Because we have stopped the Redo Apply process on the standby database, an apply lag will occur and the estimated failover time will increase.

8. Open the Incident Manager by navigating to **Enterprise | Monitoring | Incident Manager**. Refresh the page until an incident comes up about the estimated failover time. We can see an example incident in the following screenshot:

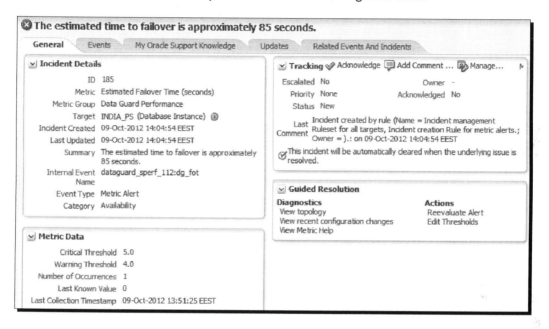

9. Stop the test application and then start the Redo Apply process on the standby database.

What just happened?

We've seen the Data Guard performance monitoring and the Incident Management properties of Cloud Control. We've also run an example to automatically create an incident on an estimated failover time metric. These incidents may help database administrators a lot, for monitoring their Data Guard environments.

RMAN integration

Backing up a database is one of the usual DBA tasks and is a mandatory job on production systems. **Recovery Manager (RMAN)** has been supplied and recommended by Oracle, and provides effective, fast, and manageable methods to back up, restore, and recover an Oracle Database. Therefore, it is the most commonly used backup and recovery manager for Oracle Databases.

When used with Data Guard, RMAN offers extra safety and effectiveness to database administrators. It's possible to use a backup taken on the standby in order to restore and recover a primary database, and vice versa. Datafile, control file, and archived log file backups are interchangeable in a Data Guard environment. So we can prefer carrying the backup load on the primary database to a standby, or back up both the primary and standby for more data security. We can also use standby databases for the **block change tracking** (**BCT**) feature; it increases the incremental backup performance by identifying the changed data blocks since the last incremental backup.

Integration requirements and best practices

We need to build an integrated environment to take advantage of using RMAN in a Data Guard configuration. Let's see the requirements and best practices for integrating these two Oracle database components.

Physical standby requirement

The most important point of this integration is the fact that only physical standby databases can be used for interchangeable backups. If you recall, logical standby databases are not block copies of the primary database, so they may be in a different physical structure from it. So it's not possible to use a logical standby backup to restore and recover a primary database. The backup consideration of logical standby databases must be dealt with separately. However, a physical standby backup can be used to restore and recover the primary or any other physical standby databases in the Data Guard configuration.

RMAN Catalog requirement

An **RMAN Catalog** application is used to record the backup information of different databases in a centrally located system for easy access and use in case of database breakdowns. It's an option that is preferred in an environment with a large number of Oracle databases; however, RMAN Catalog has to be used in a Data Guard environment for successful integration. Otherwise, it will not be possible for the databases to be aware of backups taken from others in the same Data Guard configuration without a manual operation.

We should place the RMAN Catalog in a separate server from the primary and standby database servers, so that it will be possible to access the catalog that contains the necessary backup information in the case of any database server breakdown. We should also consider the high availability and disaster recovery requirements of the RMAN Catalog database.

Using a different DB_UNIQUE_NAME

In 11*g*, databases in the Data Guard configuration should have different DB_UNIQUE_NAME values. We're saying *should* because, if it's a simple configuration with no broker, fast-start failover, TAF, and so on, it's possible to run Data Guard with the same DB_UNIQUE_NAME value on the primary and standby databases. However, this is not a recommended configuration.

When performing a backup in a Data Guard environment, RMAN records the backup information by associating it with the DB_UNIQUE_NAME value of the database. So it's important to set different values for the primary database and for all the standby databases for a proper integration.

General RMAN best practices

We should follow some general best practices when using RMAN for backing up and recovering Oracle databases. These best practices are also valid in a Data Guard configuration. Some of them are as follows:

- ◆ Enabling a fast recovery area for an effective disk backup strategy
- ◆ Keeping the flashback database on in order to return the database and objects to their state at a previous point in time without a full restore of the database
- ◆ Using SPFILE and setting AUTOBACKUP on to automate backups of SPFILE and the control file at the end of all RMAN backup operations
- ◆ Enabling block change tracking for fast increment backups
- ◆ Configuring an appropriate parallelism setting for the better performance of RMAN operations

RMAN settings for the Data Guard environment

After learning the requirements and best practices, now let's see what we should accomplish to create an integrated environment.

It is assumed that there is an RMAN Catalog database ready to use. For testing purposes, you can use your Data Guard test servers to create a catalog. Creating an RMAN catalog is not within the scope of this book, so you should follow related documentation to complete this job, which is quite easy.

Registering primary database in the catalog

We'll start with introducing the primary database to the RMAN Catalog application using the REGISTER command. Only the primary database has to be registered in the RMAN Catalog application. A physical standby database will be registered automatically when we connect it as a target to the RMAN Catalog application.

Run the following commands on the primary host to register the primary database in the RMAN Catalog application:

```
$ rman

Recovery Manager: Release 11.2.0.1.0 - Production on Wed Oct 10 13:46:15
2012

Copyright (c) 1982, 2009, Oracle and/or its affiliates.    All rights
reserved.

RMAN> CONNECT TARGET /

connected to target database: ORCL (DBID=1319333016)

RMAN> CONNECT CATALOG RMAN/RMAN@RMANCAT

connected to recovery catalog database

RMAN> REGISTER DATABASE;

database registered in recovery catalog
starting full resync of recovery catalog
full resync complete
```

Configuring RMAN settings for primary database:

After registering the primary database in the catalog, we should now configure some RMAN settings. First, specify a retention policy to specify for how long a period of time it is guaranteed to do a point-in-time recovery. Backups older than the retention policy will be marked as OBSOLETE, which means that they are not needed.

```
RMAN> CONFIGURE RETENTION POLICY TO RECOVERY WINDOW OF 7 DAYS;
```

If backups are to be run on the primary database, turn on automatic backup of the control file and turn on backup optimization; this will prevent the unnecessary backup of a datafile that has been unchanged since its last backup.

```
RMAN> CONFIGURE CONTROLFILE AUTOBACKUP ON;
RMAN> CONFIGURE BACKUP OPTIMIZATION ON;
```

We should set an archived log deletion policy for the primary database. If archived log backups will be taken from the primary database, we can set the policy to NONE in order to let the database manage the deletion regarding the FRA space or set a policy to mark the archived logs as OBSOLETE depending on the number of existing disk/tape backups.

```
RMAN> CONFIGURE ARCHIVELOG DELETION POLICY TO NONE;
```

We can also use the following command instead of the previous one:

```
RMAN> CONFIGURE ARCHIVELOG DELETION POLICY TO BACKED UP 1 TIMES TO DEVICE
TYPE DISK;
```

If archived log backups are not taken from the primary database, the retention policy will mark them as OBSOLETE as they are shipped/applied on the standby databases:

```
RMAN> CONFIGURE ARCHIVELOG DELETION POLICY TO APPLIED ON ALL STANDBY;
```

You can also use the following command:

```
RMAN> CONFIGURE ARCHIVELOG DELETION POLICY TO SHIPPED TO ALL STANDBY;
```

We'll now specify net service names for the databases in the Data Guard configuration with the following commands:

```
RMAN> CONFIGURE DB_UNIQUE_NAME TURKEY_UN CONNECT IDENTIFIER 'TURKEY';
RMAN> CONFIGURE DB_UNIQUE_NAME INDIA_PS CONNECT IDENTIFIER 'INDIAPS';
```

Using these net service names, the RMAN target database will connect to other databases of the Data Guard when the RESYNC CATALOG FROM DB_UNIQUE_NAME command is executed. This command is used to make RMAN Catalog consistent with the specified database control file. It updates physical database structure (tablespace, datafile), archived log, and backup records in the catalog. It's good practice to use the RESYNC CATALOG FROM DB_UNIQUE_NAME ALL command in the scheduled RMAN script in a Data Guard environment.

> We specified that it's not necessary to register standby databases in RMAN Catalog because they'll automatically be registered when connected as a target. The CONFIGURE DB_UNIQUE_NAME command also implicitly registers the standby database in the catalog if it has not been registered yet.

Let's check those databases of Data Guard that are known to RMAN Catalog. We'll be able to see all the databases specified with the CONFIGURE DB_UNIQUE_NAME command:

```
RMAN> LIST DB_UNIQUE_NAME OF DATABASE;
List of Databases
DB Key  DB Name  DB ID            Database Role    Db_unique_name
-------  -------  ---------------  ---------------  -----------------
2        ORCL     1319333016       PRIMARY          TURKEY_UN
2        ORCL     1319333016       STANDBY          INDIA_PS
```

Configuring RMAN settings for standby database

We should first decide whether we'll use a physical standby as the source for database backups. The best practice is to back up both the primary and the standby databases. If this is not preferred, the network between the primary and standby databases is determinant. It won't be feasible to run backups only on the standby, where it's connected to the primary database over a WAN network. This will dramatically affect the restore time on the primary database, which is not acceptable. If both databases are in the same LAN, we can consider running backups only on the standby database.

If backups are to be taken from the standby database, connect the RMAN Catalog application and the physical standby as targets to configure the settings for the standby database. We should turn on automatic backup for the control file and backup optimization.

```
RMAN> CONFIGURE CONTROLFILE AUTOBACKUP ON;
RMAN> CONFIGURE BACKUP OPTIMIZATION ON;
```

Then we should set the archived log deletion policy. We should use the similar strategy that is mentioned in the primary database RMAN settings. So if we want to back up the archived logs on the standby, we should set the deletion policy to NONE or set a policy to mark the archived logs as OBSOLETE depending on the number of existing disk/tape backups. If no archived log backup is running on the standby, use the APPLIED ON STANDBY policy for archived log deletion.

Checking the RMAN configuration

We can check the configuration for all the databases in the Data Guard configuration by connecting to any of the databases and the recovery catalog. Use the SHOW ALL command with the FOR DB_UNIQUE_NAME option to check the values of the RMAN parameters for the specified database:

```
RMAN> SHOW ALL FOR DB_UNIQUE_NAME TURKEY_UN;

RMAN configuration parameters for database with db_unique_name TURKEY_UN
are:
```

```
CONFIGURE RETENTION POLICY TO RECOVERY WINDOW OF 7 DAYS;

CONFIGURE BACKUP OPTIMIZATION OFF; # default

CONFIGURE DEFAULT DEVICE TYPE TO DISK; # default

CONFIGURE CONTROLFILE AUTOBACKUP OFF; # default

CONFIGURE CONTROLFILE AUTOBACKUP FORMAT FOR DEVICE TYPE DISK TO '%F'; #
default

CONFIGURE DEVICE TYPE DISK PARALLELISM 1 BACKUP TYPE TO BACKUPSET; #
default

CONFIGURE DATAFILE BACKUP COPIES FOR DEVICE TYPE DISK TO 1; # default

CONFIGURE ARCHIVELOG BACKUP COPIES FOR DEVICE TYPE DISK TO 1; # default

CONFIGURE MAXSETSIZE TO UNLIMITED; # default

CONFIGURE ENCRYPTION FOR DATABASE OFF; # default

CONFIGURE ENCRYPTION ALGORITHM 'AES128'; # default

CONFIGURE COMPRESSION ALGORITHM 'BASIC' AS OF RELEASE 'DEFAULT' OPTIMIZE
FOR LOAD TRUE ; # default

CONFIGURE DB_UNIQUE_NAME 'TURKEY_UN' CONNECT IDENTIFIER  'TURKEY';

CONFIGURE DB_UNIQUE_NAME 'INDIA_PS' CONNECT IDENTIFIER  'INDIAPS';

CONFIGURE ARCHIVELOG DELETION POLICY TO APPLIED ON ALL STANDBY;

CONFIGURE SNAPSHOT CONTROLFILE NAME TO '/u01/app/oracle2/product/11.2.0/
dbhome_1/dbs/snapcf_INDIAPS.f'; # default


RMAN>   SHOW ALL FOR DB_UNIQUE_NAME INDIA_PS;


RMAN configuration parameters for database with db_unique_name INDIA_PS
are:

CONFIGURE RETENTION POLICY TO RECOVERY WINDOW OF 7 DAYS;

CONFIGURE BACKUP OPTIMIZATION ON;

CONFIGURE DEFAULT DEVICE TYPE TO DISK; # default

CONFIGURE CONTROLFILE AUTOBACKUP ON;

CONFIGURE CONTROLFILE AUTOBACKUP FORMAT FOR DEVICE TYPE DISK TO '%F'; #
default

CONFIGURE DEVICE TYPE DISK PARALLELISM 1 BACKUP TYPE TO BACKUPSET; #
default

CONFIGURE DATAFILE BACKUP COPIES FOR DEVICE TYPE DISK TO 1; # default

CONFIGURE ARCHIVELOG BACKUP COPIES FOR DEVICE TYPE DISK TO 1; # default

CONFIGURE MAXSETSIZE TO UNLIMITED; # default

CONFIGURE ENCRYPTION FOR DATABASE OFF; # default

CONFIGURE ENCRYPTION ALGORITHM 'AES128'; # default
```

```
CONFIGURE COMPRESSION ALGORITHM 'BASIC' AS OF RELEASE 'DEFAULT' OPTIMIZE
FOR LOAD TRUE ; # default

CONFIGURE DB_UNIQUE_NAME 'TURKEY_UN' CONNECT IDENTIFIER  'TURKEY';

CONFIGURE DB_UNIQUE_NAME 'INDIA_PS' CONNECT IDENTIFIER  'INDIAPS';

CONFIGURE ARCHIVELOG DELETION POLICY TO NONE;

CONFIGURE SNAPSHOT CONTROLFILE NAME TO '/u01/app/oracle2/product/11.2.0/
dbhome_1/dbs/snapcf_INDIAPS.f'; # default
```

We've successfully completed the integration of the Data Guard environment with RMAN. At this stage, all the databases in the Data Guard administration will be aware of any backup taken with RMAN Catalog connection. If the backup is on tape and there is an accurate configuration between the tape library and all the database servers, any database in the Data Guard administration can use that backup for a restoration. If the backup is on the disk, it has to be on a shared filesystem across all databases of the Data Guard administration in order to be used by other databases. Otherwise, we need to transfer the backup files to other database servers and register them manually if needed.

Now let's perform a recovery scenario in which the primary datafile is lost and recovered using the backup of the standby database datafile that is then taken to the disk immediately.

Time for action – recovering a primary database using a standby database disk backup

1. Let's simulate a case where a datafile is lost by renaming one of the datafiles. Shut down the database, rename the datafile with the mv command, and start the database again. We'll see the `cannot identify/lock data file` error on startup.

   ```
   SQL> shutdown immediate


   $ mv /u01/app/oracle2/datafile/ORCL/users01.dbf /u01/app/oracle2/
   datafile/ORCL/users01.dbf.old


   SQL> startup
   ORACLE instance started.

   Total System Global Area 1603411968 bytes
   Fixed Size                  2213776 bytes
   Variable Size             872417392 bytes
   Database Buffers          671088640 bytes
   Redo Buffers               57692160 bytes
   ```

```
Database mounted.
ORA-01157: cannot identify/lock data file 4 - see DBWR trace file
ORA-01110: data file 4: '/u01/app/oracle2/datafile/ORCL/users01.
dbf'
```

2. Now we'll run an RMAN datafile backup using the standby database as the source and locating the backup file in the primary database. Connect the standby database as the target, and the primary database as the auxiliary; then back up the datafile. It's not mandatory to connect RMAN Catalog because we'll register the backup file to the primary database's control file manually.

```
$ rman
RMAN> connect TARGET sys/password@INDIAPS
RMAN> connect AUXILIARY sys/password@TURKEY
RMAN> backup as copy datafile 4 auxiliary format '/backup/users01_
bckp.dbf';

Starting backup at 10-OCT-12
allocated channel: ORA_DISK_1
channel ORA_DISK_1: SID=1239 device type=DISK
channel ORA_DISK_1: starting datafile copy
input datafile file number=00004 name=/u01/app/oracle2/datafile/
INDIAPS/users01.dbf
output file name=/backup/users01_bckp.dbf tag=TAG20121010T164250
RECID=10 STAMP=796322590
channel ORA_DISK_1: datafile copy complete, elapsed time: 00:00:25
Finished backup at 10-OCT-12
```

3. We must register the backup file to the primary database control file with the RMAN CATALOG command. On the primary database server, connect the database as the target and execute the following statements:

```
$ rman
RMAN> connect target /

connected to target database: ORCL (DBID=1319333016)

RMAN> catalog datafilecopy '/backup/users01_bckp.dbf';

using target database control file instead of recovery catalog
cataloged datafile copy
datafile copy file name=/backup/users01_bckp.dbf'
 RECID=4 STAMP=796322862
```

4. Switch the datafile 4 to the backup copy that we registered in the previous step:

   ```
   RMAN> switch datafile 4 to copy;

   datafile 4 switched to datafile copy "/backup/users01_bckp.dbf"
   ```

5. Execute the RECOVER DATABASE command on SQL*Plus and open the primary database:

   ```
   SQL> recover database;

   Media recovery complete.

   SQL> alter database open;

   Database altered.
   ```

What just happened?

We've gone through Data Guard and RMAN integration and then executed a primary database recovery example scenario in which the standby database backup was used. If the backup has been performed on the standby database to be taped periodically, we can also use these tape backups to restore files to the primary database.

Have a go hero

Now simulate the opposite situation, that is, a datafile loss on the standby database. Rename a datafile on the standby database and then recover the database using a backup of the datafile taken from the primary database.

Using block change tracking with Data Guard

Block change tracking is a useful RMAN feature that is used to increase incremental backup performance. If it's enabled, changed blocks in each datafile will be recorded in a change-tracking file. When we perform an incremental RMAN backup, this file will be used to identify the changed blocks, so it will not be necessary for the RMAN incremental backup job to scan every block in the datafiles. This considerably improves the performance of the incremental backup jobs and some minimal performance overhead on the database during normal operations.

The ability to use standby databases for block change tracking is an 11*g* feature and requires an Oracle Active Data Guard license. This feature removes the performance overhead of BCT from primary databases. We use the following SQL statement on the standby database to enable BCT:

```
SQL> ALTER DATABASE ENABLE BLOCK CHANGE TRACKING USING FILE '/backup/bct/
block_change.log';

Database altered.

SQL> SELECT FILENAME, STATUS FROM V$BLOCK_CHANGE_TRACKING;
FILENAME                          STATUS

-----------------------------     ----------

/backup/bct/block_change.log      ENABLED
```

When enabled, the block change tracking file that is 10 MB in size is created and grows as needed. It won't be wrong to estimate its maximum size as a few gigabytes.

Besides the advantages provided by block change tracking for backup performance, there are several important bugs for enabling block change tracking on the standby database; this causes the backup jobs to hang and it causes incorrect backups and data loss. These bugs (for example, bugs 9869287, 9068088, 10094823, and so on) were fixed in the later releases, so it's important to check for relevant BCT bugs in the database version before enabling it on the physical standby.

Block change tracking can be disabled with the following statement:

```
SQL> ALTER DATABASE DISABLE BLOCK CHANGE TRACKING;
```

RAC integration

Real Application Cluster (RAC) is a widely used Oracle cluster product that provides high availability and scalability for Oracle databases. When configuring Data Guard on RAC databases, there are some points that we need to take into consideration in order to build a proper integration. For a RAC primary database, we may prefer configuring single instance or RAC standby databases. These configurations will be discussed separately. A single instance primary database and RAC standby database configuration is not common and doesn't require any special attention.

A RAC primary database with a single instance standby database

Creating a single instance standby database for a RAC primary database is a very frequently encountered configuration. The following points are important when configuring a single instance standby for a RAC primary database:

♦ The `LOG_ARCHIVE_DEST_n` parameter in the primary database, which shows the standby database, must be configured with the `SID='*'` option. This will enable a redo transport service on all nodes of the primary database.

♦ Every instance of the primary database must be able to resolve the service name specified in the `LOG_ARCHIVE_DEST_n` parameter pointing to the standby database.

♦ The number of standby redo log files on the standby database must be calculated according to the number of instances and redo log groups in the primary database. The following formula can be used to determine the number of standby redo logs:

*(number of primary redo log groups + 1) * number of threads on primary*

For example, if we have three redo log groups for each instance of a two-node RAC primary database, we must create `(3+1)*2=8` standby redo log groups on the standby database. The size of the standby redo logs should be equal to that of the primary online redo logs. Use the following statement format to create standby logs:

```
ALTER DATABASE ADD STANDBY LOGFILE THREAD 1
GROUP 11 SIZE 100M,
GROUP 12 SIZE 100M,
GROUP 13 SIZE 100M,
GROUP 14 SIZE 100M,

ALTER DATABASE ADD STANDBY LOGFILE THREAD 2
GROUP 15 SIZE 100M,
GROUP 16 SIZE 100M,
GROUP 17 SIZE 100M,
GROUP 18 SIZE 100M;
```

♦ When the maximum protection mode is used, if one of the instances can't reach the standby for a pre-specified time, that instance will be shut down. Other instances that have connectivity to the standby database will continue to operate. If all instances of the primary database lose connection to the standby database for the pre-specified time, the primary database will be shut down.

♦ During the switchover operation to a physical standby, only one instance can be opened in the primary database.

A RAC primary database with a RAC standby database

Now let's see what we should pay attention to when creating a RAC standby database for a RAC primary database:

- The most important point in this configuration is the fact that recovery cannot be active on all instances of the standby database. Only one instance can be used for recovery.

- The `LOG_ARCHIVE_DEST_n` parameters must be configured properly on every instance of the primary and standby databases to show remote archiving destinations. Remote destinations configured on the standby database will be used after a switchover.

- Standby redo logs must be created on a shared location, such as a cluster file system or ASM, using the formula and format given in the previous section. All instances of the standby database must be able to access the standby redo logs.

- The local archiving destination of the standby database must be the same and it should be a shared location for all instances.

- The consideration about the maximum protection mode in the previous section is still valid.

- During a switchover, only one primary and one standby instance can be active. Other instances must be shut down.

The integration of Data Guard and RAC was covered under the titles of two different configurations where the standby database is a single instance of a RAC. Using RAC with Data Guard is a common solution that combines high availability and disaster recovery purposes in a dependable way. Oracle recommends this configuration in its **maximum availability architecture**.

Summary

We've reached the end of the chapter. The integration of Data Guard with Enterprise Manager Cloud Control, RMAN, and RAC was covered with examples. As mentioned before, it's not enough only to install a Data Guard configuration; we should also integrate it with the current Oracle database environment and the other Oracle products in use, whenever possible. This will help us build a comprehensive, effective, and highly available database system.

The next chapter will show you how to apply database patches to Oracle Data Guard environments with key points and best practices.

9
Data Guard Configuration Patching

Patching demands more from production systems to fix the existing bugs in the software to avoid outages in critical databases even when there are no workarounds available. These patches will be delivered by the development team of Oracle. Some patches come with scripts and some do not.

In this chapter we shall discuss the different types of patches, importance of patching, and how to apply patches on a database with Data Guard configuration, either on physical or logical standby databases.

What is patch and what are patch types?

Patching basically is the correction or fixing of existing bugs in the software. It can be fixing of security vulnerabilities, and any corrections will be delivered by Oracle in terms of patches, and we have to apply them in Oracle home and need to execute scripts depending on the type of patch. The different types of patches are as follows:

- Bug fix patches (for example, internal errors, memory- or SGA-related bugs, high CPU usage, and so on)
- CPU/SPU patches
- PSU patches
- How to upgrade a patch set level (11.2.0.1 to 11.2.0.3)

Interim patch

Interim patches are also known as one-off patches. For every bug that Oracle delivers, depending on the version and release, bug fixes can be delivered as patches or they will be fixed in the next releases or versions. An interim patch is a fix only for a particular bug. Bugs differ from environment to environment depending upon the OS and Oracle version. Interim patches come in a zipped format, and you have to unzip them before applying the patch. Every interim patch contains the following:

- **Metadata of patch**: This contains the patch ID, bugs that have been fixed using the patch, and so on
- **Payload**: It contains the files that will be modified by the OPatch utility
- **Custom scripts**: These contain scripts for preprocessing and postprocessing that need to run before and after the patching

CPU/SPU patches

You should not get confused between **Critical Patch Update** (**CPU**)and **Security Patch Update** (**SPU**) as CPU terminology has been changed to SPU from October 2012. Before that, the terminology was CPU. CPU patches were introduced in January 2005 and they are released every quarter, which is four times a year.

PSU patches

Patch Set Updates (**PSU**) are cumulative patches for a particular product version. They are cumulative of CPU and include security fixes, wrong results, data corruption, and additional bugs. They have a low risk and do not require changes that require recertification such as dictionary changes, major algorithm changes, and any optimizer plan changes. On an average, each PSU contains typically 25 to 100 bug fixes per PSU. For PSU-related information, you can find more details from the MOS Note:854428.1: Introduction to Database Patch Set Updates. When you apply PSU and CPU, you may come across conflicts. PSUs contain CPUs of every quarter. You can apply PSU patches on any CPU and it is very difficult to go back to CPUs from PSUs.

Patch set

A patch set provides bug fixes and it includes all the libraries that have been rebuilt to implement the bug fixes in the set. They are fully tested and integrated product fixes and are certified to work with each other. These can be applied on a database, RAC, and client software. If you are going to perform a fresh installation of a database with the latest release and patch set 11.2.0.3, then there is no need of installing 11.2.0.1 and then upgrading it to 11.2.0.3; instead of that, you can directly install the software of 11.2.0.3. This option has been introduced from 11*g*R onwards. If you have already installed 11.2.0.2 and then upgraded it to 11.2.0.3, this patch set removes the patches applied (bugs and CPU/PSUs) in the previous RDBMS version.

Patching on Data Guard

If you have already been maintaining a production database for many years, have probably applied patches to fix bugs, and also applied CPU/PSU patches for the previously discussed reasons, and if your requirement is to create a Data Guard environment for high availability of your production database, then ensure that all the patches that you have applied on the standby database are the same as the primary database. You can also consider the option of cloning ORACLE_HOME for this. It also happens to be the best option. The reason is that the standby database is an exact copy of the primary database in terms of databases and software. Hence, the environment should be compatible and same in terms of patching. If there is any incompatibility with the patch, and the requirement is to perform a switchover/ failover and in the past you have applied any patch to fix ORA-00600 on the primary and not applied the same on the standby, then the bug can hit you again. Thus, ensure that all the patches of the primary have been applied on the standby also. Consider it as a basic rule to apply patching first on a standby database and then on a primary database; the standby database can be either physical or logical.

What just happened?

We have seen what patching is, different types of patches (interim/bug, CPU/SPU, PSU, and patch set), and how patching is important in a Data Guard environment.

Best practices of patching

Before using the OPatch utility, ensure that the OPatch directory is set to the path. It is applicable for all the environments (UNIX or Windows). Then we can start using the OPatch utility as follows:

```
[oracle@oracle-primary ~]$ export PATH=$ORACLE_HOME/OPatch:$PATH
[oracle@oracle-primary ~]$ opatch -help
Invoking OPatch 11.1.0.6.6
Oracle Interim Patch Installer version 11.1.0.6.6
Copyright (c) 2009, Oracle Corporation.  All rights reserved.
```

Upgrading OPatch

If you have installed Oracle 11*g*R2, the OPatch version will be 11.1.0.6.6 by default. If you proceed to apply any latest patches of 11.2.0.1, you must upgrade the OPatch version as well. The following error will be displayed if you try to apply a higher update of the patch and if your OPatch version is lower:

```
OPatch version     : 11.1.0.6.6
. . . . . . .
```

```
ApplySession failed: Patch ID is null.
System intact, OPatch will not attempt to restore the system
OPatch failed with error code 73
```

From the logfile `/u01/home/oracle/product/11.2.0/db_1/cfgtoollogs/opatch/opatch2012-12-15_11-57-48AM.log`, the following message will be shown:

```
INFO:Starting ApplySession at Sat Dec 15 11:57:49 IST 2012
INFO:Starting Apply Session at Sat Dec 15 11:57:49 IST 2012
SEVERE:OUI-67073:ApplySession failed: Patch ID is null.
INFO:System intact, OPatch will not attempt to restore the system
INFO:Finishing ApplySession at Sat Dec 15 11:57:51 IST 2012
```

To fix this issue, first upgrade the OPatch utility by downloading `Patch 6880880` for your OS and Oracle release. Of course, the patch number will be the same even though your database version and release will be different, but you just need to select the related OS and database version. The following screenshot illustrates the same:

Patch Name	Description	Release
6880880	OPatch 9i, 10.1 (Patch)	10.1.0.0.0
6880880	OPatch 10.2 (Patch)	10.2.0.0.0
6880880	OPatch patch of version 11.1.0.9.9 for Oracle software releases 11.1.0.x (SEPTEMBER 2012) (Patch)	11.1.0.0.0
6880880	OPatch patch of version 11.2.0.3.3 for Oracle software releases 11.2.0.x (DECEMBER 2012) (Patch)	11.2.0.0.0

Then, after downloading the patch and unzipping it in the `$ORACLE_HOME` location, you should be able to apply the patch as follows:

```
[oracle@oracle-stby patches]$ opatch -help
Oracle Interim Patch Installer version 11.2.0.3.0
Copyright (c) 2012, Oracle Corporation.  All rights reserved.
```

Performing prerequisite checks of patch

Before applying any interim CPU patch that is applied through OPatch, it is strongly recommended to perform a prerequisite check in the ORACLE_HOME file that you are going to patch. Patches that are specific to security may be some of the patches that are already applied. Such a patch/patches needs to rollback and again has to apply a merge patch after applying security patches. These merge patches can be requested from Oracle support if they aren't available. Note that no down time is required to perform this check.

You can perform the prerequisite check as follows:

```
opatch prereq CheckConflictAgainstOHWithDetail -phBaseDir  /home/oracle/
patches/9711859

Oracle Interim Patch Installer version 11.2.0.3.0

Copyright (c) 2012, Oracle Corporation.  All rights reserved.

PREREQ session

Oracle Home        : /u01/home/oracle/product/11.2.0/db_1

Central Inventory : /u01/app/oraInventory

   from            : /u01/home/oracle/product/11.2.0/db_1/oraInst.loc

OPatch version     : 11.2.0.3.0

OUI version        : 11.2.0.1.0

Log file location : /u01/home/oracle/product/11.2.0/db_1/cfgtoollogs/
opatch/opatch2012-12-15_23-41-35PM_1.log

Invoking prereq "checkconflictagainstohwithdetail"

Prereq "checkConflictAgainstOHWithDetail" passed.

OPatch succeeded.

[oracle@oracle-stby 9711859]$
```

How to clean up patch history?

If you are applying any CPU, PSU, or interim patches, OPatch will consume a large amount of disk space under $ORACLE_HOME/.patch_storage. To perform a cleanup, use the file orapatch.util.cleanup. The folder patch_storage contains the backup of the affected libraries and modules that have been updated. Cleanup can be performed as follows:

```
[oracle@oracle-primary ~]$ opatch util cleanup

Oracle Interim Patch Installer version 11.2.0.3.0

Copyright (c) 2012, Oracle Corporation.  All rights reserved.

. . . . . . . . . . . . . . .

Invoking utility "cleanup"

OPatch will clean up 'restore.sh,make.txt' files and 'rac,scratch,backup'
directories.

You will be still able to rollback patches after this cleanup.

Do you want to proceed? [y|n]

y

User Responded with: Y

. . . . . . . . . . . . . . .
```

```
"/u01/home/oracle/product/11.2.0/db_1/.patch_storage" after cleanup is
79575030 bytes.

UtilSession: Backup area for restore has been cleaned up. For a complete
list of files/directories

deleted, Please refer log file.

OPatch succeeded.

[oracle@oracle-primary ~]$
```

> To find out the OPatch version, use the OPatch utility as follows:
>
> ```
> [oracle@oracle-stby admin]$ opatch version
> OPatch Version: 11.2.0.3.0
> OPatch succeeded.
> [oracle@oracle-stby admin]$
> ```

What just happened?

We have seen how to interface patching using the OPatch utility and options available with OPatch in the *Performing prerequisite of patch* and *How to clean up patch history?* sections.

Patching on Data Guard configuration

We will see how to apply patches (bug fixes and PSU) on the Data Guard configurations of physical standby and logical standby databases with and without the Data Guard broker in place. In the later part of this chapter, we will cover how to apply a patch set from 11.2.0.1 to the latest patch set level 11.2.0.3. Applying patches on physical standby is similar to doing the same on logical standby. Changes depend on what kind of patches we are applying. For bug fixes you have to apply the patch only on ORACLE_HOME, and if you are applying CPU or PSU patches, you have to run the scripts such as the catbundle.sql script. Note that it is a cumulative script.

How to apply an interim/bug patch on logical standby?

Now we will apply one bug fix Patch 9711859: ORA-600 [KTSPTRN_FIX-EXTMAP] DURING EXTENT ALLOCATION on a logical standby environment of 11.2.0.1.

Time for action – applying a patch on logical standby

1. Disable log shipping in a standby database and stop SQL Apply in it. First we need to stop SQL Apply in the standby database and disable log shipping from the primary database as follows:

```
SQL> select db_unique_name,database_role from v$database;
DB_UNIQUE_NAME   DATABASE_ROLE
---------------  ----------------
turkey_un        PRIMARY
SQL> ALTER SYSTEM SET LOG_ARCHIVE_DEST_STATE_2='DEFER';
System altered.
SQL>
```

2. Stop SQL Apply in the logical standby database as follows:

```
SQL> select db_unique_name,database_role from v$database;
DB_UNIQUE_NAME   DATABASE_ROLE
---------------  ----------------
INDIA_UN         LOGICAL STANDBY
SQL> ALTER DATABASE STOP LOGICAL STANDBY APPLY;
Database altered.
SQL>
```

3. Stop the database services of the primary and standby and perform a backup of `ORACLE_HOME`.

4. After applying a patch, more objects can become invalid. Hence. gather all the invalid objects and keep a count of them so that they can be recompiled after the activity as follows:

```
SQL> select owner,object_name,object_type,status from dba_
objects  where status <> 'VALID' and OWNER !='PUBLIC' and OBJECT_
TYPE!='SYNONYM';
```

5. Ensure a valid and latest Cold/RMAN backup prior to applying the patch, and also ensure that all the applications are stopped completely. You can check for active sessions from `v$session`.

```
SQL> shutdown immediate
Database closed.
Database dismounted.
ORACLE instance shut down.
SQL>
[oracle@oracle-primary ~]$ lsnrctl stop
```

```
LSNRCTL for Linux: Version 11.2.0.1.0 - Production on 15-DEC-2012
22:52:16

Copyright (c) 1991, 2009, Oracle.  All rights reserved.

Connecting to (DESCRIPTION=(ADDRESS=(PROTOCOL=IPC)
(KEY=EXTPROC1521)))

The command completed successfully

[oracle@oracle-primary ~]$
```

6. Make sure that no Oracle-related services are running and perform a backup of ORACLE_HOME and of Oracle's inventory using the `tar` command as follows:

```
[oracle@oracle-primary backup]$ tar -zcpvf  /home/oracle/
backup/11.2.0_Home_Inventory_Backup_$(date +%Y%m%d).tar.gz /u01/
home/oracle/product/11.2.0/db_1 /u01/app/oraInventory

/u01/home/oracle/product/11.2.0/db_1/

/u01/home/oracle/product/11.2.0/db_1/uix/

. . . . . . . . . . . . . .

/u01/app/oraInventory/ContentsXML/inventory.xml

/u01/app/oraInventory/ContentsXML/comps.xml

/u01/app/oraInventory/ContentsXML/libs.xml

[oracle@oracle-primary backup]$
```

> You can use the `tar` ball in case there are any libraries that are corrupted and you are unable to access the Oracle home after applying the patch.

7. Apply a patch on both primary and standby.

8. We apply patch 9711859, which is a fix for Patch 9711859: ORA-600 [KTSPTRN_FIX-EXTMAP] DURING EXTENT ALLOCATION on both primary and standby databases. We have already performed the prerequisite check to apply the patch and ensured that you have exported OPatch to the environment path to use the OPatch utility as follows:

```
[oracle@oracle-primary 9711859]$ export PATH=/u01/home/oracle/
product/11.2.0/db_1/OPatch:$PATH

[oracle@oracle-primary 9711859]$ opatch apply

Oracle Interim Patch Installer version 11.2.0.3.0

. . . . . . . . . . . . . .

Applying interim patch '9711859' to OH '/u01/home/oracle/
product/11.2.0/db_1'

Verifying environment and performing prerequisite checks...

All checks passed.
```

```
. . . . . . . . . . . . .
Is the local system ready for patching? [y|n]
y
User Responded with: Y
Backing up files...
Patching component oracle.rdbms, 11.2.0.1.0...
Verifying the update...
Patch 9711859 successfully applied
Log file location: /u01/home/oracle/product/11.2.0/db_1/
cfgtoollogs/opatch/9711859_Dec_15_2012_23_46_16/apply2012-12-
15_23-46-16PM_1.log
OPatch succeeded.
[oracle@oracle-primary 9711859]$
```

9. Once you initiate patching on the database server, the patch will prompt you to enter the support identifier's e-mail address for sending frequent updates on latest patches. The patch will then ask you to give a confirmation. Now verify that the patch has been applied and you are able to view it from the inventory as follows:

```
[oracle@oracle-primary ~]$ opatch lspatches -bugs
9711859;;9711859
[oracle@oracle-primary ~]$
```

or

```
[oracle@oracle-primary ~]$ opatch lsinventory|grep 9711859
Patch   9711859      : applied on Sat Dec 15 23:47:18 IST 2012
      9711859
[oracle@oracle-primary ~]$
```

10. You must perform the previous steps in both primary and standby databases.

11. Start the primary database, the logical standby databases, and listeners, and enable apply services. Enable log shipping from the primary database as follows:

```
SQL> startup
ORACLE instance started.
Total System Global Area 2238099456 bytes
Fixed Size                  2215304 bytes
Variable Size            1040188024 bytes
Database Buffers         1191182336 bytes
Redo Buffers                4513792 bytes
Database mounted.
Database opened.
```

```
SQL> alter system set log_archive_dest_state_2='enable';
System altered.
SQL>
```

12. Start the database, listener, and SQL Apply from the logical standby database as follows:

```
SQL> ALTER DATABASE START LOGICAL STANDBY APPLY IMMEDIATE;
Database altered.
SQL>

Sun Dec 16 00:02:27 2012

RFS LogMiner: Registered logfile [/u01/home/oracle/product/11.2.0/
db_1/dbs/arch1_920_788992101.dbf] to LogMiner session id [2]

LOGMINER: Alternate logfile found, transition to mining
logfile for session 2 thread 1 sequence 920, /u01/home/oracle/
product/11.2.0/db_1/dbs/arch1_920_788992101.dbf

LOGMINER: End   mining logfile for session 2 thread 1 sequence
920, /u01/home/oracle/product/11.2.0/db_1/dbs/arch1_920_788992101.
dbf
```

 If you are using logical standby with RAC, you have to perform the same steps on each of the nodes, restart the database, and then start SQL Apply.

13. Verify the logical standby SQL Apply from the standby database. Use the following query to ensure that the redo transport service is working properly in the V$DATAGUARD_STATS view:

```
SQL> SELECT NAME, VALUE, TIME_COMPUTED FROM V$DATAGUARD_STATS
WHERE NAME='transport lag';
NAME                 VALUE              TIME_COMPUTED
-------------------- ------------------ -------------------------
transport lag        +00 00:01:00      12/16/2012 00:08:37
```

14. You can also monitor the status of the redo transport service that has been transferred from the primary and the sequences that are being archived on the logical standby, using the following query:

```
SQL> SELECT PROCESS, STATUS, THREAD#, SEQUENCE#, BLOCK#, BLOCKS
FROM V$MANAGED_STANDBY;
PROCESS    STATUS        THREAD#   SEQUENCE#    BLOCK#     BLOCKS
---------  ------------  --------  ---------   ---------   ---------
ARCH       WRITING          1          5        30720        2048
ARCH       CONNECTED        0          0            0           0
```

ARCH	CONNECTED	0	0	0	0
ARCH	CLOSING	1	919	28672	1776
ARCH	CLOSING	1	920	1	1
RFS	IDLE	0	0	0	0
RFS	WRITING	1	921	149579	2048
RFS	RECEIVING	0	0	0	0

We have successfully applied a bug fix in the logical database environment and double-checked if log shipping is active after the patching, as shown previously.

> To know the applied patches on ORACLE_HOME, use the following commands. It shows the patches applied with the date and time as follows:
>
> ```
> $opatch lsinventory -all
> $opatch lsinventory -detail
> ```

What just happened?

We have seen how to apply an interim/bug fix (9711859) step by step in a Data Guard environment containing a logical standby database.

How to apply a PSU patch on physical standby database using broker?

The CPU or PSU patches are a collection of security fixes. They are released every quarter, that is, four times a year. The CPU patches contain overall security fixes of each quarter and the PSU patches, and are cumulative. Once you have applied PSU, you can further apply only PSU for future quarters until the database is upgraded to the new base version. In this example, we will see how to apply the PSU patch on the physical standby database managed by the broker.

Time for action – applying PSU on a physical standby database

1. Disable log transport and stop MRP in the standby database. Before disabling log transport in standby, cross-check the synchronization between the primary and standby database, as shown in the following screenshot:

```
DGMGRL> edit database turkey_un set state='LOG-TRANSPORT-OFF';
Succeeded.
DGMGRL> show database 'turkey_un';

Database - turkey_un

  Role:              PRIMARY
  Intended State:    TRANSPORT-OFF
  Instance(s):
    TURKEY

Database Status:
SUCCESS

DGMGRL>
```

2. Now cancel MRP using the broker; you can perform this step from any site as shown in the following screenshot:

```
DGMGRL> EDIT DATABASE 'INDIA_UN' SET STATE='APPLY-OFF';
Succeeded.
DGMGRL> show database 'INDIA_UN';

Database - INDIA_UN

  Role:              PHYSICAL_STANDBY
  Intended State:    APPLY-OFF
  Transport Lag:     0 seconds
  Apply Lag:         6 seconds
  Real Time Query:   OFF
  Instance(s):
    INDIA

Database Status:
SUCCESS

DGMGRL>
```

3. Stop the database services of the primary and standby and perform a backup of ORACLE_HOME. Prior to shutting down all the services, gather the invalid objects of each schema to check the invalid objects after the patch has been applied using the following script:

```
SQL> select owner,object_name,object_type,status from dba_
objects  where status <> 'VALID' and OWNER !='PUBLIC' and OBJECT_
TYPE!='SYNONYM';
```

4. Ensure that there is a latest and valid Cold/RMAN backup available prior to applying the patch. Also ensure that all the applications are down. You can check for active sessions from `v$session` as follows:

```
SQL> shutdown immediate

Database closed.

Database dismounted.

ORACLE instance shut down.

SQL>

[oracle@oracle-primary ~]$ lsnrctl stop

LSNRCTL for Linux: Version 11.2.0.1.0 - Production on 15-DEC-2012
22:52:16

Copyright (c) 1991, 2009, Oracle.  All rights reserved.

Connecting to (DESCRIPTION=(ADDRESS=(PROTOCOL=IPC)
(KEY=EXTPROC1521)))

The command completed successfully
```

5. If no Oracle-related services are running, perform a backup of ORACLE_HOME and of the inventory using the `tar` command as follows:

```
[oracle@oracle-primary backup]$ tar -zcpvf  /home/oracle/
backup/11.2.0_Home_Inventory_Backup_$(date +%Y%m%d).tar.gz /u01/
home/oracle/product/11.2.0/db_1 /u01/app/oraInventory

/u01/home/oracle/product/11.2.0/db_1/

/u01/home/oracle/product/11.2.0/db_1/uix/

. . . . . . . . . . . . . . . . . . . . . . . . . .

/u01/app/oraInventory/ContentsXML/inventory.xml

/u01/app/oraInventory/ContentsXML/comps.xml

/u01/app/oraInventory/ContentsXML/libs.xml

[oracle@oracle-primary backup]$
```

> You can use the `tar` ball in case there are any libraries that are corrupted and you are unable to access the Oracle home after applying a patch. The `Tar` command is applicable for UNIX systems. For Windows, the zip option can be used to compress.

6. Apply a patch on both primary and standby. We apply the PSU July 2012 (`12419378`) Patch in the Data Guard environment of both primary and physical standby databases. After applying the patch, the PSU version will be (11.2.0.1.6). Now perform the prerequisite check for any conflicts; if any conflicts are found, you have to get the merge patch on top of 11.2.0.1.6 as follows:

```
[oracle@oracle-primary 12419378]$ opatch prereq
CheckConflictAgainstOHWithDetail -phBaseDir  /home/oracle/
patches/12419378

Oracle Interim Patch Installer version 11.2.0.3.0

. . . . . . . . . . . . . . . . . . . . .

Invoking prereq "checkconflictagainstohwithdetail"

ZOP-40: The patch(es) has conflicts with other patches installed
in the Oracle Home (or) among themselves.

Prereq "checkConflictAgainstOHWithDetail" failed.

Summary of Conflict Analysis:

There are no patches that can be applied now.

Following patches have conflicts. Please contact Oracle Support
and get the merged patch of the patches :

9711859, 12419378

Following patches will be rolled back from Oracle Home on
application of the patches in the given list :

9711859

Conflicts/Supersets for each patch are:

Patch : 12419378

        Conflict with 9711859

        Conflict details:

/u01/home/oracle/product/11.2.0/db_1/lib/libserver11.a:/ktsx.o

OPatch succeeded.

[oracle@oracle-primary 12419378]$
```

7. The prerequisite applied failed because of `Patch 9711859: ORA-600 [KTSPTRN_FIX-EXTMAP] DURING EXTENT ALLOCATION` that was applied in the previous scenario. To resolve this conflict we have to request the merge patch to be applied. Now the action plan is shown as follows:

- ❏ Rollback the `9711859` Patch
- ❏ Apply PSU July 2012 `12419378`
- ❏ Apply Merge Patch `9711859` of 11.2.0.1.6

The following screenshot illustrates the action plan as discussed:

Patch Name	Description	Release
9711859	ORA-600 [KTSPTRN_FIX-EXTMAP] DURING EXTENT ALLOCATION (Patch)	11.2.0.1.6
9711859	ORA-600 [KTSPTRN_FIX-EXTMAP] DURING EXTENT ALLOCATION (Patch)	11.2.0.1.5
9711859	ORA-600 [KTSPTRN_FIX-EXTMAP] DURING EXTENT ALLOCATION (Patch)	11.2.0.1.4
9711859	ORA-600 [KTSPTRN_FIX-EXTMAP] DURING EXTENT ALLOCATION (Patch)	11.2.0.1.3
9711859	ORA-600 [KTSPTRN_FIX-EXTMAP] DURING EXTENT ALLOCATION (Patch)	11.2.0.1.2

8. A rollback is applied on `9711859` of 11.2.0.1.0 using the OPatch utility as follows:

```
[oracle@oracle-primary patches]$ opatch rollback -id 9711859
Oracle Interim Patch Installer version 11.2.0.3.0

Copyright (c) 2012, Oracle Corporation.  All rights reserved.

..........

RollbackSession rolling back interim patch '9711859' from OH '/
u01/home/oracle/product/11.2.0/db_1'

Please shutdown Oracle instances running out of this ORACLE_HOME
on the local system.

(Oracle Home = '/u01/home/oracle/product/11.2.0/db_1')

Is the local system ready for patching? [y|n]

y

User Responded with: Y

Patching component oracle.rdbms, 11.2.0.1.0...

RollbackSession removing interim patch '9711859' from inventory

Log file location: /u01/home/oracle/product/11.2.0/db_1/
cfgtoollogs/opatch/9711859_Dec_16_2012_12_12_51/rollback2012-12-
16_12-12-49PM_1.log

OPatch succeeded.

[oracle@oracle-primary patches]$
```

9. Now apply PSU July 2012 Patch `12419378` as follows:

```
[oracle@oracle-primary 12419378]$ pwd

/home/oracle/patches/12419378

[oracle@oracle-primary 12419378]$ ls

custom  etc  files  patchmd.xml  README.html  README.txt

[oracle@oracle-primary 12419378]$ opatch apply

Oracle Interim Patch Installer version 11.2.0.3.0
```

Copyright (c) 2012, Oracle Corporation. All rights reserved.

Oracle Home   : /u01/home/oracle/product/11.2.0/db_1

. . . .

Patch 12419378: Optional component(s) missing : [oracle.client, 11.2.0.1.0]

All checks passed.

. . . .

Do you wish to remain uninformed of security issues ([Y]es, [N]o) [N]:   Y

Please shutdown Oracle instances running out of this ORACLE_HOME on the local system.

(Oracle Home = '/u01/home/oracle/product/11.2.0/db_1')

Is the local system ready for patching? [y|n]

Y

User Responded with: Y

Backing up files...

Patching component oracle.rdbms.rsf, 11.2.0.1.0...

. . . .

Verifying the update...

Patch 12419378 successfully applied

OPatch Session completed with warnings.

Log file location: /u01/home/oracle/product/11.2.0/db_1/ cfgtoollogs/opatch/12419378_Dec_16_2012_12_18_09/apply2012-12-16_12-18-09PM_1.log

OPatch completed with warnings.

[oracle@oracle-stby 12419378]$

   [Dec 16, 2012 12:21:46 PM]   UtilSession: Backup area for restore has been cleaned up. For a complete list of files/directories

                              deleted, Please refer log file.

[Dec 16, 2012 12:21:46 PM]   Patch 12419378 successfully applied

10. Now apply Merge Patch 9711859 of 11.2.0.1.6 as follows:

[oracle@oracle-primary 9711859]$ ls

etc files README.txt

[oracle@oracle-primary 9711859]$ opatch apply

Oracle Interim Patch Installer version 11.2.0.3.0

Copyright (c) 2012, Oracle Corporation. All rights reserved.

```
Oracle Home        : /u01/home/oracle/product/11.2.0/db_1

Please shutdown Oracle instances running out of this ORACLE_HOME
on the local system.

(Oracle Home = '/u01/home/oracle/product/11.2.0/db_1')

Is the local system ready for patching? [y|n]

y

User Responded with: Y

Backing up files...

Patching component oracle.rdbms, 11.2.0.1.0...

Verifying the update...

Patch 9711859 successfully applied

Log file location: /u01/home/oracle/product/11.2.0/db_1/
cfgtoollogs/opatch/9711859_Dec_16_2012_12_37_13/apply2012-12-
16_12-37-13PM_1.log

OPatch succeeded.

[oracle@oracle-primary 9711859]$
```

The previous steps must be performed on both primary and standby databases and on all the instances if it is RAC.

11. Start the primary and standby databases and execute the post scripts of Catbundle.sql in the primary database. Start both primary and standby (in the Mount status if no Active Data Guard is enabled) databases including listener services. In the primary database run the Catbundle.sql script that is located at $ORACLE_HOME/rdbms/admin, which determines the last bundle in the series that was loaded in the database by the information stored in the dba_registry_history view. It processes the information in bundle_<bundle_series>.xml, which is present in each bundle patch. The following script can be used:

```
SQL> @?/rdbms/admin/catbundle.sql psu apply

PL/SQL procedure successfully completed.

PL/SQL procedure successfully completed.

.................

Generating apply and rollback scripts...

Check the following file for errors:

/u01/home/oracle/product/11.2.0/db_1/cfgtoollogs/catbundle/
catbundle_PSU_ORCL_GENERATE_2012Dec16_12_58_39.log

   6    (SYSTIMESTAMP, 'APPLY',

   7     SYS_CONTEXT('REGISTRY$CTX','NAMESPACE'),

   8     '11.2.0.1',
```

```
 9      6,
10      'PSU',
11      'PSU 11.2.0.1.6');
1 row created.
SQL> COMMIT;
Commit complete.
SQL> SPOOL off
SQL> SET echo off
Check the following log file for errors:
/u01/home/oracle/product/11.2.0/db_1/cfgtoollogs/catbundle/
catbundle_PSU_ORCL_APPLY_2012Dec16_12_58_51.log
SQL>
```

12. For any errors related to post scripts you can refer to the following logs:

```
[oracle@oracle-primary catbundle]$ pwd
/u01/home/oracle/product/11.2.0/db_1/cfgtoollogs/catbundle
[oracle@oracle-primary catbundle]$ ls
catbundle_PSU_ORCL_APPLY_2012Dec16_12_58_51.log
catbundle_PSU_ORCL_GENERATE_2012Dec16_12_58_39.log
[oracle@oracle-primary catbundle]$
```

If in case you want to rollback the patch applied with the bundle script, use the following script:

```
$opatch rollback -id 12419378
```

Start every instance dependent to ORACLE_HOME that has been patched and execute as follows:

```
sql> @$ORACLE_HOME/rdbms/admin/catbundle_
PSU_<database SID>_ROLLBACK.sql
```

13. Verify the patch status from OPatch and the database registry. Once we have applied the patch on the binaries using OPatch, we can verify the patch with an ID from the OS level as follows:

```
[oracle@oracle-primary ~]$ opatch lsinventory -bugs_fixed | grep
-i 'DATABASE PSU'
9352237    12419378  Sun Dec 16 12:21:15 IST 2012    DATABASE PSU
11.2.0.1.1
9654983    12419378  Sun Dec 16 12:21:15 IST 2012    DATABASE PSU
11.2.0.1.2 (INCLUDES CPUJUL2010)
```

```
9952216     12419378   Sun Dec 16 12:21:15 IST 2012   DATABASE PSU
11.2.0.1.3 (INCLUDES CPUOCT2010)

10248516    12419378   Sun Dec 16 12:21:15 IST 2012   database psu
11.2.0.1.4 (includes cpujan2011)

11724930    12419378   Sun Dec 16 12:21:15 IST 2012   database psu
11.2.0.1.5 (includes cpuapr2011)

12419378    12419378   Sun Dec 16 12:21:15 IST 2012   DATABASE PSU
11.2.0.1.6 (INCLUDES CPUJUL2011)

[oracle@oracle-primary ~]$
```

14. We can check the database registry using `registry$history`. This script can be executed from the standby database even in the OPEN status if the archives have been applied after running the `catbundle.sql` script as follows:

```
SQL> select namespace,version,id, comments from registry$history;
NAMESPACE        VERSION                ID COMMENTS
---------------  ----------  -----------  ---------------
SERVER           11.2.0.1               6 PSU 11.2.0.1.6
```

15. Enable redo transport in the primary, start MRP in the standby database, and verify the synchronization. After verifying the latest patch level from the primary, we can now enable the redo transport in the primary database using the Data Guard broker, as shown in the following screenshot:

```
DGMGRL> edit database turkey_un set state='ONLINE';
Succeeded.
DGMGRL>
```

16. To start redo apply services in the standby, you can give the following commands either in the primary or standby database using the Data Guard broker, as shown in the following screenshot:

```
DGMGRL> edit database 'INDIA_UN' set state='APPLY-ON';
Succeeded.
DGMGRL> show configuration;

Configuration - PACKT

  Protection Mode: MaxPerformance
  Databases:
    turkey_un - Primary database
    INDIA_UN  - Physical standby database

Fast-Start Failover: DISABLED

Configuration Status:
SUCCESS

DGMGRL>
```

17. When the MRP service starts on the standby and broker configuration, the status is SUCCESS. Now check the archives that are generated in the primary and applied in the standby using v$archived_log with the column sequence#, as shown in the following screenshot:

```
ID STATUS    DB_MODE        TYPE RECOVERY_MODE            PROTECTION_MODE      SRLs ACTIVE   ARCHIVED_SEQ#
--- --------- -------------- ---- ------------------------ -------------------- ---- ------   -------------
 1 VALID     OPEN           ARCH IDLE                     MAXIMUM PERFORMANCE     0      0             943
 2 VALID     OPEN_READ-ONLY LGWR MANAGED REAL TIME APPLY  MAXIMUM PERFORMANCE     6      1             943
```

18. In both the databases, the valid destination archived sequences are matching. Hence, the standby is in sync with the primary database.

Pop quiz

Q1. What is a terminal patch?

What just happened?

We have seen how to apply PSU Patch (11.2.0.1.6) in a Data Guard environment of a physical standby database using a Data Guard broker.

How to apply patch set on physical standby (11.2.0.1 to 11.2.0.3)?

To upgrade a database of a patch set from 11.2.0.1 to 11.2.0.3, we have to perform a complete installation of ORACLE_HOME for 11.2.0.3, and then we have to detach the old home. This procedure is called out-of-place upgrade and is introduced from 11*g*R2 onwards. In 10*g*Rx versions, we definitely have to do in-place upgrade on the same home. Even if your requirement is to create a new database of 11.2.0.3, there is no need to install 11.2.0.1 anymore.

Time for action – patch set upgrade of physical standby

For upgrading a patch set from 11.2.0.1 to 11.2.0.3 in the Data Guard environment with the SQL* Plus command line, execute the following steps:

1. Install 11.2.0.3 on the primary and standby server. Download Patch 10404530: 11.2.0.3.0 PATCH SET FOR ORACLE DATABASE SERVER from http://support.oracle.com, which comes with seven zipped files of total 5 GB, and unzip filesystem can be downloaded from https://edelivery.oracle.com/. Ensure that the unzipped directory's owner is Oracle. From the database directory, initiate runInstaller from the primary database server, as shown in the following screenshot:

```
[oracle@oracle-primary patches]$ ls
11.2.0.3   12419378   9711859   database   OPatch
[oracle@oracle-primary patches]$ cd database/
[oracle@oracle-primary database]$ ls
doc        readme.html   rpm              sshsetup   welcome.html
install    response      runInstaller     stage
[oracle@oracle-primary database]$ ./runInstaller
Starting Oracle Universal Installer...

Checking Temp space: must be greater than 120 MB.   Actual 46963 MB    Passed
Checking swap space: must be greater than 150 MB.   Actual 665 MB    Passed
Checking monitor: must be configured to display at least 256 colors.    Actual 1
6777216     Passed
Preparing to launch Oracle Universal Installer from /tmp/OraInstall2012-12-16_06
-23-45PM. Please wait ...[oracle@oracle-primary database]$ You can find the log
of this install session at:
  /u01/app/oraInventory/logs/installActions2012-12-16_06-23-45PM.log
```

2. Once the GUI is launched, you will have several options, if you would like to get security updates by adding the e-mail address, installation options, grid installation options, product languages, and so on. In these, you must choose a new ORACLE_HOME directory outside the existing ORACLE_HOME location for installation. In the installation options, you must opt for Enterprise Edition to enable the feature of Data Guard.

3. Before you start the actual installation, runInstaller performs the prerequisite check for RPM's version, kernel settings, and swap memory settings. If any of these are not adequate, you should fix them prior to the installation from the GUI. These fixes differ from one OS to the other. Note that if some of the RPMs are of a higher version, then you can acknowledge them by ignoring them and then go ahead with the installation.

4. After copying the files, linking the libraries, and setting up the files, you have to run the /u01/home/oracle/product/11.2.0/db_2/root.sh script from the root user, as shown in the following screenshot:

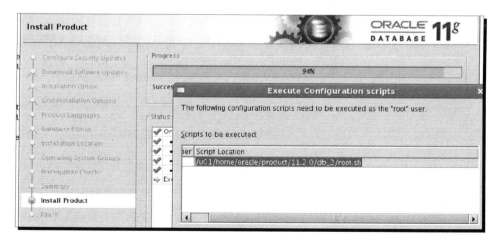

5. Open a new terminal as the `root` user and run the following script:

```
[root@oracle-primary ~]# /u01/home/oracle/product/11.2.0/db_2/
root.sh

Performing root user operation for Oracle 11g

The following environment variables are set as:

    ORACLE_OWNER= oracle

    ORACLE_HOME=  /u01/home/oracle/product/11.2.0/db_2

Enter the full pathname of the local bin directory: [/usr/local/
bin]:

The contents of "dbhome" have not changed. No need to overwrite.

The file "oraenv" already exists in /usr/local/bin.  Overwrite it?
(y/n)

[n]: y

    Copying oraenv to /usr/local/bin ...

The file "coraenv" already exists in /usr/local/bin.  Overwrite
it? (y/n)

[n]: y

    Copying coraenv to /usr/local/bin ...

Entries will be added to the /etc/oratab file as needed by

Database Configuration Assistant when a database is created

Finished running generic part of root script.

Now product-specific root actions will be performed.

Finished product-specific root actions.

[root@oracle-primary ~]#
```

6. Run the pre-upgrade scripts from 11.2.0.1 home of the primary database. From the previous 11.2.0.1 home of the database, spool the `$ORACLE_HOME/rdbms/admin/utlu112i.sql` script of 11.2.0.3 to run the pre-upgrade check as follows:

```
SQL> @/u01/home/oracle/product/11.2.0/db_2/rdbms/admin/utlu112i.
sql

Oracle Database 11.2 Pre-Upgrade Information Tool 12-16-2012
19:54:41

Script Version: 11.2.0.3.0 Build: 001
***************************************************************************

Database:
***************************************************************************
```

```
--> name:         ORCL
--> version:      11.2.0.1.0
--> compatible:   11.2.0.0.0
--> blocksize:    8192
--> platform:     Linux x86 64-bit
--> timezone file: V11
****************************************************************
Recommendations
****************************************************************
Oracle recommends gathering dictionary statistics prior to
upgrading the database.
To gather dictionary statistics execute the following command
while connected as SYSDBA:
    EXECUTE dbms_stats.gather_dictionary_stats;
****************************************************************
SQL>
```

7. Running `utlu112i.sql` is mandatory even if you are upgrading manually or using DBUA. Review the spool logfile and fix it if there are any errors and warnings; for example, invalid objects, invalid registry components, tablespaces' thresholds, and on clearing recycle bin objects.

8. Now use the script to collect the database's upgrade diagnostic information (`dbupgdiag.sql`) from MOS `note:556610.1`. If any invalid objects are found, run the `$ORACLE_HOME/rdbms/admin/utlrp.sql` script multiple times to validate these invalid objects in the database until there is no change in the number of invalid objects, shown as follows:

```
SQL> @?/rdbms/admin/utlrp.sql
TIMESTAMP
----------------------------------------------------------------
COMP_TIMESTAMP UTLRP_BGN   2012-12-16 21:16:01
. . . . . . . . . . . . . . . . . . . . . .
ERRORS DURING RECOMPILATION
---------------------------
                          0
PL/SQL procedure successfully completed.
PL/SQL procedure successfully completed.
SQL>
```

9. Disable the log transport and stop MRP in the standby database. Check the synchronization between the primary and standby databases and then proceed to defer the remote destination to send redo transport as follows:

```
SQL> alter system set log_archive_dest_state_2='defer';
System altered.
SQL>
```

10. Now stop MRP in the standby database from SQL* Plus as follows:

```
SQL> alter database recover managed standby database cancel;
Database altered.
SQL>
```

11. Take a complete backup of the database and stop the primary and standby databases, including listener services.

12. Take a backup of the entire database, either cold or hot backup, using RMAN. No need to perform a backup of ORACLE_HOME because we are installing a new 11.2.0.3 home outside 11.2.0.1 home. Now shut down the primary and standby services, including the listener services.

13. Change the environment variable's settings and run the Upgrade script in the primary database.

14. Ensure that you have modified the environment variables ORACLE_HOME and LIBRARY_PATH, PATH, and they are pointing to the newly installed home 11.2.0.3. Copy INIT/SPFILE and the network configuration files and run the catupgrade. sql script to upgrade the data dictionary objects as follows:

```
[oracle@oracle-primary ~]$ sqlplus / as sysdba

SQL*Plus: Release 11.2.0.3.0 Production on Sun Dec 16 21:26:26
2012

Copyright (c) 1982, 2011, Oracle.  All rights reserved.

Connected to an idle instance.

SQL> spool /home/oracle/upgrade.log

SQL> startup upgrade

ORACLE instance started.

Total System Global Area 2238099456 bytes

Fixed Size                  2230312 bytes

Variable Size            1056966616 bytes

Database Buffers         1174405120 bytes

Redo Buffers                4497408 bytes

Database mounted.

Database opened.
```

```
SQL> set echo on

SQL> @?/rdbms/admin/catupgrd.sql

SQL> Rem

SQL> Rem $Header: rdbms/admin/catupgrd.sql /st_rdbms_11.2.0/3
2011/05/18 15:07:25 cmlim Exp $

SQL> Rem

SQL> Rem catupgrd.sql

.........

SQL> Rem Set errorlogging off

SQL> SET ERRORLOGGING OFF;

SQL>

SQL> REM END OF CATUPGRD.SQL

SQL>

SQL> REM bug 12337546 - Exit current sqlplus session at end of
catupgrd.sql.

SQL> REM                    This forces user to start a new sqlplus
session in order

SQL> REM                    to connect to the upgraded db.

SQL> exit
```

15. Start the database in the normal mode and run the following scripts:

```
SQL> @$ORACLE_HOME/rdbms/admin/catuppst.sql;

TIMESTAMP

------------------------------------------------------------------

COMP_TIMESTAMP POSTUP_BGN 2012-12-16 22:26:56

PL/SQL procedure successfully completed.

This script will migrate the Baseline data on a pre-11g database
to the 11g database.

...                                ...

... Completed Moving the Baseline Data     ...

...                                ...

.................

  6      (SYSTIMESTAMP, 'APPLY',

  7      SYS_CONTEXT('REGISTRY$CTX','NAMESPACE'),

  8      '11.2.0.3',

  9      0,
```

```
10      'PSU',
11      'Patchset 11.2.0.2.0');
1 row created.
SQL> COMMIT;
Commit complete.
SQL> SPOOL off
SQL> SET echo off
Check the following log file for errors:
/u01/home/oracle/product/11.2.0/db_2/cfgtoollogs/catbundle/
catbundle_PSU_ORCL_APPLY_2012Dec16_22_27_18.log
SQL>
```

16. Run the `utlrp.sql` script to compile invalid objects as follows:

```
SQL> @$ORACLE_HOME/rdbms/admin/utlrp.sql;
TIMESTAMP
--------------------------------------------------
COMP_TIMESTAMP UTLRP_BGN  2012-12-16 22:28:48
ERRORS DURING RECOMPILATION
---------------------------
                          0
Function created.
PL/SQL procedure successfully completed.
Function dropped.
PL/SQL procedure successfully completed.
SQL>
```

17. Post the upgrade scripts in the primary database. Now upgrade the time zone to the latest version using `DBMS_DST`, upgrade the recovery catalog, and upgrade the `statistics` table if it is created by the `DBMS_STATS` package.

18. Synchronize the standby database with the primary database. After upgrading the primary database successfully, enable remote destination to send redo transport as follows:

```
SQL> alter system set log_archive_dest_state_2='enable';
System altered.
SQL>
DB_NAME    HOSTNAME        LOG_ARCHIVED LOG_APPLIED LOG_GAP
---------- --------------- ------------ ----------- -------
ORCL       ORACLE-PRIMARY           969         943      26
```

19. We do have around 26 archive gaps after the upgrade. Now start MRP to apply archives on the standby database. Depending on the gaps between the primary and standby databases, it will take time to synchronize.

```
SQL> alter database recover managed standby database using current
logfile disconnect from session;

Database altered.

SQL>

DB_NAME     HOSTNAME         LOG_ARCHIVED  LOG_APPLIED  LOG_GAP
----------  --------------   ------------  -----------  -------

ORCL        ORACLE-PRIMARY          972          971        1
sSun Dec 16 23:03:46 2012

RFS[1]: Selected log 10 for thread 1 sequence 973 dbid 1316772835
branch 788992101

Archived Log entry 51 added for thread 1 sequence 972 ID
0x4eede1f7 dest 3:

Recovery of Online Redo Log: Thread 1 Group 10 Seq 973 Reading mem
0

  Mem# 0: /u02/app/oracle/oradata/orcl/standby_redo01.log
```

What just happened?

We have seen how to install an out-of-place upgrade of a database from 11.2.0.1 patch set level to 11.2.0.3 patch set, including the physical standby database.

Have a go hero – in-place patch set installation

We can perform a patch set installation either in-place or out-of-place. We have just seen how to perform an out-of-place upgrade. To do an in-place patch set installation, perform the following steps:

1. Back up INIT/SPFILE and the network configuration files.
2. Detach ORACLE_HOME from the database as ./runInstaller -detachHome ORACLE_HOME= /u01/home/oracle/product/11.2.0/db_1.
3. Remove old ORACLE_HOME (11.2.0.1).
4. Install a new patch set level, 11.2.0.3.
5. Copy INIT/SPFILE and the network configuration files to the new ORACLE_HOME directory.
6. Upgrade your database (catupgrd.sql or DBUA).

Summary

We've now reached the end of this chapter. In this chapter, we have seen what are the different types of patches and the best practices involved in using the OPatch utility. Apart from that we have also seen the following:

- How to apply the interim/bug fix patch on a logical standby
- How to apply a PSU patch on a physical standby database using a Data Guard broker
- How to upgrade a patch set from 11.2.0.1 to 11.2.0.3

10

Common Data Guard Issues

Data Guard administrators need to know methods to resolve some specific issues. These issues may originate from configuration changes, misconfiguration, or user errors. Another important point is the use of diagnostic data to identify these issues. Now we'll cover handling the most common of these Data Guard issues and the methods to access and use diagnostic data.

In this chapter, we will discuss the following topics:

- ◆ Recreating the standby control file
- ◆ Dealing with redo transport authentication problems
- ◆ Dealing with UNNAMED datafiles
- ◆ Closing a gap with RMAN incremental backups
- ◆ Fixing NOLOGGING changes in a standby database
- ◆ Turning on Data Guard tracing
- ◆ Gathering diagnostic data

Let's start with renewing the standby control file of a standby database.

Recreating the standby control file

A **standby control file** essentially keeps the same information of the primary database with the control file, which is the physical structure of the database. It also contains some specific information about the Data Guard, such as whether an archive log sequence is applied or not. A standby control file is mandatory to mount a physical standby database, and we should consider keeping multiple copies of the standby control file, preferably on different disks, which is known as **multiplexing**.

In some cases, we may want to renew a standby control file by using a newly created one on the primary database. For example, before a switchover it's a good practice to renew the standby control file in order to guarantee that all of the redo, temp file structure, and historical archived log data are the same. In general, this is a three-step operation:

1. Create a copy of the standby control file from the primary database.
2. Transfer this standby control file from the primary database to the standby site.
3. Restart the standby database using a new standby control file.

In order to create a standby control file from a primary database, we can choose one of the following methods:

- Using the ALTER DATABASE CREATE STANDBY CONTROLFILE SQL statement:

  ```
  SQL> ALTER DATABASE CREATE STANDBY CONTROLFILE AS '/tmp/standby.
  ctl';
  ```

  We can directly copy the file to the standby server with FTP or SCP and use it as the new standby control file.

- Using the BACKUP CURRENT CONTROLFILE FOR STANDBY RMAN statement:

  ```
  RMAN> BACKUP CURRENT CONTROLFILE FOR STANDBY FORMAT 'standbyctl.
  bkp';
  ```

  The file will be an RMAN backup of the standby control file that we can transfer and use in order to restore the standby control file with the RESTORE STANDBY CONTROLFILE FROM RMAN statement.

This standby control file recreation operation needs some extra steps if we use **Oracle-managed files (OMF)**. OMF automatically generates datafile names, and the names will be different in the primary and standby databases. We'll not be able to mount the standby database with the newly created standby control file because it'll search for datafiles with their names in the primary database. So we need to introduce datafiles to the standby control file in some way.

Time for action – recreating the standby control file

This action shows how to renew the standby control file in a Data Guard environment with OMF.

1. In the primary database, create a backup of the standby control file with the following RMAN statements:

   ```
   $rman target /

   Recovery Manager: Release 11.2.0.1.0 - Production on Wed Dec 19
   22:18:05 2012

   Copyright (c) 1982, 2009, Oracle and/or its affiliates.  All
   rights reserved.

   connected to target database: ORCL (DBID=1319333016)


   RMAN> BACKUP CURRENT CONTROLFILE FOR STANDBY FORMAT 'standbyctl.
   bkp';

   Starting backup at 19-DEC-12

   using target database control file instead of recovery catalog

   allocated channel: ORA_DISK_1

   channel ORA_DISK_1: SID=149 device type=DISK

   channel ORA_DISK_1: starting full datafile backup set

   channel ORA_DISK_1: specifying datafile(s) in backup set

   including standby control file in backup set

   channel ORA_DISK_1: starting piece 1 at 19-DEC-12

   channel ORA_DISK_1: finished piece 1 at 19-DEC-12

   piece handle=/u01/app/oracle2/product/11.2.0/dbhome_1/dbs/
   standbyctl.bkp tag=TAG20121219T221811 comment=NONE

   channel ORA_DISK_1: backup set complete, elapsed time: 00:00:01

   Finished backup at 19-DEC-12
   ```

   You'll see that a file named standbycf.bkp is generated under the $ORACLE_HOME/dbs directory. This file will be used to restore the standby control file in the standby database.

2. Copy this backup file from the primary database to the standby site by using the scp or ftp protocols:

   ```
   scp $ORACLE_HOME/dbs/standbyctl.bkp standbyhost:/tmp/standbyctl.
   bkp
   ```

3. Query the current online and standby logfile paths in the physical standby database:

```
SQL> SELECT * FROM V$LOGFILE WHERE TYPE = 'ONLINE';

GROUP# STATUS  TYPE  MEMBER                                           IS_
------ ------  ------ -----------------------------------------------  ---

3      ONLINE  /u01/app/oracle2/datafile/ORCL/redo03.log     NO
2      ONLINE  /u01/app/oracle2/datafile/ORCL/redo02.log     NO
1      ONLINE  /u01/app/oracle2/datafile/ORCL/redo01.lo      NO


SQL> SELECT * FROM V$LOGFILE WHERE TYPE = 'STANDBY';

GROUP# STATUS   TYPE  MEMBER                                          IS_
------ -------  ----  -----------------------------------------------  ---

4      STANDBY  /u01/app/oracle2/.../ol_mf_4_85frxrh5_.log    YES
5      STANDBY  /u01/app/oracle2/.../ol_mf_5_85fry0fc_.log    YES
6      STANDBY  /u01/app/oracle2/.../ol_mf_6_85fry7tn_.log    YES
7      STANDBY  /u01/app/oracle2/.../ol_mf_7_85fryh0n_.log    YES
```

4. Shut down the standby database and delete all the online and standby logfiles:

```
$ sqlplus / as sysdba
SQL> SHUTDOWN IMMEDIATE
$ rm /u01/app/oracle2/datafile/ORCL/redo0*.log
$ rm /u01/app/oracle2/fra/INDIA_PS/onlinelog/ol_mf_*.log
```

Depending on whether you use the filesystem or the ASM to store the database files, you must run the `rm` command on the shell or on `asmcmd` respectively.

5. Start up the physical standby database in the NOMOUNT mode:

```
$ sqlplus / as sysdba
SQL> STARTUP NOMOUNT
```

6. On the standby server, connect to RMAN and restore the standby control file from the backup file:

```
$rman target /
RMAN> RESTORE STANDBY CONTROLFILE FROM '/tmp/standbyctl.bkp';

Starting restore at 19-DEC-12
using target database control file instead of recovery catalog
```

```
allocated channel: ORA_DISK_1
channel ORA_DISK_1: SID=1 device type=DISK
channel ORA_DISK_1: restoring control file
channel ORA_DISK_1: restore complete, elapsed time: 00:00:01
output file name=/u01/app/oracle2/datafile/INDIAPS/control01.ctl
Finished restore at 19-DEC-12
```

7. Mount the standby database as follows:

```
RMAN> ALTER DATABASE MOUNT;
database mounted
released channel: ORA_DISK_1
```

8. If OMF is not being used, and the datafile paths and names are the same for both the primary and standby databases, skip this step and continue with the next step.

   At this stage, in an OMF-configured Data Guard environment, the physical standby database is mounted, but the control file doesn't show the correct datafile names because it still contains the primary database's datafile names. We need to change the datafile names in the standby control file. Use the RMAN CATALOG and SWITCH commands for this purpose:

   ```
   RMAN> CATALOG START WITH '/oradata/datafile/';
   ```

   For ASM, use the following commands:

   ```
   RMAN> CATALOG START WITH '+DATA1/MUM/DATAFILE/';
   RMAN> SWITCH DATABASE TO COPY;
   ```

9. If the flashback database is ON, turn it off and on again in the standby database:

   ```
   SQL> ALTER DATABASE FLASHBACK OFF;
   Database altered.


   SQL> ALTER DATABASE FLASHBACK ON;
   Database altered.
   ```

10. If standby redo logs exist in the primary database, we only need to execute the clear logfile statement in the standby database so that they will be created automatically (the log_file_name_convert parameter must already be set properly):

    ```
    SQL> SELECT GROUP# FROM V$STANDBY_LOG;

    GROUP#
    ----------
    4
    ```

```
5
6
7

SQL> ALTER DATABASE CLEAR LOGFILE GROUP 4;
Database altered.

SQL> ALTER DATABASE CLEAR LOGFILE GROUP 5;
Database altered.

SQL> ALTER DATABASE CLEAR LOGFILE GROUP 6;
Database altered.

SQL> ALTER DATABASE CLEAR LOGFILE GROUP 7;
Database altered.
```

If standby redo logs don't exist in the primary database, the following query will not return any rows. In this case, we need to create the standby redo logs manually:

```
SQL> SELECT GROUP# FROM V$STANDBY_LOG;
no row selected

SQL> ALTER DATABASE ADD STANDBY LOGFILE GROUP 4 SIZE 50M;
Database altered.

SQL> ALTER DATABASE ADD STANDBY LOGFILE GROUP 5 SIZE 50M;
Database altered.

SQL> ALTER DATABASE ADD STANDBY LOGFILE GROUP 6 SIZE 50M;
Database altered.

SQL> ALTER DATABASE ADD STANDBY LOGFILE GROUP 7 SIZE 50M;
Database altered.
```

11. Start a media-recovery process in the physical standby database. The online logfiles will be cleared automatically.

```
SQL> ALTER DATABASE RECOVER MANAGED STANDBY DATABASE USING CURRENT
LOGFILE DISCONNECT FROM SESSION;
Database altered.
```

What just happened?

We've successfully changed the standby control file using the primary database as a source. With a new standby control file, some database information such as the size and number of the temporary files and the size and number of the online redo logs, will be updated in the physical standby database. These infrastructural changes are not replicated to the standby databases automatically. So if we don't apply these changes manually in the standby database, a new standby control file will fix these inconsistencies.

Dealing with redo transport authentication problems

By default, the SYS user is used for redo transport in Data Guard configurations. Data Guard communication uses password files in the standby databases to authenticate redo transport sessions. If we change the password of the SYS user in the primary database, redo transport sessions will not be authenticated because the password file in the standby site will be outdated. So redo transport will raise the ORA-01017: invalid username/password or ORA-01031: insufficient privileges error. The primary database alert logfile will include the following lines:

```
Error 1017 received logging on to the standby

PING[ARC0]: Heartbeat failed to connect to standby 'INDIAPS'. Error is
16191.
```

It can also include the following lines:

```
ORA-01031: insufficient privileges

PING[ARC2]: Heartbeat failed to connect to standby 'INDIAPS'. Error is
1031.
```

Time for action – changing the SYS password in a Data Guard environment

The way to change the SYS password without breaking the redo transport service includes copying the primary database's password file to the standby server after changing the password. The following steps show how this can be done:

1. Stop redo transport from the primary database to the standby database. We can execute the DEFER command to defer the log destination with the ALTER SYSTEM statement:

```
SQL> ALTER SYSTEM SET LOG_ARCHIVE_DEST_STATE_2 = 'DEFER';

System altered.
```

If the Data Guard broker is being used, we can use the following statement:

```
DGMGRL> EDIT DATABASE TURKEY_UN SET STATE = 'LOG-TRANSPORT-OFF';
```

2. Change the `SYS` user's password in the primary database:

```
SQL> ALTER USER SYS IDENTIFIED BY newpassword;

User altered.
```

3. Copy the primary database's password file to the standby site:

```
$ cd $ORACLE_HOME/dbs
```

```
$ scp orapwTURKEY standbyhost:/u01/app/oracle/product/11.2.0/
dbhome_1/dbs/orapwINDIAPS
```

4. Try logging into the standby database from the standby server using the new `SYS` password:

```
$ sqlplus sys/newpassword as sysdba
```

5. Start redo transport from the primary database to the standby database:

```
SQL> ALTER SYSTEM SET LOG_ARCHIVE_DEST_STATE_2 = 'ENABLE';

System altered.
```

If the Data Guard broker is being used, we can use the following statement:

```
DGMGRL> EDIT DATABASE TURKEY_UN SET STATE = 'ONLINE';
```

6. Check whether the redo transport service is running normally by switching the redo logs in the primary database:

```
SQL> ALTER SYSTEM SWITCH LOGFILE;

System altered.
```

Check the standby database's processes or the alert log file to see redo transport service status:

```
SQL> SELECT PROCESS, STATUS, THREAD#, SEQUENCE#, BLOCK#, BLOCKS
FROM V$MANAGED_STANDBY ;
```

PROCESS	STATUS	THREAD#	SEQUENCE#	BLOCK#	BLOCKS
ARCH	CLOSING	1	3232	1	275
ARCH	CLOSING	1	3229	1	47
ARCH	CONNECTED	0	0	0	0

ARCH	CLOSING	1	3220	2049	1164
RFS	IDLE	0	0	0	0
RFS	IDLE	0	0	0	0
RFS	IDLE	0	0	0	0
MRP0	APPLYING_LOG	1	3233	122	102400
RFS	IDLE	1	3233	122	1

> Also, if the password file of the standby database is somehow corrupted, or has been deleted, the redo transport service will raise an error and we can copy the primary password file to the standby site to fix this problem.

Pop quiz – the redo transport authentication problem in only one instance of the primary database

Suppose we have an RAC primary database, and all instances successfully transmit redo to the standby database except one. One of the primary instances shows an authentication error in the alert log file. What do we need to do to fix this issue?

What just happened?

We've now changed the SYS user's password in a Data Guard environment without causing any errors in the redo transport service. Database administrators have to consider standby databases when changing a SYS password in the primary database of a Data Guard configuration. Otherwise, the redo transport will fail, and if it is not noticed quickly, this may cause data loss in case of any failover.

If we often need to change the SYS user's password in the primary database, it may be troublesome to copy the password file to the standby site every time, especially when there's more than one standby destination. In this case, the REDO_TRANSPORT_USER parameter comes to our rescue. It's possible to change the default redo transport user from SYS to another database user by setting this parameter.

Time for action – changing the redo transport user

Follow these steps to change the redo transport user in the Data Guard configuration:

1. Create a new database, which will be used for redo transport in the primary database. Grant the SYSOPER privileges to this user and ensure that the standby database has applied these changes:

   ```
   SQL> CREATE USER DGUSER IDENTIFIED BY SOMEPASSWORD;

   SQL> GRANT SYSOPER to DGUSER;
   ```

Don't forget that if the password expires periodically for this user, this will pose a problem in Data Guard redo transport. So ensure that the default profile does not include the `PASSWORD_LIFE_ TIME` and `PASSWORD_GRACE_TIME` settings. If it does, choose another profile for this user.

2. Stop the redo transport from the primary database to the standby databases. We can execute the `DEFER` command to defer the log destination with the `ALTER SYSTEM` statement:

```
SQL> ALTER SYSTEM SET LOG_ARCHIVE_DEST_STATE_2 = 'DEFER';
```

3. Change the redo transport user by setting the `REDO_TRANSPORT_ USER` parameter in the primary and standby databases:

```
SQL> ALTER SYSTEM SET REDO_TRANSPORT_USER = DGUSER;
```

4. Copy the primary database's password file to the standby site:

```
$ cd $ORACLE_HOME/dbs

$ scp orapwTURKEY standbyhost:/u01/app/oracle/product/11.2.0/
dbhome_1/dbs/orapwINDIAPS
```

5. Start redo transport from the primary database to the standby databases:

```
SQL> ALTER SYSTEM SET LOG_ARCHIVE_DEST_STATE_2 = 'ENABLE';
```

6. Check whether the redo transport service is running normally by switching redo logs in the primary database:

```
SQL> ALTER SYSTEM SWITCH LOGFILE;
```

Check the standby database processes or the alert log file to see redo transport service status:

```
SQL> SELECT PROCESS, STATUS, THREAD#, SEQUENCE#, BLOCK#, BLOCKS
FROM V$MANAGED_STANDBY ;
```

What just happened?

The default user, who is the user for the redo transport authentication, is now changed from `SYS` to another database user. As mentioned, this may be useful if we change the `SYS` password often in the primary database.

Dealing with UNNAMED datafiles

There are some reasons for a file being created as UNNAMED in the standby database, including insufficient disk space on the standby site, non-privileged directory structure on standby database, or improper parameter settings related to file management.

The STANDBY_FILE_MANAGEMENT parameter enables or disables automatic standby file management in Data Guard. When automatic standby file management is enabled, file additions and deletions in the primary database are replicated to the standby database.

For example, we add a datafile in the primary database when the STANDBY_FILE_MANAGEMENT parameter on the standby database is set to MANUAL. Due to this parameter setting, it will create an UNNAMED file under $ORACLE_HOME/dbs, and this will cause the MRP process to be killed. Errors in the alert log file will be as follows:

```
Errors in file /u01/app/oracle2/diag/rdbms/india_ps/INDIAPS/trace/
INDIAPS_pr00_691.trc:
ORA-01111: name for data file 10 is unknown - rename to correct file
ORA-01110: data file 10: ' /u01/app/oracle2/product/11.2.0/dbhome_1/dbs/
UNNAMED00010'
ORA-01157: cannot identify/lock data file 10 - see DBWR trace file
```

Time for action – resolving UNNAMED datafile errors

Now we'll see how to resolve an UNNAMED datafile issue in a Data Guard configuration:

1. Check for the datafile number that needs to be recovered from the standby database:

   ```
   SQL> SELECT * FROM V$RECOVER_FILE WHERE ERROR LIKE '%MISSING%';

       FILE# ONLINE  ONLINE_ ERROR               CHANGE# TIME
   ---------- ------- ------- ----------------- ---------- ----------
          10 ONLINE  ONLINE  FILE MISSING                0
   ```

2. Identify datafile 10 in the primary database:

   ```
   SQL> SELECT FILE#,NAME FROM V$DATAFILE WHERE FILE#=10;

       FILE# NAME
   ---------- -------------------------------------------------
         536 /u01/app/oracle2/datafile/ORCL/users03.dbf
   ```

3. Identify the dummy filename created in the standby database:

```
SQL> SELECT FILE#,NAME FROM V$DATAFILE WHERE FILE#=10;

    FILE# NAME
---------- -----------------------------------------------------------
      536 /u01/app/oracle2/product/11.2.0/dbhome_1/dbs/
UNNAMED00010
```

4. If the reason for the creation of the UNNAMED file is disk capacity or a nonexistent path, fix the issue by creating the datafile in its original place.

5. Set STANDBY_FILE_MANAGEMENT to MANUAL:

```
SQL> ALTER SYSTEM SET STANDBY_FILE_MANAGEMENT=MANUAL;

System altered.
```

6. Create the datafile in its original place with the ALTER DATABASE CREATE DATAFILE statement:

```
SQL> ALTER DATABASE CREATE DATAFILE '/u01/app/oracle2/
product/11.2.0/dbhome_1/dbs/UNNAMED00010' AS '/u01/app/oracle2/
datafile/ORCL/users03.dbf';

Database altered.
```

If OMF is being used, we won't be allowed to create the datafile with the preceding statement. We'll come across the following error:

```
SQL> ALTER DATABASE CREATE DATAFILE '/u01/app/oracle2/
product/11.2.0/dbhome_1/dbs/UNNAMED00010' AS '/u01/app/oracle2/
datafile/ORCL/users03.dbf';

    *

ERROR at line 1:

ORA-01276: Cannot add file

/u01/app/oracle2/datafile/ORCL/users03.dbf. File has an Oracle
Managed Files file name.
```

In order to avoid the error, run the following command:

```
SQL> ALTER DATABASE CREATE DATAFILE '/u01/app/oracle2/
product/11.2.0/dbhome_1/dbs/UNNAMED00010' AS NEW;

Database altered.
```

7. Set STANDBY_FILE_MANAGEMENT to AUTO and start Redo Apply:

```
SQL> ALTER SYSTEM SET STANDBY_FILE_MANAGEMENT=AUTO SCOPE=BOTH;

System altered.
```

```
SQL> SHOW PARAMETER STANDBY_FILE_MANAGEMENT
NAME                                   TYPE          VALUE
------------------------------------   -----------   ------------------
standby_file_management                string        AUTO


SQL> ALTER DATABASE RECOVER MANAGED STANDBY DATABASE USING CURRENT
LOGFILE DISCONNECT FROM SESSION;
Database altered.
```

8. Check the standby database's processes, or the alert log file, to monitor Redo Apply:

```
SQL> SELECT PROCESS, STATUS, THREAD#, SEQUENCE#, BLOCK#, BLOCKS
FROM V$MANAGED_STANDBY;
```

What just happened?

We've fixed a datafile creation error in the standby database by using the ALTER DATABASE CREATE DATAFILE statement. Usage of this statement varies depending on the use of Oracle-managed files.

Have a go hero

Simulate the datafile creation error in your test environment. In the primary database, you can create a datafile in a path that the Oracle user doesn't have privilege to on a standby server, or fill the disk on the standby database server where datafiles reside and create a new datafile in the primary database. Then fix the datafile creation error with the method mentioned previously.

Closing a gap with an RMAN incremental backup

When a standby database falls behind the primary database in time because of any interruption in redo transport or apply, the database can be synchronized again by applying the archived logs produced in the no-synchronization period. However, even if one of the necessary archived logfiles is not accessible, there is nothing to do for Data Guard to close the gap.

In such a case, we have to restore these archived logfiles from backups if they exist. If not, the only way to close the gap is by using an RMAN incremental backup taken from the primary database, especially to close the gap in question. We use the BACKUP INCREMENTAL FROM SCN RMAN statement for this special-purpose backup.

Time for action – closing a gap with an RMAN incremental backup

Let's see all the required steps to practice this recovery operation:

1. In this practice, assume that there are missing archived logs (gap) in the standby database, and we're not able to restore these archived logs. We'll synchronize Data Guard using the RMAN incremental backup. To represent this situation, execute the DEFER command to defer the log destination in the primary database, and execute the following operation that will generate redo in the primary database:

```
SQL> ALTER SYSTEM SET LOG_ARCHIVE_DEST_STATE_2 = 'DEFER';
```

2. Now we have a standby database behind the primary database, and we'll use RMAN to reflect the primary database's changes to the standby database. Stop Redo Apply in the standby database:

```
SQL> ALTER DATABASE RECOVER MANAGED STANDBY DATABASE CANCEL;
```

3. Query the current **system change number** (**SCN**) of the standby database that will be used as the limit for an incremental backup of the primary database. Run the following statement on the standby database:

```
SQL> SELECT MIN(FHSCN) FROM X$KCVFH;


MIN(FHSCN)
----------------
20606344
```

4. Run an RMAN incremental backup of the primary database by using the obtained SCN value.

 This backup job will check all the blocks of the primary database and back up the blocks that have a higher SCN. So even if the backup size is small, it may take a long time.

```
RMAN> BACKUP INCREMENTAL FROM SCN 20606344 DATABASE FORMAT '/tmp/
Standby_Inc_%U' tag 'STANDBY_INC';


Starting backup at 20-DEC-12
using target database control file instead of recovery catalog
allocated channel: ORA_DISK_1
channel ORA_DISK_1: SID=165 device type=DISK
backup will be obsolete on date 27-DEC-12
```

```
archived logs will not be kept or backed up

channel ORA_DISK_1: starting full datafile backup set

channel ORA_DISK_1: specifying datafile(s) in backup set

input datafile file number=00001 name=/u01/app/oracle2/datafile/
ORCL/system01.dbf

...

input datafile file number=00007 name=/u01/app/oracle2/datafile/
ORCL/system03.dbf

channel ORA_DISK_1: starting piece 1 at 20-DEC-12

channel ORA_DISK_1: finished piece 1 at 20-DEC-12

piece handle=/tmp/Standby_Inc_03nt9u0v_1_1 tag=STANDBY_INC
comment=NONE

channel ORA_DISK_1: backup set complete, elapsed time: 00:01:15

using channel ORA_DISK_1

including current control file in backup set

channel ORA_DISK_1: starting piece 1 at 20-DEC-12

channel ORA_DISK_1: finished piece 1 at 20-DEC-12

piece handle=/tmp/Standby_Inc_04nt9u3a_1_1 tag=STANDBY_INC
comment=NONE

channel ORA_DISK_1: backup set complete, elapsed time: 00:00:01
Finished backup at 20-DEC-12
```

5. Copy the backup files from the primary site to the standby site with FTP or SCP.

```
scp /tmp/Standby_Inc_* standbyhost:/tmp/
```

6. Register the backup files to the standby database control file with the RMAN
   CATALOG command, so that we'll be able to recover the standby database using
   these backup files:

```
RMAN> CATALOG START WITH '/tmp/Standby_Inc';


using target database control file instead of recovery catalog
searching for all files that match the pattern /tmp/Standby_Inc


List of Files Unknown to the Database
=====================================
File Name: /tmp/Standby_Inc_03nt9u0v_1_1
File Name: /tmp/Standby_Inc_04nt9u3a_1_1
```

```
Do you really want to catalog the above files (enter YES or NO)?
YES

cataloging files...

cataloging done


List of Cataloged Files

========================

File Name: /tmp/Standby_Inc_03nt9u0v_1_1

File Name: /tmp/Standby_Inc_04nt9u3a_1_1
```

7. Recover the standby database with the RMAN RECOVER statement. The Recovery operation will use the incremental backup by default as we have already registered the backup files:

```
RMAN> RECOVER DATABASE NOREDO;


Starting recover at 20-DEC-12

allocated channel: ORA_DISK_1

channel ORA_DISK_1: SID=1237 device type=DISK

channel ORA_DISK_1: starting incremental datafile backup set
restore

channel ORA_DISK_1: specifying datafile(s) to restore from backup
set

destination for restore of datafile 00001: /u01/app/oracle2/
datafile/INDIAPS/system01.dbf

...

destination for restore of datafile 00007: /u01/app/oracle2/
datafile/INDIAPS/system03.dbf

channel ORA_DISK_1: reading from backup piece /tmp/Standby_
Inc_03nt9u0v_1_1

channel ORA_DISK_1: piece handle=/tmp/Standby_Inc_03nt9u0v_1_1
tag=STANDBY_INC

channel ORA_DISK_1: restored backup piece 1

channel ORA_DISK_1: restore complete, elapsed time: 00:00:01

Finished recover at 20-DEC-12
```

8. In this step, we'll create a new standby control file in the primary database and open the standby database using this new control file. We've performed this process at the beginning of this chapter, so we won't be explaining it again; only the statements are given as follows:

In the primary database you will see the following command lines:

```
RMAN> BACKUP CURRENT CONTROLFILE FOR STANDBY FORMAT '/tmp/Standby_
CTRL.bck';

scp /tmp/Standby_CTRL.bck standbyhost:/tmp/
```

In the standby database you will see the following command lines:

```
RMAN> SHUTDOWN;

RMAN> STARTUP NOMOUNT;

RMAN> RESTORE STANDBY CONTROLFILE FROM '/tmp/Standby_CTRL.bck';

RMAN> SHUTDOWN;

RMAN> STARTUP MOUNT;
```

If OMF is being used, execute the following commands:

```
RMAN> CATALOG START WITH '+DATA/mystd/datafile/';

RMAN> SWITCH DATABASE TO COPY;
```

9. If new datafiles were added during the time when Data Guard had been stopped, we will need to copy and register the newly created files to the standby system, as they were not included in the incremental backup set.

We will determine if any files have been added to the primary database, as the standby current SCN will run the following query:

```
SQL>SELECT FILE#, NAME FROM V$DATAFILE WHERE CREATION_CHANGE# >
20606344;
```

10. If the flashback database is ON in the standby database, turn it off and on again:

```
SQL> ALTER DATABASE FLASHBACK OFF;

SQL> ALTER DATABASE FLASHBACK ON;
```

11. Clear all the standby redo log groups in the standby database:

```
SQL> ALTER DATABASE CLEAR LOGFILE GROUP 4;

SQL> ALTER DATABASE CLEAR LOGFILE GROUP 5;

SQL> ALTER DATABASE CLEAR LOGFILE GROUP 6;

SQL> ALTER DATABASE CLEAR LOGFILE GROUP 7;
```

12. Start Redo Apply in the standby database:

```
SQL> ALTER DATABASE RECOVER MANAGED STANDBY DATABASE USING CURRENT
LOGFILE DISCONNECT FROM SESSION;
```

What just happened?

We've recovered a Data Guard configuration where the standby database is behind the primary database because of a gap, and the necessary archived logfiles to recover the standby database are missing. We used the RMAN `BACKUP INCREMENTAL FROM SCN` statement for this purpose.

Pop quiz – using a tape for SCN incremental backup

Is it possible to use tape backups in order to close a Data Guard gap with the RMAN incremental backup method?

Fixing NOLOGGING changes on the standby database

It's possible to limit redo generation for specific operations on Oracle databases, which provide higher performance. These operations include bulk inserts, creation of tables as select operations, and index creations. When we work using the `NOLOGGING` clause, redo will not include all the changes to data on the related segments. This means if we perform a restore/recovery of the related datafile, or of the whole database after the `NOLOGGING` operations, it'll not be possible to recover the data created with the `NOLOGGING` option.

The same problem exists with Data Guard. When the `NOLOGGING` operation is executed in the primary database, Data Guard is not able to reflect all the data changes in the standby database. In this case, when we activate a standby database or open it in the read-only mode, we'll see the following error messages:

```
ORA-01578: ORACLE data block corrupted (file # 1, block # 2521)
ORA-01110: data file 1: '/u01/app/oracle2/datafile/INDIAPS/system01.dbf'
ORA-26040: Data block was loaded using the NOLOGGING option
```

For this reason, Data Guard installation requires putting the primary database in the `FORCE LOGGING` mode before starting redo transport between the primary and standby database. The `FORCE LOGGING` mode guarantees the writing of redo records even if the `NOLOGGING` clause was specified in the SQL statements. The default mode of an Oracle database is not `FORCE LOGGING`, so we need to put the database in this mode using the following statement:

```
SQL> ALTER DATABASE FORCE LOGGING;
```

In this section, we'll assume that the primary database is not in the FORCE LOGGING mode, and some NOLOGGING changes were made in the primary database. One method to fix this situation in the standby database is restoring the affected datafiles from backups taken from the primary database after the NOLOGGING operation. However, in this method we have to work with backup files that are most likely much bigger in size than the amount of data that needs to be recovered. A method that uses the RMAN BACKUP INCREMENTAL FROM SCN statement is more efficient because the backup files will include only the changes from the beginning of the NOLOGGING operation.

We'll now see two scenarios. We'll use the BACKUP INCREMENTAL FROM SCN statement for an incremental datafile backup in the first scenario, and use the same statement for an incremental database backup in the second one. For a small number of affected datafiles and relatively less affected data, choose the first scenario. However, if the number of affected datafiles and amount of data are high, use the second scenario that takes an incremental backup of the whole database.

Time for action – fixing NOLOGGING changes on a standby database with incremental datafile backups

As a prerequisite for this exercise, first put the primary database in the no-force logging mode using the ALTER DATABASE NO FORCE LOGGING statement. Then perform some DML operations in the primary database using the NOLOGGING clause so that we can fix the issue in the standby database with the following steps:

1. Run the following query to identify the datafiles that are affected by NOLOGGING changes:

```
SQL> SELECT FILE#, FIRST_NONLOGGED_SCN FROM V$DATAFILE WHERE
FIRST_NONLOGGED_SCN > 0;


FILE#       FIRST_NONLOGGED_SCN
----------  -------------------
         4             20606544
```

2. First we need to put the affected datafiles in the OFFLINE state in the standby database. For this purpose, stop Redo Apply in the standby database, execute the ALTER DATABASE DATAFILE ... OFFLINE statement, and start Redo Apply again:

```
SQL> ALTER DATABASE RECOVER MANAGED STANDBY DATABASE CANCEL;

SQL> ALTER DATABASE DATAFILE 4 OFFLINE FOR DROP;

SQL> ALTER DATABASE RECOVER MANAGED STANDBY DATABASE USING CURRENT
LOGFILE DISCONNECT;
```

3. Now we'll take incremental backups of the related datafiles by using the FROM SCN keyword. SCN values will be the output of the execution of the queries in the first step. Connect to the primary database as an RMAN target and execute the following RMAN BACKUP statements:

```
RMAN> BACKUP INCREMENTAL FROM SCN 20606544 DATAFILE 4 FORMAT '/
data/Dbf_inc_%U' TAG 'FOR STANDBY';
```

4. Copy the backup files from the primary site to the standby site with FTP or SCP:

```
scp /data/Dbf_inc_* standbyhost:/data/
```

5. Connect to the physical standby database as the RMAN target and catalog the copied backup files to the control file with the RMAN CATALOG command:

```
RMAN> CATALOG START WITH '/data/Dbf_inc_';
```

6. In order to put the affected datafiles in the ONLINE state, stop Redo Apply on the standby database, and run the ALTER DATABASE DATAFILE ... ONLINE statement:

```
SQL> ALTER DATABASE RECOVER MANAGED STANDBY DATABASE CANCEL;

SQL> ALTER DATABASE DATAFILE 4 ONLINE;
```

7. Recover the datafiles by connecting the standby database as the RMAN target. RMAN will use the incremental backup automatically because those files were registered to the control file previously:

```
RMAN> RECOVER DATAFILE 4 NOREDO;
```

8. Now run the query from the first step again to ensure that there're no more datafiles with the NOLOGGING changes:

```
SQL> SELECT FILE#, FIRST_NONLOGGED_SCN FROM V$DATAFILE WHERE
FIRST_NONLOGGED_SCN > 0;
```

9. Start Redo Apply on the standby database:

```
SQL> ALTER DATABASE RECOVER MANAGED STANDBY DATABASE USING CURRENT
LOGFILE DISCONNECT;
```

What just happened?

We've successfully recovered the standby database that didn't include the NOLOGGING changes performed in the primary database. We used the datafile incremental backup method because the number of affected datafiles was small. For a high number of affected datafiles, the method explained in the next section will be more suitable.

Time for action – fixing NOLOGGING changes in the standby database with incremental database backups

1. Determine the SCN that we'll use in the RMAN incremental database backup by querying the minimum `FIRST_NONLOGGED_SCN` column of the `V$DATAFILE` view in the standby database:

   ```
   SQL> SELECT MIN(FIRST_NONLOGGED_SCN) FROM V$DATAFILE WHERE FIRST_
   NONLOGGED_SCN>0;


   MIN(FIRST_NONLOGGED_SCN)

   ------------------------
                   20606544
   ```

2. Stop Redo Apply on the standby database:

   ```
   SQL> ALTER DATABASE RECOVER MANAGED STANDBY DATABASE CANCEL;
   ```

3. Now we'll take an incremental backup of the database using the `FROM SCN` keyword. The SCN value will be the output of the execution of the query in the first step. Connect to the primary database as the RMAN target and execute the following RMAN `BACKUP` statement:

   ```
   RMAN> BACKUP INCREMENTAL FROM SCN 20606344 DATABASE FORMAT '/data/
   DB_Inc_%U' TAG 'FOR STANDBY';
   ```

4. Copy the backup files from the primary site to the standby site with FTP or SCP:

   ```
   scp /data/DB_Inc_* standbyhost:/data/
   ```

5. Connect to the physical standby database as the RMAN target and catalog the copied backup files to the control file with the RMAN `CATALOG` command:

   ```
   RMAN> CATALOG START WITH '/data/DB_Inc_';
   ```

6. Recover the standby database by connecting it as the RMAN target. RMAN will use the incremental backup automatically because those files were registered to the control file previously:

   ```
   RMAN> RECOVER DATABASE NOREDO;
   ```

7. Run the query in the first step again to ensure that there're no more datafiles with `NOLOGGING` changes:

   ```
   SQL> SELECT FILE#, FIRST_NONLOGGED_SCN FROM V$DATAFILE WHERE
   FIRST_NONLOGGED_SCN > 0;
   ```

8. Start Redo Apply on the standby database:

```
SQL> ALTER DATABASE RECOVER MANAGED STANDBY DATABASE USING CURRENT
LOGFILE DISCONNECT;
```

 If the state of a tablespace that includes the affected datafiles is READ ONLY, those files will not be backed up with the RMAN BACKUP command. We need to put these tablespaces in the read-write mode before the backup operation. Change the state of a tablespace with the following statements:

```
SQL> ALTER TABLESPACE <TABLESPACE_NAME> READ WRITE;
SQL> ALTER TABLESPACE <TABLESPACE_NAME> READ ONLY;
```

9. Put the primary database in the FORCE LOGGING mode:

```
SQL> ALTER DATABASE FORCE LOGGING;
```

What just happened?

We've fixed the adverse affect of executing the NOLOGGING operation in the primary database in a Data Guard configuration. If this problem is not fixed in the standby database, we'll face the ORA-26040 error when we attempt to open the standby database as read-only or read-write.

Turning on Data Guard tracing

When database administrators work on a Data Guard problem or plan an important Data Guard operation such as role transition, they generally prefer to gather comprehensive trace information about the activity of Data Guard-related processes. For this purpose, Oracle offers the LOG_ARCHIVE_TRACE parameter. By setting this parameter to an appropriate value, it's possible to have detailed information about log archiving, redo transport, and Redo Apply activities.

The default value of this initialization parameter is 0, which means the additional tracing feature is off, and Oracle will continue generating its default alert and trace entries related to error conditions. It's possible to change the value of this parameter in the primary and/or standby databases online using the ALTER SYSTEM statement. For example, look at the following statement:

```
SQL> ALTER SYSTEM SET LOG_ARCHIVE_TRACE=15;
```

In the Real Application Cluster database it's possible to set different tracing levels for different instances, if necessary.

Keep in mind that additional tracing may produce more trace files with larger sizes. This will fill the diagnostic destination filesystem quickly. So if the parameter change is intended for temporary purposes, do not forget to set the LOG_ARCHIVE_TRACE parameter back to 0.

The following table shows the values and meanings of the LOG_ARCHIVE_TRACE parameter levels. It's also possible to turn on tracing for multiple levels. For this purpose, set the parameter to the sum of the intended levels. For example, if we want comprehensive tracing for real-time apply activity and LGWR redo shipping network activity, which are level 4096 and 512 respectively, we can set the LOG_ARCHIVE_TRACE parameter to 4608.

Level	Meaning
0	Disables archived redo log tracing (default setting)
1	Tracks archiving of redo log files
2	Tracks archive status by each archive log file destination
4	Tracks archive operational phase
8	Tracks archive log destination activity
16	Tracks detailed archive log destination activity
32	Tracks archive log destination parameter modifications
64	Tracks ARCn process state activity
128	Tracks the FAL server process activity
256	Tracks the RFS logical client
512	Tracks the LGWR redo shipping network activity
1024	Tracks the RFS physical client
2048	Tracks the RFS/ARCn ping heartbeat
4096	Tracks the real-time apply activity
8192	Tracks the Redo Apply activity (media recovery or physical standby)
16384	Tracks archived I/O buffers
32768	Tracks the LogMiner dictionary archiving

Have a go hero

Turn on Data Guard tracing with some of the given levels in the primary and standby databases, and observe the alert log and trace entries. See which extra information is given in which tracing level.

Gathering diagnostic data

We need to access diagnostic data about the Data Guard configuration, especially when there's a problem in the Redo Apply or redo transport services. After the first diagnosis of the problem, it's possible to decide whether to search for detailed information in the primary database or in the standby database. If the issue is about sending redo, it's more likely that the necessary information can be found on the primary site. However, if it's about Redo Apply, it's better to search for detailed information on the standby site.

No matter where we search for diagnostic data, we need to know where to search for the related logfiles and how to query diagnostic data in the database. The most commonly referenced files in a Data Guard issue are the primary and standby alert log files. If the Data Guard broker is used in the configuration, **Data Guard Monitor** (**DMON**) logfiles can also be helpful for troubleshooting. If necessary, we can also query Data Guard-related dynamic performance views to get information about the issue.

Now let's look at the details of using these methods to access diagnostic data in a Data Guard configuration.

Alert log and trace files

Alert log files are the first step to start investigating an Oracle Database issue. It's also the same for Data Guard. We can find the directory that contains the alert log and the trace files using the following query:

```
SQL> SELECT NAME,VALUE FROM V$DIAG_INFO  WHERE NAME LIKE 'Diag%';


NAME               VALUE
---------------    ----------------------------------------------------------
Diag Enabled       TRUE
Diag Trace         /u01/app/oracle2/diag/rdbms/india_ps/INDIAPS/trace
Diag Alert         /u01/app/oracle2/diag/rdbms/india_ps/INDIAPS/alert
Diag Incident      /u01/app/oracle2/diag/rdbms/india_ps/INDIAPS/incident
Diag Cdump         /u01/app/oracle2/diag/rdbms/india_ps/INDIAPS/cdump
```

Here, the `Diag Trace` directory is the location of the background process trace files, the server process trace files, the SQL trace files, and the text-formatted version of the alert log file. The `Diag Alert` directory keeps the XML-formatted version of the alert log. Incident logfiles are under the `Diag Incident` directory, and the core dump files are under the `Diag Cdump` directory.

Let's go to the `Diag Trace` directory and list the alert log file; we can use the `tail` command to see the last lines of the file:

```
$ cd /u01/app/oracle2/diag/rdbms/india_ps/INDIAPS/trace
$ ls -al alert*
-rw-r----- 1 oracle dba 2533843 Dec 20 01:56 alert_INDIAPS.log
$ tail -100 alert_INDIAPS.log
.

.

.

Media Recovery Waiting for thread 1 sequence 3273 (in transit)
Recovery of Online Redo Log: Thread 1 Group 5 Seq 3273 Reading mem 0
  Mem# 0: /u01/app/oracle2/datafile/ORCL/std5.log
RFS[20]: Selected log 4 for thread 1 sequence 3274 dbid 1319333016 branch
791552282
Thu Dec 20 01:48:19 2012
Archived Log entry 450 added for thread 1 sequence 3273 ID 0x4eea7a49
dest 1:
Media Recovery Waiting for thread 1 sequence 3274 (in transit)
Recovery of Online Redo Log: Thread 1 Group 4 Seq 3274 Reading mem 0
  Mem# 0: /u01/app/oracle2/datafile/ORCL/std4.log
Thu Dec 20 01:56:08 2012
RFS[20]: Selected log 5 for thread 1 sequence 3275 dbid 1319333016 branch
791552282
Thu Dec 20 01:56:08 2012
Archived Log entry 451 added for thread 1 sequence 3274 ID 0x4eea7a49
dest 1:
Thu Dec 20 01:56:09 2012
Media Recovery Waiting for thread 1 sequence 3275 (in transit)
Recovery of Online Redo Log: Thread 1 Group 5 Seq 3275 Reading mem 0
  Mem# 0: /u01/app/oracle2/datafile/ORCL/std5.log
```

Another method to monitor the alert log is the ADRCI command-line tool, which is an Oracle Database 11g feature to manage Oracle Database diagnostic data. Using ADRCI, it's possible to manage the entire alert log and trace files in the diagnostic directories (database, ASM, listener alert log files, and so on), view the health monitor reports, and zip incident and problem information into a file to send to Oracle Support.

Time for action – monitoring the database alert log using ADRCI

Let's see an example of monitoring the database alert log using the ADRCI utility:

1. Ensure that the ORACLE_HOME and PATH environment variables are set properly. The PATH environment variable must include the ORACLE_HOME/bin directory.

   ```
   export ORACLE_HOME=/u01/app/oracle2/product/11.2.0/dbhome_1
   export PATH=$PATH:$ORACLE_HOME/bin
   ```

2. Start the ADRCI command-line tool:

   ```
   $ adrci

   ADRCI: Release 11.2.0.1.0 - Production on Thu Dec 20 02:06:49 2012

   Copyright (c) 1982, 2009, Oracle and/or its affiliates.  All
   rights reserved.

   ADR base = "/u01/app/oracle2"
   ```

3. We can run the HELP command to get help on the usage of this utility:

   ```
   adrci> HELP

   HELP [topic]
      Available Topics:
            CREATE REPORT
            ECHO
            EXIT
            HELP
            HOST
            IPS
            PURGE
            RUN
            SET BASE
            SET BROWSER
            SET CONTROL
            SET ECHO
            SET EDITOR
            SET HOMES | HOME | HOMEPATH
            SET TERMOUT
   ```

```
SHOW ALERT

SHOW BASE

SHOW CONTROL

SHOW HM_RUN

SHOW HOMES | HOME | HOMEPATH

SHOW INCDIR

SHOW INCIDENT

SHOW PROBLEM

SHOW REPORT

SHOW TRACEFILE

SPOOL
```

There are other commands intended to be used directly by Oracle, type "HELP EXTENDED" to see the list

It's possible to get help for a specific command by specifying the topic in the HELP command:

```
adrci> HELP SHOW ALERT


  Usage: SHOW ALERT [-p <predicate_string>]   [-term]

                    [ [-tail [num] [-f]] | [-file <alert_file_
name>]]
  Purpose: Show alert messages.


  Options:
     [-p <predicate_string>]: The predicate string must be
double-quoted.
     The fields in the predicate are the fields:
          ORIGINATING_TIMESTAMP        timestamp
          NORMALIZED_TIMESTAMP         timestamp
          ORGANIZATION_ID              text(65)
          COMPONENT_ID                 text(65)
          HOST_ID                      text(65)
          HOST_ADDRESS                 text(17)
          MESSAGE_TYPE                 number
          MESSAGE_LEVEL                number
          MESSAGE_ID                   text(65)
```

MESSAGE_GROUP	text(65)
CLIENT_ID	text(65)
MODULE_ID	text(65)
PROCESS_ID	text(33)
THREAD_ID	text(65)
USER_ID	text(65)
INSTANCE_ID	text(65)
DETAILED_LOCATION	text(161)
UPSTREAM_COMP_ID	text(101)
DOWNSTREAM_COMP_ID	text(101)
EXECUTION_CONTEXT_ID	text(101)
EXECUTION_CONTEXT_SEQUENCE	number
ERROR_INSTANCE_ID	number
ERROR_INSTANCE_SEQUENCE	number
MESSAGE_TEXT	text(2049)
MESSAGE_ARGUMENTS	text(129)
SUPPLEMENTAL_ATTRIBUTES	text(129)
SUPPLEMENTAL_DETAILS	text(129)
PROBLEM_KEY	text(65)

[-tail [num] [-f]]: Output last part of the alert messages and output latest messages as the alert log grows. If num is not specified, the last 10 messages are displayed. If "-f" is specified, new data will append at the end as new alert messages are generated.

[-term]: Direct results to terminal. If this option is not specified,

    the results will be open in an editor. By default, it will open in

    emacs, but "set editor" can be used   to set other editors.

[-file <alert_file_name>]: Allow users to specify an alert file which

may not be in ADR. <alert_file_name> must be specified with full path. Note that this option cannot be used with the -tail option

Examples:

```
show alert
show alert -p "message_text like '%incident%'"
show alert -tail 20
```

4. Type the following statement to list the ADR home directories:

```
adrci> SHOW HOMES
ADR Homes:
diag/rdbms/india_ps/INDIAPS
diag/asm/+asm/+ASM
diag/tnslsnr/india_ps/listener
```

5. Set the database ADR HOME to work on:

```
adrci> SET HOME diag/rdbms/india_ps/INDIAPS
```

6. Monitor the last 20 lines of the database alert log file with the following statement:

```
adrci> SHOW ALERT -TAIL 20


2012-12-20 01:46:25.303000 +02:00
Archived Log entry 445 added for thread 1 sequence 3268 ID
0x4eea7a49 dest 1:
Media Recovery Waiting for thread 1 sequence 3269 (in transit)
Recovery of Online Redo Log: Thread 1 Group 5 Seq 3269 Reading mem
0
  Mem# 0: /u01/app/oracle2/datafile/ORCL/std5.log
2012-12-20 01:46:28.383000 +02:00
RFS[20]: Selected log 4 for thread 1 sequence 3270 dbid 1319333016
branch 791552282
  .

  .

  .


Archived Log entry 451 added for thread 1 sequence 3274 ID
0x4eea7a49 dest 1:
Media Recovery Waiting for thread 1 sequence 3275 (in transit)
Recovery of Online Redo Log: Thread 1 Group 5 Seq 3275 Reading mem
0
  Mem# 0: /u01/app/oracle2/datafile/ORCL/std5.log
adrci>
```

7. Run the following statement to monitor the alert log messages that contain the string `ORA-`:

```
adrci> SHOW ALERT -P "MESSAGE_TEXT LIKE '%ORA-%'"

...

Errors in file /u01/app/oracle2/diag/rdbms/india_ps/INDIAPS/trace/
INDIAPS_pr05_22496.trc:

ORA-27090: Unable to reserve kernel resources for asynchronous
disk I/O

Additional information: 3

Additional information: 128

Additional information: 268423168

Errors in file /u01/app/oracle2/diag/rdbms/india_ps/INDIAPS/trace/
INDIAPS_pr06_22498.trc:
```

8. It's also possible to list the incidents with the `SHOW INCIDENT` command:

```
adrci> SHOW INCIDENT

ADR Home = /u01/app/oracle/diag/rdbms/sb2db/SB2DB1:
*********************************************************************
INCIDENT_ID       PROBLEM_KEY            CREATE_TIME
-----------       --------------         ----------------------------
320729            ORA 1578               2012-12-20 00:03:50.538000 +02:00
1 rows fetched
```

What just happened?

We've seen an example of using the ADRCI command-line tool to monitor alert log files. In a Data Guard-related problem, the first place to check will be the alert log files of the primary and standby databases. Using ADRCI, it's easy to read alert log files of all Oracle components and also list specific problems that are recorded in the alert log files.

Data Guard broker logs

For each database of a Data Guard configuration where a Data Guard broker is being used, the DMON process writes log data into a logfile. This logfile resides in the same directory as the alert log and is named `drc<$ORACLE_SID>.log`. It contains important information about the Data Guard's status that can be used to troubleshoot Data Guard's failures.

Chapter 10

Let's check this file in our standby database:

```
$ cd /u01/app/oracle2/diag/rdbms/india_ps/INDIAPS/trace
$ tail -50 drcINDIAPS.log

...
2012-12-20 02:15:37.050                              Property
'LogFileNameConvert' has inconsistent values:METADATA='', SPFILE='',
DATABASE='/u01/app/oracle2/datafile/ORCL, /u01/app/oracle2/datafile/ORCL'
2012-12-20 02:15:37.050                 RSM0: HEALTH CHECK WARNING:
ORA-16714: the value of property LogFileNameConvert is inconsistent with
the database setting
2012-12-20 02:15:37.066                 RSM Warning: Property
'LogArchiveTrace' has inconsistent values:METADATA='0', SPFILE='0',
DATABASE='8192'
2012-12-20 02:15:37.066                 RSM0: HEALTH CHECK WARNING:
ORA-16714: the value of property LogArchiveTrace is inconsistent with the
database setting
2012-12-20 02:15:37.077 00000000  2049726439 Operation HEALTH_CHECK
continuing with warning, status = ORA-16792
2012-12-20 02:15:37.078 00000000  2049726439 Operation HEALTH_CHECK
continuing with warning, status = ORA-16792
```

Dynamic performance views

Dynamic performance views are special database views that are dynamically updated by the database itself and contain important information about the status and performance of database components. It's not possible to insert or update data in these views. DBAs only query them to gather information about the status of the database.

Here, we'll see some of the dynamic performance views that contain information about Data Guard's configuration or status:

♦ V$DATABASE: This view includes a lot of general information about the database. In a Data Guard configuration, it's possible to query the role of the database, the protection mode, and the switchover status using this view. Run the following query in the databases in your Data Guard environment:

```
SQL> SELECT PROTECTION_MODE, PROTECTION_LEVEL, DATABASE_ROLE ROLE,
SWITCHOVER_STATUS FROM V$DATABASE;
```

```
PROTECTION_MODE          PROTECTION_LEVEL      ROLE            SWITCHOVER_
STATUS

-------------------   -----------------   ----------------  ----------

MAXIMUM PERFORMANCE   MAXIMUM PERFORMANCE  PHYSICAL STANDBY
NOTALLOWED
```

- **V$DATAGUARD_CONFIG**: This view lists the `DB_UNIQUE_NAME` parameters of the databases existing in the Data Guard configuration. You can query this view on any of the databases:

```
SQL> SELECT * FROM V$DATAGUARD_CONFIG;


DB_UNIQUE_NAME

-----------------------------

INDIA_PS

turkey_un

INDIA_UN
```

- **V$ARCHIVE_DEST_STATUS**: This view shows the configuration information for the archived redo log destinations. By running the following query in the primary database, we can display the recovery mode at the archival destination:

```
SQL> SELECT RECOVERY_MODE FROM V$ARCHIVE_DEST_STATUS where dest_
id=2;


RECOVERY_MODE

----------------------

MANAGED REAL TIME APPLY
```

- **V$MANAGED_STANDBY**: We query this view in a physical standby database to monitor the current status of specific Data Guard processes. Run the following query in the physical standby database and see which sequence is being applied and which sequences are being transferred from the primary database to the standby database:

```
SQL> SELECT PROCESS, STATUS, THREAD#, SEQUENCE#,BLOCK#, BLOCKS
FROM V$MANAGED_STANDBY;
```

PROCESS	STATUS	THREAD#	SEQUENCE#	BLOCK#	BLOCKS
ARCH	CLOSING	1	3272	18432	2043
ARCH	CLOSING	1	3274	20480	1
ARCH	CONNECTED	0	0	0	0

ARCH	CLOSING	1	3273	18432	2034
RFS	IDLE	0	0	0	0
RFS	IDLE	0	0	0	0
RFS	IDLE	0	0	0	0
MRP0	APPLYING_LOG	1	3275	4098	102400
RFS	IDLE	1	3275	4098	1

◆ V$ARCHIVED_LOG: This view contains detailed information about the archived logfiles of databases. In a physical standby database, the APPLIED column shows whether the archived logfile was applied or not. The following query shows the archived log sequences that are received from the primary database but not applied:

```
SQL> SELECT THREAD#, SEQUENCE#, FIRST_CHANGE#,NEXT_CHANGE# FROM
V$ARCHIVED_LOG where APPLIED='NO';

no rows selected
```

◆ V$DATAGUARD_STATUS: This view contains messages that are recently written to the alert log or trace files, related with Data Guard services. In case of a Data Guard issue, it's a good method to check errors using this view.

```
SQL> ALTER SESSION SET NLS_DATE_FORMAT = 'DD-MON-YYYY HH24:MI:SS';

SQL> SELECT TIMESTAMP, MESSAGE FROM V$DATAGUARD_STATUS WHERE
TIMESTAMP>SYSDATE-1 ORDER BY TIMESTAMP;

TIMESTAMP               MESSAGE
--------------------    -------------------------------------------
20-DEC-2012 01:48:13 Media Recovery Waiting for thread 1 sequence
 3272 (in transit)

20-DEC-2012 01:48:16 ARC0: Beginning to archive thread 1 sequence
    3272 (20612121-20612129)

20-DEC-2012 01:48:16 ARC0: Completed archiving thread 1 sequence
3272
 (0-0)

...

20-DEC-2012 01:56:08 ARC1: Beginning to archive thread 1 sequence
 3274 (20612140-20612682)

20-DEC-2012 01:56:08 ARC1: Completed archiving thread 1 sequence
3274
 (0-0)

20-DEC-2012 01:56:09 Media Recovery Waiting for thread 1 sequence
    3275 (in transit)
```

◆ `V$ARCHIVE_GAP`: If there is a gap in a standby database that is blocking recovery, we can query the missing archived logfiles using this view. If there is no gap, the query will not return any rows.

```
SQL> DESC V$ARCHIVE_GAP

 Name                                        Null?    Type
 ------------------------------------------- -------- --------------

  THREAD#                                              NUMBER

  LOW_SEQUENCE#                                        NUMBER

  HIGH_SEQUENCE#                                       NUMBER


SQL> SELECT * FROM V$ARCHIVE_GAP;


no rows selected
```

◆ `V$LOGSTDBY_PROCESS`: We can monitor SQL Apply in a logical standby database by querying this view. If SQL Apply is not running, the query will not return any rows.

```
SQL> SELECT SID, SERIAL#, SPID, TYPE, HIGH_SCN FROM V$LOGSTDBY_
PROCESS;
```

SID	SERIAL#	SPID	TYPE	HIGH_SCN
48	6	11074	COORDINATOR	7178242899
56	56	10858	READER	7178243497
46	1	10860	BUILDER	7178242901
45	1	10862	PREPARER	7178243295
37	1	10864	ANALYZER	7178242900
36	1	10866	APPLIER	7178239467
35	3	10868	APPLIER	7178239463
34	7	10870	APPLIER	7178239461
33	1	10872	APPLIER	7178239472

Summary

In this chapter, we have covered common Data Guard issues using diagnostic data in a Data Guard environment. As Data Guard administrators, we have to identify the underlying reason of a Data Guard issue using this diagnostic data, and resolve the issue in the correct way. We think that the information and examples that we've seen in this chapter will be helpful for this purpose. The next chapter is about Data Guard best practices.

11
Data Guard Best Practices

In many Data Guard installation cases, people may think that seeing the main functions of Data Guard running is enough for a successful deployment of Data Guard. In other words, if redo is being transferred from the primary database to a standby database(s), and is being applied on the standby, it's a smooth Data Guard configuration. However, if the configuration is prepared keeping in mind best practices, which is the topic of this chapter, it will be more robust, effective, and complete.

In this chapter, we will discuss the following topics:

♦ Configuring connection failover

♦ Archived log deletion policy on a standby database

♦ Using flashback on a standby database

♦ Database rolling upgrade using a transient logical standby

♦ Corruption detection, prevention, and automatic repair with Oracle Data Guard

Let's start with configuring a connection failover in a Data Guard environment.

Configuring a connection failover

Building a configuration in which database clients are able to automatically connect to a new primary database after a role change is vital in Data Guard. If we skip this important aspect, it may be very hard to configure connections of all database users to the new primary database.

Now, let's learn about the important connection failover terms – **Transparent Application Failover (TAF)**, **Fast Connection Failover (FCF)**, and **Fast Application Notification (FAN)**.

Transparent Application Failover (TAF)

TAF is a connection failover configuration of **Oracle Call Interface** (**OCI**) that is used for high-availability environments such as Oracle Data Guard, **Oracle Real Application Clusters** (**RAC**), and Oracle Fail Safe.

When using this configuration, clients can automatically establish a prespecified connection to the database after a failure of the database instance. In RAC, this means connecting to one of the surviving instances and in Data Guard it means connecting to the new primary database after failover.

We can configure TAF in two ways – client-side configuration and server-side configuration:

♦ **Client-side TAF configuration**: The TNS connect string is configured to specify the failover details.

♦ **Server-side TAF configuration**: The database service attributes are configured to specify the failover details. This method will be more effective when there are many client connections.

 If both client- and server-side TAF configurations exist in the database environment, the server-side configuration properties will be valid regarding the order of precedence.

TAF will not only establish a new connection to the database, but also re-run a `select` statement and reposition the cursor if preferred. We can configure TAF only for establishing a new connection, which is called **session failover**, or for the recovery of the session and query, which is called **select failover**. With the select failover mode, the number of rows fetched by the cursor is tracked and when the connection is lost, it's recovered by TAF by repositioning the cursor. So, the client doesn't restart but resumes fetching rows. This is especially good for long-running, time-critical reports and data extractions.

 TAF cannot failover inserts, updates, or deletes. The Oracle database rolls back these DML operations in case of a failure.

It's possible to monitor TAF properties of sessions using the `V$SESSION` dynamic performance view. The following query result will show the service name, failover type, failover method, and failover failovers, if occurred, for the clients connected to the database:

```
SQL> SELECT USERNAME, SERVICE, FAILOVER_TYPE, FAILOVER_METHOD, FAILED_
OVER FROM V$SESSION;
```

Configuring the client-side TAF

The client-side TAF is configured using the TNS connection string. The following string is an example of a Data-Guard-enabled client-side TAF configuration where primary and standby databases are 11gR2 RAC with **Single Client Access Names (SCAN)** being used:

```
OLTP =
  (DESCRIPTION =
    (LOAD_BALANCE=OFF)
    (FAILOVER=ON)
    (ADDRESS_LIST =
      (ADDRESS = (PROTOCOL = TCP)(HOST = PRIMARY_SCAN)(PORT = 1521))
      (ADDRESS = (PROTOCOL = TCP)(HOST = STANDBY_SCAN)(PORT = 1521))
    )
    (CONNECT_DATA =
      (SERVICE_NAME = OLTP)
      (SERVER = DEDICATED)
        (FAILOVER_MODE =
          (TYPE = session)
          (METHOD = BASIC)
          (RETRIES = 15)
          (DELAY = 10)
        )))))
```

Configuring the server-side TAF

In 11gR2, we configure the server-side TAF using **Server Control Utility (SRVCTL)**. The `srvctl add service` command adds a new service, and the `srvctl modify service` command changes settings for a predefined service. The following is an example of creating a TAF-enabled database service on a RAC and Data Guard configuration. We must create this service both in the primary and standby hosts with the following commands:

- For the primary cluster, use the following:

  ```
  srvctl add service -d ORCL_PRIM -s OLTP -r prim_node1,prim_node2
  -l PRIMARY -q TRUE -e SESSION -m BASIC -w 10 -z 15
  ```

- For the standby cluster, use the following:

  ```
  srvctl add service -d ORCL_STD -s OLTP -r std_node1,std_node2 -l
  PRIMARY -q TRUE -e SESSION -m BASIC -w 10 -z 15
  ```

The following table lists the definitions of the command options:

Option	Description
-d	This gives a unique name for the database.
-s	This gives the service name.
-r	For RAC databases, this gives the list of preferred instances on which the service runs.
-l { [primary] | [physical_standby] | [logical_standby] | [snapshot_standby] }	This gives the service role. Service is automatically started when the database is in this role.
-q {TRUE | FALSE}	This indicates whether AQ HA notifications should be enabled for this service.
-e {NONE | SESSION | SELECT}	This gives the failover type – session failover, select failover, or none.
-m {NONE | BASIC}	This gives the failover method. If the session failover or select failover type is selected, you should use BASIC for this option. NONE means TAF is disabled.
-z	This gives the number of failover retries.
-w	This gives the time delay between failover attempts.

If we're going to use the physical standby database with active Data Guard for reporting, we should create a service for this purpose on both primary and standby hosts. For example:

- For the primary cluster, create the following service:

```
srvctl add service -d ORCL_PRIM -s REPORTING -r prim_node1,prim_
node2 -l PHYSICAL_STANDBY -q TRUE -e SESSION -m BASIC -w 10 -z 15
```

- For the standby cluster, create the following service:

```
srvctl add service -d ORCL_STD -s REPORTING-r std_node1,std_node2
-l    PHYSICAL_STANDBY -q TRUE -e SESSION -m BASIC -w 10 -z 15
```

In this case, the service will be created at the cluster level but the service definition will not be applied to the standby database because it's read-only. For this reason, we run the DBMS_SERVICE.CREATE_SERVICE procedure for the REPORTING service on the primary database, and the service definition will be replicated to the standby database with Redo Apply.

```
EXECUTE DBMS_SERVICE.CREATE_SERVICE( service_name => 'reporting'
network_name => 'reporting' goal => 'NULL' dtp => 'NULL' aq_ha_
notifications => 'TRUE' failover_method => 'BASIC' failover_type =>
'SESSION' failover_retries => 15 failover_delay => 10 clb_goal =>
'NULL');
```

Using the previous server-side TAF configuration (the OLTP and REPORTING services), it's not necessary to configure TAF at the client side in the tnsnames.ora file. The following TNS entry is an example that can be used to connect the OLTP service:

```
OLTP=
  (DESCRIPTION_LIST=
  (LOAD_BALANCE=OFF)
  (FAILOVER=ON)
(DESCRIPTION=
  (CONNECT_TIMEOUT=3)(TRANSPORT_CONNECT_TIMEOUT=2)(RETRY_COUNT=3)
    (ADDRESS_LIST=
    (LOAD_BALANCE=ON)
    (ADDRESS=(PROTOCOL=TCP)(HOST=PRIMARY_SCAN)(PORT=1521)))
      (CONNECT_DATA=(SERVICE_NAME=OLTP)))
(DESCRIPTION=
  (CONNECT_TIMEOUT=5)(TRANSPORT_CONNECT_TIMEOUT=3)(RETRY_COUNT=3)
    (ADDRESS_LIST=
    (LOAD_BALANCE=ON)
  (ADDRESS=(PROTOCOL=TCP)(HOST= STANDBY_SCAN)(PORT=1521)))
    (CONNECT_DATA=(SERVICE_NAME=OLTP))))
```

In this TNS entry, both the primary and standby SCAN hostnames are involved. Just below DESCRIPTION_LIST, we can see LOAD_BALANCE=OFF. This means that the client will try to connect the DESCRIPTION definitions in order. If it can't connect to the primary database, it'll try to connect to the standby database. However, below the DESCRIPTION definitions, we see LOAD_BALANCE=ON. This is about the connection to the RAC database and new connections are going to be assigned to three IP addresses of the SCAN name randomly.

For each DESCRIPTION definition, we can see some TNS string parameters set. CONNECT_TIMEOUT specifies the total time to establish an Oracle net connection to a database. It includes the TRANSPORT_CONNECT_TIMEOUT value, which is the time taken by a client to establish a TCP connection to the database server. It's possible to set the CONNECT_TIMEOUT value globally for a database instance in the sqlnet.ora file using the SQLNET.OUTBOUND_CONNECT_TIMEOUT parameter. Also, we can set the TCP.CONNECT_TIMEOUT parameter for a global TRANSPORT_CONNECT_TIMEOUT value. The last parameter, RETRY_COUNT, specifies the maximum number of connection attempts for the DESCRIPTION definition.

In this configuration, the following algorithm will be applied when clients connect to a database using the OLTP service:

1. The PRIMARY_SCAN hostname is resolved to three IP addresses.

2. One of the IP addresses is randomly selected and a connection attempt is performed.

3. If the IP address doesn't respond in the time we set in TRANSPORT_CONNECT_ TIMEOUT, which is two seconds, or the IP address responds but a connection can't be established in three seconds (CONNECT_TIMEOUT), it'll try the next IP address. There will be a maximum of three retry attempts because of the RETRY_COUNT setting.

4. When the client can't connect to the primary database with the first DESCRIPTION definition, it'll try to connect the second DESCRIPTION definition, which is the standby database.

5. The STANDBY_SCAN hostname will be resolved to three IP addresses.

6. One of the IP addresses is randomly selected and an attempt for a connection is performed. The same settings are defined for the standby database description.

Note that automatically controlling the startup of services by assigning a role to the service with SRVCTL is an 11*g*R2 feature. In earlier releases, we can create a trigger to ensure that the service is started only for the specified database role, such as the following example:

```
create trigger TAF_TRIGGER after startup on database
declare
 db_role varchar(30);
begin
 select database_role into db_role from v$database;
 if db_role = 'PRIMARY' then
 DBMS_SERVICE.START_SERVICE('OLTP');
 else
 DBMS_SERVICE.STOP_SERVICE('OLTP');
 end if;
end;
/
```

Fast Connection Failover (FCF)

Fast Connection Failover is the equivalent of Transparent Application Failover for **Java Database Connectivity (JDBC)** clients. TAF works for OCI clients and FCF works for JDBC clients.

Time for action – configuring FCF for JDBC connections

Let's see an example of how we can configure FCF for JDBC clients.

1. In order to run FCF as we configured it, we need to create database services where TAF or aq_ha_notifications is disabled. As we discussed, in 11*g*R2, it's possible to create role-specific database services so that service is automatically enabled or disabled whenever there is a role change. The following statements can be run on the primary and standby clusters to create a database service for a production service OLTP:

❑ For the primary cluster, use the following:

```
srvctl add service -d ORCL_PRIM -s OLTP -r prim_node1,prim_
node2 -l PRIMARY -q FALSE -e NONE -m NONE -w 0 -z 0
```

❑ For the standby cluster, use the following:

```
srvctl add service -d ORCL_STD -s OLTP -r std_node1,std_
node2 -l    PRIMARY -q FALSE -e NONE -m NONE -w 0 -z 0
```

If needed, the following statements will create a read-only service for reporting on the physical standby database:

❑ For the primary cluster, use the following:

```
srvctl add service -d ORCL_PRIM -s REPORTING -r prim_
node1,prim_node2 -l PHYSICAL_STANDBY -q FALSE -e NONE -m
NONE -w 0 -z 0
```

❑ For the standby cluster, use the following:

```
srvctl add service -d ORCL_PRIM -s REPORTING -r std_
node1,std_node2 -l PHYSICAL_STANDBY -q FALSE -e NONE -m NONE
-w 0 -z 0
```

 Create the REPORTING service with the DBMS_SERVICE. CREATE_SERVICE procedure on the primary database so that standby knows about this service through redo transmission.

2. Now we configure the JDBC clients with the proper CONNECT descriptor.

```
"jdbc:oracle:thin:@" +
"(DESCRIPTION_LIST=" +
  "(LOAD_BALANCE=off)" +
  "(FAILOVER=on)" +
  "(DESCRIPTION=" +
    "(ADDRESS_LIST=" +
    "(LOAD_BALANCE=on)" +
    "(ADDRESS=(PROTOCOL=TCP)(HOST=PRIMARY_SCAN)(PORT=1521)))" +
    "(CONNECT_DATA=(SERVICE_NAME=OLTP)))" +
  "(DESCRIPTION=" +
    "(ADDRESS_LIST=" +
    "(LOAD_BALANCE=on)" +
    "(ADDRESS=(PROTOCOL=TCP)(HOST=STANDBY_SCAN)(PORT=1521)))" +
   "(CONNECT_DATA=(SERVICE_NAME=OLTP))))";
```

3. The JDBC client should set the `TCP_CONNTIMEOUT_STR` property so that the connection attempt fails over to the next host in the `ADDRESS_LIST` list after the specified time.

```
Properties prop = new Properties(); prop.put(oracle.net.
ns.SQLnetDef.TCP_CONNTIMEOUT_STR, ""+5000); // 5000ms pds.
setConnectionProperties(prop);
```

4. Enable FCF and configure the application to connect to all of the primary and standby ONS daemons.

```
pds.setFastConnectionFailoverEnabled(true);
pds.setONSConfiguration("nodes=prim_node1:6200,prim_
node2:6200,std_node1:6200,std_node2:6200");
```

What just happened?

We've successfully configured FCF for JDBC client connections.

Fast Application Notification (FAN)

FAN is a notification mechanism in which Oracle doesn't wait for clients to detect any database status changes (such as service, instance, or if the database goes up or down), and quickly (as its name implies) informs clients about the events. If FAN is not used, clients need to wait for the TCP timeout duration to fail over to another specified connection. This duration can be very long and not suitable for our failover time target.

 If the Data Guard broker is used in a failover, the FAN event is automatically sent to the clients.

In addition to up/down events, FAN also notifies clients with load-balancing advisory events. Clients use this information and connect to the instance with the best response time.

It's possible to take advantage of FAN with the following methods:

1. If an integrated Oracle client is used, the client application can use FAN without programmatic changes. The integrated clients for FAN events are Oracle database 11*g* JDBC, **Oracle Universal Connection Pool (UCP)** for Java, Oracle database 11*g* ODP.NET, and Oracle database 11*g* **Oracle Call Interface (OCI)**.

 JDBC clients subscribe to ONS daemons and receive FAN events only if FCF is configured on the clients.

2. Implement FAN server-side callouts on your Database Tier.

What just happened?

Connection failover methods are important pieces of the database high-availability feature, and we've gone through configuring automatic connection failover for Oracle database clients in an RAC and Data Guard environment.

The archived log deletion policy on the standby database

The continuously transferred redo transaction is archived at the standby database before or after being applied, depending on the configuration. At the end, we're faced with lots of files filling the log destination either on the filesystem or ASM disk group. We need to build an automatic structure on the standby site, where applied archived logs are deleted automatically based on a specific logic.

There are several methods for archived log deletion. It's possible to delete archived logs with the rm command of the operation system or ASM. However, if we use rm, the control file will not be updated about the deletion of archived logfiles. Thus, in order to update the control file with the deletion operation, we must run crosscheck and delete expired RMAN commands as follows:

```
RMAN> crosscheck archivelog all;
RMAN> delete expired archivelog all;
```

Another option is scheduling an RMAN job that deletes applied archived logs on the standby database. The RMAN command's delete archivelog command updates the control file related to the delete operation. This method is easier than using the rm command; however, for both methods we have a job-maintenance issue. If the scheduled job doesn't run for some reason, the log destination will fill up and manual operation will be required.

The recommended method to keep deleting the archived logfiles on standby databases is simply leaving this task to Oracle. We use the fast recovery area for this purpose.

Time for action – the recommended configuration for archived log maintenance on a standby database

Let's see an example of configuring automatic maintenance of the archived logs on a standby database:

1. Enable the fast recovery area on the standby database by setting the DB_RECOVERY_FILE_DEST and DB_RECOVERY_FILE_DEST_SIZE parameters:

    ```
    SQL> ALTER SYSTEM SET DB_RECOVERY_FILE_DEST='/data/FRA';
    SQL> ALTER SYSTEM SET DB_RECOVERY_FILE_DEST_SIZE=500G;
    ```

If we're using ASM, we can specify a disk group as `DB_RECOVERY_FILE_DEST`.

```
SQL> ALTER SYSTEM SET DB_RECOVERY_FILE_DEST='+FRA';
```

2. Set the `LOG_ARCHIVE_DEST_1` parameter as follows so that the archived logfiles will be created at the `DB_RECOVERY_FILE_DEST` parameter:

```
SQL> ALTER SYSTEM SET LOG_ARCHIVE_DEST_1='LOCATION=USE_DB_
RECOVERY_ FILE_DEST';
```

3. Set the `RMAN` archived log deletion policy as follows. With this setting, the applied archived logs will be automatically deleted when there is a space constraint in FRA, depending on `DB_RECOVERY_FILE_DEST_SIZE`. If the archived logs are not applied, they will not be deleted.

```
RMAN> CONFIGURE ARCHIVELOG DELETION POLICY TO APPLIED ON STANDBY;
```

Automatic deletion of archived logs in a logical standby database is already covered in *Chapter 3, Configuring Oracle Data Guard Logical Standby Database*, in detail.

What just happened?

We've mentioned methods to maintain the applied archived logfiles on the standby database. The recommended method of using FRA is described step by step. With this method, deletion of applied archived logs is maintained by Oracle and it's guaranteed that the archived logs that are not applied yet will not be deleted.

Using flashback on a standby database

Flashback is a useful feature introduced in Oracle database version 9*i* and more properties were added on in the next versions, 10*g* and 11*g*. When enabled, the flashback feature helps us recover data loss, corrupted data, or logical errors easily. In the following scenarios, we can use flashback with **PITR (Point-in-Time Recovery)** to recover data:

- Dropped tables
- Truncated tables
- Massive changes by inserts / updates / deletes
- Logical errors

If we're not using flashback, the steps to restore a table loss will be as follows:

1. Restore the full database on a separate server using a backup performed before the table's `drop` operation.

2. After restoring the database, perform the `until time` recovery.

3. Open the database with `resetlogs`.

4. Export the table from the restored database and import it into the production database.

If you are using flashback, you can use it to recover the table. However, if there is no standby database, this will be a disadvantage because we'll need to flash back the whole database to that particular time. So there will be loss of transactions.

Time for action – using flashback on a standby database

Now we are going to see how to recover a dropped/truncated table if a standby database exists, and using the flashback feature. We won't make any changes to the primary database and even the flashback feature may be off on the primary database.

1. **Enabling flashback**: To perform recovery of an object, flashback must be enabled on the standby database. Ensure MRP is cancelled before enabling flashback.

```
SQL> alter database recover managed standby database cancel;
Database altered.
SQL> alter database flashback on;
Database altered.
SQL> select db_unique_name,flashback_on from v$database;
DB_UNIQUE_NAME   FLASHBACK_ON
--------------   ------------------

INDIA_UN         YES
```

On the alert log, you will get the following:

```
Thu Dec 20 15:22:21 2012
RVWR started with pid=25, OS id=7900
Thu Dec 20 15:22:24 2012
Allocated 3981120 bytes in shared pool for flashback generation
buffer
Flashback Database Enabled at SCN 6082371
Completed: alter database flashback on
```

2. **Adjusting the flashback retention period on the standby database**: In order to perform recovery of an object with flashback, the object's drop/truncate time must not be more than the value specified in DB_FLASHBACK_RETENTION_TARGET and all the flashback and archive logs should be available.

```
SQL> show parameter db_flashback_retention_target
NAME                                 TYPE        VALUE
------------------------------------ ----------- --------db_
flashback_retention_target           integer     5760
```

3. **Gathering table information before truncation**: We can collect the following data from the primary database before truncating the table, in order to ensure that we'll recover the same number of rows after the flashback:

```
SQL> select segment_name,sum(bytes/1024/1024) from dba_segments
where segment_name='PACKT' group by segment_name;
SEGMENT_NAME     SUM(BYTES/1024/1024)
---------------- --------------------
PACKT                            7738
SQL> select count(*) from packt;
      COUNT(*)
--------------
      88080384
```

The PACKT table's size is around 7.7 GB with 88080384 rows.

4. **Truncating the table and capturing the time**: From the primary database, let's truncate the table:

 This truncate operation is only for testing purposes. Please do not perform this on production databases.

```
SQL> truncate table packt;
Table truncated.
SQL> select count(*) from packt;
COUNT(*)
--------
0
SQL> select sysdate from dual;
SYSDATE
---------
20-DEC-2012 16:11:41
```

The table was truncated on 20-DEC-2012, at 16:11:41.

5. **Verifying the data on a standby database**: We're using the standby database with real-time apply and active Data Guard features. So the transactions will be quickly replicated with no delay.

```
SQL> select db_unique_name,database_role from v$database;
DB_UNIQUE_NAME   DATABASE_ROLE
---------------  ----------------
INDIA_UN         PHYSICAL STANDBY
SQL> select count(*) from packt;
  COUNT(*)
----------
         0
```

The number of rows for the table PACKT on standby is also 0, so the truncate operations are applied on the standby database.

6. **Performing a time-based flashback on a standby database**: Now connect as SYSDBA, cancel recovery, shut down the standby database, and start in MOUNT status:

```
SQL> connect / as sysdba
Connected.
SQL> recover managed standby database cancel;
Media recovery complete.
SQL> shutdown immediate
SQL> startup mount
Database mounted.
```

From step 4, we have captured the time of the table's truncate operation, and now will use that time to flash back the standby database:

```
SQL> flashback database to timestamp to_date('20-DEC-2012
16:10:00','DD-MON-YYYY HH24:MI:SS');
Flashback complete.
```

On the alert log, you will get the following:

```
Thu Dec 20 16:26:04 2012
flashback database to timestamp to_date('20-DEC-2012
16:10:00','DD-MON-YYYY HH24:MI:SS')
Flashback Restore Start
Flashback Restore Complete
Flashback Media Recovery Start
Serial Media Recovery started
Flashback Media Recovery Log /u02/app/oracle/flash_recovery_area/
INDIA_UN/archivelog/2012_12_20/o1_mf_1_985_8f5vcxhj_.arc
Incomplete Recovery applied until change 6090032 time 12/20/2012
16:10:01
```

```
Flashback Media Recovery Complete
Completed: flashback database to timestamp to_date('20-DEC-2012
16:10:00','DD-MON-YYYY HH24:MI:SS')
```

 If there is any difference in time zones, you can use the log miner to analyze the archived redo logfiles and see at exactly what time the table was truncated.

In the previous command, we used flashback 10 minutes prior to when the drop and flashback operations were successful.

7. **Verifying the data after flashback on a standby database**: Now open the database and check the number of rows that have been recovered.

```
SQL> select db_unique_name,database_role,resetlogs_change# from
v$database;
DB_UNIQUE_NAME   DATABASE_ROLE     RESETLOGS_CHANGE#
--------------   ---------------   -----------------
INDIA_UN         PHYSICAL STANDBY             945184
SQL> select count(*) from packt;
  COUNT(*)
----------
  88080384
```

We can now compare the actual rows before truncating with the number of rows after the flashback operation. In steps 3 and 7, the number of rows are the same. So we've successfully recovered the data.

8. **Exporting the table from a standby database**: We should now export the table from the standby database. If we create a DB link in the primary database pointing to the standby database, we can use NETWORK_LINK to export the table from standby. We have already discussed this option in *Chapter 7*, *Active Data Guard, Snapshot Standby, and Advanced Techniques*. You should perform the following steps from the primary database; it will export data from standby using NETWORK_LINK.

    1. Create a database link in the primary database to point to standby.

```
SQL> create public database link exp_turkey connect to
system identified by "free2go" using 'india';
Database link created.
```

    2. Export the PACKT table.

```
[oracle@oracle-primary expdp]$expdp system/free2go
directory=EXPDP_INDIA network_link=exp_turkey tables=oracle.
packt dumpfile=Packt_table.dmp logfile=packt_table.log
```

```
Connected to: Oracle Database 11g Enterprise Edition Release
11.2.0.3.0 - 64bit Production
With the Partitioning, OLAP, Data Mining and Real
Application Testing options
Starting "SYSTEM"."SYS_EXPORT_TABLE_02":  system/********
directory=EXPDP_INDIA network_link=exp_turkey tables=oracle.
packt dumpfile=Packt_table.dmp logfile=packt_table.log
Estimate in progress using BLOCKS method...
Processing object type TABLE_EXPORT/TABLE/TABLE_DATA
Total estimation using BLOCKS method: 7.556 GB
Processing object type TABLE_EXPORT/TABLE/TABLE
Processing object type TABLE_EXPORT/TABLE/STATISTICS/TABLE_
STATISTICS
. . exported "ORACLE"."PACKT"
3.386 GB 88080384 rows
Master table "SYSTEM"."SYS_EXPORT_TABLE_02" successfully
loaded/unloaded
******************************************************************
**********
Dump file set for SYSTEM.SYS_EXPORT_TABLE_02 is:
  /u02/backups/expdp/Packt_table.dmp
Job "SYSTEM"."SYS_EXPORT_TABLE_02" successfully completed at
17:24:18
```

9. **Importing the table in a primary database**: This process checks the status of the database and row count in the `packt` table.

```
SQL> select db_unique_name,database_role,resetlogs_change# from
v$database;
DB_UNIQUE_NAME      DATABASE_ROLE      RESETLOGS_CHANGE#
------------------- ----------------- -----------------
turkey_un           PRIMARY                      945184
SQL> select count(*) from packt;
  COUNT(*)
----------
         0
```

We have the table metadata in the database, so we only need to perform import of data using the parameter `CONTENT=DATA_ONLY`:

```
[oracle@oracle-primary expdp]$ impdp system/free2go
directory=EXPDP_INDIA tables=scott.packt dumpfile=Packt_table.dmp
logfile=packt_table_imp.log content=data_only
Import: Release 11.2.0.3.0 - Production on Thu Dec 20 17:31:06
2012
Copyright (c) 1982, 2011, Oracle and/or its affiliates.  All
rights reserved.
```

```
Connected to: Oracle Database 11g Enterprise Edition Release
11.2.0.3.0 - 64bit Production
With the Partitioning, OLAP, Data Mining and Real Application
Testing options
Master table "SYSTEM"."SYS_IMPORT_TABLE_01" successfully loaded/
unloaded
Starting "SYSTEM"."SYS_IMPORT_TABLE_01":  system/********
directory=EXPDP_INDIA tables=scott.packt dumpfile=Packt_table.dmp
logfile=packt_table_imp.log content=data_only
Processing object type TABLE_EXPORT/TABLE/TABLE_DATA
. . imported "SCOTT"."PACKT"                              3.386 GB
88080384 rows
Job "SYSTEM"."SYS_IMPORT_TABLE_01" successfully completed at
17:50:43
```

10. **Verifying the table data after importing into a primary database**: From the previous step, we successfully imported data into the primary database and the number of the rows is same as in step 3.

```
SQL> select db_unique_name,database_role,resetlogs_change# from
v$database;
DB_UNIQUE_NAME        DATABASE_ROLE      RESETLOGS_CHANGE#
-------------------- ---------------- -----------------
turkey_un            PRIMARY                     945184
SQL> select count(*) from packt;
  COUNT(*)
----------
   88080384
```

11. **Starting MRP on a standby database to synchronize with a primary database**: Start the recovery on a standby database to synchronize it with the primary database after importing.

```
SQL> alter database recover managed standby database using current
logfile disconnect from session;
Database altered.
```

On the alert log, you will get the following:

```
Waiting for all non-current ORLs to be archived...
All non-current ORLs have been archived.
Media Recovery Waiting for thread 1 sequence 1036 (in transit)
Recovery of Online Redo Log: Thread 1 Group 11 Seq 1036 Reading
mem 0
```

What just happened?

We have seen how to recover a huge truncated table from the primary database by using the flashback technique and the Export/Import procedures.

Database rolling upgrade using the transient logical standby database

To perform upgrade of a production database from 11*g*R1 to 11*g*R2 or to perform any patch set upgrade (for example, from 11.2.0.1 to 11.2.0.3), we need downtime. When upgrading a production database that includes movement of the database to new binaries, database upgrade, and post upgrade tasks, we may need a few hours or more downtime depending on the database size, runtime errors, and so on. However, with the feature of **Rolling Upgrade Using Transient Logical Standby**, we may only need a few minutes of downtime. We can also run load tests to check the performance on the upgraded logical standby database when keeping the primary database with the old version without any upgrade. If the performance test results in a good response, we can go ahead to perform the further steps.

Time for action – performing a rolling upgrade using the transient logical standby database

We will now see a step-by-step approach to upgrade a database from 11.2.0.1 to 11.2.0.3.

1. **Ensuring protection mode and compatibility**: Ensure the protection mode is in either maximum performance or maximum availability.

```
SQL> select * from v$version;
BANNER
------------------------------------------------------------
--Oracle Database 11g Enterprise Edition Release 11.2.0.1.0 -
64bit Production
PL/SQL Release 11.2.0.1.0 - Production
CORE    11.2.0.1.0      Production
TNS for Linux: Version 11.2.0.1.0 - Production
NLSRTL Version 11.2.0.1.0 - Production
SQL> select protection_mode from v$database;
PROTECTION_MODE
--------------------
MAXIMUM PERFORMANCE
```

The `COMPATIBLE` initialization parameter should be same as the software release version. Once we upgrade to the new release and after all the post checks, we can change the compatible parameter value.

```
SQL> show parameter compatible
NAME               TYPE      VALUE
----------------   --------  -------------
compatible         string    11.2.0.0.0
```

2. **Disabling the Data Guard broker**: If the database is managed with the Data Guard broker, disable it; we can enable it after the successful upgrade of the database.

```
SQL> show parameter dg_broker_start
NAME                 TYPE      VALUE
------------------   --------  -------
dg_broker_start      boolean   FALSE
```

3. **Enabling flashback in the primary and standby databases**: Now check flashback database status and then enable it on both primary and standby databases:

```
SQL> select db_unique_name,flashback_on from v$database;
DB_UNIQUE_NAME   FLASHBACK_ON
---------------- ------------------
INDIA_UN         NO
SQL> alter database flashback on;
Database altered.
SQL> select db_unique_name, flashback_on from v$database;
DB_UNIQUE_NAME   FLASHBACK_ON
---------------- ------------------
turkey_un        YES
```

On the alert log, you will get the following:

```
Sun Dec 30 21:42:53 2012
alter database flashback on
Starting background process RVWR
Sun Dec 30 21:42:57 2012
RVWR started with pid=20, OS id=21651
Sun Dec 30 21:43:18 2012
Allocated 3981120 bytes in shared pool for flashback generation
buffer
Sun Dec 30 21:43:33 2012
Flashback Database Enabled at SCN 955828
Completed: alter database flashback on
```

In 11*g*R2, we no longer need to restart database to the `mount` state in order to enable or disable `flashback` on a primary database. Therefore, we can enable/disable `flashback` when the database is in the read-write mode. However, we can't enable or disable flashback on a standby database when MRP is running (`ORA-01153: an incompatible media recovery is active`). In order to perform this on the standby database, we must stop Redo Apply.

4. **Creating a guaranteed restore point on the primary and standby databases**: Create a guaranteed restore point on both the primary and standby databases. We may need to flash back the database to this point in case of any failures during the upgrade.

```
SQL> create restore point Rolling_Upgrade_Turkey guarantee
flashback database;
Restore point created.
SQL> select name,guarantee_flashback_database,scn from v$restore_
point;
NAME                                GUA     SCN
------------------------------- --- ----------
ROLLING_UPGRADE_TURKEY              YES     972018
```

On the alert log, you will get the following:

```
Sun Dec 30 22:09:19 2012
Created guaranteed restore point ROLLING_UPGRADE_TURKEY
```

Now create a guaranteed restore point on the standby database. In order to create a restore point, we must cancel the recovery.

```
SQL> alter database recover managed standby database cancel;
Database altered.
SQL> create restore point Rolling_Upgrade_India guarantee
flashback database;
Restore point created.
```

5. **Creating a log miner dictionary on a primary database**: This package enables supplemental logging on the primary database, which ensures that the updates contain enough information to identify each modified row that is needed for a logical standby configuration.

```
SQL> execute dbms_logstdby.build;
PL/SQL procedure successfully completed.
```

In the alert log, add the following:

```
SUPLOG:  unique = ON, foreign key = OFF, all column = OFF
SUPLOG:  procedural replication = OFF
Completed: alter database add supplemental log data (primary key,
unique index) columns
```

```
alter database add supplemental log data for procedural
replication
SUPLOG: Previous supplemental logging attributes at scn = 998811
```

6. **Converting the physical standby database into a logical standby database**: Now convert the physical standby database into a logical standby database with the KEEP IDENTITY clause so that the database name and DBID remain the same as those in the primary database.

```
SQL> alter database recover managed standby database cancel;
Database altered.
SQL> shutdown immediate
ORACLE instance shut down.
SQL> startup mount exclusive;
Database mounted.
SQL> alter database recover to logical standby keep identity;
Database altered.
```

On the alert log, you will get the following:

```
Online log /u01/app/oracle/oradata/orcl/redo03.log: Thread 1 Group
3 was previously cleared
Standby became primary SCN: 1003598
Mon Dec 31 00:49:04 2012
Setting recovery target incarnation to 3
RECOVER TO LOGICAL STANDBY: Complete - Database mounted as logical
standby
Completed: alter database recover to logical standby keep identity
```

7. After completing the conversion, open the database and check for the new database role.

```
SQL> select open_mode from v$database;
OPEN_MODE
--------------------
MOUNTED
SQL> alter database open;
Database altered.
SQL> select database_role from v$database;
DATABASE_ROLE
----------------
LOGICAL STANDBY
```

8. **Starting SQL Apply and monitoring the apply status**: On the new logical standby database, issue the following command to start SQL Apply:

```
SQL> alter database start logical standby apply immediate;
Database altered.
```

On the alert log, you will get the following:

```
Some indexes or index [sub]partitions of table SYSTEM.LOGMNR_
DICTIONARY$ have been marked unusable
Indexes of table  SYSTEM.LOGMNR_ATTRCOL$ have been rebuilt and are
now usable
Indexes of table  SYSTEM.LOGMNR_ATTRIBUTE$ have been rebuilt and
are now usable
Indexes of table  SYSTEM.LOGMNR_CCOL$ have been rebuilt and are
now usable
SQL> SELECT NAME, VALUE, TIME_COMPUTED FROM V$DATAGUARD_STATS
WHERE NAME='transport lag';
NAME            VALUE            TIME_COMPUTED
------------- --------------- ------------------------------
transport lag +00 00:00:00    12/31/2012 00:59:25
```

If any active DDLs/DMLs are in progress, you can monitor them using `v$logstdby_state`.

```
SQL> select state from v$logstdby_state;
STATE
-------------
APPLYING
SQL> /
STATE
-------------
IDLE
```

9. **Upgrading a logical standby database**: Stop sending redo on the primary database by changing the remote destination status to `defer`.

```
SQL> alter system set log_archive_dest_state_2='defer';
System altered.
SQL> select dest_id,status from v$archive_dest where dest_id=2;
      DEST_ID STATUS
--------------- ---------
            2 DEFERRED
```

Stop SQL Apply from the logical standby database.

```
SQL> alter database stop logical standby apply;
Database altered.
```

On the alert log, you will get the following:

```
Mon Dec 31 01:06:16 2012
LOGSTDBY status: ORA-16128: User initiated stop apply successfully
completed
Completed: alter database stop logical standby apply
```

10. Create another restore point prior to the upgrade.

```
SQL> create restore point Rolling_Upgrade_India2 guarantee
flashback database;
Restore point created.
SQL> select name from v$restore_point;
NAME
----------------------------------
ROLLING_UPGRADE_INDIA
ROLLING_UPGRADE_INDIA2
```

11. Now the database version is 11.2.0.1. Install the new ORACLE_HOME locations of 11.2.0.3 and upgrade the database after setting the environment variables to point to the new home, 11.2.0.3. Then run the upgrade scripts as shown in the following code:

```
[oracle@oracle-stby ~]$ sqlplus / as sysdba
SQL*Plus: Release 11.2.0.3.0 Production on Mon Dec 31 01:14:12
2012
Copyright (c) 1982, 2011, Oracle.  All rights reserved.
Connected to an idle instance.
SQL> startup upgrade
Database mounted.
Database opened.
SQL> @?/rdbms/admin/catupgrd.sql
DOC>###########################################################
DOC>###########################################################
DOC>
DOC>   The first time this script is run, there should be no error
messages
DOC>   generated; all normal upgrade error messages are
suppressed.
.............
SQL> REM END OF CATUPGRD.SQL
SQL>
SQL> REM bug 12337546 - Exit current sqlplus session at end of
catupgrd.sql.
SQL> REM              This forces user to start a new sqlplus
session in order
```

```
SQL> REM                        to connect to the upgraded db.
SQL> exit
Disconnected from Oracle Database 11g Enterprise Edition Release
11.2.0.3.0 - 64bit Production
With the Partitioning, OLAP, Data Mining and Real Application

Testing options
```

On the alert log, you will find the following:

```
Database Characterset is WE8MSWIN1252
Updating 11.2.0.1.0 NLS parameters in sys.props$
-- adding 11.2.0.3.0 NLS parameters.
.............
Mon Dec 31 01:30:10 2012
SERVER COMPONENT id=CATPROC: timestamp=2012-12-31 01:30:10
SERVER COMPONENT id=RDBMS: status=VALID, version=11.2.0.3.0,
timestamp=2012-12-31 01:30:15
```

12. Now start the upgraded logical standby and check for the registry components' status from DBA_REGISRY.

```
SQL> select comp_name, status from dba_registry;
COMP_NAME                                      STATUS
---------------------------------------------- -----------
OWB                                            VALID
Oracle Application Express                     VALID
Oracle Enterprise Manager                      VALID
OLAP Catalog                                   VALID
Spatial                                        VALID
Oracle Multimedia                              VALID
```

13. **Starting SQL Apply**: After the successful upgrade, we'll enable redo transport from the primary database and start SQL Apply on the logical standby database.

Enable redo transport by running the following statement on the primary database.

```
SQL> alter system set log_archive_dest_state_2='enable';
System altered.
```

14. On the primary database, perform some DML transactions for verification.

```
SQL> select count(*) from packt;
      COUNT(*)
--------------
            14
SQL> insert into packt select * from packt;
14 rows created.
```

```
SQL> commit;
Commit complete.
SQL> select count(*) from packt;
      COUNT(*)
--------------
            28
```

15. Start SQL Apply on the standby database and check for the number of rows from packt.

```
SQL> alter database start logical standby apply immediate;
Database altered.
SQL> select db_unique_name,database_role from v$database;
DB_UNIQUE_NAME        DATABASE_ROLE
--------------------  ----------------

INDIA_UN              LOGICAL STANDBY
SQL> select count(*) from scott.packt;
  COUNT(*)
----------
        28
```

16. **Switchover to upgraded 11.2.0.3**: Until this step, there is no downtime on the production database. Now perform the switchover steps as shown in the following code:

First issue the switchover command from the primary database.

```
SQL> alter database commit to switchover to logical standby;
Database altered.
SQL> select db_unique_name,switchover_status,open_mode from
v$database;
DB_UNIQUE_NAME    SWITCHOVER_STATUS    OPEN_MODE
---------------   --------------------  --------------------
turkey_un         NOT ALLOWED          READ WRITE
```

On the alert log, you will find the following:

```
Mon Dec 31 02:22:20 2012
NSA2 started with pid=26, OS id=12227
Beginning log switch checkpoint up to RBA [0x34.2.10], SCN:
1009787
...........
LOGSTDBY: Switchover complete (TURKEY)
LOGSTDBY: enabling scheduler job queue processes.
JOBQ: re-enabling CJQ0
Completed: alter database commit to switchover to logical standby
```

17. Now issue the `switchover` command from the upgraded logical standby database:

```
SQL> select db_unique_name,switchover_status,open_mode from
v$database;
DB_UNIQUE_NAME        SWITCHOVER_STATUS    OPEN_MODE
------------------- -------------------- --------------------
INDIA_UN              TO PRIMARY           READ WRITE
SQL> alter database commit to switchover to logical primary;
Database altered.
SQL> select db_unique_name,switchover_status,open_mode from
v$database;
DB_UNIQUE_NAME        SWITCHOVER_STATUS    OPEN_MODE
------------------- -------------------- --------------------
INDIA_UN              NOT ALLOWED          READ WRITE
```

18. **Retransforming into the physical standby database**: Now the new logical standby is running under Oracle lower patch set level (11.2.0.1) as a transient logical standby database, and it cannot receive and apply redo from the new primary database. Let's convert it into the old physical standby database state.

```
SQL> alter system set log_archive_dest_state_2='defer';
System altered.
```

Now flash back to the restore point before the upgrade.

```
SQL> select db_unique_name,database_role from v$database;
DB_UNIQUE_NAME  DATABASE_ROLE
-------------- ----------------
turkey_un       LOGICAL STANDBY
SQL> shutdown immediate
ORACLE instance shut down.
SQL> startup mount
Database mounted.
SQL> select name from v$restore_point;
NAME
-------------------------------
ROLLING_UPGRADE_TURKEY
SQL> flashback database to restore point ROLLING_UPGRADE_TURKEY;
Flashback complete.
SQL> shutdown immediate
ORACLE instance shut down.
```

19. Starting a logical standby database from new version binary (11.2.0.3): Copy PFILE/SPFILE, the password file, and network configuration files to the new installed ORACLE_HOME location and start the database in the MOUNT status.

```
[oracle@oracle-primary ~]$ sqlplus / as sysdba
SQL*Plus: Release 11.2.0.3.0 Production on Mon Dec 31 02:43:45
2012
Copyright (c) 1982, 2011, Oracle.  All rights reserved.
Connected to an idle instance.
SQL> startup mount
Database mounted.
SQL> alter database convert to physical standby;
Database altered.
```

Shut down instance and start up in the MOUNT status using the following code:

```
SQL> shutdown immediate
ORA-01507: database not mounted
ORACLE instance shut down.
SQL> startup mount
Database mounted.
```

20. Enabling redo transport from a primary database and starting to recover on a standby database: Issue the following command from the new primary database to send redo data to the new physical standby database.

```
SQL> alter system set log_archive_dest_state_2='enable';
System altered.
```

Now start Redo Apply on the standby database to apply all the redo of the upgrade script.

```
SQL> alter database recover managed standby database using current
logfile disconnect;
Database altered.
```

On the alert log, you will see the following:

```
Mon Dec 31 02:51:28 2012
MRP0 started with pid=26, OS id=13970
MRP0: Background Managed Standby Recovery process started (TURKEY)
Serial Media Recovery started
Managed Standby Recovery starting Real Time Apply
...........
ORA-19906: recovery target incarnation changed during recovery
Managed Standby Recovery not using Real Time Apply
Completed: alter database recover managed standby database using
current logfile disconnect
```

The previous errors are expected; if any archives are unable to fetch, copy the archive logs from the primary database and then catalogue them with the database using the RMAN command catalog start with 'arch location'.

```
Mon Dec 31 04:08:50 2012
alter database recover managed standby database disconnect from
session
Attempt to start background Managed Standby Recovery process
(TURKEY)
..................
Media Recovery Log /u01/app/oracle/flash_recovery_area/TURKEY_UN/
archivelog/2012_12_31/1_55_803436544.dbf
Media Recovery Log /u01/app/oracle/flash_recovery_area/TURKEY_UN/
archivelog/2012_12_31/1_56_803436544.dbf
Media Recovery Waiting for thread 1 sequence 57
```

21. **Verifying the upgraded standby database**: Now the standby database is completely synchronized with the primary database.

On the primary database, add the following:
```
SQL> select max(sequence#) from v$archived_log;
MAX(SEQUENCE#)
-------------
           56
```

On the standby database, add the following:
```
SQL> select max(sequence#) from v$archived_log where
applied='YES';
MAX(SEQUENCE#)
-------------
           56
```

Verify once if all the components of the registry are valid.

```
SQL> @?/rdbms/admin/utlu112s.sql
Component                    Current     Version     Elapsed Time
Name                         Status      Number      HH:MM:SS
.
Oracle Database 11.2 Post-Upgrade Status Tool          12-31-2012
04:18:17
.
Component                    Current     Version     Elapsed Time
Name                         Status      Number      HH:MM:SS
.
Oracle Server
```

```
            .                                    VALID      11.2.0.3.0
..............
Gathering Statistics

            .
00:03:27
Total Upgrade Time: 00:46:51
PL/SQL procedure successfully completed.
```

So far the downtime is only for the switchover. However, at this point
we moved the production database to the standby server. In order to
keep clients connected to the new primary database, the connection
failover should be configured for the database clients.

What just happened?

We have seen how to perform a rolling upgrade using the transient logical standby database
with very little downtime. With this method, 96 percent of upgrade downtime can be avoided.

Have a go hero – one last switchover

If you want to use your original primary server as the production server, you should perform
a switchover again, to move the primary server into the original server.

Corruption detection, prevention, and automatic repair with Oracle Data Guard

Corruption in an Oracle database block means that a block doesn't contain the data that
the database expects to find. This can be caused by various failures in the hardware
environment, including disks, disk controllers, memory or network components or software
errors in the operating system, firmware, the volume manager, and the Oracle database
software itself.

Oracle offers some initialization parameters to control the level of corruption prevention
and detection. Of course, a higher level brings performance issues with it. In a Data Guard
configuration, using the standby database for corruption detection and prevention will bring
higher data protection and availability with less performance effect on the primary database.

Let's first start with learning the three types of block corruption in Oracle databases.

- **Physical block corruption:** In a physically corrupted database block, the block header may be corrupted, the block may be misplaced or fractured, or the block checksum may be invalid. These types of corruptions are reported by the Oracle database as a ORA-01578 error in the alert log.

- **Logical block corruption:** In a logical block corruption, the block contains a valid checksum; however, the block content is corrupt. This corruption is not reported in the alert log but if db_block_checking is enabled, ORA-600 internal errors may show up.

- The third type of Oracle database corruptions are caused by stray writes, lost writes, or misdirected writes. In this case, the block may not be corrupted as described in the first two types; however, the content of the block is older, stale, or in the wrong location.

Now we'll learn about preventing and detecting these corruptions, especially in a Data Guard configuration, by studying the related initialization parameters. There are three important parameters in this study: DB_BLOCK_CHECKSUM, DB_BLOCK_ CHECKING, and DB_LOST_ WRITE_PROTECT.

DB_BLOCK_CHECKSUM

This is the initialization parameter used to detect physical corruptions in a database. As we know, a checksum is the data calculated from the arbitrary data with a specific function. It can be recalculated anytime and compared with the stored result of the previous instance to ensure integrity of data. When we use DB_BLOCK_CHECKSUM, the Oracle database calculates a checksum and stores it in the header of each data block when writing to the disk. The following are the possible values of this initialization parameter:

- OFF (FALSE): Checksums are calculated only for the SYSTEM tablespace data blocks. The user's tablespace and log checksum are not performed. The FALSE value is preserved for backward compatibility, and has the same effect as OFF.

- TYPICAL (TRUE): When a block of any tablespace is read, checksum is calculated and compared. Also, at the last write of the block, the new checksum is stored. The TRUE value is preserved for backward compatibility and has the same effect as TYPICAL.

- FULL: In addition to checksum calculations in the TYPICAL mode, Oracle also verifies checksum before the update/delete statements. Also, Oracle gives every log block a checksum before writing it to the current log. Before 11*g*, log block checksum was performed by LGWR; however, in 11*g*, the database creates foreground processes for this purpose for better performance. Note that, when checksum validation fails in the FULL mode, Oracle will try to recover the block using the data version on disk and redo data.

In a Data Guard environment, Oracle recommends setting this parameter to FULL on both primary and standby databases. Oracle also indicates that setting it to FULL causes 4 percent to 5 percent overhead in a primary database, whereas the TYPICAL mode causes 1 percent to 2 percent overhead. If setting FULL in the primary database has unacceptable performance degradation, consider setting it as TYPICAL on the primary database and FULL on the standby database.

DB_BLOCK_CHECKING

This parameter specifies whether the database will perform block checking for database blocks and detect logical corruptions. Oracle controls the header and the data in the block if it's logically consistent.

The following are the possible values of this initialization parameter:

- OFF (FALSE): Only semantic block checking is performed for the blocks of the SYSTEM tablespace. No block checking is performed for the other tablespaces.

- LOW: Only block header checks are performed when the block content changes. This setting has very limited benefit for corruption detection and prevention, because there's no block checking on the data blocks itself.

- MEDIUM: Block checking is performed for all objects except indexes.

- FULL (TRUE): All the LOW and MEDIUM checks are performed for all objects. When MEDIUM or FULL is being used, block corruptions detected in memory will be automatically repaired using the data version on disk and redo data.

In a Data Guard environment, Oracle recommends setting this parameter to FULL at both the primary and standby databases for the highest level of detection and prevention against logical corruptions. However, the performance effect of using this checking can be very high. Oracle states that block checking typically causes 1 percent to 10 percent overhead on the primary database; for update- and insert-intensive applications, the performance effect may me even higher. We should test its effect on the primary database and if the FULL value is unacceptable in terms of performance effect, we should consider setting it to MEDIUM or LOW.

When we cannot set it to FULL or MEDIUM on the primary database because of performance issues, it becomes more important to enable it on the standby database. The performance effect of block checking on Redo Apply may also be high; in some cases it may halve the Redo Apply rate. So we must test and evaluate the effect. We can sum up by saying that it's good practice to set the highest degree of logical corruption detection and prevention on a standby database using the DB_BLOCK_ CHECKING parameter.

DB_LOST_WRITE_PROTECT

Lost-write corruption is a serious type of corruption that occurs on the storage layer. The I/O subsystem acknowledges to the database that the write operation is completed, but it is actually not. The DB_LOST_WRITE_PROTECT initialization parameter can be used to detect the lost write. Lost-write detection on the standby database is an 11*g* feature and it's most effective when used with Data Guard.

The following are the possible values of this initialization parameter:

◆ NONE: Lost-write detection is disabled.

◆ TYPICAL: Lost-write detection is enabled for read-write tablespaces. Buffer cache reads are recorded in the redo log and this information is used to detect lost writes. When set in the physical standby database, the MRP process will check for lost writes in read-write tablespaces and stop recovery if detected. Thus, corruption will not be applied on the standby database.

◆ FULL: Lost-write detection for read-only tablespaces is included besides read-write tablespaces.

The recommended setting is FULL for both primary and standby databases, and for most cases its performance effect on the primary database and Redo Apply is negligible.

Automatic block media repair

In Oracle 11*g*R2, when Active Data Guard is being used with Real-Time Apply, if a physical corruption is detected on the primary database, Oracle will automatically try to repair the corruption using the non-corrupted block on the standby database. This operation is also valid in the opposite direction, which means standby database corruption will be repaired using the data block on the primary database. A notification will be printed in the alert log about the automatic block media repair operation in the meantime; this repair operation is completely transparent to database users.

In order to run ABMR successfully, the following initialization parameters must be configured:

◆ The LOG_ARCHIVE_CONFIG parameter with a DG_CONFIG list on both the primary and standby databases

◆ The LOG_ARCHIVE_DEST_n parameter for the primary database

◆ The FAL_SERVER parameter for the standby database with the Oracle Net service name pointing to the primary database

We can also manually repair a corrupted data block with the RMAN command's RECOVER BLOCK command. By default, this command will try to use an Active Data Guard physical standby database if it exists. In order to exclude the standby database as a source to repair corruption, we must use the EXCLUDE STANDBY option of this command.

Summary

We've reached the end of *Chapter 11*, *Data Guard Best Practices*. In this chapter, we've seen the most important best practices of Oracle Data Guard configurations. Using the features and methods mentioned in this chapter, it's possible to make the Data Guard environment more robust and effective.

In this book, we've started with the foundations and configuration of Data Guard and continued with learning details, features, common issues, and best practices. At this stage, you've learned everything you need in order to effectively administrate Data Guard systems. You also exercised real-world examples and hands-on tasks. We recommend you to glance over the book again to consolidate what you've learned.

Pop Quiz Answers

Chapter 1, Getting Started

Pop quiz – real-time apply consideration

Q1	User-based errors on the primary database such as an inadvertent table drop will be instantly replicated to the standby database. In order to get rid of this kind of data loss risk, we must use "Flashback Database" feature on primary or standby database.

Chapter 5, Data Guard Protection Modes

Pop quiz – precautions for primary database availability issue in maximum protection mode

Q1	Oracle recommends using two physical standby databases on separate locations to overcome this issue. If we don't have two separate locations we can still install two standby databases on the same location or use Real Application Cluster on the standby database and use redundant network between primary and standby database.

Chapter 6, Data Guard Role Transitions

Pop quiz

Q1	Use the following statement to cancel switchover from the primary or standby databases:
	`SQL> ALTER DATABASE PREPARE TO SWITCHOVER CANCEL;`

Chapter 9, Data Guard Configuration Patching

Pop quiz

Q1	Terminal patch can be named as final patch and it can be either CPU or PSU. It will be the last patch to be released on a particular platform of Oracle Database release.

Chapter 10, Common Data Guard Issues

Pop quiz – redo transport authentication problem in only one instance of primary database

Q1	In this case, password file is not correct for the primary instance that shows authentication error. We can simply copy password file from one of the other RAC servers to the failing server to fix this issue.

Pop quiz – using tape for SCN incremental backup

Q1	No, only disk backups can be used to resolve a gap with RMAN SCN incremental backups, because backups on tape cannot be cataloged.

Index

NET_TIMEOUT 51
NOAFFIRM 49
REOPEN 50
SYNC 48
VALID_FOR 47
interim/bug patch
applying, on logical standby 282-286
interim patches
about 278
custom scripts 278
metadata 278
payload 278
issues, Data Guard
about 305
Data Guard tracing, turning on 326
diagnostic data, gathering 328
gap, closing with RMAN incremental backup 317
NOLOGGING changes, fixing on standby database 322
redo transport authentication issues, dealing with 311
standby control file, recreating 306-311
UNNAMED datafiles, dealing with 315

J

Java Database Connectivity (JDBC) clients 344

L

LOCATION attribute 47
LOG_ARCHIVE_CONFIG parameter 45
LOG_ARCHIVE_DEST_n parameter 46
LOG_ARCHIVE_DEST_STATE_n parameter 52
LOG_ARCHIVE_MAX_POCESSES parameter 46
LOG_FILE_NAME_CONVERT parameter 55
logical block corruption 367
logical standby database
about 10
cons 80, 81
creating 82, 87
interim/bug patch, applying 282-286
physical standby database, converting into 90-93
physical standby database environment, making ready for conversion 88, 89

properties 79
pros 80-82
unsupported data types 10
logical standby database configuration
any table row uniqueness, checking 85-87
primary database,preparing 82, 83
unsupported data types, checking 83-85
logical standby database customization
about 98
automatic deletion process 111
database objects, creating 106
Data Guard settings 103
DBMS_LOGSTDBY.SKIP procedure, using 99-102
DML replication, disabling 99
selective replication 98
skip rules, creating 98
logical standby database verification
about 94
redo transport service status, checking 94-96
services, checking in broken configuration 98
SQL Apply service status, checking 96, 97
loop detection 32
LSP0 (Logical Standby Coordinator Process) 29
LSP1 (Logical Standby Dictionary Build Process) 29
LSP2 (Logical Standby Set Guard Process) 29

M

Managed recovery process (MRP) 9
management, with Data Guard broker
broker configuration, disabling 131, 132
broker configuration, enabling 131
configuration, changing 134
database properties, changing 135
performing 131
standby database, disabling 133
standby database, enabling 132, 134
MAX_CONNECTIONS attribute 49
MAX_FAILURE attribute 50
maximum availability architecture 275
Maximum Availability mode 155, 156
Maximum Performance mode 155
Maximum Protection mode
about 154
considerations 154

Thank you for buying
Oracle Data Guard 11gR2 Administration Beginner's Guide

About Packt Publishing

Packt, pronounced 'packed', published its first book "*Mastering phpMyAdmin for Effective MySQL Management*" in April 2004 and subsequently continued to specialize in publishing highly focused books on specific technologies and solutions.

Our books and publications share the experiences of your fellow IT professionals in adapting and customizing today's systems, applications, and frameworks. Our solution-based books give you the knowledge and power to customize the software and technologies you're using to get the job done. Packt books are more specific and less general than the IT books you have seen in the past. Our unique business model allows us to bring you more focused information, giving you more of what you need to know, and less of what you don't.

Packt is a modern, yet unique publishing company, which focuses on producing quality, cutting-edge books for communities of developers, administrators, and newbies alike. For more information, please visit our website: www.PacktPub.com.

About Packt Enterprise

In 2010, Packt launched two new brands, Packt Enterprise and Packt Open Source, in order to continue its focus on specialization. This book is part of the Packt Enterprise brand, home to books published on enterprise software – software created by major vendors, including (but not limited to) IBM, Microsoft and Oracle, often for use in other corporations. Its titles will offer information relevant to a range of users of this software, including administrators, developers, architects, and end users.

Writing for Packt

We welcome all inquiries from people who are interested in authoring. Book proposals should be sent to author@packtpub.com. If your book idea is still at an early stage and you would like to discuss it first before writing a formal book proposal, contact us; one of our commissioning editors will get in touch with you.

We're not just looking for published authors; if you have strong technical skills but no writing experience, our experienced editors can help you develop a writing career, or simply get some additional reward for your expertise.

Oracle Database 11gR2 Performance Tuning Cookbook

ISBN: 978-1-84968-260-2   Paperback: 542 pages

Over 80 recipes to help beginners achieve better performance from Oracle Database applications

1. Learn the right techniques to achieve best performance from the Oracle Database

2. Avoid common myths and pitfalls that slow down the database

3. Diagnose problems when they arise and employ tricks to prevent them

4. Explore various aspects that affect performance, from application design to system tuning

Oracle Database 11g – Underground Advice for Database Administrators

ISBN: 978-1-84968-000-4   Paperback: 348 pages

A real-world DBA survival guide for Oracle 11g database implementations

1. A comprehensive handbook aimed at reducing the day-to-day struggle of Oracle 11g Database newcomers

2. Real-world reflections from an experienced DBA—what novice DBAs should really know

3. Implement Oracle's Maximum Availability Architecture with expert guidance

4. Extensive information on providing high availability for Grid Control

Please check **www.PacktPub.com** for information on our titles

Oracle Warehouse Builder 11g R2: Getting Started 2011

ISBN: 978-1-84968-344-9   Paperback: 424 pages

Extract, Transform, and Load data to build a dynamic, operational data warehouse

1. Build a working data warehouse from scratch with Oracle Warehouse Builder

2. Cover techniques in Extracting, Transforming, and Loading data into your data warehouse

3. This second edition covers great new features of 11gR2 such as the new user interface and a whole new chapter on code templates that implement knowledge module functionality from Oracle Data Integrator

OCA Oracle Database 11g: Database Administration I: A Real-World Certification Guide

ISBN: 978-1-84968-730-0   Paperback: 582 pages

Learn how to become an Oracle-certified database administrator

1. Prepare for Oracle Database Administration I certification

2. Learn real world skills in database administration

3. Written in an example driven format with step-by-step real world examples

Please check **www.PacktPub.com** for information on our titles

Made in the USA
Middletown, DE
29 December 2016